Psychology AS
for OCR

Louise Ellerby-Jones
and Karon Oliver with Moira Donald

DYNAMIC LEARNING

HODDER EDUCATION
AN HACHETTE UK COMPANY

Figures 2.9, 2.10, 2.11, 2.12, 2.13, 2.14, 2.15, 2.16 are all reproduced from Reicher and Haslam (2006) 'Rethinking the psychology of tyranny; The BBC prison study', *British Journal of Social Psychology*, 45: 1–40. Copyright © 2006, British Psychological Society. Reproduced with permission of John Wiley & Sons Ltd.

Orders: please contact Bookpoint Ltd, 130 Milton Park, Abingdon, Oxon OX14 4SB. Telephone: (44) 01235 827720. Fax: (44) 01235 400454. Lines are open from 9.00–5.00, Monday to Saturday, with a 24 hour message answering service. You can also order through our website www.hoddereducation.co.uk

If you have any comments to make about this, or any of our other titles, please send them to educationenquiries@hodder.co.uk

British Library Cataloguing in Publication Data
A catalogue record for this title is available from the British Library

ISBN: 978 1 444 12338 8

First Published 2011
Impression number   10 9 8 7 6 5 4 3 2 1
Year   2015, 2014, 2013, 2012, 2011

Hachette UK's policy is to use papers that are natural, renewable and recyclable products and made from wood grown in sustainable forests. The logging and manufacturing processes are expected to conform to the environmental regulations of the country of origin.

Cover photo © Image Source/ Getty Images
Illustrations by Barking Dog Art
Typeset by DC Graphic Design Ltd, Swanley Village, Kent.
Printed in Italy for Hodder Education, An Hachette UK Company, 338 Euston Road, London NW1 3BH

Contents

Introduction

This book has been written for students following the OCR AS Psychology course, although we hope it might be useful for students taking any AS course or any student interested in finding out about psychology. The specification outlined below is specific to OCR students.

The OCR AS Exams

The OCR AS Psychology assessment is formed of two exams:

Psychological Investigations

This is a one hour written paper accounting for 60 marks (30 per cent of the marks available at AS). It will be formed of three sections and you will answer ALL of the questions. The purpose of this exam is to test your understanding of the methods that Psychologists use to investigate behaviour.

Core Studies

This is a two hour written paper accounting for 120 marks (70 per cent of the marks available at AS). The purpose of this exam is to introduce you to some classic and modern studies that introduce you to the subject matter of psychology. It will be formed of three sections, in section A you will answer all of the questions, and you will answer one question in both sections B and C.

You will be tested on three assessment objectives:

Assessment objective 1 (A01): this will be testing your knowledge and understanding and how well you can communicate this.

Assessment objective 2 (A02): this tests how you can analyse and evaluate scientific information and assess its validity and reliability. Examiners will be looking at whether you can apply your understanding to unfamiliar situations.

Assessment objective (A03): This focuses on your knowledge of practical techniques, being able to make, communicate and evaluate observations and methods.

Our other title *OCR Research Methods for Psychology AS and A2* will teach you everything you need to know about the methods used in psychological research and ensure you maximise your potential in both the AS and A2 exams.

Walk Through

This book is divided into nine chapters, the first six of which outline all of the core studies you will need to know. Chapters seven to nine describe the research methods, issues, approaches and perspectives that you will be tested on. There are certain regular features throughout the book which will help you strengthen your learning.

The Study

Containing the core information on each of the studies you will need to know about for the AS exam this feature is accompanied by background information and commentary.

Key Concept

Clear definitions of important terms and ideas that you will come across in the course of your study.

Activity

These encourage you to get thinking and looking more deeply at the material.

Revision Activity

These activities will help you apply your knowledge and practice skills that will be tested in the exams.

Exam Focus

Exam style questions will help you avoid any surprises in the exam!

Photo Credits

The author and publishers would like to thank the following for permission to reproduce material in this book;

Figure 2.1 © Bettmann/CORBIS; Figure 2.2 From the film Obedience © 1968 by Stanley Milgram, © renewed 1993 by Alexandra Milgram; Figure 2.4 © AP/Press Association Images; Figure 2.5 courtesy of Williamson-Dickie Mfg. Co.; Figure 2.7 © P. G. Zimbardo Inc.; Figure 2.8 © BBC; Figure 3.2 © UNITED ARTISTS/THE KOBAL COLLECTION; Figure 3.6 © Marzanna Syncerz – Fotolia; Figure 3.7 © Autism Research Centre, Department of Psychiatry, University of Cambridge; Figure 3.8a and b © Autism Research Centre, Department of Psychiatry, University of Cambridge; Figure 3.9 © Viktor Pravdica – Fotolia; Figure 3.10 © http://commons.wikimedia.org/wiki/File:Hans_Pr%C3%BCfung_1907.jpg/from Karl Krall, Denkende Tiere, Leipz. 1912, Tafel 1; Figure 3.11 © Mark Kauffman//Time Life Pictures/Getty Images; Figure 3.12 © HO/Reuters/Corbis; Figure 3.13 © The Great Ape Trust; Figure 3.14 © SUSAN KUKLIN/SCIENCE PHOTO LIBRARY; Figure 3.15 © The Great Ape Trust; Figure 3.16 © The Great Ape Trust; Figure 3.17 © The Great Ape Trust; Figure 4.1 © Russi & Morelli – Fotolia; Figure 4.2 © sonya etchison – Fotolia; Figure 4.4 © George Marks/Retrofile/Getty Images; Figure 4.5 © Hufton + Crow / View Pictures/Rex Features; Figure 4.6 © Kathy Libby – Fotolia.com Figure 4.8 © Bettmann/CORBIS; Figure 4.9 © Nina Leen/Time & Life Pictures/Getty Images; Figure 4.10 © ALBERT BANDURA, STANFORD CENTER ON ADOLESCENCE, STANFORD UNIVERSITY; Figure 4.11 © AP/Press Association Images; Figure 4.12 © Monkey Business – Fotolia; Figure 4.13 © Christine Stuermer – Fotolia; Figure 4.14 © Kitch Bain – Fotolia; Figure 5.1 © Vladimirs Koskins – Fotolia; Figure 5.8 © uwimages – Fotolia; Figure 6.1 © Ints Vikmanis – Fotolia; Figure 6.3 © Design Pics Inc./Alamy; Figure 6.4 © Lorelyn Medina – Fotolia; Figure 6.6 © sharky1 – Fotolia; Figure 6.8 © 20TH CENTURY FOX/THE KOBAL COLLECTION; Figure 6.9 © kentoh – Fotolia; Figure 6.10 © AP/Press Association Images; Figure 6.11 © Joggie Botma – Fotolia; Figure 6.14 © Sean Gladwell – Fotolia; Figure 6.15 © Monkey Business – Fotolia; Figure 7.3 © 2005 Kay Ransom – Fotolia; Figure 7.4 © sculpies – Fotolia; Figure 7.5 © Archives of the History of American Psychology, Center for the History of Psychology – The University of Akron; Figure 8.2 © picsfive – Fotolia; Figure 8.3 © Chris Brignell – Fotolia; Figure 8.4 © Vanessa van Rensburg – Fotolia; Figure 8.7 © Jakub Jirsák – Fotolia; Figure 8.13 © Megapress/Alamy; Figure 9.1 © Laurence Gough – Fotolia.

Every effort has been made to obtain necessary permission with reference to copyright material. The publishers apologise if inadvertently any sources remain unacknowledged and will be glad to make the necessary arrangements at the earliest opportunity.

1 Introduction to psychology

Why do people do what they do, and why do they not do the same things that I do? How can they do things that I would never do or would never want to do? Why do they think the way they do and why do not they seem to think the same way that I do? How can people believe in things that I do not believe in? Do people feel the same things that I'm feeling?

If these are the kind of questions that interest you, then you have chosen the right subject – psychology. What psychology actually is, however, is not commonly understood. Here is a psychology teacher's story.

> When I meet new people, one of the questions they ask is, 'What do you do?' I hate this question, so I try to avoid telling them, and go for half the story: 'I'm a teacher,' I say. Then their next question is, 'What do you teach?' Well, I can hold them off with the facetious answer, 'Students', but that's a bit rude, so I have to admit it: 'Psychology,' I say eventually. This is then, as often as not, followed by them saying, 'Ooh! I'll have to be careful what I say now, won't I? You're going to be reading my mind,' or they say, 'You're going to be analysing me now, aren't you?'
> Typically they might ask me something along the lines of: 'I had this dream about being chased by a giant snail round a 400 metre running track and it was wearing a baseball cap and calling out my name. What does it mean?' or 'I must introduce you to my brother, Rick. We think he's bipolar. Maybe you could confirm it for us?'

Psychologists do not tell you what your dreams mean. Psychologists do not diagnose mental disorders. That's the job of psychiatrists – medical doctors who have specialist psychiatric training. They do not offer you therapy or counselling. That's the job of psychotherapists, not psychologists. Psychologists do not read your mind. No one can do that.

What psychologists actually do is systematically investigate human behaviour and experience, with the aim of trying to explain, understand, predict or manage behaviour. It is to be hoped that what they discover helps us to live better, happier lives and makes a positive contribution to human welfare. Psychologists are best thought of as researchers or scientists, and never as therapists, doctors, gurus or magicians.

Psychology is considered to have begun in the 1870s in Leipzig, in modern Germany, when Wilhelm Wundt and his colleagues opened their 'psychology laboratory'. Their method of studying psychology was to take an introspective approach – asking themselves questions such as: What do I feel? Why do I feel like this? How do I behave? How does my memory work?

However, this was rejected as a way of studying behaviour on the grounds that it was too subjective. Despite Wundt and his colleagues focusing on collecting data about behaviour, their attempts to understand psychology were always going to be limited by the fact that they were just a handful of people and their interpretations of their own behaviour were always going to be biased.

Modern psychology, on the other hand, tries to follow an objective scientific methodology in investigating human behaviour. This means that theories are generated which are then tested by gathering empirical evidence. To be taken seriously as an academic discipline, psychology has, for the most part, taken a scientific approach to studying behaviour.

The aim of science is to determine causality by carrying out controlled experiments to test hypotheses. The findings from experiments provide support for or against a theory. The findings need to stand up on replication so that if you do the study again you must get similar results. These features of science are important in psychological investigations and you will learn a great deal about how data is gathered and analysed as you progress through this book or through your programme of study. If you are reading this because you are following the OCR examination for AS level, you will do a whole exam paper on research methodology called the Psychological Investigations paper.

In general terms, psychologists have investigated aspects of human behaviour under five headings or 'approaches'. These are:

- The **social approach**, which investigates how the social context, including the presence and behaviour of other people, impacts on how people behave.

- The **cognitive approach**, which investigates how we think, perceive, pay attention, problem-solve and remember.

- The **developmental approach**, which investigates how our thinking changes as we mature and grow older; the development of personality – for example, Freud's psychoanalytic perspective; and how we learn – for example, the behaviourist perspective.

- The **physiological approach**, which investigates how biology, especially neurobiology (the biology of the brain), impacts people's behaviour.

- The **individual differences approach**, which investigates the differences between people, such as abnormality and mental illness.

In reality, these approaches overlap, but in terms of developing an understanding of what psychologists do, they provide you with a useful starting point.

The aim of the OCR AS level, and therefore of this book, is to give you a grounding in these key approaches to psychology. In order to do this, three studies from each approach have been included for you to study:

Approaches	Studies		
Social psychology	Milgram – obedience	Piliavin *et al.* – Subway Samaritan	Reicher and Haslam – BBC prison experiment
Cognitive psychology	Loftus and Palmer – eyewitness testimony	Baron-Cohen *et al.* – autism in adults	Savage-Rumbaugh *et al.* – ape language
Developmental psychology	Samuel and Bryant – conservation	Bandura *et al.* – imitating aggression	Freud – Little Hans
Physiological psychology	Maguire *et al.* – taxi drivers' brains	Dement and Kleitman – sleep and dreaming	Sperry – split brains
Psychology of individual differences	Rosenhan – being sane in insane places	Thigpen and Cleckley – multiple personality disorder	Griffiths – cognitive bias in gamblers

You will also study methods and issues and relate these to the 15 core studies.

Methods	Issues
Experimental method (laboratory and field)	Ethics
Case study	Ecological validity
Self-report	Longitudinal and snapshot
Observation	Qualitative and quantitative data
Methodological issues such as reliability and validity	

Much of the psychological terminology that you will have to get to grips with will be in relation to research methodology. To help with this we have explained key research methods concepts for you as each one crops up. We have also explained key concepts that relate to specific studies in a similar way.

Well, we have told you that as psychologists we cannot read your mind. However, we can infer what is going on in your mind from your behaviour. That is, if you are reading this book, then either you must be interested in finding out about psychology or you have already started to study psychology for AS or A level.

And if you want a bit of magic, then we can definitely predict the future for you: you are going to love psychology. Why? Psychology is fascinating because it is all about people, and what could be more fascinating than us?

2 Social psychology

Humans are innately social creatures who actually *need* to interact with other people. Past research has indicated that one of the cruellest types of punishment is to keep someone in solitary confinement. This is not only because we enjoy the company of others; it seems also that we are biologically programmed to be social creatures. Deprivation studies have shown that if we are kept apart from other people our brain 'manufactures' them in the form of dreams or hallucinations (many of the main psychology textbooks give information about social deprivation studies). You may argue that some people actually choose to live a life of social isolation, avoiding any kind of unnecessary interaction, but even people who are antisocial have to have some form of contact with others (for work or shopping, for example) in order to survive.

It will probably be clear by now that if humans need to interact with each other, this will guide their behaviour. If you need something enough, you will sometimes do things which go against what you actually feel or believe in order to get what you want. An example of this would be being nice to or doing things for people who you do not really like, because you would rather have their company than be on your own. This is the basis of much of our social interaction – we need something from others and will do what is necessary to get it.

The topic of social psychology is divided into two sub-areas.

First, social interaction is concerned with how we interact with each other and how our position in society has a strong effect on the type of behaviour we demonstrate. It also takes into account the factors which affect this behaviour, such as our past experiences, the roles we are playing or our perceived vulnerability. You might think that the way you behave is entirely unique to you, but the truth is that we all tend to follow certain patterns of behaviour, and in some cases these patterns are entirely predictable. The two studies which focus on this area of psychology are the study by Milgram, which investigates obedience, and the study undertaken by Reicher and Haslam, who investigated the effect that group identity and group inequalities have on our behaviour.

Second, social cognition involves how we think and feel about current social experiences and how we try to make sense of them, much of which is affected by past memories. The study which relates to social cognition is the Piliavin *et al.* study, which looks at the factors which make us willing to help another person.

Milgram's study on obedience

What is obedience?

Being obedient means that we give up our personal responsibility to make decisions and go along with the decisions of an authority figure as to how we should act and what we should do. In other words, we do as we are told. There are a number of different reasons why we are obedient:

Self-preservation

First, obedience may be a form of self-preservation, especially if the authority figure who is telling us what to do has some kind of power and could harm us if we disobey. In such situations we do not necessarily have to see the authority figure as being legitimate (although it helps), because no matter what we feel, we are looking after our own welfare. This can be taken to extremes. In the army, soldiers may be court-martialled if they do not do as they are told. At home, if we do not do as we are told by our parents, we may face being grounded or having our allowance stopped, for example.

Socialisation

The second reason that we are inclined to obey is that we have been taught to be obedient. We have been socialised to toe the line, and it is more acceptable for us to be obedient than to go against the orders or rules, especially when these are set by someone perceived as being a legitimate authority figure.

When we are very young, we are trained to be obedient by our parents or carers and our teachers, and we are taught that these forms of authority are legitimate and have our best interests at heart. We can all remember the many occasions that our parents or carers said to us, 'Do as you are told.' This will often have been backed up with threats if you were naughty, and praise if you were obedient. What happens is that we internalise the need for obedience and therefore become conditioned to obey voluntarily in most situations. This seems to become set as a default position, which means that eventually disobeying becomes the difficult action. Obedience therefore becomes the norm, and to be defiant or disobedient is perceived as abnormal, drawing the disapproval of others.

What is wrong with being obedient?

Most of the time there is nothing wrong with being obedient. Obedience fulfils an important function for us. It is necessary to maintain social harmony, for without some form of obedience to an authority we would end up with a state of anarchy. Stanley Milgram (1963) wrote: 'it must not be thought all obedience entails acts of aggression against others. Obedience serves numerous productive functions… Obedience may be ennobling and educative and refer to acts of charity and kindness as well as to destruction.'

On the other hand, we also have to remember that blind obedience is an undesirable state and can result in acts of destruction and damage to others. This brings us to why obedience has been studied by psychologists. What kind of person could obey orders or instructions that would lead to the injury or death of innocent people? Examples often cited are the Holocaust and the Vietnam War, where innocent civilians were slaughtered as a result of orders given by authority figures. However, research has suggested that the people who committed these atrocities were not always amoral monsters.

Eichmann was perhaps one of the worst offenders in the Second World War. He was responsible for arranging the transportation of Jews to ghettos and concentration camps. Following the war he escaped to Buenos Aires, but he was caught in 1961 and put on trial for his part in the killing of millions of Jews. While the case was being prepared he was interrogated for a total of 275 hours, as it was believed he must have been some kind of monster to have allowed this genocide to occur. Captain Avner W. Less, who interrogated Eichmann for the duration of the 275 hours, wrote:

> *'My first reaction when the prisoner finally stood facing us in the khaki shirt and trousers and open sandals was one of disappointment. I no longer know what I had expected – probably the sort of Nazi you see in the movies: tall, blonde, with piercing blue eyes and brutal features expressive of domineering arrogance. Whereas this rather thin, balding man not much taller than myself looked utterly ordinary.'*
> *(Von Lang and Sibyll (eds) 1983, in R. Brown 1986: 3)*

Figure 2.1 Eichmann was described by the man who interrogated him for war crimes as looking 'utterly ordinary' and not a monster at all

In fact, Hannah Arendt (1965), who reported on the trial of Eichmann, concluded that he was simply a commonplace bureaucrat like any other, who obeyed orders given to him without question.

The other frequently cited evidence of how obedience to authority can be destructive comes from the case of Lieutenant William Calley's part in the My Lai massacre during the Vietnam War in 1970. Calley was the commander of a platoon of American soldiers. He received orders to round up all the inhabitants of a village called My Lai and was told that there were Vietcong in the village, and that the soldiers should round up all the members of the village and 'waste them' (shoot them dead). The inhabitants were mainly women, old men and children and yet they were all wiped out.

Again, the nature of the man who was at fault was questioned. How could a normal person agree to order his men to shoot obviously innocent children? However, Calley had shown no criminal tendencies before My Lai, and after his sentence he continued to live quietly as an average American civilian. In 1972 a survey was carried out in the USA to gauge the reaction of the public to Calley's trial. The results were that 51 per cent of the sample said they would follow the same orders by killing the inhabitants of the village if that is what they had been instructed to do, because the orders came from a legitimate authority.

Whether or not we agree with Eichmann's or Calley's actions, the reasons for their obedience are perhaps easy to understand. First, the consequences of disobedience were perhaps too high – court martial and imprisonment or execution. Everyone else was obeying orders at the time, so they were conforming to group norms. It therefore becomes evident that there is more than one simple reason why people are obedient.

The Study

Stanley Milgram (1963) 'Behavioural study of obedience', *Journal of Abnormal and Social Psychology*, **67: 371–8**

Background

Is the type of person who is seemingly blindly obedient really very different to the rest of the population, representing perhaps a few in every thousand? Perhaps there is just a sadistic minority who get drawn into situations which enable them to gratify their impulses to injure others? Or is it possible that in certain circumstances it is in fact the majority of us who would obey orders, behaving in cruel ways which we would normally like to believe we were incapable of?

Stanley Milgram is the author of the core study which focuses on obedience. Milgram began his career working at Princeton University in the USA as a research assistant to Solomon Asch and moved on to Yale University where he took up his first teaching position. Having studied conformity with Asch, Milgram became interested in obedience to authority. One question he considered was that perhaps there was something unique about certain members of the German nation who were prepared to commit what could be seen as mass murders during the Holocaust. If this were the case, maybe other members of society, like William Calley, shared the same characteristics. On the other hand, Milgram pointed out that the inhumane policies of the Nazis 'could only be carried out on a massive scale if a very large number of persons obeyed orders'. So perhaps the unquestioning obedience to authority of the thousands who took part in administering the policies may have demonstrated what most ordinary people would do when subjected to extraordinary social influences.

Milgram's study attempted to show whether there is an 'obedient type' – someone who follows orders to be cruel to others – or whether this type of obedience is something of which we are all capable of in certain circumstances, therefore contributing to the debate on individual vs situation explanations.

Aim

The aim of the study was to investigate what level of obedience would be shown when subjects were told by an authority figure to administer electric shocks to another person.

Key concept

Individual and situational explanations of behaviour and determinism

Is it the characteristics of individuals that make them behave the way they do, or is it the situation in which they find themselves that influences their behaviour? This is an important question in social psychology. Its origins lie in philosophy and the question of determinism: how far our behaviour is a result of our own free will and how far it is outside our control, being governed or determined by outside forces, such as society and culture, or by internal forces, such as our genes and personality.

Method

The study was carried out in the laboratory, using observation to collect data. The data consisted of a record of the maximum level of shock the subject administered to the 'victim', together with recordings of the sessions, occasional photographs through a one-way mirror and notes of any unusual behaviour.

Subjects

The subjects who took part in Milgram's study were 40 males between the ages of 20 and 50, who came from the New Haven (Connecticut) area in the USA, from a range of occupations and educational backgrounds. They were recruited by a newspaper article and direct mail advertising, which asked for volunteers to take part in a study of memory and learning at Yale University. This was, therefore, a volunteer or self-selected sample. They were to be paid $4.50 and were told this was simply for turning up at the university and was theirs to keep whatever happened.

... continued

Key concept

Subjects/participants and samples

'Subject' means a person whose behaviour is being studied. The standard abbreviation is S, and Ss for the plural 'subjects'. You will also see 'participant' (P) and 'participants' (Ps). These terms are interchangeable, but ethical guidelines that form a code of conduct for psychologists suggest that we should refer to those who take part as 'participants', and modern studies do this. Where the original studies use 'subjects', as is the case in Milgram's study, we have also referred to those taking part as 'subjects'.

'Sample' refers to the whole group of participants being studied. A sample should be selected so that it is representative of the group, or target population, from which it has been drawn. If a sample is biased (e.g. all-male or all-female), represents only a narrow age range, is very small or represents only one culture or group (that is, it has an ethnocentric bias), this limits the ability of the researchers to generalise the findings from the study. There are various ways of selecting a sample and we shall come across some of these as we go through the core studies.

Key concept

Volunteer or self-selected samples

As its name suggests, this type of sample is formed when participants are asked to volunteer to take part in the study. Typical ways of obtaining such a sample include putting an advert in a newspaper or a notice on a noticeboard, and sending out postal questionnaires. Those who respond to the ad or notice, and those who fill in and return the questionnaires are volunteering to take part in the study.

This can be a cost-effective and convenient way for researchers to obtain participants to take part in their research, but the drawback is that since the vast majority of people do not volunteer (for example, the return rate for a postal questionnaire is only about 30 per cent), the sample is fundamentally biased. It is only representative of those people who volunteer, and since they are atypical, this limits the usefulness of findings of studies which use self-selected samples.

Apparatus and setting

Two rooms were used within Yale University. One room contained what looked like an electric-shock generator, which had a row of 30 switches ranging from 15 to 450 volts in 15-volt increments. There were also descriptions about the type of shocks (e.g. slight shock, strong shock, intense shock, danger: severe shock, and, finally, the last switches were marked XXX). In the other room was a chair with restraining straps where the learner was to receive the shocks via his wrist. There was also a tape recording of responses which were played according to which switch was depressed, ensuring that all subjects heard the same responses in the same order from the learner.

Two male confederates took part in the study:

- The experimenter (standard abbreviation: E) – a 31-year-old 'stern' biology teacher who wore a grey lab technician's coat.

- The learner – a 47-year-old accountant who appeared mild-mannered and likeable.

Procedure

The subject was introduced to the learner and told the cover story that the study was about the effects of punishment on learning. The subject and the confederate drew lots to see who was to be teacher or learner, although the situation was rigged: both slips of paper said 'teacher'. The teacher then saw the learner taken to the other room and strapped into the chair, and his wrist attached to the equipment that would deliver the shocks. At this point the learner explained that he had a slight heart condition and asked if the shocks were dangerous. He was told by the experimenter that although the shocks could be extremely painful, they caused no permanent tissue damage.

... continued

The teacher and experimenter returned to the first room and the teacher sat at the desk with the shock generator before him. Since the learner was located in the anteroom, neither the teacher nor the experimenter would be able to see him during the study. The teacher was then told that the learner had to learn word pairs such as 'fat neck', 'blue box' and 'nice day'. The teacher had to read out the first word of the word pair and another four words, one of which was correct, and the subject had to choose the correct word. The way the learner would indicate the correct answer to the teacher was by pressing one of four switches in front of him, which lit up one of four corresponding lights on the top of the shock generator. If the subject got the answer wrong, the teacher was told to give the subject an electric shock by flicking a switch on the shock generator.

The teacher was then told that for each mistake the shocks would increase; in order to do this the subject was instructed to 'move one level higher on the shock generator each time the learner flashes a wrong answer' (Milgram 1963: 374). Although no shocks were actually given to the learner, the teacher was always given a 'test shock' of 45 volts (switch 3). A battery was installed in the shock generator for this purpose – it was not really plugged in to the electrical supply! This added to the authenticity of the study and made the teacher believe the learner was truly being given shocks.

As the teacher administered the 'shocks', all subjects experienced the same feedback from the 'learner'. This consisted of standardised answers which came through the 'answer box' (a buzzer

showed which answer the learner had selected), always in the same sequence. No vocal protest was made by the learner in this version of Milgram's study (although in later versions Milgram introduced a tape recording of the learner crying out in pain, and you may have seen this on a video of the study). The only response from the learner in this version was the predetermined set of answers which implied that he was taking part in the experiment, then, at 300V (the twentieth switch on the shock generator), the learner pounded heavily on the wall and no answer came through the answer box. The teacher was told to treat no answer as a wrong answer and to use the shock generator in the same way.

Figure 2.2 Milgram's shock generator – 30 switches, with verbal descriptions underneath, from 15 volts to 450 volts

The learner again gave no answer and after the shock at 315V he pounded on the wall again. After this, the teacher found that when he continued with the task he received no more answers, nor heard any more pounding from the learner, leaving him to assume that the learner may be unconscious, or even dead!

When the teacher protested that he did not want to continue if the learner might be hurt, it was the experimenter's task to instruct the teacher to carry on. He used four verbal 'prods' to pressurise the subject to continue with the experiment. If the subject disobeyed all four prods the experiment was ended. The prods used by experimenter were:

- Prod 1: Please continue/Please go on.
- Prod 2: The experiment requires that you continue.
- Prod 3: It is absolutely essential that you continue.
- Prod 4: You have no other choice, you must go on.

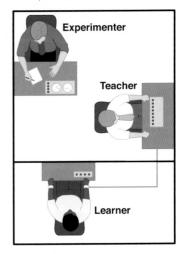

Figure 2.3 Layout of the laboratory

... continued

Further prods used by the experimenter if the subject questioned the welfare of the learner were: 'Although the shocks may be painful, there is no permanent tissue damage, so please go on', and, 'Whether the learner likes it or not, you must go on until he has learned all the words correctly. So please go on'.

Key concept

Standardising instructions and procedures

Standardisation means keeping the test conditions the same for every participant. It is a method of controlling situational variables, or environmental factors, which might have an influence on the participants' behaviour. If participants were treated differently, this would mean that fair comparisons between their responses could not be made. Standardisation of the instructions, the learner's taped responses and the sequence of prods used by the experimenter are examples of how Milgram controlled situational variables in this study.

At the end of the study, the teacher was reunited with the learner, assured that no shocks had been given, and was thoroughly debriefed about the true nature and purpose of the experiment. Milgram also interviewed the subjects using open-ended questions, projective measures (tests intended to predict whether the experience may result in any possible long-term consequences), and attitude scales to ensure (as far as possible) that the subject left the laboratory 'in a state of well-being'.

Key concept

Quantitative and qualitative data

When we think of measurement, we tend to assume this means that numbers will be used to tell us how much or how many of something there is. This is precisely what you get with quantitative data. An advantage of using numbers to measure variables is that it allows for easy comparisons to be made between subjects (e.g. on a memory test, subject one scored 10 out of 100 and subject two scored 90). We can also summarise quantitative data easily, using averages or percentages. For example, Milgram found that 65 per cent of his subjects went up to 450 volts.

Another advantage of quantitative data is that it allows for inferential statistics to be used and hypotheses to be tested, as you will see when you are doing your practical folder. It is also easier to establish the reliability of results when quantitative data are collected, as you can repeat the test to see if the findings are replicable.

Quantitative data alone can be quite narrow, however, and can also lack ecological validity. For example, if you ask someone, 'How are things with you?' they are more likely to say, 'Pretty good, thanks', than, 'On a scale of 0 to 100, where 0 is terrible and 100 is unqualified bliss, I'd say today I am scoring 65'.

In order to increase the level of detail and the validity of findings, qualitative data can be gathered. These usually consist of descriptions in words of what was observed. For example, Milgram tells us subjects were seen 'to sweat, tremble, stutter, bite their lips…[and] these were characteristic rather than exceptional responses to the experiment' (Milgram 1963: 375). This tells us a lot more about the experience of subjects in the experiment than just the fact that 65 per cent of them went to the end on the shock generator.

Qualitative data can also be reports of interviews, responses to open questions in questionnaires and reports of what subjects said and did during a study. Using this type of information gives a richness and detail to the findings and is more valid. However, it is harder to make comparisons between subjects' responses or to summarise qualitative data.

... continued

Results

The dependent variable being measured in this study was obedience. This was measured quantitatively by recording how far the subject was prepared to go on the shock generator.

Prior to the commencement of the study, Milgram had questioned a number of psychology students, adults and psychiatrists as to how many people they predicted would administer fatal electric shocks to others as part of a psychology experiment. The estimate from all groups was 0–3 per cent of subjects (mean 1.2 per cent). In the context of these predictions, Milgram's results were surprising. This illustrates well that what we think we might do is not what we actually do when faced with a situation.

All 40 subjects gave shocks up to 300 volts, with five refusing to go beyond this point. Between 315 volts and 375 volts a further nine subjects stopped obeying. This meant that 26/40, a staggering 65 per cent of subjects tested, went all the way up to 450 volts.

In addition to these statistics, Milgram had invited objective observers to record what they observed during the study. Their reports provide qualitative data. He reported that although 26 of the subjects had been obedient to the experimenter's authority right up to 450 volts, they displayed signs of extreme stress. They sweated, trembled, stuttered in their speech, bit their lips, groaned, dug their fingernails into their hands or appeared to be crying; many laughed, not in amusement, but as a nervous reaction; three subjects had violent convulsions. Milgram says that the results were also surprising to the observers, who expressed disbelief at the behaviour of the subjects. Milgram quotes one observer.

> *'I observed a mature and initially poised businessman enter the laboratory smiling and confident. Within 20 minutes he was reduced to a twitching, stuttering wreck, who was rapidly approaching a point of collapse. He constantly pulled on his earlobe and twisted his hands. At one point he pushed his fist into his forehead and muttered "Oh God, let's stop it." And yet he continued to respond to every word of the experimenter, and obeyed to the end.' (Milgram 1963: 377)*

Discussion

The level of obedience was totally unexpected. Apparently normal men had obeyed to the point where they believed they might have seriously injured a man just like themselves – the power of obedience outweighing their personal moral beliefs that it was wrong to injure others.

Milgram suggested a number of reasons to explain why the obedience rate was so high in these circumstances:

- The fact that the study was carried out at a prestigious university influenced subjects as to the worthiness of the study and the competence of the experimenter.
- The subjects believed that the learner had also volunteered and that the allocation of roles was due to chance.
- The subjects had agreed to an implicit social contract by agreeing to take part and being paid for their participation, and therefore they felt obliged to continue.
- The subjects were told that the shocks were not harmful.
- The situation was entirely new for the subjects, so they had no past experience to guide their behaviour.
- There was no obvious point at which the subjects could stop administering shocks, because each shock was only a small amount more than the previous shock.
- The subjects who did withdraw from the study did so when the 'natural break' occurred – when the subject ceased to reply.

Milgram suggested that the subjects in his study faced a number of conflicts. First, there was the conflict which arose from being asked to meet the competing demands of the experimenter and the

... continued

learner. To meet the demands of one was to fail to meet the demands of the other. The teacher was forced into making a decision, to stop or continue, and this put him in a public conflict with no satisfactory solution.

More generally, there is the conflict the subjects experienced internally: which of two ingrained behaviour dispositions should they respond to? Should they respond to their belief that one should not harm others and therefore refuse to go on with the study? Or should they respond to their equally ingrained tendency to obey authority figures, and therefore continue?

Commentary: Methods and issues

Research method, design and data gathering

Milgram carried out his research under the controlled conditions of a laboratory setting. Although it is referred to as the 'obedience experiment', it does not qualify as an 'experiment' in the true sense. (Details of what is meant by an experiment can be found in the commentary at the end of the next core study, by Piliavin *et al.*)

Milgram collected both quantitative data, measuring obedience by how far people were willing to go on the shock generator, and qualitative data, obtained by observing their behaviour and reactions during the study.

Does the study raise any ethical concerns?

For a review of the ethical guidelines that psychologists ought to follow today, see Chapter 9.

Milgram's study has been one of the most highly criticised in the whole of psychological research and provoked an investigation after it was published, during which time Milgram's membership of the American Psychological Association was suspended.

Milgram justified his work by saying that he had not anticipated his results. Although subjects were deceived by the cover story, and therefore informed consent was not obtained, this was necessary in order for the study to be carried out. He argued that although the study did encourage the subjects to continue, as that was its purpose, the fact that some subjects could and did withdraw illustrates that this was always a choice for those taking part. Milgram denied that his subjects had been harmed by the study – either by the stress they experienced at the time, or as a result of any self-knowledge they gained as a result of their participation in the study. This second point was confirmed by an independent psychiatrist, who followed up with subjects a year after the study.

Milgram thoroughly debriefed his subjects at the end of the study, introducing them to the learner and telling the 'obedient' ones that their behaviour was normal. All subjects received a report on the findings of this and subsequent studies, and 92 per cent responded to a questionnaire regarding their feelings about having taken part. Less than 2 per cent said they were sorry to have taken part, with 84 per cent saying they were glad to have been involved. Milgram himself saw this point as a key defence. If those who had taken part in the study were glad to have done so and felt it was worthwhile, this justified the study on ethical grounds. However, the participants' enthusiasm for the study may simply have been a way of reducing their cognitive dissonance.

Cognitive dissonance is a state of discomfort or anxiety, caused by holding two opposing attitudes or beliefs about a situation (e.g. I smoke and smoking is bad for me, or, I am giving electric shocks and I shouldn't be giving another person electric shocks for something as silly as a memory test). To claim that they had learned something of personal significance from the study and that it had high scientific value would have reduced the subjects' dissonance.

In the end, Milgram's work was deemed to be ethical and it is regarded as one of the most significant pieces of social psychological research to date.

Is the study useful?

Key concept

Usefulness of psychological research

Are the findings of a study useful? The questions we must ask are: useful *for what* and *to whom*? Findings may be useful to psychologists in that they help to explain or predict behaviour, or useful generally in helping to explain behaviours and solve problems in the real world.

Studies can be useful to psychology itself. A study or theory may be highly generative, that is, it leads to a great deal of further research, both testing and refining the conclusions drawn in a particular area of study. Examples include Freud's theory of psychosexual development, and Piaget's theory of cognitive development (which we will look at later in this book).

It follows that studies which contribute to the debate in a particular area are also useful to psychology (e.g. Samuel and Bryant's work contributes to the debate concerning children's cognitive development by providing support for the sequence of Piaget's stages, but also suggesting refinements to the timing of the stages, as their work proposes that he underestimated young children's abilities).

Usefulness can be assessed by asking: Are the conclusions or findings from the study of any use in helping to solve problems in the real world?

Note that the usefulness of a study will be reduced if:

- The study is low in ecological validity and therefore findings cannot be easily generalised to a real-life setting.
- The study is reductionist and ignores other important factors or variables which affect behaviour.
- The validity of the findings of the study can be challenged (e.g. if demand characteristics could have affected the findings, if sample biases mean the findings are not generalisable to a broad population).

Milgram's study is useful to psychology as an explanation of why people obey in certain situations. In terms of the influences on our behaviour, Milgram's study shows us that we do not always act in the way we might predict. He argues that obedience 'comes easily and often', and that if we are in a situation where obedience is demanded of us by a legitimate authority, we can be encouraged by that authority to act in a way that may harm another person, even though this means acting in opposition to our own personal morality.

In terms of individual and situational explanations of behaviour, Milgram's study demonstrates how it can be the situation you are in which influences your behaviour, and that we abdicate control when we are in the 'agentic state'. We are socialised to obey.

Are the conclusions we can draw from this study useful in helping to solve problems in the real world? Many writers see Milgram's work as illustrating the inevitability of good people being drawn into malevolent systems and the likely repetition of events such as the Holocaust in Nazi Germany. However, by knowing that we are socialised to obey, we are armed with the knowledge which suggests that another holocaust is far from inevitable. In terms of politics, we have the power to choose whom we obey. Good people are easily integrated into a malevolent system, and therefore it is up to us to ensure that such a system is not put into place. Use your vote wisely!

Validity and reliability of the study

Key concept

Internal validity (design validity)

When we ask, 'Are the findings of a study valid?', what we are really asking is, 'Can we believe the findings? Are there any reasons to believe that they might not be true?'

Internal validity is determined by the extent to which a study is free of design faults which might affect the result, meaning that the test is not a true test of what it intended to measure. Factors which reduce the validity (internal validity) of findings include the following:

- Low generalisability of findings (e.g. sample biases, ethnocentric bias, difficulty extrapolating to other groups of people or settings). If the findings are not generalisable, they are not valid.
- If demand characteristics might have affected the study (see the key concept below on demand characteristics).
- If the findings of the study do not prove to be reliable (see the key concept below on reliability).
- If it is possible that a confounding variable has operated systematically alongside the independent variable this might affect the validity of the findings (we will look at this in more detail in later chapters).
- If it is possible that the study is out of date or has lost validity over time. This is a particular problem for studies in social psychology. Social, political, cultural and technological changes can mean that a study only represents the time and place in which it was carried out. We cannot generalise the findings to the present day.

Is this study valid? In terms of the generalisability of Milgram's sample, we might question whether conclusions could be drawn about a broader population of people's obedience to authority. It contains a number of ethnocentric biases, such as age, gender, all being from New Haven, and so on, and it is also a volunteer sample. These give us reason to question the generalisability and therefore the validity of his findings.

Did the subjects really believe they were administering shocks? It has been claimed that subjects were not really deceived by the study and did not genuinely believe that they were administering electric shocks to another person, that their behaviour was simply a response to demand characteristics present in the study.

Key concept

Demand characteristics

Demand characteristics are the clues or cues given consciously or unconsciously by the researcher, or elements in the procedure of the study that reveal the purpose of the study. If subjects can work out what the researcher is trying to investigate, it is possible for them to falsify their results to please the researcher, to make sure that the study 'works'. Alternatively, subjects may adopt the 'screw you' approach, making sure they do not behave in the way they believe they are expected to, thus spoiling the study.

If results have been affected by subjects responding to demand characteristics, this will mean that they are not valid (i.e. they have not tested what they intended to test), which reduces the scientific value and usefulness of the research. However, when Milgram asked his subjects whether they believed they were administering real shocks in the questionnaire they completed a year after the study, only 2.4 per cent claimed to be 'certain' the learner was not receiving shocks. Unless they were all talented actors, the signs of tension shown by the teachers suggested they really did believe in the study at the time. Also, if they did not believe shocks were actually being given, why did some of the teachers feel it necessary to stop before they reached 450 volts?

In social psychological studies researchers can often justify the use of deception, telling participants a cover story to hide the true purpose of the study, as this is essential in order to avoid demand characteristics influencing participants' responses. Imagine how Milgram's results would have differed if he had told subjects that he was trying to see how far the experimenter could coerce them into going on the shock generator.

Key concept

Ecological validity

Is the behaviour that the participants are being asked to perform in the study comparable with behaviours that people might carry out in the course of their everyday life? In other words, how realistic is the study? If the behaviour in a study is very like real-life behaviours, the study is said to be high in ecological validity. If the behaviours required of participants in a study are not like real-life behaviours, the study is low in ecological validity and this limits its usefulness.

Since people tend to behave differently in a lab when they know they are being tested, and due to the artificial nature of the laboratory environment itself, social psychological studies carried out in the lab tend to be low in ecological validity.

This study took place in a laboratory, which was essential to convince subjects that it was a valid piece of research. However, this may mean that the subjects' behaviour was only typical of the behaviour they would display in a laboratory, so the study lacks ecological validity on this count.

Key concept

Reliability

Reliability refers to the consistency of a measurement. A test or measure is reliable if it gives similar results when carried out again in similar circumstances. In other words, if the findings prove to be replicable (consistent) when the same or a similar researcher carries out the study again, the test or measure is reliable. If the study is not reliable, that is, if the repeat of the study gives different results from the original, this gives us reason to question the validity of the original research. Reliable findings can help to support the validity of research.

However, the relationship between reliability and validity is not straightforward, as a test could prove to be reliable but still not be valid. For example, if a researcher decided that the cleverest people in the world had two or more 'h's in their name, Stephen Hawking (with two 'h's) would be cleverer than Albert Einstein (no 'h's!). We could count the 'h's again and find that the result is reliable: two 'h's for Stephen Hawking and none for Einstein is a consistent finding. However, it is not true that 'h's in your name make you clever, so the finding is not valid.

Validity over time is related to reliability; what it means is that the findings remain consistent when the study is replicated after the passage of time. Milgram's study was carried out more than 40 years ago. Do you think this study would give the same results if we carried it out in, say, Blackpool, on a sample of similar men today?

Piliavin *et al.* study: Subway Samaritan

Is there such a thing as altruism?

The definition of altruism is when you do something for someone else without gaining anything for yourself. But do you think we ever do anything to help another person without getting back something for ourselves, even if it is just a good feeling that we helped or avoiding the bad feeling we might get if we didn't? Can you think of a truly altruistic act?

The murder of Kitty Genovese and the altruism debate

The debate surrounding the existence of altruism alone would be sufficient to provoke research into the area, but perhaps a greater provocation occurred in America in 1964, with the murder of a 28-year-old woman called Kitty Genovese.

Coming home from work at about 3 a.m. Kitty was attacked on three separate occasions, within a 35-minute period, by a man with a knife, although it was not until the third attack that he actually succeeded in killing her. Kitty had parked her car and was within about 100 metres of her home. At one point in the attack apparently frightened off by neighbours shouting from their windows, the attacker actually drove away in his car, but when the neighbours turned their lights off he returned, this time to kill Kitty. What made this case infamous was that 38 people actually saw the killer from the windows of their homes, but none of them reported the incident to the police until it was too late. No one was prepared to come forward and help, either by intervening or by telephoning the police until, finally, one man got a neighbour to call after phoning a friend in a different county for advice. By the time the call was made Kitty was dead.

Figure 2.4 Kitty Genovese

The incident was reported in the *New York Times* in March 1964 and contained the following condensed extracts.

Twice the sound of their voices and the sudden glow of their bedroom lights interrupted him and frightened him off. Each time he returned, sought her out and stabbed her again. Not one person telephoned the police during the assault; one witness called after the woman was dead.
Kitty Genovese was returning home from her job as manager of a bar in Hollis. She parked her red Fiat in a lot adjacent to the Kew Gardens Long Island Rail Road Station … She turned off the lights of her car, locked the door and started to walk the 100 feet to the entrance of her apartment… She got as far as a street light in front of a bookstore before the man grabbed her.

She screamed. Lights went on in the ten-storey apartment house … Windows slid open and voices punctured the early morning stillness.

Miss Genovese screamed: 'Oh, my God, he stabbed me! Please help me! Please help me!'

From one of the upper windows in the apartment house, a man called down: 'Let that girl alone!'

The assailant looked up at him, shrugged and walked down Austin Street toward a white sedan parked a short distance away. Miss Genovese struggled to her feet.

Lights went out. The killer returned to Miss Genovese, now trying to make her way around the side of the building by the parking lot to get to her apartment. The assailant grabbed her again. 'I'm dying!' she shrieked. 'I'm dying!'

Windows opened again, and lights went on in many apartments. The assailant got into his car and drove away. Miss Genovese staggered to her feet …

The assailant returned. By then, Miss Genovese had crawled to the back of the building where the freshly painted brown doors to the apartment house held out hope of safety. The killer tried the first door; she wasn't there. At the second door… he saw her slumped on the floor at the foot of the stairs. He stabbed her a third time – fatally.

… the police received their first call from a man who was a neighbour of Miss Genovese. In two minutes they were at the scene… The man explained… 'I didn't want to get involved.'

There are numerous cases where bystanders did nothing to help victims of varying crimes. Just typing 'bystanders did nothing' into Google, you will find example after example of cases where people have not responded to cries for help. It is very easy to criticise, but imagine that you saw a woman screaming at a small tearful child, possibly even hitting the child. Would you go up to the woman and stick up for the small child? If not, why not? Now imagine you are walking along a street, you turn the corner and see a man holding on to a woman's arm and shouting at her, while she screams back at him and looks as if she is pulling away. Would you feel that you could 'interfere' in this situation?

If we decide to intervene in such situations, we would have to consider the circumstances carefully because both of these are ambiguous – that is, we have no idea what is really happening here because we do not have all the facts. We would therefore have to make attributions about the nature of the situation and decide who was to blame (if anyone) or whether the person actually needed help or not.

The Genovese case sparked a great deal of research in social psychology, looking into some of the reasons why people do and don't help. Key researchers in this area were Latané and Darley (1968) who were social psychologists teaching in New York at the time of the Kitty Genovese incident. They were interested in whether the presence of other people affected helping behaviour. Using the Kitty Genovese incident as a stimulus, they decided to look at the idea of the 'unresponsive bystander'. They thought that it was because there were so many witnesses to her murder that she was not helped.

Latané and Darley asked male college students to sit in a waiting room and fill in a questionnaire before taking part in a study of people's attitudes toward the problems of urban life. They were sitting either alone or in groups of three. The researchers arranged for smoke to pour in through a small ventilation grille and secretly watched the students' behaviour over the next six minutes.

You would expect that the moment smoke started coming through the vent they would feel very uncomfortable and become concerned that the building was on fire. When they were on their own, 75 per cent reported the smoke within the six-minute period, and half of these reported it within the first two minutes. However, what happened with the subjects waiting together was quite different. Only 12 per cent of these students reported the smoke within two minutes, and only 38 per cent of the groups reported the smoke within the six-minute period, which meant that the other 62 per cent carried on working for the full six minutes, even though the room was completely full of smoke.

The subjects later explained their actions. The ones who were waiting together had looked to each other for guidance as to how to behave. As none of them knew what to do, and no one moved, they redefined the situation as harmless. Latané and Darley called this redefinition **pluralistic ignorance**, although this situation can only occur when people are not actually aware of *all* the facts.

Another factor which influences whether others are prepared to help or not is when **diffusion of responsibility** occurs. Diffusion of responsibility is where the responsibility for the situation is actually spread, or diffused, among the people present. This means that the more people present, the more a potential helper believes that the responsibility is spread out, so they feel less personally responsible and are less likely to help as a result. This should mean that the more potential helpers present, as in the Genovese witnesses, the less likely a person is to help.

Darley and Latané (1968) thought that if there were lots of people present this might decrease the likelihood of helping behaviour. They decided to investigate this by manipulating the size of a group again. In this case, however, none of the group could see each other, yet all were apparently aware of exactly what was happening.

They recruited their subjects from a group of female students and told them they were to take part in a discussion group where college students were to talk about the kinds of personal problems they were experiencing. They were told that the way they would be assured of anonymity was to stay in separate cubicles and talk over a kind of intercom. It was also explained that this was to ensure that they could talk openly without embarrassment.

At the beginning of the discussion students were led to believe that they were taking part in the discussion with either five other students, three other students or one other student. They were also told that they would each have a chance to speak for two minutes and that the other members of the group would then each have a turn to comment on what the student had just said. The reason for this was in fact because there was only one subject per group, and all the other 'subjects' were actually pre-recorded voices. Soon after they started the discussion, the stooge would explain that she had epilepsy and would imply that she was prone to seizures as she was quite stressed by urban living. Shortly afterwards she could be heard to make a series of noises and gasps for help, crying out that she was having a seizure and then falling silent.

Darley and Latané noted the number of subjects who actually left their cubicle to find out what was happening to the victim or to find someone to help:

- When they believed they were the only ones present, 85 per cent helped within 60 seconds.

- When they thought there was one other person besides themselves hearing the 'victim', the speed of response was slower, and only 62 per cent helped within 60 seconds.

- When the subjects thought there were four other students besides themselves and the seizure victim, only 31 per cent helped in the first 60 seconds.

The conclusion was that the likelihood of people helping in an emergency situation will go down as the number of people who witness the situation goes up. This is the bystander effect, where the responsibility is diffused among the people present, and the more people there are, the less responsibility each one takes.

Piliavin *et al.* (1969), however, wondered if the effects that were being shown in these laboratory studies really happened in emergency situations. Could it be that these laboratory based studies of helping behaviour, where in fact there was only one possible helper, the subject themselves, were low in ecological validity? Piliavin *et al.* also considered that the level of help offered would be affected by the nature of the victim, and theorised that a man who was seemingly ill would be helped more than a man who seemed to be drunk.

The Study

Irving M. Piliavin, Judith A. Rodin and Jane Allyn Piliavin (1969) 'Good Samaritanism, an underground phenomenon?', *Journal of Personality and Social Psychology*, 13 (4): 289–99

Background

Prior to this study, research had already suggested that there were a number of factors which would influence the likelihood of helping behaviour occurring. However, many of the past studies had confounding factors which may have influenced the results, such as ambiguity or a lack of ecological validity. Where the 'accident' occurred out of sight there was ambiguity: Had someone else helped? Was the emergency over now? Where the incident was set up under laboratory conditions within a controlled setting there might be low ecological validity, especially where a large number of confederates had been told to do nothing, as in real life we are not in a situation where most of the potential helpers or responders present have been primed from the outset not to react.

Piliavin *et al.* (1969) designed their study to take place in a natural environment, to improve ecological validity, and to stage an incident where the ambiguity of the situation was reduced to a minimum so that pluralistic ignorance should not enter the equation. People would be able to see the 'emergency' face to face, so the person's need for help, and whether or not he had already been helped, would be obvious as it was happening right in front of the subjects.

Aims and hypotheses

The aims of the study were to see, in a face-to-face situation in a real-life setting, from which there would be no clear escape route:

... continued

- whether an ill person would get more help than a drunk person
- whether there would be ethnocentric behaviour in helping (i.e. people would help someone of their own race more than someone of another race)
- whether the intervention of a model (a confederate of the experimenters, who would step in and offer help) would influence others' helping behaviour.

Method

For this study the experimental method was used.

A field experiment was carried out using covert observation techniques to gather data (see Commentary, below, for explanations of these concepts).

Piliavin *et al.* engaged 16 general studies students from the University of Columbia in the USA to carry out the study and gather the data. These 16 were split into four teams of researchers, giving four members in each team, two of whom were female. Each team member was given a role; they always performed the same role in each trial and they always worked in the same teams.

Below is a description of the roles played by the team members.

> ### Key concept
>
> #### Experimental method
> The experimental method (or scientific method, as it is also known) is a research method which can establish causal relationships between variables. A hypothesis is formulated to predict the effect of one variable, known as the independent variable (IV), on another variable, known as the dependent variable (DV). Usually two conditions are operated, with one testing subjects in the experimental condition, where the IV is introduced, and one testing subjects in the control condition. The control condition is used for comparison to see if the IV has affected the DV.

Table 2.1

Team member	Role, appearance and behaviour
Victim	The victims were standardised in their appearance and behaviour across the four teams.
	They were always male, between the ages of 26 and 35.
	Their dress was identical: Eisenhower jacket, old trousers, no tie. An Eisenhower jacket is a waist-length casual jacket, first designed as part of Eisenhower's military uniform – easier to drive in than a full-length jacket or coat, and easy to wear a sidearm with; in civilian life it is probably the ease with which you can get to your small change or your car keys that ensures this short jacket style maintains its popularity.
	They got on the train and went to stand near the pole in the centre of the carriage (critical area), waited 70 seconds, then staggered forwards and collapsed on the floor, looking up at the ceiling.
	In order to operationalise the IV 'drunk' or 'ill', the victim played these two roles on alternate days. On the drunk day he smelled of alcohol and carried a liquor bottle in a brown paper bag. On the ill days he carried a black cane (walking stick).
	In order to test whether same-race helping occurred, one of the models was black and three were white (the only black male student who had volunteered to carry out the study was allocated to the role of victim).

... continued

Table 2.1 *continued*

Team member	Role, appearance and behaviour
Observer 1 and Observer 2	These were female, and appeared to be just ordinary passengers on the train. They would get on with the other team members and make their way to be as close to their allotted position in the adjacent areas as possible.
	Observer 1 would then observe and record: the race, sex and location of passengers in the critical area, the total number of passengers in the whole carriage and the total number of helpers who assisted the victim, and their race, sex and original position in the carriage.
	Observer 2 would observe and record: the race, sex and location of passengers in the critical area, the total number of passengers in the whole carriage and the total number of helpers who assisted the victim. She also measured how long it took for the first helper to arrive and, in the model conditions, how long it took for a subsequent helper to arrive.
	Both spoke to the person immediately next to them after the event took place, noting down what they responded and also making a note of any other spontaneous comments made by passengers.
Model	Since laboratory studies had suggested that people did not help, a further team member was used who was to step in and help to see if his actions would bring in others to assist. The model was always male, aged 24–29, and casually dressed. The model was to help by getting the victim to a seated position and staying with him until the train arrived at the next stop.
	To see if the model had any effect, and whether which side of the carriage he was in or how long it took him to help would affect others helping, five model conditions were devised:
	Critical area, early help (i.e. he stood in the critical area when he got on the train and helped approximately 70 seconds after the victim fell).
	Critical area, late help (late meant after approximately 150 seconds).
	Adjacent area, early help.
	Adjacent area, late help (for both 'adjacent area' conditions he would have to cross the carriage to help).
	No model: this was to act as a control condition to see what would happen with no model intervention.

Location

The study took place in the New York subway, between 59th and 125th Street stations on the 8th Avenue line. This particular run of track was selected as there was a non-stop ride of 72 minutes, giving enough time for the procedure to be carried out. The trials took place between April and June 1968, between the hours of 11 a.m. and 3 p.m. The teams only selected the old-style trains with two-seater seats.

... continued

Figure 2.5 An Eisenhower jacket of the type 'victims' were wearing

Subjects

Over the three-month period approximately 4,450 unsolicited subjects were observed over the trials. The racial mix was about 55 per cent white and 45 per cent black, and the mean number of people present in the whole carriage was 43, with a mean of 8.5 for the critical area where the incident took place.

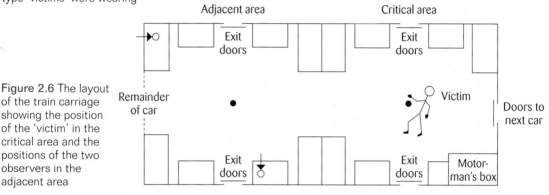

Figure 2.6 The layout of the train carriage showing the position of the 'victim' in the critical area and the positions of the two observers in the adjacent area

Source: Piliavin *et al.* (1969) 'Good Samaritanism, an underground phenomenon?' *Journal of Personality and Social Psychology*, 13(4) 289–99. Copyright American Psychological Association Reproduced with permission.

Variables

There were three independent variables:

- whether the victim appeared drunk or ill
- whether the victim was black or white
- the manipulation of the actions of the model (the effect of the presence or absence of the model, manipulations in the time delay before the model helped and which side of the carriage the model was originally standing in).

The dependent variables measured included:

- the number of helpers and the speed at which they offered help
- the race and gender of helpers
- if anyone moved out of the critical area
- the comments made by passengers during the incident.

Procedure

The teams entered the train through different doors and the victim enacted his 'collapse' after 70 seconds. By consulting a random number table drawn up before the trials, the model would have worked out which condition he was in and he would stand on the appropriate side of the carriage and time himself ready to step in. The observers made their recordings as unobtrusively as possible. They were participant observers.

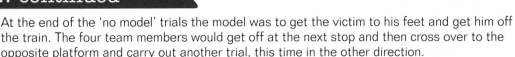

... continued

At the end of the 'no model' trials the model was to get the victim to his feet and get him off the train. The four team members would get off at the next stop and then cross over to the opposite platform and carry out another trial, this time in the other direction.

The teams were supposed to alternate the victim condition daily (drunk or ill), but the victim for team 2 did not like performing the drunk condition, which meant that the ill condition was carried out more often. A total of 103 trials were recorded, 65 in the ill condition and 38 in the drunk condition.

Results

One of the main findings was that, unlike the studies carried out under laboratory conditions, people generally helped and were quick to help. So for 79 per cent of the trials the model was not required, and the amount of trials where the model was required was too small to fully analyse the effects of his original location or speed of helping.

The nature of the victim influenced levels of helping. The ill victim received spontaneous help from a fellow passenger before 70 seconds had elapsed after his collapse on 62 out of 65 trials, and the drunk victim on 19 out of 38 trials. This confirmed that someone who appears ill is more likely to receive help than someone who appears drunk. Not only was there more help for the ill victim, but help also came more quickly (a median of five seconds rather then 109 seconds for the drunk condition).

Of the 81 first helpers, 90 per cent were males (even though the gender breakdown for the critical area was 60 per cent male and 40 per cent female); this leads to the conclusion that men were more likely to help in this sort of scenario than women.

No one left the compartment during any of the trials, but in 21 of the 103 trials, 34 people moved from the critical area to the adjacent area, with more leaving in the drunk than the ill trials.

No significant tendency for same-race helping was seen, although there was a slight tendency for same-race helping to occur more in the drunk condition than the ill condition.

There was no evidence of diffusion of responsibility. Remember, this was the hypothesis derived from laboratory studies, that the more people there are present, the less help would be offered. This was supposed to be because each person would feel less personally responsible the more people there were available to share the responsibility. In the Piliavin *et al.* study, a slight trend was shown in the opposite direction – with more help being offered when the carriage was fuller.

Table 2.2   Results for the ill condition, with no model (help came spontaneously before 70 seconds from when the victim collapsed), showing the help received by black and white victims.

	No. of trials	No. of times helped	Overall % of helping
White victim	54	54	100%
Black victim	8	8	100%

Source: adapted from Piliavin *et al.* (1969)

Table 2.3   Results for the ill condition, with model, showing the help received by white victims. (There were no trials with the black victim in this condition.)

	No. of trials	No. of times helped	Overall % of helping
White victim	3	3	100%

Source: adapted from Piliavin *et al.* (1969)

Table 2.4   Results for the drunk condition, with no model (help came spontaneously before 70 seconds from when the victim collapsed), showing the help received by black and white victims.

	No. of trials	No. of times helped	Overall % of helping
White victim	11	11	100%
Black victim	11	8	73%

Source: adapted from Piliavin *et al.* (1969)

... continued

Table 2.5   Results for the drunk condition, with model, showing the help received by black and white victims.

	No. of trials	No. of times helped	Overall % of helping
White victim	13	10	77%
Black victim	3	2	66%

Source: adapted from Piliavin *et al.* (1969)

Discussion

What explanation do Piliavin *et al.* offer for the findings? They propose a model of helping which included the assumptions that observation of an emergency creates an emotional state in the bystander, that is, it induces a state of arousal (interpreted negatively in this instance as either disgust, fear or sympathy), and that we are motivated to reduce this negative arousal. This can be achieved by the following actions:

- helping directly
- going to get help
- leaving
- not offering help because you have decided the victim does not deserve it.

Additionally, the action we choose in order to reduce arousal will depend on us carrying out a cost–benefit analysis. This means we will carry out the action that we assess as giving us the greatest benefit and the least cost. Costs of helping include effort, disgust and embarrassment; and there are also the costs of not helping to weigh up, such as self-blame and our worry about what others will think of us if we do not help. Benefits might include self-praise or the praise of others.

Piliavin *et al.* suggested that this model is consistent with all their findings. For example, the drunk is helped less because the costs of helping are higher – he may get angry, over-friendly or may even vomit! – and the costs of not helping are lower, as we may feel less guilt for not helping because we believe he is at least partially to blame for the position he is in.

Women help less in this study because the costs of helping (effort) are high, and the costs of not helping are low – as it is not a woman's place to help in such a situation, she will feel less self-blame or have less fear of judgement by others.

Why was no diffusion of responsibility recorded in this study? Piliavin *et al.* suggested that this may be because the subjects on the train were face to face with the victim and could not either conclude that there was no emergency, or, if no helper came along, that the emergency was over. These are two possible assumptions which might have led the subjects in the earlier laboratory-based studies not to offer help.

Perhaps the reason why diffusion of responsibility was not evident in the subway study was because there were more potential helpers present here than in laboratory experiments. All past research had involved the use of only one subject, with the rest being stooges of the experimenter. Therefore, there was only one potential helper and that potential helper may have been looking to everyone else to guide them as to what they should do. Bearing in mind that all the other people 'taking part' did nothing as part of the study, perhaps the phenomenon of pluralistic ignorance could explain the results of past research in this area. In the subway study there were large numbers of potential helpers, and this may have resulted in more helping behaviour rather than less, and as the group size increased, the potential number of helpers grew.

It may therefore be that diffusion of responsibility is only an artefact of laboratory-based studies with one potential helper, the naive subject.

Commentary: Methods and issues

Research method, design and data gathering

The study used the experimental method. It was a field experiment, using an independent groups design comparing, for example, the helping response to an ill or drunk victim, the helping response to a victim of the same or a different race, and so on.

Key concept

Laboratory vs field experiments

The following table provides a breakdown of the strengths and weaknesses of each experimental setting.

Table 2.6

Location	✅ Strengths	❌ Weaknesses
Laboratory	In the controlled environment of the lab it is easier to isolate the IV as a causal factor and keep all extraneous variables constant or controlled. In the lab, technical equipment can be used to measure variables (e.g. EEG machine).	One problem with the lab setting is that subjects have consented to attend and be studied. This means that all lab studies can be affected by subject reactivity, with subjects responding to demand characteristics. This leads us to question the internal validity of lab-based studies. Since the lab setting is often constrained and unlike real-life settings, lab studies of social behaviour also tend to lack ecological validity.
Field (natural or real-life setting)	By carrying out a study in a real-life setting, the ecological validity of a study of social behaviour can be improved. (**Note:** Be careful not to assume that all studies carried out in a real-life setting are ecologically valid. For example, if the study involved 300 clowns riding bikes through a supermarket to see how people react, this would not be ecologically valid, as the experience of subjects would not be realistic!)	In the field it is harder to isolate the IV as a causal factor and keep all extraneous variables constant or controlled, so the possibility of other variables affecting the DV, becoming confounding variables, is higher in the field. It can be harder to transport and set up sensitive technical equipment in the field.

The data-gathering method used in this study was participant, covert observation.

Key concept

Observation as a data-gathering technique

Observation can be carried out either covertly, that is, undercover and without the knowledge of those being observed, or overtly, where subjects are either aware or have been informed of the fact that they are being observed.

The advantage of covert observation is that you are sampling 'real' behaviour, uncontaminated by the subjects' desire to respond to demand characteristics. Some researchers believe that the only valid way to sample typical human behaviour is by covert observation in a field setting, the method used by Piliavin *et al.* in this study.

Observation can also be carried out as participant or non-participant observation. This means that the researcher is either a part of the setting or event they are observing (participant), or is outside the setting (non-participant). The advantage of being a participant, as in the Piliavin *et al.* study, is that you get an insight into the experience yourself, and also you have a good vantage point for your observations. However, your mere presence may change the course of the events you are observing. It could be that the inactivity of some potential helpers in the adjacent area in the trials was because of the inactivity of the two observers; we cannot know for sure.

It is also possible that if you are observing as a participant for a longer period of time, you may become too involved in the setting to be objective about your observations.

Does the study raise any ethical concerns?

There is a problem with carrying out the study using covert observation techniques. An unsolicited subject cannot be briefed about the nature of the study and give their informed consent. Nor is it always possible for the subject to be debriefed and later asked for permission to use their data. This means that this study raises ethical concerns about consent and invading people's privacy. Don't we have the right to go about our daily business without being monitored for the purposes of scientific research without our knowledge?

Also, deception is used in the study. The victim is not really in need of help, just play-acting a role for the purposes of the study. Seeing someone fall, and the anxiety such an event can arouse, may have upset some of the passengers on the train, who would never know that this was not a real collapse. They might also have to confront their conscience about their lack of willingness to help, and this self-knowledge might have caused distress to some subjects.

Is the study useful?

The study offers a useful model where helping behaviour is described in terms of the emotional and cognitive processes which a person responds to in making a decision to offer assistance. The study is also useful in that it shows the care that must be taken when trying to generalise findings from the social psychology laboratory to real-life settings.

Even though the study does contradict the earlier laboratory studies, and shows a much higher level of helping than the laboratory studies would have predicted, there is still no suggestion that people act out of pure altruistic motives. Piliavin *et al.* see them as acting out of 'a selfish desire to rid oneself of an unpleasant emotional state'.

Validity and reliability of the study

Given that the study took place on a real train in a real setting, and that the behaviour enacted by the victim, although uncommon, is a possible scenario people may encounter, the study is high in ecological validity. The internal validity of the study is also increased by the fact that the subjects were unaware that they were being observed, which would suggest that their behaviour was as it would have been if the event were actually real and not part of a psychological investigation. In other words, demand characteristics were less likely to be a threat to the validity of the findings.

It is possible to question the generalisability of the sample, however, and this means that the validity of the study's findings may be affected. The study is now around 40 years old – do you think people would be as helpful today as they were back then? Is it possible that the study's findings have lost validity over time? As this study was a field experiment and used an independent groups design, it is also possible that the behaviour of the subjects was affected by variables other than those tested by the researcher, and these extraneous variables may have confounded the study.

Key concept

Extraneous and confounding variables

For an experiment to establish that it is the IV causing any observed change in the DV, all other variables, known as extraneous variables, need to be controlled or kept constant. The experimenter has to make sure the subjects are not too dissimilar from each other, and must control situational variables, for example by standardising procedures and instructions.

Variables which are not controlled operate alongside the IV, making it impossible to establish whether it is the IV or this second variable, which has become a confounding variable, which has caused any change in the DV. If it is possible that the study has been affected by confounding variables then the study's validity can be questioned. Field experiments and studies which employ an independent groups design are most likely to be affected by extraneous and confounding variables.

Reicher and Haslam: BBC prison study

Roles

Social influence comes into play when we take on one of the many roles that are part of our daily lives: daughter or son, student, grandchild, employee, and so on. Your behaviour is influenced by the role you adopt, and the role may also change the status you have in relation to others. In fact, a role does not exist unless it involves some kind of interaction with others. You cannot be a nurse unless you have a patient, or a teacher unless you have a student.

A role is usually defined as 'the behaviours expected of a person occupying a certain position in a group'. How far do the roles we adopt have an influence on our behaviour? Could the role we have adopted or been given override our individual will and make us behave in ways in which we would not behave if we were not fulfilling the role? Psychology has considered some of the dangers of subjugating our will to fulfil what we perceive is our role in a situation. A famous study that seemed to illustrate this was the Stanford prison experiment carried out by Haney, Banks and Zimbardo (1973).

The Stanford Prison Experiment (SPE)

Imagine a type of community which might be affected by some of the factors that might lead a person to conform to their role rather than act individually. These include the nature of the role assigned to the person – do they have power or are they in a subordinate role? Are they the only member taking that role or are they a member of a group each taking the same role?

One such community might be a prison. Prisoners would have their individual identity removed by wearing uniforms and being given a prison number. Prison officers would also be deindividuated because they would be wearing uniforms. This would give them anonymity when dealing with prisoners or if they were operating in a group, and they might be perceived as being less human and therefore potential perpetrators of aggression. Finally, the role played by the prison inmates would be very likely to affect the way they behave. All these factors lead us to considering one of the most famous pieces of social psychological research, undertaken by Haney, Banks and Zimbardo (1973) and known as the Stanford Prison Experiment.

This study was funded by the US Navy and the Marine Corps, with the aim of helping to explain the causes of conflict between guards and prisoners in its prison system, where brutality was not unknown. Previous explanations had focused on the disposition of the people involved, with the belief that the prisoners were likely to be 'typical' criminals who would have little regard for the welfare of others and who would be likely to act in an aggressive and impulsive way. On the other hand, the guards were thought to have been attracted to the job because they were potentially insensitive and controlling. Zimbardo was interested in looking at the situational impact on the behaviour of individuals, because if the situation was the reason for the behaviour, the problems could be addressed more easily.

If you are of the opinion that prison should be punitive, you might think it is desirable for the experience of those incarcerated to be brutal and harsh, teaching them a lesson. However, Zimbardo *et al.*'s research in prisons, talking to current and ex-inmates and those working as guards, showed that the system went beyond brutal but fair and into the realms of the inhumane, rife with both sexual and physical abuse. This has an impact on prisoners on their release, as Haney (1973: 2) pointed out: 'The experience of prison creates undeniably almost to the point of cliché, an intense hatred and disrespect in most inmates for the authority and the established order of society into which they will eventually return.'

The study was therefore designed to find out whether it was possible to explain what was going on within the prison environment by attributing the causes to either situational or dispositional reasons. It was not possible to research this in a natural, real prison setting because the structure of the prison setting and the nature of those involved were variables already present and would therefore confound each other. This would mean that it would be impossible to answer the question of which was leading to the brutality. Therefore a simulated prison was set up in the basement of Stanford University in the USA and the student participants were recruited through a local newspaper advert, calling for volunteers to take part in a study of the psychological effects of prison life.

The applicants were given diagnostic interviews and personality tests in order to exclude those with psychological or mental problems, or a history of crime or drug abuse. This left a sample of 24 male college students, who were healthy, intelligent and middle-class, from the USA and Canada. They were randomly divided into two groups by the toss of a coin, so that, in effect, there were no differences between the two groups. One group was assigned the role of prisoners and one group was assigned the role of guards. Zimbardo set up conditions that would result in the prisoners being disorientated, depersonalised and emasculated, and for deindividuation to take place, which included 'uniform' for both the prisoners and the guards.

The prison study was supposed to last for 14 days, but was actually terminated after six days due to the extreme behaviours of the guards and the intense responses of the prisoners. Prisoners experienced sadistic and humiliating treatment from the guards, and the high levels of discomfort they felt initially caused them to rebel. The differences between the two groups became obvious within a very short space of time, with the guards tormenting the prisoners and imposing physical punishments and even sexual humiliation. The guards volunteered to work extra hours; the prison became dirty and inhospitable; the right to use the bathroom suddenly became a frequently denied privilege; and some prisoners were forced to clean toilets with their bare hands. Over time, the regime resulted in the prisoners accepting the behaviour of the guards and becoming overly passive. During the study, four prisoners showed severe emotional disturbances and had to be 'released' early.

Figure 2.7 A 'guard' in the Stanford Prison Experiment keeps a 'prisoner' in line

The results of the study demonstrated how social roles (which are environmental factors) can have a significant influence on behaviour, thus supporting the situational rather than the dispositional hypothesis. The conclusions of the researchers were that the structure of prisons and not the nature of those who inhabit them is the source of brutality. In this study, the participants seemed to accept their roles and behaved accordingly. The brutal regime operated by the guards, who were normal middle-class students, was caused by them accepting and responding to the role they perceived that they were being asked to play. Zimbardo theorised that the guards became brutal because they were affected by the power that their roles gave them over the prisoners, and that this power made them behave in the way that they did. He called this the pathology of power and used it to explain, in part, how tyranny can arise.

Social identity theory

In addition to responding to the roles we have been assigned, situations can affect us in other ways too. There is another group process which may help to explain some of the behaviours we will cover in this chapter. This is the way in which we need to feel that the group we are a part of is the best group, and so we behave in ways that make this seem true, such as favouring our own group or group members over other groups.

Have you ever thought about your group of friends and compared them to other groups of people you know? The expectation would be that you would rate your friends more highly than other groups. Similarly, if you rated your psychology class in comparison to other classes, it is more than likely that you would believe yours to be the best.

You must have come across people who, no matter what it is, always seem to have one better or bigger than yours. Well, this kind of group thinking is very similar, where the belief is that the group to which we belong is bigger and/or better than everyone else's. We also tend to think that our group is the norm, and therefore everyone else will be judged by our standards, which, of course, are the best. It is almost like being egocentric about your group, and this kind of group self-centredness is known as **ethnocentrism**. Another way of looking at ethnocentrism is to think of it as being centred on our ethnic group (but exchange the word 'ethnic' for 'social group').

Ethnocentrism seems to occur the minute people are divided into groups. It does not matter what that group is, or on what basis it was formed, but we perceive the group we belong to as being superior to other groups and we develop an **in-group bias** (we are biased in favour of the group we are in). This bias is demonstrated by consistently rating the abilities and characteristics of the group we belong to as much higher than those of other people, even when this is not the case.

Ethnocentricity is linked to the process of stereotyping, which involves grouping people – other than ourselves – (usually) on the basis of some superficial physical characteristic, such as colour, and then attributing the same characteristics to all the group members. In this section we are going to focus on ethnocentricity rather than stereotyping, although often the results are the same because they may both lead to a kind of discrimination.

According to Tajfel (1982), the process of trying to give ourselves some kind of positive self-identity seems to explain why people demonstrate an in-group bias. If we are assigned to a group – any group – either by birth, colour, gender or design, we immediately seem to feel a kind of innate automatic preference for that group over any other group, and somehow elevate the group to a higher status than any other. This in-group preference is really a tactic to increase our self-esteem, and even if the reasons why the groups have been formed are minimal, if our group wins over another group, it will strengthen our feelings of pride in belonging to the winning group and consequently increase our self-esteem still further.

This process was described by Tajfel and Turner (1986) in what is known as **social identity theory.** This theory states that people actually get their identity from the group to which they perceive they belong. However, to gain an identity, we need to make comparisons between our group and other groups, and in order for our identity to be positive we need to see our group as being superior to other groups. If a group believes it is less worthy than other groups, it will be much more likely to accept any discrimination and disadvantage shown towards it without complaint, because it will believe that the discrimination is probably justified. This will result in the group being very unwilling to fight for its cause.

In the core study that follows, Steve Reicher and Alex Haslam explored both role theory and social identity theory as explanations of the behaviour of groups given unequal status.

The Study

Stephen Reicher and S. Alexander Haslam (2006) 'Rethinking the psychology of tyranny: The BBC prison study', *British Journal of Social Psychology,* **45: 1–40**

Background

Reicher and Haslam introduce the study by covering a number of issues. They begin by pointing out that the events of the Second World War, especially the systematic extermination of six million Jews, shattered the generally held belief in society that human beings were becoming more civilised over time. These events not only affected the population as a whole, but also had a huge impact on social psychologists, who began to try to understand how humans can be so driven by discrimination and hatred towards their fellow man, and how 'the seeds of authoritarianism, social dominance and power abuse are sown and cultivated' (Reicher and Haslam 2006: 1). They explain that the question which concerned them most was how we seem 'to condone the tyranny of others or else act tyrannically ourselves' (p.2). They pointed out that research, which initially focused on the nature of the individual who perpetrated acts against humanity, had now shifted and was more interested in the nature of the group processes that managed to change inoffensive individuals into monsters (e.g. Milgram 1974; Sherif 1966; Tajfel 1982).

Taking the argument one stage further, the suggestion was that extreme acts against our fellow man *must* be considered by looking at the group; and that, generally, the actions of groups tend to become antisocial in the extreme. Reicher and Haslam also explain that, in their opinion, the psychology of tyranny occurs when one group is more powerful than another, and that the powerful group uses its power in an 'arbitrary or oppressive' way. However, this is not always the case, and the authors make very clear that they do not automatically accept that once a group is given power, it will turn on another group and subject its members to some kind of tyrannical rule.

Reicher and Haslam accept that research by psychologists such as Zimbardo *et al.*'s Stanford Prison Experiment (SPE) was necessary, and it was this research which helped to change our understanding of the causes of behaviour. Before this work, people often explained the behaviour of individuals by suggesting they were innately evil. However, following the SPE, Zimbardo and his colleagues formulated the theory that it is the role a person takes on which leads to them adopting brutal behaviour – a case of 'the uniform made me do it'. They argued that the tyranny of the guards in the SPE was typical of how people respond to a role that offers an individual the opportunity to exert power over others. Reicher and Haslam tell us (p.3) that 'Zimbardo and colleagues explained their findings by commenting that guard aggression "was emitted simply as a 'natural' consequence of being in the uniform of a 'guard' and asserting the behaviour inherent in that role" (Haney *et al.,* 1973, p.12)'.

A strong argument against this theory, however, comes from the evidence in the SPE itself. Not all the guards behaved in the same way, not all were arbitrarily unfair in their dealings with the prisoners, not all behaved brutally and not all of them liked the role they had been assigned. If adopting a powerful and authoritarian role does indeed lead to a person taking on the role without recourse to their own conscience, then surely all the guards would have behaved in a similar way? The fact that they did not contradicts the rather deterministic view that roles dictate behaviour in the way that Zimbardo implies, and perhaps this situational deterministic view was overplayed by Zimbardo *et al.* in their analysis of their findings.

They also point out that the other enormous impact of Zimbardo's work was to highlight concerns about how ethical the study was and how acceptable it was generally to put participants through such a traumatic experience as the SPE. Consequently, it was not possible to assess the reliability of the study as it had not been ethically permissible (until the present study) to carry out a replication of the SPE: 'the ethical concerns that have placed the SPE "off-limits"…have led to a situation in which the results of that study have become almost inviolate and social psychological inquiry into tyranny has effectively ground to a halt' (p.3). In other words, for researchers who might challenge

... continued

Zimbardo *et al.*'s role theory explanation of their findings, there was no way to repeat the study and see if the findings proved replicable.

Consequently, there was a lack of any further 'realistic' research, and future investigations were laboratory-based and therefore often unrelated to important social psychological issues. This resulted in a lack of opportunity to look at 'the role of personal and group history or the development of interactions over time', or to 'undertake studies that create, manipulate and systematically investigate the effects of social environments on human interaction [which can therefore] be seen to have contributed to the increasing dominance of explanations based upon inherent and essentially unavoidable genetic, biological, or psychological propensities.' (p.3)

Moreover, Reicher and Haslam argued that the interventions by Zimbardo himself, rather than the spontaneous response to their roles, might account for the behaviour of the guards in the SPE. To begin with, Zimbardo, who played the role of the superintendent in the prison, was the guards' 'boss', and he told them:

> *'You can create in the prisoners feelings of boredom, a sense of fear to some degree, you can create a notion of arbitrariness that their life is totally controlled by us, by the system, you, me and they'll have no privacy … They have no freedom of action – they can do nothing, say nothing, that we don't permit. We're going to take away their individuality in various ways. In general what this all leads to is a sense of powerlessness …' (cited in Reicher and Haslam 2006: 4)*

Given that this was said to them at the start of the study by their 'leader', one interpretation of the guards' behaviour in the SPE was simply that they were obeying the instruction to create a brutal environment, rather than showing how tyranny might be created.

Bearing in mind the time that had elapsed since the SPE was carried out, and the progress made in social psychological explanations of tyranny, Reicher and Haslam considered that Zimbardo *et al.*'s explanations of tyranny might not be adequate. They argued that there were two reasons to believe they were not:

- The data produced for the SPE was selective and not all interactions were either filmed or subsequently revealed in the written reports by the authors.

- The video film data that was produced showed 'that both prisoners and guards challenged their roles not only at the start, but throughout the entire study. In the case of the guards … while some exploited their power, others sided with the prisoners, and yet others were tough but fair. Such diversity sits uneasily with the notion that role acceptance is simply determined by the situation…' (p.4)

Social identity approach

Developments in our understanding of group psychology have resulted in us no longer believing that simply by adopting some kind of role, our normal behaviour suddenly changes in a negative way, or that being a member of a group can lead us to become antisocial. The social identity approach which incorporates **social identity theory** (Tajfel and Turner 1979) and **self-categorisation theory** (Turner 1985) provides an alternative explanation of group behaviour. The social identity approach proposes that groups can have a positive as well as a negative effect on an individual's behaviour. It suggests that the person does not simply act according to a role given to them by someone else, but that their decision to act with or against the group is dependent on whether they 'internalize such [group] memberships as part of the self concept'. (Turner, 1982)

In other words, if group membership is an important and integrated part of the person's identity, and the behaviour of the group contributes to their sense of belonging and self-esteem, they will act with the group and/or for the benefit of the group. According to this theory, some groups may use their

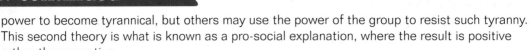

... continued

power to become tyrannical, but others may use the power of the group to resist such tyranny. This second theory is what is known as a pro-social explanation, where the result is positive rather than negative.

Researchers in this area have focused on trying to work out *when* people will act as a group to change inequalities between groups (resistance). This means identifying dominant and subordinate groups and seeing when those in subordinate groups would resist. Social identity explanations predict that the members of dominant and subordinate groups are likely to behave in different ways. Those people:

'who are positively valued by virtue of their group membership (i.e. members of dominant groups)… would identify with and act in terms of the group. For people who are negatively valued by virtue of their group membership (i.e. members of subordinate groups), collective action depends upon two factors in particular: [permeability and security].' (p.5)

In terms of resistance, it is the behaviour of people in subordinate groups that is important. You need to understand the key terms 'permeability' and 'security' in order to understand the authors' interventions and explanations in this study.

Key concept

Permeability and security

Permeability of group boundaries refers to the beliefs a person has about their ability to advance through the social system despite their group membership. If they believe they can advance (the permeability of group boundaries is possible), this belief encourages them to act in ways that might lead to their individual advancement. However, if they believe that they cannot advance (permeability is impossible), they are more likely to see themselves as group members and act collectively as a group.

Security is a second factor that affects whether a person acts individually or collectively. It is the perceived security of inter-group relations. This is split into two parts: the perceived fairness of inter-group inequalities (legitimacy) and perceived stability.

According to these concepts, people are more likely to act collectively if permeability is impossible. According to this theory, whether they then challenge inequalities depends on whether the inequalities are perceived to be unstable and illegitimate (unfair): 'people should be most inclined to resist domination when they see inequality as both illegitimate and unstable and can thus envisage cognitive alternatives to it' (p.5). That is, they are able to imagine 'cognitive alternatives to the status quo'. In other words, they can imagine how things could be different.

In more simple terms:

If the situation is: fair + unstable = no challenge to authority.

If the situation is: fair + stable = no challenge to authority.

If the situation is: unfair + stable = no challenge to authority.

But:

If the situation is unfair + unstable = challenge to authority is more likely, as more alternative situations can be imagined.

Reicher and Haslam sought to investigate group behaviour in relation to these concepts.

A further reason for revisiting the SPE is given by Reicher and Haslam. They suggest that the dominance of the SPE, and the use of role theory in describing a range of behaviours beyond the SPE itself, 'from prison behaviour to terrorism' (p.6), should be reconsidered. In their study, Reicher and Haslam aimed to test the validity of the claim that 'people "naturally" assume roles' (p.6), because they believed that the analysis of the SPE

... continued

'has profound and troubling implications… if people cannot help but act in terms of assigned role, it implies that they have little choice, and hence little responsibility, for their social actions. This makes it more difficult to hold tyrants to account for what they do. Moreover, in communicating the message that resistance is futile, the analysis discourages the oppressed from attempting to challenge tyranny…' (p.6)

Using the social identification approach, Reicher and Haslam planned to revisit some of the issues raised by the SPE:

- What are the psychological consequences of inter-group inequality?

- When do people seek to impose such inequality? And when do they resist it?

This study also aimed to test the validity of Zimbardo *et al.*'s analysis of the SPE and their role-based explanation of group behaviour and tyranny. They did this through a study similar but, for both ethical and theoretical purposes, not identical to the SPE, and in association with the BBC. This was called the BBC prison experiment and was carried out in December 2001.

Figure 2.8 The participants in the BBC prison experiment

Aims

The authors point out that they did not aim to replicate the SPE, which would not have been possible for ethical reasons anyway. They also indicate that they did not intend to try to simulate a prison, but to assemble another sort of 'institution' which would create inequalities that were real to the participants. This would then provide a setting in which the issues raised by the SPE could be addressed, with the intention of investigating whether the descriptions of group behaviour, specifically role theory, would be evident in this study, or whether the concepts of the social identity approach would offer a better explanation of the behaviour observed.

This was not to be a direct comparison with the SPE, but, it was hoped, would answer some of the questions raised by the SPE, such as:

> *'Do participants accept their roles uncritically? Do those accorded group power exercise it without constraint, and do those without group power accept their subordination without complaint? After all, if the process of role enactment is indeed 'natural', then it should apply in all cases and any exception is troubling for the overall claim.' (p.7)*

The overall aims of the study were as follows:

(a) To provide comprehensive and systematic data pertaining to the unfolding interactions between groups of unequal power and privilege.

(b) To analyse the conditions under which people (i) define themselves in terms of their ascribed group memberships and act in terms of group identities, and (ii) accept or else challenge intergroup inequalities. Specifically, we predict that dominant group members will identify with their group from the start and impose their power. However, subordinate group members will only identify collectively and challenge intergroup inequalities to the extent that relations between groups are seen as impermeable and insecure.

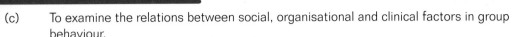
... continued

(c)   To examine the relations between social, organisational and clinical factors in group behaviour.

(d)   To develop protocols that provide a practical and ethical framework for examining social psychological issues in large-scale studies. (p.7)

Method and design

A social psychological field study was carried out. The authors describe their study as an 'experimental case study of the behaviour of members in dominant or subordinate positions and of the developing relations between them'. Although it was conducted with the BBC, and formed the basis of four one-hour programmes on television, the study was independently designed and run by the authors and was therefore 'an ordinary piece of research' (p.6). The researchers describe the study as 'original science filmed', explaining that it was unlike reality TV-style shows, which are designed by TV companies for entertainment purposes, and where academics might be invited to comment on the goings-on (although they did not mention *Big Brother*, this fits the bill of the type of programme they were disassociating themselves from). The authors downplay the role of the BBC in organising or influencing the study, claiming the organisation had a limited role (creating the environment, in line with the authors' guidelines; filming the study; preparing the material for broadcast).

The study aimed to create a hierarchical society in Elstree Film Studios, to the north of London, where the participants would live for a maximum of 10 days. The aim was:

> 'to create an institution that in many ways resembled a prison (but also other hierarchical institutions such as a school, an office, a barracks; see Morgan, 1979) as a site to investigate the behaviour of groups that were unequal in terms of power, status and resources. What is critical, then, is not that the study environment replicated a real prison (which no such environment ever could), but that it created inequalities between groups that were real to the participants.' (p.8)

There were three-person lockable cells to house the prisoners. These, and showers for the prisoners, led off a central area (the atrium). Guards' quarters were separated by a lockable steel-mesh fence. Guards had a dormitory, a bathroom and a mess room.

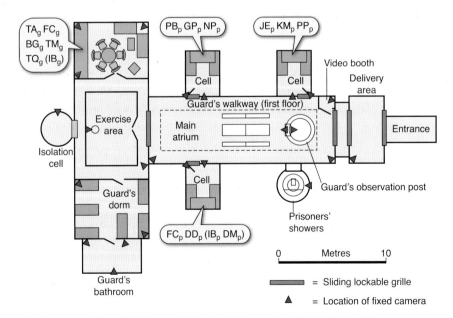

Figure 2.9 Plan of the prison showing the layout and the initials of the participants, who were either prisoners or guards (Reicher and Haslam, 2006)

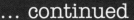

... continued

Participants

The recruitment of participants was done through screening those who responded to adverts for male volunteers in the national press or leaflets. Males only were studied so that comparisons with the SPE could be made, and also to avoid the ethical concerns about mixing men and women in the 'prison'. From a pool of 332 applicants, 27 men were selected by a three-phase screening process. A final sample of 15 was chosen to ensure diversity of age, social class and ethnic background.

In the screening process:

- Prospective participants completed a battery of psychometric tests that measured both social variables (authoritarianism, social dominance, modern racism) and clinical variables (depression, anxiety, social isolation, paranoia, aggressiveness, demotivation, self-esteem, self-harm, drug dependence).
- Prospective participants underwent a full weekend assessment by independent clinical psychologists.
- Medical and character references were obtained, and police checks were conducted.

The selected participants were all people who were well adjusted and pro-social. This was done, first, for ethical reasons, and second, to ensure that the sample was generalisable to a broader population and comparable to the participants in the SPE.

The authors claim that the final 15 were randomly divided into two groups of five guards and ten prisoners. However, this was done only after they had been put into matched groups of three, as closely matched as possible on personality variables 'potentially implicated in tyranny: modern racism, authoritarianism and social dominance' (p.9). From each group of three, a guard and two prisoners were randomly allocated. This process acted as a control to ensure that the personality types were spread out across the guards and prisoners. As a further control, this process was carried out blind, with the experimenters not knowing who was being allocated to which role.

Because of the planned interventions in the study, it began with nine prisoners and five guards, with a tenth prisoner introduced at a later stage in the study.

Procedure

The authors present an overview of the study:

> 'Over a period of 8 days, the study examined the behaviour of 15 men who were placed in a social hierarchy of guards and prisoners within a purpose-built environment. Their behaviour was video- and audio-recorded over the entire period, and this was complemented by daily psychometric and physiological measures. The video data were edited into four 1-hour long documentaries screened in May 2002...' (p.7)

Of course, with eight full days of observations, interventions and daily psychometric measures, there is much more to it than this!

Let us start at the beginning, by considering the set-up of the study.

Set-up of the study: guards

In setting up the study, the guards were invited to a hotel the night before the study was to begin. Here they were briefed as follows:

- Informed they would have the role of guards in the study.
- Shown the prison timetable (e.g. cleaning rota, work duties, prisoner roll calls, exercise and recreation time).
- Told they would be responsible for making sure that the institution ran smoothly and ensuring the prisoners performed all their tasks.

... continued

- Asked to draw up a series of prison rules, under headings given by the authors, and to draw up punishments should the prisoners violate the rules. They were given no guidance on how to do this, except that they must respect a set of ethically determined rights for prisoners.
- As in the SPE, the guards were informed that no physical violence would be tolerated, but beyond this it was stressed that they could act as they pleased (p.11).

Day 1 of the study: guards

On the morning of Day 1, guards were taken in a blacked-out van to the institution. The blacked-out van was used so that the inside of the prison would be the guards' total sensory experience of their environment for the duration of the study. They were briefed about the layout of the prison and resources available to them to help enforce their authority, including keys to all doors, the guards' observation post, with full cell surveillance system installed, access to an upper level, a social isolation cell for punishment, and resources such as snacks and cigarettes that they could give or withhold as punishment or reward. They could also put the prisoners on a bread-and-water diet. The guards had well-made uniforms, which they put on after the briefing, and prepared for the arrival of the prisoners by practising the procedure for introducing a prisoner to the prison.

Set-up of the study, Day 1: prisoners

Prisoners arrived one at a time. On arrival they had their heads shaved and were given a uniform consisting of a T-shirt printed with a three-digit number, loose trousers and flimsy sandals. The prisoners were given no information other than the prison rules and a list of prisoners' rights, which were posted in their cells. The only other information they received was a short loudspeaker announcement by the researchers, which told them that no violence was permissible and that, since the allocation process might not have been reliable, the guards would be looking for 'guard-like' qualities in the prisoners, with a possibility for 'promotion' on Day 3 (see the permeability intervention below).

Planned interventions

In contrast to the SPE, which the authors of this study describe as 'exploratory', this study had a theoretical basis and was intended to test the social identification approach as an explanation of group behaviour, so the authors planned to introduce variables through a set of time-series interventions. Three interventions were to be made:

1. **Permeability**: A possibility for the promotion to the role of guard from the role of prisoner was introduced. Guards were told they had been selected for their reliability and initiative, but that these measures were not always reliable, so they were to check out any prisoners who showed 'guard-like' qualities to suggest that they might be promoted. Prisoners were also informed of this possibility of advancement to the other group (permeability) on arrival, through a loudspeaker announcement.

   The incentive to want to move from prisoner to guard was apparent in the inequalities between the two groups:

   - Guards had all the power and authority.
   - Guards had superior and well-made uniforms.
   - Guards had superior living conditions, including superior food and extra drinks and snacks.

   On Day 3 such a promotion was made by the guards, using a selection procedure suggested by the researchers, after which there was an announcement that there would be no further promotions or demotions (the prisoners would now believe that permeability was impossible).

2. **Legitimacy:** Three days after the promotion (Day 6), all guards and prisoners were to be informed that the allocation to roles had actually been random, and there was no real difference between guards and prisoners, but it was too late to make changes now. This would mean that the division of groups which had previously appeared legitimate now lost its legitimacy.

... continued

3. **Cognitive alternatives**: A day after the legitimacy intervention, a tenth prisoner was to be introduced. Although he was no better informed about the study than all other participants, he was chosen specifically as he had a background as an experienced trade union official. It was assumed he would raise the possibility of group-based negotiations (given that the set-up would by then be illegitimate and changeable): 'it was envisaged that his introduction would enable the prisoners (and the participants more generally) to envisage the achievement of a more equal set of social relations' (p.11). In other words, it was expected that he would encourage the participants to imagine cognitive alternatives to the status quo.

Data gathering and recording

1. Observational data: The prison set-up was designed so that all participants could be both audio- and video-recorded at all times. All audio channels and four video channels were recorded at any one time throughout the study.

2. Self-report data: Participants completed a daily set of psychometric tests. The key variables reported here were:

    (a) social variables: social identification, awareness of cognitive alternatives, right-wing authoritarianism

    (b) organisational variables: compliance with rules, organisational citizenship

    (c) clinical variables: self-efficacy, depression. (p.10)

To prevent test fatigue, not every test was given every day (see Results, below).

3. Biochemical measures: A daily saliva swab was taken, from which measures of cortisol were taken, as an indication of stress levels. (The data for stress are not reported in this version of the study.)

Results

The authors divide the results into two phases:

1. **Rejecting inequality**: In the first phase of the study the guards did not identify with their roles, and therefore did not stick together as a group. Initially, the prisoners failed to identify as a group and acted individually in the hope of promotion, but after the promotion on Day 3, they increasingly identified as a group and worked collectively to challenge the guards. 'This led to a shift of power and ultimately to the collapse of the prisoner–guard system' (p.12).

2. **Embracing inequality**: In this phase, the participants decided to operate the study as a single self-governing 'commune', on an equal footing. However, this was not successful as it did not develop a system for dealing with internal dissent, and was unsustainable in the face of opposition which arose. By the end, participants seemed more predisposed to tolerate a harsher guard–prisoner system which some now proposed.

Phase 1: Rejecting inequality

Social identification

The pattern of **social identification** in the prisoners was as predicted. While they believed that permeability was possible, there was less collective action and more individual action towards the goal of promotion. However, after the promotion on Day 3, and once it was apparent that group boundaries were impermeable, the prisoners acted more collectively against the guards.

Reicher and Haslam quote the behaviour of one cell of prisoners before and after the promotion to fully illustrate this. (Note: Participants are identified only by initials; 'g' or 'p' after their initials indicates their role, 'p' for prisoner and 'g' for guard.) In this cell the three prisoners were JEp, KMp – both of whom had worked hard to get promotion and failed – and PPp. After the promotion, all three realised that the only way to improve their position was to change the system. From the outset all had been very unhappy with the unequal conditions of guards and prisoners: JEp had said he wanted to be a guard 'because they get all the luxuries' (p.13).

... continued

The authors quote this extract to show how the prisoners planned and justified collective resistance:

> JEp: Hopefully we'll get [TQg] in. That's the person, he's the target.
> KMp: No. I mean obviously I think it's going to be a lot of fun for us to do this but I don't think [TQg]…I feel so…I just feel…
> PPp: Listen, listen mate I, you've got to, you've got to start forgetting about other people's feelings and what they're doing because the days when you're sitting here starving hungry and you've got f**k all and you've got nothing mate and you've got a ratty little bed and a stupid little blanket to sit under and they're under there in their duvets, they've got everything they want and they're not giving two f**ks about you. So – think on and f**k them.
> KMp: I think they do care about us. But guys I'm going to back you all the way. You should not doubt me. (p.13)

Before the promotion the prisoners were interested in 'what *I* will do'; after the promotion it changed to 'what *we* will do'. Their behaviour changed from compliance with the authority of the guards to conflict.

For the guards, the results were not as predicted. In contrast to the SPE, and against the authors' predictions, the guards here failed to identify with their high-status, positively valued role in the prison, resulting in a failure to cohere as a group. The authors note that some guards were reluctant to impose their authority, and their failure to internalise their role led to a weak sense of group identity.

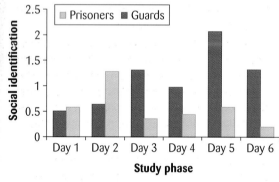

Figure 2.10 Social identification as a function of assigned group and time

The self-report data (psychometric testing giving quantitative data) confirm the observational data, showing that although the guards started out with the higher sense of social identification, this reduced after Day 2 when they had to enforce the system, whereas the social identification of the prisoners increased, as predicted, after the promotion on Day 3.

Security of inter-group relations

The aim had been to create insecurity by use of the legitimacy intervention, but this proved not to be necessary as the way the groups emerged naturally created a sense of illegitimacy. The prisoners became more cohesive and collectively challenging of the guards, whereas the guards failed to act as a group, and their weak and ineffective management of the institution led to beliefs that the original groupings were not legitimate – the guards were just not up to the job.

An illustration of the challenge of the prisoners to the guards' authority was when the three prisoners of Cell 2 set up a challenge to see what would happen. JEp threw his plate to the floor and demanded better food, and as guards tried to deal with this, KMp and PPp chipped in with their own demands – for a cigarette and a plaster for a blister. The guards could not decide whether to take an authoritarian role or make concessions. In the end, TQg decided to give a cigarette to PPp to get all the prisoners back in their cell. The prisoners' response to this was that they were delighted, saying things like 'that was f**king sweet'. The guards, however, bickered among themselves, with TAg saying: 'This is only day 4. They can see what happened today and now they can do whatever they want' (p.15). From this we can see that both the prisoners and the guards clearly understood that the system could be changed (they could imagine cognitive alternatives to the status quo).

... continued

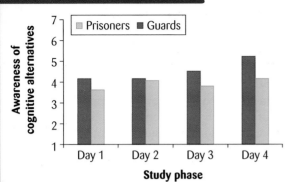

Figure 2.11 Awareness of cognitive alternatives as a function of assigned group and time

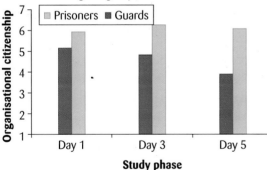

Figure 2.12 Compliance with prison rules as a function of assigned group and time

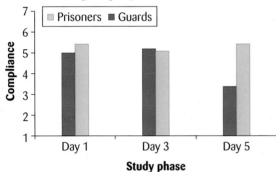

Figure 2.13 Organisational citizenship as a function of assigned group and time

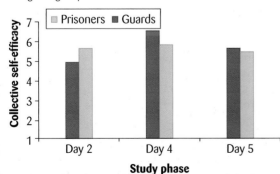

Figure 2.14 Collective self-efficacy as a function of assigned group and time

The introduction of the tenth prisoner (DMp) had been planned to introduce cognitive alternatives, but since these were already apparent he might not have been necessary. However, since he had been told he would join the study, the authors introduced him as planned on Day 5. What he did do was to offer further alternatives to the status quo, especially questioning the whole idea of the prisoner–guard division, encouraging collective action against the researchers, for example in relation to the level of heat in the institution.

Quantitative measures show how cognitive alternatives to the status quo became more apparent to participants through the study.

Acceptance of the unequal regime: Compliance and organisational citizenship
As the study progressed, the impact of social identification and security became apparent in the reducing compliance of the prisoners to the guards' regime over time.

Measurement of a further variable also shows how the prisoners were less willing to support the guards' authority as time progressed. This variable, organisational citizenship, measured the willingness of the participant to act above and beyond what was required to make the system work.

Observations of the prisoners' behaviour confirmed this decline in compliance and lack of cooperation with the system; for example, being insubordinate at the prisoner roll call, or the complaints about food made collectively by a group of prisoners.

Collective self-efficacy and mental health
The prisoners became more successful in their challenges and undermining of the guards' authority. This can be seen in the quantitative measurement of collective self-efficacy and depression over time.

The results show that the prisoners' sense of group success increased over time, whereas this variable decreased for the guards. This matches the data for social identification. The guards' lack of ability to act collectively led to more observed despondency among them than these quantitative data suggest.

... continued

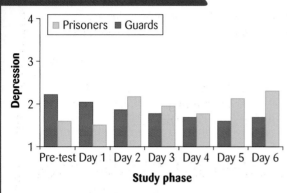

Figure 2.15 Depression as a function of assigned group and time

In terms of depression, the graph shows clearly that although the prisoners were more depressed at the start of the study, this trend had reversed completely by the end.

The combined impact of these variables was that by Day 6 the prisoners were strong enough to plan and execute a plot to destroy the guards' now weak and ineffective regime. This culminated in a breakout of prisoners from Cell 2 and their occupation of the guards' quarters, bringing the guards' regime to an end.

Phase 2: Embracing inequality

After the collapse of the guards' regime all but two of the participants agreed for the study to continue as a 'commune', with all participants working on an equal basis. Successful at first, the commune failed since those who had challenged the guards' regime felt marginalised in the commune, and they challenged and undermined it, for example, by not doing their chores, then by violating communal rules, and then plotting to overturn the commune. The commune had not developed a way to deal with disciplining rule breakers and this made it difficult for it to succeed in the face of subordination.

A chance factor, a poor-quality breakfast on the commune's second day, Day 8, was interpreted as a sign of the researchers' disapproval of the commune, and what was now proposed by some (one ex-guard and three ex-prisoners) was a new regime, more harsh than the first. PBp's comments show what the new regime was to be like: 'We want to be the guards and f**king make them toe the line, I mean *on the f**king line*. No f**king talking while you are eating. Get on with your food and get back to your f**king cell' (p.22).

The supporters of the commune were passive and despondent in the face of this. In debriefing, some said that although prior to the study they would not openly support such a harsh regime as the one now being proposed, they found they were less opposed to it after their experience in the study.

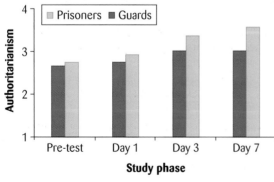

Figure 2.16 Right-wing authoritarianism as a function of self-selected group and time

Why would this be the case? The authors considered changes to the attitudes of the participants over the course of the study in terms of a right-wing authoritarian scale. As you can see clearly from the graph comparing the allocated prisoners and guards, both groups increased on this variable through the course of the study. The breakdown of the commune and the willingness to let someone else take responsibility for making the system work might account for the increase in authoritarianism. This increase in authoritarianism occurred in conjunction with the proposal for the new regime.

Interestingly, analysis of the authoritarianism of those proposing the new regime showed that those wanting to be the new guards were more authoritarian in their opinions throughout the study.

Since the authors considered that the new regime could not be enforced without a level of force not permitted in the study, and because the existing system had failed, the authors report that they

... continued

considered the study to be gridlocked and to have come to a 'natural point of termination' (p.24). The study was therefore ended at noon on Day 8, with participants remaining for a further day for debriefing.

Discussion

Before giving their explanation of group behaviour based on the social identity approach, the authors try to pre-empt and account for four possible criticisms that might be made of their study. The following table sets out these criticisms and the authors' responses.

Table 2.7

Criticism	Authors' response
The role of television Participants were only play-acting and faking their roles, and looking for 'celebrity status' Surveillance explains the behaviour observed	Play-acting was unlikely over an extended period (eight days), and the psychometric data, which is harder to fake, supported the observational data, suggesting the observed behaviour was valid. Play-acting does not explain the observed behaviour, especially in terms of the willingness to accept the move towards tyranny in the final stages. Surveillance cannot account for changes in behaviour that occurred: surveillance remained constant, but attitudes and behaviour changed, and, importantly, changed in the ways the study had predicted. The authors argue that 'surveillance is everywhere (anyway)' and that it is a normal part of our everyday lives, so the study should not be discounted simply because it was broadcast on TV.
The role of personality The personalities of certain people, especially prisoners JEp, PPp and PBp, and not group processes explain the behaviour that was observed	The authors agree that personalities play a part, but point out, for example, that PPp had always personally opposed the guards' regime, but was unable to *actively* oppose it until this became the will of his group (i.e. after the promotion on Day 3), so the impact of an individual's will was dependent on the group will; it did not happen just because he was personally 'rebellious'. This was also true of the environmentalist prisoner, FCp, quiet for six days, then becoming prominent in setting up the commune, when the group will allowed his particular skills, knowledge and personality to direct them. Their relationship to the group thus influenced participants' success as individuals, in directing group action according to their personalities. In addition, changes in personality variables seemed to occur across the study; for example, authoritarianism increased. It could therefore be argued that the study impacted on personalities, and not the other way round.

... continued

Criticism	Authors' response
The authors failed to create real power and inequalities between the groups, so the study tells us little about group processes and tyranny *The guards did not have any real power to wield, even if they were inclined to do so*	The guards' behaviour in the study was not because they had too little power, but because they had too *much* power and were reluctant to use it (e.g. they had the power to reward and punish, were able to make the prisoners perform roll calls, etc., and were given the power to promote a prisoner). It seems that they were afraid of being seen as authoritarian. The study appears to have given them a fear of their potential power, not too little power in the first place.
The study's claim to be an 'experimental case study' can be questioned because the manipulation of the independent variables (e.g. the promotion as an example of permeability) may not have had the claimed effects	As in all studies, there are difficulties operationalising variables, even more so in a complex study such as this one. However, the researchers used manipulation checks to establish the validity of their interventions, specifically checking that the observed behaviour could be explained in terms of the social identity principles on which interventions were based. They also used their multiple sources of data to confirm their findings (e.g. see the data graph on cognitive alternatives – Figure 2.11).

In the case of all these criticisms, the authors argue that while each one impacts on the study, none alone can adequately account for the study's results in their entirety. In order to explain fully the observed and recorded behaviour in the study, an explanation based on a social identity approach offers the best explanation.

The authors' social identity account of tyranny

Before giving their explanation of the findings, the authors make a very clear statement that the analysis of their findings is at odds with the analysis of the SPE by Zimbardo *et al.*: 'the simplest and clearest finding of our study is that people do not automatically assume roles that are given to them in the manner suggested by the role account that is typically used to explain events in the SPE'.

An alternative account to role theory is thus offered, where the components of the social identity approach are used to explain the findings. For example, the move from permeability to impermeability (the promotion) had a strong influence on prisoner group identification, as predicted. The increasing insecurity in inter-group relations affected the willingness of prisoners to challenge the guards' authority. The concept of legitimacy explains why the prisoners challenged the guards (when it was clear the guards were not functioning properly as a group and therefore not up to doing their job). This factor of legitimacy also explains why the participants as a whole did not challenge the researchers, as to do so would be a breach of their agreement to take part. There were two occasions however, when the researchers were considered to be breaking their side of the bargain (it was too hot in the prison, the guards' supplies were not replenished), and in both cases talk of 'mutiny' (p.30) was the result, again showing that loss of legitimacy can lead to challenges to inequalities and unfairness in a system.

The consequences of social identification are also discussed by the researchers. They suggest that to understand fully the impact of factors on group behaviour from this theoretical approach (e.g. the role of collective self-efficacy and social support) further study is required.

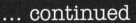

... continued

The impact of TV cameras

The researchers suggest that the presence of the TV cameras had an impact on the study in two ways:

- The response of the guards and their reluctance to be seen as authoritarian shows that because they were able to consider the judgements made of their behaviour beyond the context of the prison, extreme situational explanations of group behaviour (such as role theory) really do not account for their behaviour.

- It seemed to confirm that 'extreme behaviours can be restrained by making actors visible, and hence, accountable to broader or yet-to-be encountered audiences' (p.30).

The authors' explanation of tyranny

The results pf the BBC Prison study agree with the SPE that it is not from the individual that tyranny arises, but that in order to understand tyranny we have to consider the impact of group processes on behaviour. The authors of the BBC Prison study disagree with the conclusion from the SPE that it is powerful groups that cause tyranny and that a successful dominant group with power abuses their power to create a tyrannical regime. Instead, Reicher and Haslam's study suggests that tyranny can be explained by the *failure* of dominant groups. It is the powerlessness of groups to maintain order that leads to the conditions from which tyranny might arise.

From this study they cite two examples of group failure: the failure of the guards to fulfil their role, which led to the collapse of the guards' regime; and the inability of the commune to use discipline to enforce its rule, which led to the collapse of the commune.

The authors argue that after the failure of a group and the breakdown of a system, people are willing to give up some of their core principles in order to establish a system that works. For example, the guards had been willing to give up their power so that the commune might work. At the collapse of the commune, the participants were willing to accept a new, harsher system, even though they would not have supported such a system openly at the outset. Indeed, all the participants opposed the inequalities of the system designed by the researchers, so what would induce them now to create a system that was even more unequal? The authors explain this:

'rather than people "naturally" preferring any given form of social order, it appears that, when group members fail to impose an order based on their own existing norms and values, they are willing to adapt those values (or adopt new ones) in order to create viable order rather than have no order at all.' (p.32)

Conclusions

The authors conclude that their results agree with the SPE in that to understand tyranny it has to be investigated in terms of group processes and not on an individual basis. However, where they disagree with the SPE is in the *explanation* of the group processes that lead to tyranny.

Whereas the SPE concluded that 'the toxic combination of groups and power lead to tyranny' (p.33), the authors of this study argue that strong groups can, depending on their norms and values, behave either antisocially or pro-socially, so tyranny is not an inevitable outcome.

On the other hand, failing groups do seem to lead to a situation in which tyranny can seem an attractive alternative – a viable system being preferable to an unworkable one: 'in short it is the breakdown of groups and the powerlessness of groups that creates the conditions under which tyranny can triumph' (p.33).

Supporting this argument, the authors argue three points:

- It is consistent with contemporary thinking in social psychology (social identity approach).

... continued

- It is consistent with the accounts of the rise of tyranny from other disciplines. For example, the historian Hobsbawm wrote in 1995:

  'the optimal conditions for the triumph of the ultra-right were an old state and its ruling mechanisms which could no longer function; a mass of disenchanted, disoriented and disorganised citizens who no longer knew where their loyalties lay; strong socialist movements threatening or appearing to threaten social revolution, but not actually in a position to achieve it... These were the conditions that turned movements of the radical right into powerful, organised and sometimes uniformed and paramilitary force.' (p.33)

- It can be used as an alternative analysis of what happened in the SPE. After their initial rebellion and being led by their ringleader to believe that Zimbardo would not permit them to leave, the failure of the prisoners to act as a group allowed the tyranny of the guards to emerge and prevail, much as the failure of the commune might have allowed a tyranny to emerge in the BBC experiment.

The SPE, it seemed, had closed debate about the nature of tyranny by suggesting that studies could not be carried out ethically in this area. However, the authors say that a major strength of the BBC study is that it shows how such studies can be operated ethically and that the debate on tyranny can be reopened, especially in light of the fact that the findings of this study are in contrast with those of the SPE.

They do admit, however, that their analysis contains 'large and controversial claims', and they invite further research on this topic. They claim that this is essential if their discipline of social psychology is to advance.

Commentary: Methods and issues

Research method, design and data gathering

The authors describe this as an 'experimental case study', and it was carried out as role-play simulation (similar to the SPE). The study was audio- and video-recorded, and finally edited into four one-hour programmes broadcast on BBC TV. The authors themselves attempt to address two problems with these methods. First, the problem that the nature of role play and the TV recording might mean that all the participants were doing was play-acting; and second, the problem of controlling and recording the effect of the variables they attempted to manipulate in the study (see Discussion, above).

Being a case study, along with audio- and video-recording for eight days, as well as carrying out daily psychometric tests, this study offers a great deal of both qualitative and quantitative data. This is a strength of the study, as is the fact that the researchers used a wide range of data-gathering methods – observation, self-report and biochemical measures – in their study.

Does the study raise any ethical concerns?

For this study to be justified in the first place there had to be good reason for attempting to create a situation similar to the SPE, given the ethical concerns that were raised by the behaviour of the guards in that study. The researchers' justification was to further the understanding of how groups behave and how tyranny might emerge. Their aim also included the introduction of variables, such as permeability and legitimacy, to see if this had an impact on challenges to inequality, as was suggested by the social identity approach.

To ensure the study was carried out ethically, the researchers discussed it with colleagues, and proposals were submitted both to the University of Exeter's ethics panel and to the Chair of the British Psychological Society's Ethics Committee. In addition, the following (ethical) safeguards were built into the study:

(a) Potential participants went through three-phase clinical, medical and background screening to ensure that they were neither psychologically vulnerable nor liable to put others at risk…

(b) Participants signed a comprehensive consent form. Among other things, this informed them that they may be subject to a series of factors – including physical and psychological discomfort, confinement, constant surveillance and stress – which may involve risk.

(c) Two independent clinical psychologists monitored the study throughout, and had the right to see any participant at any time or to demand that any participant be removed from the study.

(d) A paramedic was on constant standby in case of illness or injury.

(e) On-site security guards were provided with detailed protocols clarifying when and how to intervene in cases of dangerous behaviours by participants.

(f) An independent five-person ethics committee – chaired by a British Member of Parliament – monitored the study throughout. This committee had the right to demand changes to the study's set-up or to terminate it at any time. (pp.8–9)

The study might have run for 10 days, but was brought to a stop on Day 8. Although this was not done explicitly for ethical reasons, it was clear that the proposed new regime might have been too harsh to be permitted under the ethical guidelines all the participants had agreed to follow, and it was also clear that the previous system, the commune, had broken down. Otherwise, the researchers report that the study raised no ethical concerns and none of the safeguards had to be used: 'After the study, the ethical committee published an independent report and characterized the conduct of the study as "exemplary"'(p.9).

Is the study useful?

By reopening the discussion about the emergence of tyranny by conducting this study, the authors have made a positive contribution to the discipline of social psychology. Also, by suggesting that tyranny is not an inevitable outcome where powerful groups exist, and that powerful groups can also act pro-socially (for example, to resist tyranny), the authors argue that this study might help psychologists to 'reconnect with policy makers'. In other words, there might be positive changes to society that social psychology could advise on and contribute to.

Even Zimbardo, who does not have much that is positive to say about the BBC study, confirms that it has one very important implication.

> *'I want to thank these researchers for demonstrating a point that I have long argued in favour of as a means to reduce prisoner abuses, namely greater surveillance of guard–prisoner interactions. This BBC-TV research shows that such violence can be eliminated if all parties in a prison setting realize that their behaviour is open for scrutiny and evaluation…' (Zimbardo 2006: 53)*

The study itself seemed to confirm that 'extreme behaviours can be restrained by making actors visible, and hence, accountable to broader or yet-to-be encountered audiences' (Reicher and Haslam 2006: 30). The implication here is that if surveillance equipment were introduced in prisons, the brutality and abuses reported to take place could be reduced or eliminated.

Validity and reliability of the study

Throughout their BBC prison study, Reicher and Haslam were at pains to point out and counter possible criticisms against their conclusions. In addition, they used their different data sources to support the reliability, and therefore the validity, of their findings. For example, they used the data from the psychometric testing to confirm their observational data.

Reicher and Haslam have presented a challenge to the validity of the analysis made by Zimbardo *et al.* of the way that tyranny emerges, based on their SPE. Does this study refute the theory that powerful groups and roles lead to tyranny and adequately replace it with a social identity-based explanation of tyranny? As the researchers modestly point out, this is just one study, and further research is necessary if their theory is to be confirmed.

Does the study lack ecological validity?

Of course, given that both the SPE and the BBC study were simulations that required participants to role-play as guards or prisoners, it could be argued that the studies lack sufficient validity to be used as explanations of how tyranny really emerges, or of the impact of groups on behaviour in the real world. The emergence of tyranny occurs in a complex socio-economic, political and psychological context which would be impossible to replicate in any simple, simulated environment, especially ones as controlled and short-lived as these two studies have presented us with.

Zimbardo was invited by the *British Journal of Social Psychology* to write an article in which he responded to the BBC study. He largely dismissed the study as a 'scientifically irresponsible "made-for-TV-study"'. What do you think?

Revision Activity

To help you consider the ecological validity of this study, copy and complete the following table, listing as many similarities and differences as you can.

Ways in which the BBC Prison was like a real prison	Ways in which the BBC prison was different from a real prison

3 Cognitive psychology

Almost everything we do causes us to think but before the invention of computers, our understanding of how we processed information was limited. Much of the work in psychology involved simply looking at behaviour by observing the type of responses that were produced by different types of stimuli. There was little research on what happened between the stimulus and the response. However, the computer analogy opened up a whole new way of looking at the way the brain processes information. This information-processing approach works as follows:

1. Input – through one of the senses.

2. Processing – this occurs using currently installed software (previous experience and knowledge).

3. Response – which may be action or chosen inaction.

Cognitive psychology is involved in understanding the middle process; how the information is processed and what kind of choices are made. Many of the choices we make may not be rational. For example, we may know that chocolate is fattening and that we desperately want to lose weight, but we still buy a large bar of chocolate and eat it. This information-processing model has opened up study in this area, allowing us to investigate these processes. It is somewhat removed from the perspective of reductionism, which suggests that all our responses can be reduced to the most basic explanation.

Cognitive psychology therefore covers a number of areas – memory, perception, language, thinking and attention – and all these processes are interconnected. For example, you cannot identify an object you have seen without thinking what it is called. In fact, you will not even try to identify it unless you happen to be looking in the right place at the right time (paying attention to it); and if you identify it as something frightening, you will have to work out how to escape.

This chapter focuses on three areas of cognition:

1. The topic of memory is addressed by looking at the structure and function of our memories and how accurate they really are.

2. We will then consider social cognition, by addressing how we integrate and assimilate social information in order to facilitate relationships, and will consider how people with autism have difficulty with these skills.

3. The last section focuses on whether language is an innate ability in humans or is simply learned, and whether it is beyond the capability of other species to acquire language.

Loftus and Palmer study: Eyewitness testimony

Memory

We will begin this section by looking at one of the most fundamental and complex of human cognitive abilities: the human memory. In fact, when considering cognition, it is hard to start anywhere else, because what we have stored in our memory forms the basis of what makes us who we are and dictates how we behave.

What is memory? It is difficult to find a precise definition of 'memory', but it is often referred to as the ability to retain information and demonstrate retention through behaviour. If we could not retain and use information that we have already discovered, it would mean that for every new experience we would have to process huge amounts of information, which could be very costly in terms of the time it might take.

Memory is a fundamental part of each of us and our everyday lives. Our memories serve to tell us who we are, to help us make sense of the situations in which we find ourselves, and to enable us to make plans for the future. In fact, memory is so much a part of what and who we are that it is almost impossible to imagine what it must be like to have no recollection of anything. Think of all the things you do automatically every day which rely on stored knowledge, such as getting dressed, finding your way round, talking, writing and reading, recognising people, remembering past events or information you have been told. Is there anything you can do without referring to something you have stored in your memory?

People who have lost their memory, for whatever reason, are called amnesics. The classic portrayal of amnesics in the media tends to suggest that they forget everything, but this is rarely the case. If you think of the things we learn and store in our memories, such as a knowledge of language or how to dress ourselves, you will realise that amnesics rarely lose these abilities. What they seem to lose is the memory of who they are, because they have no information relating to their past. These past memories are not stored as if they were recorded on videotape – although this is a commonly held belief by people who do not understand how memory works. Television dramas tend to support this idea, with dramatic scenes of hypnotherapists gaining access to previously lost information by hypnotising their clients. What actually happens is that we seem to unconsciously select information to store, and overwrite similar experiences until they become merged into one memory. Memory is a dynamic process which is constantly being updated or changed by our experiences.

Although psychologists often consider what happens when memory becomes disrupted, they are also interested in how memory is structured and how it actually works. The structures are the various component parts, like short-term memory and long-term memory, and the processes are how information is taken in and stored and then recalled.

Psychologists have discovered that there are a number of factors which influence whether information is stored or simply forgotten. You do not remember all the information you are told: you may remember the gist of it, or a reasonable amount, but only for a limited period, no matter how hard you tried to learn it (think of examination revision). However, it has been found that we do tend to store information on a more long-term basis if it is very different to other information, if it is rich in detail, if it is connected to other things we know, or if it is personally important to us.

Is memory like a tape recorder?

No. Our memory does not document everything we experience and recall it as necessary. In fact, many of the things we experience are not stored, and other things are stored inaccurately.

> It was a cold afternoon in late September and two women were standing talking, outside their adjacent front gates. Both carried bags of shopping and one woman had a young girl standing by her side.
> 'I can't believe your Emily is going off to university. It only seems like yesterday when she was playing in the front garden with our Paul,' said the other woman to the girl's mother.
> The young girl shuffled. God, she was bored, and all she wanted to do was go inside and watch TV.
> 'Come on, Mum, I'm cold, and I want to finish packing.'
> 'I remember the first day your mum and I took you to school,' said the other woman, totally ignoring her comment. 'You had a cream-coloured coat on, and just as you were going into the school you slipped over on the ice and made your coat all dirty, and you cried and cried. You refused to go in and you were clinging to your mum's hand and begging her to take you home. It only seems like yesterday.'
> 'No, Elsie, that wasn't her first day at school. That was when we took the children to see Father Christmas, and she had asked me if she could wear her new coat so she would look smart when she went in to tell him what she wanted for Christmas. Don't you remember, it was your Paul who pushed her over on the way into the shop?' said Emily's mother.
> 'No, it wasn't,' said Emily. 'I remember that coat and falling over, but it was when I was on my way to Sophie's birthday party, and I didn't want to go in because I had mud on my knees.'

How do we know which was the true story? Each version was true for the teller, but the actual truth may have been a different version altogether!

The next section helps to explain how we use our memories in order to make sense of our environment, rather than simply having a list of information that we draw on as and when necessary. It will also help you to understand how our memories become distorted – or positively inaccurate.

Schema theory

Schema theory helps to explain many pieces of research, especially the work of Loftus and Palmer, the core study described later, which focuses on memory.

Endel Tulving (1972) suggested that we have two different types of memory: episodic memory, which is a memory of episodes (or events in our lives), and semantic memory, which is a memory of facts (e.g. trees lose their leaves in winter). Sometimes the experience of an episode leads us to learn new facts.

Often (even when we do not have a damaged memory) we remember the facts rather than the actual episode. Why this happens can be explained in part by schema theory.

Constructing schemata

Each fact that we learn as a result of our experiences becomes part of a schema, which is a kind of packet of information about something. It may help you to think of schemata (plural of schema) as files in a filing cabinet. You have schemata about school, work, holidays, clubs, picnics, parties, and so on. You simply open the drawer of the filing cabinet in your head, take out the relevant file and look up the information, in a fraction of a second.

We have schemata for all different types of objects, events and situations, and they are put together from the experiences we have had and the information we have gathered. They seem to contain a kind of prototype which develops from this information, and the amount of detail they contain will vary accordingly.

Think back to your fifth birthday. What do you think you did on that day? The majority of you would say that you had a party with a cake, and cards and presents. It is very unlikely that you actually remember your fifth birthday, but you will have no problem thinking what it was probably like. You make inferences about the situation, using information about what happens at birthday parties, stored from past experiences and acquired information. In other words, you are describing what your schemata lead you to believe it was like, rather than how it really was. As you will see in the Loftus and Palmer study, the expectations caused by our schemata can lead to us to produce inaccurate and distorted versions of events. This is another example of the errors in human processing that make us question the machine analogy proposed by the information-processing model.

Schema theory shows how we make use of our memory to enable us to repeat quickly and efficiently behaviours or experiences that occur regularly in our lives, or to manage experiences similar to those we have lived through before. Our knowledge of a typical (or perhaps stereotypical) trip to the supermarket means we are able to do the weekly shop efficiently, without having to keep learning how to do it. By putting schemata in order, we are able to produce a script, or template, for what to expect and how to behave. As we have seen, schema theory emphasises the fact that what we remember is influenced by what we already know. It also helps to explain how the ideas, beliefs and attitudes we hold have an effect on what we will remember about an event.

If you were asked to imagine going to a restaurant, and told to list 20 things that happened during the course of your time there, you would include many of the same things as other people, such as being seated, reading the menu, ordering food, having drinks and paying the bill. Such a study, conducted by Bower, Black and Turner (1979), involving 32 people, found that 73 per cent included the following six events on their list: sitting down, looking at a menu, ordering, eating, paying the bill and leaving the restaurant.

The subjects in this piece of research named the same events, as they obviously had experience of restaurants and knew exactly what went on. Now imagine you are a small child and the only 'restaurant' you have been to is McDonald's. What sort of things would you describe if you were asked the same question? Then you visit a Harvester or Beefeater restaurant, and your knowledge of restaurants increases enormously, as you realise that restaurants involve sitting down at a table, reading the menu and having food brought to you rather than having to queue for it. Then you visit somewhere like the Savoy in London, and things would be different again.

With growing experience and knowledge, the packet of information contained in your brain which stores information about a certain event will increase in size as you get older. You will be able to use this stored knowledge to answer questions and interpret conversations without having to have all the details presented to you. You would understand what was meant by, 'We went to the Harvester last night and the service was excellent,' without wondering what on earth the person was talking about.

How do schemata affect memories?

They can affect them in the following ways:

1. A schema guides the selection of what is encoded and stored in memory. You are unlikely to remember irrelevant details of events (e.g. what clothes you wore when you sat your GCSEs, assuming that it was not school uniform). A schema also provides a framework to store new information, like a file marked 'restaurant'.

2. You abstract information from events. This means that you take out and store only some of the information from different events, if there are a number of them which are all very similar. To return to the example of your fifth birthday, it is likely that all you can remember is general information about birthdays – presents, cakes, parties, and so on. This also happens with conversations – you only remember the gist of them, not all the contents.

3. Because we have integrated lots of information into our schemata, they help us to interpret different situations about which we have very limited knowledge. We may end up having to use inferences in the light of past knowledge and previous experiences.

4. Memories can also be distorted to fit prior expectations, and in order to make them consistent with your existing schemata they may actually be transformed. This is how eyewitness testimony gets blurred – you see what you expect to see.

5. A schema may also aid retrieval. You can sometimes remember what happened by searching through the information you have already stored in a schema, to see if you recognise what is required.

Schemata and stories

The idea of schema theory was introduced by Frederick Bartlett in 1932, in order to explain why, when people remember stories, they regularly leave out some details and introduce what he called 'rationalisations', which they use to

make the stories make sense. He investigated this using a story called 'The war of the ghosts', asking people to recall a story which contained unfamiliar information. He found that they did not remember the story as it was told, but made errors in their recall, because they used their schemata to interpret the story and provide information which they believed was included, rather than what was actually there.

Bartlett asked people to recall the story at intervals over time, showing that distortions occurred. The story was made more westernised, for example, with 'fishing' substituted for 'hunting' seals. In addition, the amount recalled decreased over time, and there were further distortions.

Bartlett believed that when people remember stories, there is a tendency for them to sacrifice detailed recall in favour of 'making sense' of the information provided. He demonstrated that rather than being like computer memory, where input information is retrieved unaltered, human memory is reconstructive in nature. When we process information, we try to make it logical, sensible and coherent. As we have already seen (above), this means that we include what could or should have happened, according to our expectations, so our memory is likely to be an imperfect record of events, and can be a complete distortion, governed by our biases and prejudices. You may be unaware of ever doing this, as it is not a conscious process, but if you want to see it in real life, just ask two squabbling siblings for their version of events and see how much they differ.

The Study

E.F. Loftus and J.J. Palmer (1974) 'Reconstruction of automobile destruction: An example of the interaction between language and memory', *Journal of Verbal Learning and Verbal Behaviour*, 13: 585–9

Background

Bartlett's ideas are still widely accepted, as they explain how the information we take in is affected by already existing schemata representing previous knowledge. His work, however, has its critics. His findings were largely qualitative, as it is very difficult to establish objective measures of memory distortion. Later researchers, however, have undertaken laboratory studies to investigate scientifically the reconstructive nature of human memory, and to consider some of the factors which lead to these distortions. An eminent researcher in this field is Elizabeth Loftus, who, along with colleagues, has carried out a series of studies, particularly concerning the reliability of eyewitness testimony.

It is interesting that eyewitness testimony was once considered one of the most important factors in court cases. Many suspects were found guilty as a result of their identification by witnesses and witness reports of events. But if human memory is reconstructive, should we rely on this in a court of law?

Loftus was concerned not only with the fragility of memory, but also with the effects of stress on the ability of victims to recall facts. Loftus and Burns (1982) showed their subjects a film of a hold-up and then tested their memory for details. The experimental group saw a violent version of the film, where one of the members of a group of young boys is shot and collapses on the floor, clutching his bleeding face. The control group saw the same film, but this scene was omitted. Instead, their film changed to a scene inside the bank, where the manager is explaining to staff and customers exactly what has happened.

Loftus and Burns found that subjects who saw the violent version had significantly less memory for details of events before the shooting. Most subjects failed to mention that one of the boys had a

... continued

large number '17' on his jersey, which was very obvious from the film. There were actually 16 items that subjects could have recalled, but those who had seen the violent version of the film recalled significantly less than the other group on 14 of those items.

The core study that we are concerned with here focuses on the effects of language on memory changes. Loftus suggested that there are two types of information that affect our memory of an event:

- information gained at the time of the event.
- information gained after the event (subsequent information).

Loftus was interested in how you can actually change a witness's recollection of an incident by subtly introducing new and subsequent information during questioning, that is, *after* the event. This depends on how language is used. For example, one study showed how changing the structure of a question could lead people to reconstruct an event and 'remember' false facts. In the study, film clips were shown and the independent variable was manipulated by asking one of two versions of the critical question:

- In one condition, subjects were asked: 'Did you see a broken headlight?' – this question suggests that there may or may not have been a broken headlight.
- In the second condition, subjects were asked: 'Did you see the broken headlight?' – the use of the definite article 'the' here suggests that there definitely was a broken headlight, so the subject should have seen it.

The results showed that more of those in the second condition reported seeing a broken headlight, even though there was no broken headlight in the film.

Aim

Loftus and Palmer carried out two experiments to investigate the effects of language on memory. Their expectation was that information received after the event in the form of leading questions would be integrated into a person's memory. It would form part of the memory and cause the event to be recalled in a way that was consistent with the subsequent information they were given.

Method

Two experiments were carried out to see whether leading questions could change a person's memory of an event. The first experiment also tested the established theory that witnesses are not very good at estimating the speed of vehicles.

Experiment 1

Method and design: This was a laboratory experiment, and the experimental design used was independent groups.

Subjects: Forty-five student subjects were tested in groups of various sizes. For test purposes, it was designed that overall there would be five conditions, with nine subjects providing data for each condition.

Apparatus: Equipment was needed to screen seven film segments from the Evergreen Safety Council of the Seattle Police Department. Each segment lasted between five and 30 seconds. The films were

> ### Key concept
>
> **Leading questions**
>
> Loftus and Palmer point out that it was already known that 'some questions are... more suggestive than others', and that a legal concept of 'leading questions' existed, along with rules for the use of such questions in the courtroom.
>
> Their definition is as follows: 'A leading question is simply one that, by its form or content, suggests to the witness what answer is desired or leads him to the desired answer.' We have already considered the example of the broken headlight. Examples from everyday life might include: 'You don't mind babysitting your little brother, do you?' or 'My bum doesn't look too big in these jeans, does it?'

... continued

Key concept

Critical questions

In an experiment, the critical question (or questions) is what is used to measure the dependent variable. It is common for these to be masked in a questionnaire by the use of distracter questions, so that subjects cannot respond to the demand characteristics present when just one question is asked. The fewer questions that are asked, the more likely it is that subjects will work out the purpose of the study and behave so as to support the hypothesis or scupper the study. This needs to be avoided, as it affects the internal validity of the study.

safety promotion films, and four of the seven clips contained staged crashes. (There would have been serious ethical concerns about showing real crashes.) The staged crashes had the advantage that the speed at which the vehicles were travelling when they crashed was known: for two of the films it was 40mph, for one 20mph, and for another 30mph. This meant the accuracy of speed estimates could be measured.

There were also sets of questionnaires corresponding to the film clips for each subject, to be completed after each clip.

Procedure: All the subjects were shown the seven film clips and were given a questionnaire to complete after each clip. There were two parts to each questionnaire. First, they were asked to 'Give an account of the accident you have just seen', and second, to answer a set of questions relating to the accident. Of the questions asked, the one the researchers were interested in was about the speed of the vehicles at the time of the accident.

In order to counteract order effects, the groups were presented with a different order of films. The entire experiment lasted about an hour and a half.

The independent variable was manipulated by changing the wording of the critical question about the speed of vehicles at the time of the accident, using a different verb in the question. The authors theorised that the stronger the verb, the higher the speed estimate would be. The standard format of the critical question was: 'About how fast were the cars going when they _____ each other?' There were five verb conditions: 'contacted', 'hit', 'bumped', 'collided' and 'smashed'.

Each subject received one of the five critical questions in their questionnaires. This means that the independent variable in this experiment was which verb condition the subject was tested in. The dependent variable was the mean speed estimate in miles per hour per condition, thus giving a quantitative measure.

Results: We will look at these in two parts.

1. How accurate are the witnesses' speed estimates?

The accuracy of subjects' speed estimates in miles per hour for the four staged crashes were as follows:

Table 3.1

Film	Actual speed (mph)	Mean estimated speed (mph)
1	20	37.7
2	30	36.2
3	40	39.7
4	40	36.1

Source: adapted from Loftus and Palmer (1974)

These results support previous studies in that they indicate that people are not very good at judging how fast a vehicle is actually travelling.

... continued

2. Does changing the verb in the critical question affect speed estimates?

The mean speed estimates in miles per hour for each of the five verb conditions were as follows:

Inferential analysis of these results showed that they were significant, at the $p < 0.05$ level. This shows that the form of the question affected the witnesses' answers.

Why does the wording affect the subject? Loftus and Palmer offer two interpretations. First, it may be due to response bias. This is the tendency to give a response in a certain direction according to the situation. If a subject cannot decide between 30 and 40, the word 'smashed' may cue the response of 40, as it suggests a higher speed. Second, it may be that the language used causes a change in the subject's memory representation of events. Loftus and Palmer say: 'The verb "smashed" may change a subject's memory such that he "sees" that accident as being more severe than it was.'

Loftus and Palmer carried out a second experiment to try to establish which of these interpretations was true. They theorised that if the person's memory had been changed, then they could be expected to 'remember' other details which did not occur, but which would fit in with their belief that the accident took place at a higher speed.

Table 3.2

Verb	Mean estimated speed (mph)
Smashed	40.8
Collided	39.3
Bumped	38.1
Hit	34
Contacted	31.8

Source: adapted from Loftus and Palmer (1974)

Experiment 2

Aim: The aim of the second experiment was to see if subjects asked the 'smashed' question would be more likely than two other groups to report seeing broken glass in a filmed accident, when tested one week later. They were compared to a group asked the 'hit' question, and a control group not asked to make a speed estimate. Broken glass would be expected in an accident occurring at high speed, but no broken glass was actually shown in the film. A positive report of broken glass would suggest that the memory of the event was being reconstructed as a result of information (in the form of leading questions) received after the event.

Method and design: This was also a laboratory experiment, using independent groups.

Subjects: One hundred and fifty student subjects were divided into three groups, with 50 subjects in each condition.

Apparatus: Equipment was needed to screen a film showing a multiple car crash. The clip lasted less than one minute, with the accident itself lasting less than four seconds.

Each subject completed two questionnaires. The questionnaires completed immediately after viewing the film clip asked subjects to describe the accident in their own words and to answer a series of questions (Questionnaire 1). The critical question asked subjects to estimate the speed of the vehicles.

There were three conditions, with two conditions being asked leading questions about the speed of the vehicles:

- 50 subjects were asked: 'About how fast were the cars going when they smashed into each other?'
- 50 subjects were asked: 'About how fast were the cars going when they hit each other?'
- 50 subjects were not asked about the speed of vehicles, and thus acted as a control condition.

A second questionnaire (Questionnaire 2) contained ten questions about the accident. The critical question was: 'Did you see any broken glass?' Subjects responded to this by ticking yes or no.

... continued

Procedure: This was a two-part procedure, with subjects seeing the film and filling in one of the three versions of Questionnaire 1 on one day, and returning a week later to complete Questionnaire 2.

Results: Subjects in the 'smashed' condition gave a significantly higher speed estimate than those in the 'hit' condition, 10.46mph and 8mph respectively, supporting the finding from the first experiment that the wording of the question can have a considerable effect on the estimate of speed.

Subjects in the 'smashed' condition were also significantly more likely to answer 'yes' to the question, 'Did you see any broken glass?' than those in the 'hit' and control conditions. The differences between the control and the 'hit' conditions were negligible.

The distribution of yes and no responses to the question 'Did you see any broken glass?' was as follows:

Table 3.3

Response	'Smashed' condition	'Hit' condition	Control
Yes	16	7	6
No	34	43	44

Source: adapted from Loftus and Palmer (1974)

Discussion

The conclusion of the second experiment was that the verb not only affected the estimate of speed, but also the likelihood of subjects thinking they had seen broken glass. Loftus and Palmer explain this by suggesting that subjects took in information from the original scene and then merged this with information given after the event. This produced a memory of the event made up of some of the original information and subsequent information received when they were questioned about it. We are inclined to make our memory make sense, so those subjects who believed the accident had taken place at a higher speed, and was therefore more severe (those in the 'smashed' condition), were more likely to think that broken glass was present.

Commentary: Methods and issues

Research method, design and data gathering

The experimental method was used in this study, with both experiments employing an individual groups design. The strengths and weaknesses of this method and design can be applied here, so the study had a high level of control enabling the effect of the IV to be isolated and recorded and a causal relationship to be inferred. As is often the case in a highly controlled laboratory experiment, there are some concerns about the ecological validity of the task subjects were asked to perform in the study.

Quantitative data was gathered and the data-gathering method was self-report by questionnaire.

Key concept

Strengths and weaknesses of self-report data-gathering methods

Self-report data are the data gathered from interviews, questionnaires and psychometric tests, and the detailed notes made in case studies, such as those by Freud (Little Hans) and by Thigpen and Cleckley (The three faces of Eve).

Self-report data can also mean simply asking subjects to answer questions, such as 'Which has more?' in the Samuel and Bryant study on conservation.

The advantages of using self-report data are that we are able to measure cognitive variables such as memory, knowledge and attitudes, which cannot be either observed directly or tested for in any biological test. Without self-report, the study by Loftus and Palmer on memory and language would not be possible, for example.

However, the validity of self-report data can be questioned where subjects are able to deliberately falsify their answers. This may be because they are responding to demand characteristics present in the study, or because of evaluation apprehension: they lie to give a socially desirable answer in order to avoid being judged negatively.

Does the study raise any ethical concerns?

Although the subjects knew that this was a test of memory, the hypothesis about leading questions was not revealed to them, and distracter questions were used to further conceal the exact hypothesis. This was necessary in this study to ensure that demand characteristics did not affect the findings. The researchers chose to show clips of car crashes from safety films which did not contain gruesome images (not even any broken glass!), so they should not have upset the subjects or caused them harm.

Given the findings of the study, we could describe it as ethically worthy, since it contributes to the debate about how witnesses to events should or should not be questioned in order to get a true picture of what happened.

Is the study useful?

Loftus and Palmer's study is one in a series of studies which showed that it is possible to distort the memories of witnesses. This has considerable repercussions for the police. Such studies have led to a great deal of research being carried out into the best way for police officers to question witnesses.

Look again at the responses of subjects in the second experiment. Of 150 subjects questioned, 121 answered 'no' correctly, including over two-thirds of the subjects in the 'smashed' condition. So perhaps it is not so easy to change a memory for an important event, and we must be careful not to exaggerate the extent to which the recall of witnesses is affected by leading questions. Also, if the misleading information is blatantly incorrect, people are less likely to take it in and overwrite previous information.

Validity and reliability of the study

One of the challenges to the external validity is that the findings of the study are low in generalisability. Where college students are used as subjects in psychological research, generalisability beyond the sample, and to the wider population, is low. For both experiments, Loftus and Palmer drew their sample from a population of university students.

Key concept

Students as subjects

Since most psychologists undertake research while working at a university, the student body provides them with a convenient opportunity sample. The researcher just needs to put up an ad on the noticeboard with the offer of money (or, for psychology students, the possibility of marks towards their course) and stand back to avoid being killed in the rush. Perhaps that is an exaggeration, but the fact is that students are plentiful on campus, and many researchers have benefited from using the time- and cost-effective sample that an undergraduate sample base can provide. The researcher is able to carry out the study from the comfort of their workplace, and students earn some money. So why are student samples a problem? In order for a sample to be generalisable to the wider population, you need a broader sample than that enticed out of the university library or the student bar. Sears (1986) reviewed the use of student samples in psychology and considered the problems presented in terms of biasing factors that reduce generalisability, and the consequences of basing our view of human psychology on such a narrow sample base.

Biasing factors include the fact that students tend to represent only a narrow age range, and the upper levels of family income and educational background. This means that they present us with a biased sample, as other age groups are under-represented. Moreover, students are not even typical of their own age group, as they are university students because they have displayed the academic skills required to gain entry, and in order to do this they tend to be more compliant to authority than their peers in general. Sears goes on to say that laboratory studies, such as that by Loftus and Palmer, compound the problems, since the students will be more willing to comply with researchers' requests, especially if studies they participate in form part of their course. So we should always be cautious when making generalisations from studies using student samples. (For a well-written and concise review of Sears' work, see Banyard and Grayson 2000.)

In terms of the reliability of the findings, both the experiments carried out provided evidence that memory of an event can be distorted by information introduced afterwards. This supports the reliability of the theory that language – in this case, leading questions – can distort memory.

Since the findings of the two experiments agree, we describe them as being concurrently valid, that is, each supports the validity of the other.

As the study is carried out in the controlled conditions of the laboratory, it is low in ecological validity. In the study, the subjects were asked to watch the film clips and were prepared to recall what they had seen. Accidents happen spontaneously in the real world, and our memories of such events will obviously be different without the luxury of prior warning. We also have to question whether watching film clips of staged accidents leads to memories being laid down or recalled in the same way as they might be under the stressful and distressing circumstances of being a witness to a real car crash involving real people.

Baron-Cohen *et al.* study: Adults with autism and theory of mind

Autism and the theory of mind

We are going to look at how important cognitions are to another area of our lives – social interactions. Although this may not seem at first to be linked directly to cognitive psychology, our ability to take in all available information, process it effectively and draw accurate conclusions affects not only our learning ability but also our social skills. If we are unable to use our 'social cognitions' effectively, we can misinterpret or misunderstand different situations, and this can have a dramatic effect on our relationships with others.

In this section we are going to consider what happens when some children do not develop effective social cognitions and the impact this has on their lives. These children have a condition known as autism, and one thing that seems to be common to children with autism is that they have tremendous difficulty with social relationships. Dr Simon Baron-Cohen has identified a core deficit in people with autism: they have an underdeveloped theory of mind. This means that they do not develop at the same rate as people without autism the understanding that they, and other people, have thoughts, beliefs, feelings and knowledge that can and do differ from one another. This deficit can be used to explain many of the social difficulties experienced by people with autism.

Diagnosis of autism

Autism used to be a relatively rare condition, which, according to Uta Frith, writing in 1993, affected only one or two children in every 1,000. More recently, Baird *et al.* (2006) writing in *The Lancet*, suggested that the prevalence of autism and related autistic spectrum disorders is much higher than was previously recognised. They suggest the minimum number of children with some form of autistic spectrum disorder is one in 100. This statistic suggests that over half a million people in the UK have autism. However, they do discuss the fact that the increase may also be influenced, in part, by better diagnosis or the broadening of diagnostic criteria.

Although autism was first recognised in 1943 by Kanner, it was not accepted as an official diagnosis until 1980. Until this point it had been considered a type of childhood schizophrenia – the 'aloneness' of the autistic child is very like the behaviour of people with schizophrenia, whose disordered thoughts cut them off from others. However, it became clear that this was not the case, as autistic children do not develop schizophrenic symptoms as adults. Nowadays, autism is a medical diagnosis which has specific criteria laid down in ICD-10 (International Classification of Diseases from the World Health Organization) and DSM-IV (Diagnostic and Statistical Manual of Mental Disorders, a US publication).

People who are diagnosed with autism will have a tremendous variation in the degree to which they are affected. This means that no two children with the disorder will be totally alike, as some have little or no speech, while others may have fluent speech; some may shy away from social contact, while others will tolerate considerable interaction. A child on the more extreme end of the autistic spectrum is likely to suffer from severe disabilities, which will continue into adulthood. Thus autism is not simply a childhood disorder, but rather one which may extend the dependence we associate with childhood across the adult lives of those with the condition, leaving families and authorities to deal with the individuals who need lifelong care.

Oliver Sacks (1995) has written about Temple Grandin, an autistic adult who holds a PhD in animal sciences, teaches at Colorado State University and runs her own business. Temple has developed ways of coping with the symptoms of her autism and is able to live a full and independent life, although it has to be

pointed out that her social skills remain highly impaired – she chooses to live alone, and admits she has a better understanding of the feelings of cattle than she has of the feelings of her fellow humans. The way she deals with human interaction is to refer consciously to a kind of database in her memory, which has stored factual information about how to behave and respond, rather than having the kind of innate skills that most of us have.

The autistic spectrum

One technique which has attempted to address the issue of identifying the variation in the presentation of autistic disorders is to consider the difficulties that children experience as being somewhere on an autistic spectrum. This relatively new term includes the sub-groups within the spectrum of autism, such as children with high-functioning autism and Asperger's syndrome (children who show the same characteristics of autism to a greater or lesser extent, but are of average or above-average intelligence, and give the appearance of having good communication skills, although this may not really be the case). If you imagine a line with autism at one end and Asperger's syndrome at the other, which then borders on normality, this may be a helpful way of picturing what is meant by the autistic spectrum.

The variation in severity of each impairment from one child to the next presents problems when it comes to reaching a diagnosis. What makes matters even more confusing is that children may have one or two of the impairments which will affect their ability to interact with others, but will

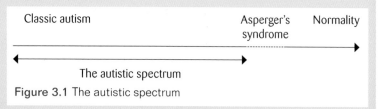

Figure 3.1 The autistic spectrum

not be sufficiently impaired in all three areas to be labelled 'autistic'. Similarly, how do you quantify an 'impairment'? What is normal, and who decides? Is this not just a little bit subjective?

Autism and autistic spectrum disorders

Autism is often referred to as a communication disorder and is characterised by three main areas of difficulty, all of which relate to social interactions. These three main areas of difficulty are known as the **triad of impairments**, and are used to help identify children who have autistic spectrum disorder. These areas of difficulty are:

- Difficulties with social interaction: Difficulties in relating to other people or understanding other people and social situations.

- Difficulties with communication: At the extreme end of the spectrum, children with autism may have minimal language, or difficulty with both verbal and non-verbal communication (e.g. taking language literally, or not being able to read facial expressions or gestures).

- Difficulties with imagination: A lack of imaginative ability which will affect the quality of play. These difficulties with imagination are often replaced by obsessive, repetitive behaviours, such as watching things that spin, tapping and scratching, flicking fingers, rocking, and showing a strong resistance to change.

Looking in more detail at the impact of these difficulties will help you to gain an insight into the challenges faced by people with an autistic diagnosis.

Difficulties with social interaction

Autistic children find it difficult to form meaningful relationships with others, including their parents, and this usually results in a degree of heartbreak for the parents. In normal development, the bond between parent/caregiver and child develops very early on. Babies make eye contact with their parents when being fed; they cry for attention or to be picked up; they smile from about four weeks of age – they are active in their communication with parents, and quickly learn how a smile, giggle or happy scream can draw attention from others. From about seven months they develop stranger fear and separation anxiety, showing that they have developed emotional attachments.

Autistic children do not develop in this way. Those on the extreme end of the spectrum do not seek attention as babies, unless they are uncomfortable or wet. They do not make eye contact, even seeming to look through you, rather than at you. They do not smile and they appear to be unaware of others. Not until they are two or three do they form some sort of attachment to their caregivers/ parents, and even then this may not be of the same quality as a normal child– parent bond.

Difficulties with communication

Just focusing on language for a moment, it is worth mentioning that children with an autistic spectrum disorder often fail to communicate in any way, either verbally or non-verbally, to the extent that they may not use eye contact. This is because they do not see any reason to communicate with other people. When there is no communication, the child will not explore their ability to vocalise or learn new sounds, so their language acquisition will not develop effectively, leading to a delay. Alongside the delay may come frustration because the child will be unable to make their wishes known. When they do speak, they are unlikely to use eye contact or hand gestures.

Lack of eye contact in children with autism is often the first indication of their poor communication skills. As mentioned, their language development is very slow, and in fact 50 per cent of people with autism never learn to speak. The language they do develop may differ from the normal use of language, for instance, they may repeat what others say. The child is not responding to the meaning of what is being said, but simply repeating the words. This is known as echolalia. If all the child does is repeat back, parrot fashion, what you have said, then the conversation is non-existent.

These difficulties with play and communication lead to severe social difficulties for the autistic child. In the most extreme cases, the child can be left in total isolation, in an apparently impenetrable world of their own.

Difficulties with imagination

An autistic child will join in and play only if an adult insists. They usually play alone, and tend to focus on repetitive actions with an object, such as spinning a hoop on their arm or passing keys from one hand to the other. They do not engage in what is called socio-dramatic play, or pretend play, as normal children do, such as playing house, pretending to be Superman or dressing up. Normal children also engage in shared games, where they take on different roles and act out scenarios together, using their imaginations and social skills to move the plot forwards.

Difficulties with imagination often result in an obsessive insistence on particular routines or interests as a way of coping with a world that appears confusing and unintelligible. If you can imagine not understanding the rules of the social world that you live in, it must seem like a scary place – unpredictable and sometimes hostile. In order to manage it, you would probably like to retreat into your own world where things are predictable, ordered and manageable. In fact, many of the ritualistic and repetitive actions of autistics, such as twiddling objects or tapping, are simply a way to reduce over-arousal and consequent discomfort, by focusing on one small and apparently meaningless action. This would help to explain why people with autism get extremely distressed when things are changed or disorganised.

In the film *Rain Man*, Dustin Hoffman gives a very good portrayal of an autistic adult, Raymond. The character is extremely upset by any change in his routine. Any alteration, however small, can cause a person with autism to demonstrate inexplicable rage, where they will scream wildly and lash out, and may be very difficult to calm down. Their resistance to any change, and their extremely negative responses to any changes in routine, can make living and dealing with autistic adults and children very challenging.

Figure 3.2 In the film *Rain Man*, Dustin Hoffman accurately portrayed the fear and discomfort of an autistic person subjected to a change in routine

In addition to an obsession with routine, autistic children and adults develop obsessions with specific tasks or objects. As children in the playground, we were all familiar with the idea of crazes, such as collecting and swapping football stickers, playing marbles, and so on. The obsessions of the autistic person are extreme versions of this type of behaviour. They become focused on one particular activity or interest, and the level of detailed and complex knowledge acquired can be mind-boggling. The focus of these obsessions varies according to the age of the child. Many young children are fixated on dinosaurs or Thomas the Tank Engine, while older children may become obsessed with trains or astronomy, or even something as bizarre as different types of burglar alarm system.

It may be through such enthusiasms that one in ten people with autism seem to develop a particular skill or gift. Baron-Cohen calls these **islets of ability**. The autistic person paradoxically develops skills which normal people cannot, such as playing a piece of music immediately after hearing it, being able to draw architecturally detailed drawings of buildings from memory, or specific and unusual mathematical skills, such as the card-counting skill that Raymond has in *Rain Man*. A real-life example comes from Oliver Sacks (1985), who described the particular skills of John and Michael, 26-year-old twins with autism. They both had a remarkable memory for digits and could remember up to 300 digits with ease, even though they could not manage simple addition or subtraction. If you gave them a date, in the past or the future, they could immediately tell you on what day of the week it fell or would fall.

While the existence of such skills is academically fascinating and attracts a great deal of attention, it is not usually the case that they are of any benefit to the individual who possesses them.

Central coherence and autism

Recent research has indicated that people with autism seem to have difficulty integrating information so that it makes sense, and this may help to explain some of the problems associated with the condition. Frith (1989) suggested that people with autism have a cognitive deficit in what she calls their 'central coherence'. In order to understand what she means, we will consider some examples.

If you were asked to describe the figure below, you are quite likely to say it is a triangle, whereas it is actually three lines. You have integrated the information so that it makes sense to you.

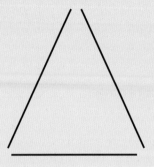

Figure 3.3

Is the image below a 'P', or is it lots of S's?

```
SSSSSS
S SSSSS SS
SSSSSSS S
S SSSSS SS
SSSSSS
S
S
S
S
```

Figure 3.4

What you are probably doing here is seeing the 'bigger picture'. You are integrating the parts so that they have more meaning. This ability was first identified by the Gestalt psychologists, based in Germany, who put forward the idea that 'the whole is greater than the sum of its parts'. They suggested that we integrate information in order to make sense of it, rather than looking at each individual component.

Frith suggested that people with autism do not tend to be affected by the context of an object, but are able to see each part for what it is, rather than perceiving (or misperceiving) it as a whole. This has been investigated by looking at people's ability on an embedded figures test, where you have to find a simple shape embedded in a larger figure.

Happé (1997) looked for further evidence of lack of central cohesiveness by investigating a sample of 16 participants with autism. She found that they mispronounced homophones (words which are spelt the same but pronounced differently), despite reading them in a context which would have indicated the correct pronunciation. For example, if you read the sentence, 'There was a tear in her eye', you are unlikely to pronounce the word 'tear' as you would if you read the sentence, 'There was a tear in her dress'. This provided further evidence that the autistic participants were not looking at the 'whole' when reading, but simply reading each word individually.

Campbell *et al.* (1995) also found that children with autism can identify a famous person just as well being given part of their face or the whole face, presumably because they look at each part of a person's face, rather than the face as a whole. Perhaps this lack of executive function – the ability to bring together all the pieces of information – can help to explain the difficulties people with autism have in making sense of social interactions and social situations.

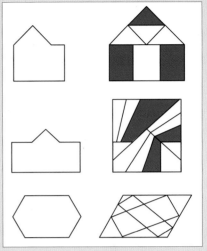

Figure 3.5 Can you see the embedded figures in these illustrations?

Social relationships

As children grow up in a social world, they need to learn the way in which social relationships, which are a feature of their lives from birth, actually operate. The ability to make friends and to behave appropriately is quite a complex task, which we are not taught directly. We might be instructed in social etiquette (table manners, saying please and thank you, and not interrupting when someone is speaking to us), but we are not taught to look at another person when they talk to us, or to retain an appropriate social distance.

We develop an understanding of gestures and facial expressions, we can sense uncomfortable atmospheres and we do not always have to ask how someone is. We can also understand that language does not need to be interpreted literally, and that people do not always say what they mean. For example, if you were told to pull your socks up when you had failed an assignment, you would not immediately bend over and literally pull up your socks. You would know that the person was telling you that you would have to make more effort in the future. Most of us are also able to put ourselves into another person's shoes – imagining how they must feel or what they might want, without actually experiencing their lives.

All these skills develop as we get older, and as our cognitive ability matures, so does our capacity to process all the information we gather from our experiences. By the time we reach our teenage years, we are likely to be proficient 'social interactors' and 'mindreaders'. In other words, we have a well-developed theory of mind.

Figure 3.6 It is interesting to note that most children who have no developmental problems seem to share an understanding of unwritten social rules

False beliefs

Researchers have investigated the theory of mind by looking at children's abilities to understand false beliefs. There are two types of 'beliefs' that are investigated in the research on false beliefs:

- A first-order belief task requires the child to think about another person's thoughts about a real event. For example, the child would have to explain that 'Jack believes that the shop is closed, even if the shop is open'. Children with normal development should pass these tests by the age of about four years.

- Second-order beliefs require the child to think about a second person's thoughts about a third person's thoughts about an event. For example, the child would have to explain that 'Jack believes that John believes that the shop is closed, even if the shop is open'. Children with normal development should pass these tests between the ages of six and seven years.

One of the original studies was undertaken by Heinz Wimmer and Josef Perner (1983), and involved a small boy called Maxi and a bar of chocolate. The story required children of different ages to attribute a false belief (using a first-order belief task) to another person, and it was acted out with dolls. The story went something like this.

> Maxi puts his chocolate in a red cupboard and then goes to play outside. Unknown to Maxi, his mother moves the chocolate to a blue cupboard. Maxi then comes back from playing and wants to get his chocolate. A child who has observed this will be asked, 'Where will Maxi look for the chocolate when he comes back?'

Obviously the correct answer is the red cupboard, because that is where Maxi put it and where he believes it still is. If the child has an understanding of false beliefs, he will realise that Maxi will have a false belief as to where his chocolate will be found. If, on the other hand, the child does not understand that people can see things differently from the way that the child himself sees them, he will answer that Maxi will look for the chocolate in the blue cupboard because that is where it really is.

Wimmer and Perner found that all children younger than four years typically said that Maxi would look in the blue cupboard. This indicated that they could not take into account the fact that Maxi did not know that the chocolate had been moved.

Lacking a theory of mind

Having an idea of how children develop a theory of mind, and how important this is to their social functioning, we can imagine how awful it must be for a child who has no concept of how other people think and feel. If they are unaware that other people have thoughts and beliefs which are totally different from their own, they will be unable to 'mind-read', that is, to understand how other people feel and how they will react to different situations. Imagine being unable to assess how someone is responding to you when you meet them? How would you feel if you were not sure whether they liked you or not, or whether they were angry, upset or bored with your company? Under

normal circumstances, having a theory of mind would help you in the following interaction.

> 'Do you like my new dress, Miriam?' squeaked Edna, as she wrestled with the buttons at the front of the vivid purple dress. 'I think it is soooo sexy, and I love the way the front shows off my cleavage.' Miriam grimaced. The buttons looked like they were on maximum tension, hanging on to both sides of the dress and trying to hold back the flow of excess flesh between them. One more inhalation of breath would result in the whole row just popping off and projecting across the other side of the room. As for the cleavage, it was more like two giant marshmallows trying to escape from the tight line of the bodice. If she bent over, they would escape, smothering the top of the dress. And why that colour? It would make someone with even the strongest constitution feel nauseous.
> 'Yes, it looks lovely!'

Now imagine the same situation, but in this instance Miriam has no theory of mind. Her answer would have been something along the lines of: 'It looks absolutely awful. You are much too fat to wear it and the buttons look like they are about to burst. And the colour makes me feel sick!'

What would Edna's response be to this? She would likely become either extremely upset or incredibly angry, but Miriam would have no concept of what her response would be because she had simply told Edna the truth.

Autistic children have an underdeveloped theory of mind, and even high functioning autistic children of above average IQ may only develop the theory of mind of a nine year old by the time they are 16. Having a theory of someone else's mind is a higher-order skill, which requires integrating a considerable amount of information. If a child can only process one piece of information at a time, it is not surprising that children with autism find this extremely difficult. It is a very complex task to try to see things from someone else's point of view and to identify their mistaken beliefs.

Autism and gender

According to the National Autistic Society, the ratio of boys to girls with autism is estimated at 4:1, but apart from this difference, autism is a disorder that is found across all socio-economic classes and across all racial and ethnic groups.

Simon Baron-Cohen (1999) has suggested that autism is no more than an extreme form of the male brain. In his paper he cites studies which provide evidence that men and women from the general population differ in the area of cognition, suggesting that women are better at language tasks, tests of social judgement, measures of empathy, perceptual speed, matching tasks, fluency of ideas and fine motor coordination, mathematical calculation tests and pretend play in childhood. On the other hand, men are better than women at mathematical reasoning, tasks where they are required to find embedded figures in an abstract drawing, tasks where they have to imagine how an object will look when rotated, some (not all) spatial skills and target-directed motor skills such as gliding.

Baron-Cohen also talks about two skills, **systemising** and **empathising**. In 2005, he was interviewed by Randall F. White, MD, FRCPC, for the American clinician's website, Medscape. In the interview he described systemising as follows:

'as the drive to analyze or construct a system. It could be any kind of system – a mechanical system such as a computer, or a natural system such as the circulatory system of the body. Or it could be an abstract system like mathematics. The key thing is that when you systemize, you identify the rules or the laws that govern that system in order to predict how it will behave. Empathizing is completely different. It's about being able to imagine what someone else is thinking or feeling, and having an emotional response to the other person's feelings.'

He continues by explaining that:

'In the general population, you find that, on average, males have a stronger drive to systemize and females have a stronger drive to empathize. Those are the two cognitive processes we've been focusing on to try to understand autism and why it should be more common among boys than girls. We've found that people on the autistic spectrum show an exaggeration of the male profile.'

It also appears that people with autism are even more skilled at the male-superior tasks, and less skilled than 'normal' males at the female-superior tasks.

Work by Baron-Cohen and his colleagues attempted to find what he called a core deficit in autism – the idea being to find one difficulty that all people with autism have in common. If a core deficit were found, it might help to explain why people with autism behave as they do, but perhaps more importantly, it would help to eliminate the subjectivity that may occur when trying to diagnose the condition. Baron-Cohen *et al.* (1985) conducted research investigating whether autistic children had a theory of mind by using a false belief task, the Sally-Anne Test. The results indicated that only 20 per cent of the high functioning autistic children could pass the test, and some of the children in the control groups could not. The results indicated that a theory of mind was underdeveloped in autistic children.

Baron-Cohen has continued to conduct further research in this area, looking in greater detail at the methodology that has been used in past studies and investigating theory of mind in adults.

The Study

S. Baron-Cohen, T. Jolliffe, C. Mortimore and M. Robertson (1997) 'Another advanced test of theory of mind: Evidence from very high functioning adults with autism or Asperger syndrome', *Journal of Child Psychology and Psychiatry*, 38: 813–22

Background

Do very high-functioning adults with autism and Asperger's syndrome (AS) have difficulty with mind-reading in the same way that children do? If lacking a theory of mind is a core deficit of autism, then it should be apparent in people of all ages and across the autistic spectrum.

Research by Baron-Cohen (1989) had suggested that adults with autism do have problems mind-reading. However, a number of researchers dispute the fact that theory of mind is a general problem in the population of very high-functioning adults with autism and AS. For example, Ozonoff (1991) and Bowler (1992) tested adults and found that some of them passed the theory of mind tests.

In this study, Baron-Cohen *et al.* question the validity of these findings as evidence that adults with autism or AS have an intact theory of mind on the basis that the tests given were too easy. Common tests of theory of mind for children fall into two categories: first-order and second-order tests.

... continued

Second-order tests are more difficult, but even these are designed to measure the theory of mind of a normal child aged six years, as Baron-Cohen and his colleagues point out.

> *'Finding a 30-year-old individual with autism, of normal intelligence, who can pass a theory of mind test at the level of a normal six year old does not lead to the conclusion that they are necessarily normal in this domain. All we can conclude is that they have intact theory of mind skills at the level of a six year old.' (pp.813–14)*

Obviously, if an adult could read a picture book designed for a six-year-old, we would not consider them to have the normal reading level of an adult, and Baron-Cohen *et al.* are saying that the same goes for very high-functioning adults with autism and AS when considering theory of mind.

What Baron-Cohen *et al.* suggest is that previous researchers had failed to note that neither first- nor second-order tests are complex tests of theory of mind. The fact that adults can pass these tests does not mean that mind-reading poses no problem for them. It may be that the tests have a ceiling effect, that is, they are too easy, so everyone tested can achieve full marks.

The authors go on to describe the method used to test theory of mind by Happé (1994), who tested adults with autism and AS on what they refer to as an 'advanced' test of theory of mind. Happé's method was called the strange stories task, which required the subjects to understand the characters' mental states in order to demonstrate theory of mind. Adults with autism and AS had more difficulty with this than the controls, again providing evidence to support Baron-Cohen's earlier work that adults with autism and AS have difficulties with theory of mind. This test, however, measured the level of theory of mind of a normal child aged eight to nine years. Although this was advanced in terms of being beyond what typical first- and second-order tasks assess (the six-year-old level), it is still not really an adult test of theory of mind.

In order to test whether very high-functioning adults with autism or AS have problems with theory of mind, a new adult test of theory of mind was devised for this study. The task extended Happé's ideas and was called the 'Reading the mind in the eyes task', or the 'Eyes task' for short.

The eyes task

In the eyes task, subjects have to interpret parts of faces, by choosing one from a pair of given mental state terms to describe what the face suggests the person is thinking or experiencing.

The design of the materials and the way they were presented to subjects were standardised as follows:

* The photos were always of the same area of the face.
* The photos were always the same size.
* The photos were always black and white.
* The faces were taken from magazine photos.
* Each picture was shown for three seconds, with a forced choice between two mental state terms printed under each picture.
* The experimenter said to the subject: 'Which word best describes what this person is feeling or thinking?'
* The 'foil' (wrong) word was always the semantic opposite of the target (correct) word. (Whether the correct mental state concept was presented on the left or the right was randomised across the subjects.)

Figure 3.7 The picture shows a 'serious' image, with the subject given the choice of 'Serious message' or 'Playful message' in their interpretation of the mental state depicted

The total score possible (all correct) on this test is 25. Here is an example:

... continued

Both basic and complex mental state terms were included in the test. Basic terms included 'happy', 'sad', 'angry' and 'afraid'. Complex terms included 'reflective', 'scheming' and 'arrogant'. The full list is shown below.

Table 3.4

Target Mental State Terms, and Their Foil Terms

No.*	Target term	Foil
1	Concerned	Unconcerned
2	Noticing you	Ignoring you
3	Attraction	Repulsion
4	Relaxed	Worried
5	Serious message	Playful message
6	Interested	Disinterested
7	Friendly	Hostile
8	Sad reflection	Happy reflection
9	Sad thought	Happy thought
10	Certain	Uncertain
11	Far away focus	Near focus
12	Reflective	Unreflective
13	Reflective	Unreflective
14	Cautious about something over there	Relaxed about something over there
15	Noticing someone else	Noticing you
16	Calm	Anxious
17	Dominant	Submissive
18	Fantasising	Noticing
19	Observing	Daydreaming
20	Desire for you	Desire for someone else
21	Ignoring you	Noticing you
22	Nervous about you	Interested in you
23	Flirtatious	Disinterested
24	Sympathetic	Unsympathetic
25	Decisive	Indecisive

*Stimulus number.

Source: adapted from Baron-Cohen *et al.* (1997)

... continued

Construction of the eyes task

Baron-Cohen *et al.* explain the construction of their eyes task as follows (p.4).

> 'In discussion, the target word for each pair was generated by four judges, two male and two female.
>
> A "foil" word (the semantic opposite of the target word in all cases) was selected. These were tested on a panel of eight judges (four male, four female), all independent raters and blind to the hypothesis of the study.
>
> All eight independent raters agreed unanimously on the application of the target words to the eye pairs.'

Validity of the eyes task

The authors stated that 'The Eyes task is designed to be a "pure" theory of mind test, at an advanced level.' By this, they mean that the test is not affected by executive function (no attention switching, planning, and so on), and there is no central coherence component – by presenting only parts of the faces there is no 'whole context' to interpret.

The authors say that the eyes task could equally be called a test of mind-reading (in the sense of working out what someone is thinking or feeling), and the authors use the terms 'theory of mind' and 'mind-reading' interchangeably in this study.

To establish the validity of the eyes task as a test of theory of mind, subjects were also tested using Happé's strange stories test (described above). If both these tests were indeed relatively advanced tests of theory of mind, then if the subject had difficulties with one test, they should also have difficulties with the other.

In order to discount the fact that problems with other cognitive processes, such as difficulties with face perception or emotion recognition, might account for any difficulties subjects had on the eyes task, two control tasks were included: a basic emotion recognition task and a gender recognition task.

The study acknowledged the common belief that females are better than males at mind-reading, so it also aimed to investigate gender differences on the eyes task in the normal population.

Aims

The study tested the following predictions:

- Adults with autism or AS, despite being of normal or above-average IQ, would nevertheless be impaired on a subtle theory of mind test.
- Within the normal population, females would be significantly better on this test of theory of mind than males.

Method and design

This was an experiment using an independent groups design. Each subject was tested individually in a quiet room, either in their own home, in the researcher's clinic, or in a laboratory at Cambridge University.

Subjects

Three groups were tested.

Group 1:

- 16 subjects with high-functioning autism (HFA) or AS (four had HFA and 12 had AS).
- 13 male, 3 female.
- Age range = 18–49 years, mean age = 28.6 years.
- Those with HFA had shown the classic signs of autism (autism compared with language delay) and met the criteria for autism on DSM-IV.

... continued

- Those with AS met the same criteria for autism, but without language delay, and met the criteria for AS defined in ICD-10.

These subjects were selected for being of at least normal intelligence (IQ of greater than 85 – average is 100), as assessed on the WAIS-R (Wechsler Adult Intelligence Scale Revised) test. In this, the group was quite rare, described by Baron-Cohen *et al.* as being cases of 'pure' autism or AS, that is, without the mental handicap that is so commonly associated with autism. They were recruited through clinical sources known to the researchers and from volunteers who responded to an advert in *Communication* (the magazine for the National Autistic Society in the UK).

Group 2:

- 50 normal, age-matched adults.
- 25 male, 25 female.
- Age range = 18–48 years, mean age = 30 years.

These subjects were selected from the general population of Cambridge (although members of the university were excluded from this group). It was established by self-report that none of them had a history of any psychiatric condition. The subjects were selected randomly from a subject panel held in the university department. They were assumed to have IQ in the normal range.

Group 3:

- 10 adult patients with Tourette's syndrome.
- Age-matched with groups 1 and 2 (age range = 18–47 years, mean age = 27.77 years).
- 8 male, 2 female, all diagnosed by Dr Mary Robertson on the basis of DSM-IV criteria for Tourette's syndrome.

All these subjects were attending a referral centre in London. They were selected for being in the normal IQ range, established by the use of the short form of the WAIS-R (the short form was used with these subjects as they were only available for study for a limited time).

Groups 1 and 3 were also tested using first- and second-order false belief tests. If they had failed these tests they would have been excluded from the study, although none failed. This was carried out as a control, so that any difference on the eyes task could be attributed to problems in these two groups beyond the level of which a normal six-year-old was capable.

The similarities between the subjects in this study with autism or AS and those with Tourette's syndrome are as follows:

- All had intelligence in the normal range.
- All had suffered from a developmental disorder from childhood.
- All these disorders cause disruption to both normal schooling and normal peer relations.
- It is suggested that all these disorders involve abnormalities in the frontal cortex of the brain (although in different areas of the frontal cortex in Tourette's from autism and AS).
- There is a lot of evidence to suggest that these disorders have a genetic cause.
- All these disorders affect males more than females (p.6).

The authors theorised that if the problem with theory of mind in adults with autism

Key concept

Controlling extraneous subject variables
The group with Tourette's syndrome was included as a control in this study to ensure that any difficulties on the eyes task experienced by the HFA and AS subjects were not caused because they had an organic, childhood-onset psychiatric disorder. The authors point out that while autism and AS are different from Tourette's syndrome in many ways, they share enough similarities for the inclusion of these Tourette's subjects to act as a control.

... continued

and AS was indeed caused by their autism, and not from just 'having any disorder', then the subjects with Tourette's should have no difficulties on the eyes task. They predicted that the Tourette's syndrome group would not differ from the normal group on the eyes task.

Procedure

Each subject was tested on four tasks, and the presentation of tasks was randomised to control for order effects. The four tasks were:

- the eyes task
- the strange stories task
- two control tasks:
    - the gender recognition task
    - the basic emotion recognition task.

On the gender recognition task, the subjects were shown the same sets of eyes used in the eyes task, but on this test they were asked to identify the gender of the person in the photograph. This had a maximum score of 25, the same as the eyes task.

The basic emotion recognition task (the emotion task) involved judging photographs of whole faces displaying the basic emotions (based on Ekman categories). Six faces were used, showing: 'happy', 'sad', 'angry', 'afraid', 'disgust' and 'surprise'. Two examples are shown below.

Results

As predicted, the findings showed that the adults with autism and AS did have more difficulties on the eyes task than both the control groups. There was also no difference between the normal subjects and those with Tourette's syndrome on the eyes task.

Table 3.5

The eyes task: results by condition

Condition	Mean score (total = 25)
Adults with high-functioning autism or AS	16.3
Normal adults	20.3
Adults with Tourette's syndrome	20.4

Source: Baron-Cohen *et al.* (1997)

The analysis of gender difference in performance on the eyes task also gave results in the predicted direction: males had more difficulties than females.

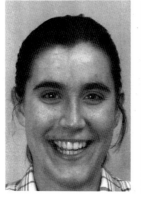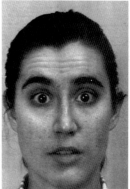

Figure 3.8 Two faces from the basic emotion recognition task

Table 3.6

The eyes task: gender difference in the normal subjects

Condition	Mean score (total = 25)
Normal males	18.8
Normal females	21.8

Source: Baron-Cohen *et al.* (1997)

... continued

Even when the adults with autism or AS were compared just with the normal males, there was still a significant difference between them.

There were no differences on the gender recognition task between the groups, and all subjects scored top marks in the emotion task.

Discussion

Do adults with autism or AS have problems with theory of mind?

The conclusions the authors drew from their findings were that despite having normal or above-average IQ, adults with autism or AS had difficulties on a subtle theory of mind test, the eyes task, suggesting that not only children, but also adults with autism have problems with theory of mind and attributing mental states to others. This shows that individuals with autism or AS have difficulties with mind-reading at stages of development and at higher IQ levels than previous studies had suggested.

The authors give four reasons to support the validity of the eyes task as a measure of theory of mind:

- The target terms are mental state terms.
- The target words are not just emotion terms, so it is more than just an emotion test.
- The same results are found on Happé's strange stories test as on the eyes task, making the results from the eyes task concurrently valid with an 'existing advanced test of theory of mind'.
- There was no difference between the adults with autism or AS on the two control tasks (gender and emotion), suggesting that their poor performance in the eyes task was not due to other perceptual or social cognitive skills.

The authors found no correlation between the IQ and eyes task scores of the adults with autism or AS, and the fact that some of these subjects had university degrees suggests that the ability to mind-read, as required by the eyes task, is an ability independent of general intelligence.

The fact that the subjects with Tourette's syndrome did not differ from the controls on their performance in the eyes task suggests that the difficulties demonstrated by those with autism or AS were not due to having any developmental neuropsychiatric disorder.

How do the findings from the eyes task relate to studies on gaze direction in children with autism?

The difficulties that the autistic and AS subjects had with the eyes task mirrors difficulties that young children with autism have in understanding the importance in the eyes in signalling mental states:

- Toddlers with autism often fail to understand that gaze direction is a signal of attention.
- Young children with autism fail to understand that gaze direction might indicate what a person is focusing their intention on or referring to, or may act as an expression of their goals or desires.
- Pre-school children with autism, unlike children without autism of the same age, also fail to recognise gaze direction as a cue to indicate when someone is thinking.

Are females better at mind-reading than males?

As predicted, within a normal population, this study showed that normal females were better at recognising mental states on the eyes task than normal males. The authors point out that while this study indicates that there is a difference, it does not explain why: 'the female advantage on the mind-reading task could be taken to reflect genetic or socialization factors … This remains to be investigated further'.

Note: Baron-Cohen did investigate these findings further in 1999, when his research indicated that women are better at language tasks, tests of social judgement, measures of empathy, perceptual speed, matching tasks, fluency of ideas and fine motor coordination, mathematical calculation tests and pretend play in childhood.

Commentary: Methods and Issues

Research method, design and data gathering

The study employs the experimental method, using an independent groups design, comparing very high-functioning adults with autism and AS with normal subjects and subjects with Tourette's syndrome. The normal males were also compared with the normal females.

The data-gathering method was self-report, as all subjects verbally reported their responses to the researcher in each task.

Data gathered was quantitative, and statistical analysis was carried out to establish any differences between conditions.

Does the study raise any ethical concerns?

The study was carried out according to the British Psychological Society (1993) ethical guidelines. The subjects were not deceived; they gave their informed consent; they had the right to withdraw; and they were generally not negatively affected by their experience.

Is the study useful?

This study has intrinsic value as a piece of psychological research. It furthers our understanding of the extent of the problem of theory of mind across the autistic continuum. It demonstrates that the problem extends beyond childhood, showing that not only children but also adults have problems mind-reading – interpreting the mental states of others. It also shows that the problems seem to be unrelated to levels of general intelligence.

In terms of real-world applications, one area where the study may be of use is in helping to understand how best to assist people with autistic spectrum disorders to develop more effective social skills. People with autism may be able to learn how to interpret eyes more effectively by taking account of other visual cues, such as mouth or body language, in order to understand someone else's state of mind. The tasks may also be useful as an aid to the diagnosis of people with autistic disorders who are at the mild end of the spectrum.

Validity and reliability of the study

The authors discuss the validity of the eyes task as a measure of theory of mind (see 'Discussion' above). They employ control tasks to increase the validity of the task by accounting for other perceptual or social cognitive skills that could account for difficulties on the eyes task. In addition, they establish concurrent validity of the eyes task with Happé's strange stories test.

Key concept

Concurrent validity

If the outcome of a test of a particular behaviour correlates with scores on an established test of the same behaviour that has previously been agreed as valid, then the second test is described as being concurrently valid with the first.

In this case, the test that was already validated as an 'advanced' test of theory of mind was Happé's strange stories test. By showing that subjects' scores on this test correlated with their scores on the new test of theory of mind, the eyes task, the authors were able to provide evidence for the validity of their new test as a true measure of theory of mind.

There are problems with the ecological validity of the eyes task. In their discussion, the authors raise the point that their 'very advanced test' of theory of mind, the eyes task, is still simpler than having to interpret people's mental states in a real-life social situation. To begin with, the test is static, showing only partial faces, and this is not typically how we see people – usually they are whole and animated!

The authors suggest that a better stimulus might be to show films to the subjects, as this might be more like a real-life situation. However, this would involve other perceptual and social cognitive skills which might confound the study. Therefore, they defend their choice to use the eyes task in this study, calling it a 'pure' test of theory of mind.

Savage-Rumbaugh *et al.* study: Ape language

The last area of cognition that we are going to consider is language. A question over which there has been much psychological debate is whether the ability to learn language is pre-programmed or hard-wired into the human brain, or whether it is dependent on the environment in which the child is raised. In other words, language development has been a core topic in the nature–nurture debate.

The core study on language raises questions not only about what we mean by language, but also about whether language is a species-specific behaviour which sets humans apart from other animals.

Language – the last bastion of human uniqueness?

Are humans the only species with the capacity for language? If you were asked if animals communicate, your initial response would probably be to say, 'Of course they do', and you would be right. But what we need to be aware of here is exactly what we mean by communication. Most other animals communicate with each other by gesture, by smell and even by sound. The bee dances as a way of communicating to the other members of the hive where they can find pollen. If it dances in a sickle shape, this indicates a different direction to dancing in a figure of eight. Monkeys can indicate whether impending danger is in the sky or on the ground according to what kind of shriek they make. Dogs, foxes and cats communicate their territory by scent. Most animals and birds communicate threats to others of the same species by patterns of behaviour that are easily understood. The male stickleback, for example, uses the red underside of his belly as a way of demonstrating territorial aggression to other sticklebacks.

However, most commentators are quick to distinguish between communication and language. If you were asked if animals have language, you might not be so quick to say yes. Although you may have heard people say, 'My dog understands every word I say to him', or even believe this yourself, it seems extremely unlikely that this is true. Evidence shows that although dogs can be trained to respond to verbal instructions such as 'sit' or 'stay', they cannot identify these words if they are hidden in a sentence.

Whether or not an animal can learn language has been investigated by attempting to teach language to other species. If we are biologically programmed to learn language and no other species has this ability, perhaps it is an innate ability which only humans have evolved. However, if other species can be taught to use language, it might support the theory that language is learned. It might also suggest that we are not so different from our close relatives in the animal kingdom, and would question the position taken by some that animals are inferior creatures over whom our dominance is morally justified.

Figure 3.9 Humans seemingly overestimate their pets' ability to understand them

You will no doubt be familiar with Charles Darwin's theory of evolution and know that, in evolutionary terms, our closest relatives are the great apes. There are four great apes: gorillas, orang-utans, chimpanzees and bonobos. (The last of these might not be familiar, but you will learn more about bonobos in the core study at the end of this section.) In order to find out whether another species was capable of learning a language, it made sense to start with our close relatives.

Thanks to films such as *King Kong* and *Congo*, most of us would think twice about poking a gorilla with a big stick. However, *Tarzan* and his sidekick chimp, Cheetah, and those cute tea adverts on the television have given the common chimpanzee an altogether cuddlier image. Trixi and Allan Gardner, who took on the task of raising a female chimpanzee, Washoe, in a human environment, in the first attempt to teach sign language to a chimpanzee, were under no illusions. Specialists in rats and spiders, they were more used to animals that were bred for study and could be kept in a box on the laboratory counter. They were quick to point out that 'affectionate as chimps are, they are still wild animals'. It is important to remember this as we discuss attempts to teach language to animals.

Can an ape learn language?

It seems that the answer to this, like the answer to so many questions is 'It depends'. First, it depends on what you mean by 'language', and second, it depends on what you mean by 'ape'. In order to consider whether animals have the capacity for language, we first need to consider what we mean by language.

What is language? According to Banyard (1996), language is 'a small number of signals (sounds, letters, gestures) that by themselves are meaningless, but can be put together according to certain rules to make an infinite number of messages'. The key factors here are the rules that we use which are well defined. An example of one of the rules we use is the rule of syntax, the order of the words we use in a sentence (e.g. subject – verb – object).

He hat the put on.

The lorry green out of the garage rolled.

Although you may think you know very little about English grammar, you will know that the sentences above are obviously wrong.

As we know, language is important to humans because it is necessary to help us socialise with others, and we are creatures who need to be social. Deaf people use sign language, which has the same grammatical structure as spoken language and can transmit the same information. For humans, language is vital for the transmission of ideas, to help us understand the world and to organise our thoughts; and language acts as a useful tool for learning about our personalities from how other people react to us. Language also enables us to communicate our intentions and to exert control over our environment.

A number of researchers have described lists of features which seem to be the essence of language. Hockett (1959) listed 13 design features, while Aitchison (1983) proposed that there were only ten which she considered essential to make the difference between communication and language:

- Use of the vocal/auditory channel.

- Arbitrariness (use of neutral symbols (words) to denote objects, etc.).

- **Semanticity (use of symbols to mean or refer to objects/actions)**.

- Cultural transmission (handing down the language from generation to generation).

- Spontaneous usage (freely initiating speech, etc.).

- Turn-taking (conversation is a two-way process).

- Duality (organisation into basic sounds and combinations or sequences of these).

- **Displacement (reference to things not present in time or space)**.

- **Structure dependence (the patterned nature of language and use of 'structured chunks', e.g. word order)**.

- **Creativity (what Brown (1973) calls productivity; the ability to produce and understand an infinite number of novel utterances, including combining words to increase meaning)**.

It is obvious that many of these do not seem to be present in the communications of animals. In fact, the four features in bold are those which Aitchison considered to be unique to humans. This is a useful definition of language for us to use

here, although we should consider whether this description of language is somewhat ethnocentric. It is a bit like the goalkeeper in a game of football selecting a place to put the goalposts after the match has finished. One of the problems with deciding whether an animal has language or not is that definitions of language change. In other words, the goalposts are moved, and this has frustrated some researchers who work in the field of primate language. Still, we have to accept that language needs to be defined, and the above outline will serve our purposes for the time being.

What is an ape?

Having decided on what we mean by language, we now have to consider what we mean by 'ape'. Since the 1930s, attempts have been made to raise common chimpanzees (and, more recently, gorillas) to communicate linguistically. As the great apes are supposedly our closest relatives on the evolutionary scale, you can see why they were seen as the most likely candidates in attempts to teach an animal language. The problem was that early attempts were unsuccessful, which is not surprising, as the vocal equipment of apes is not adequate to deal with the range of sounds used in human language. Although they make lots of different sounds, these are more like shrieks and are very unrefined. They are usually made when the chimps are either excited or frightened, and seem to relate to the situation they are in. The rest of the time they are silent, so we could interpret the sounds they do make as being a very primitive, situation-specific noise rather than anything else. In fact, it is quite hard to imagine why the researchers believed that chimps could speak in the first place.

Teaching chimpanzees sign language and symbols

Kellogg and Kellogg (1933) were the first to attempt this and raised a female chimpanzee with their own child, but she never managed to utter a word! Hayes and Hayes (1951) tried with another female chimpanzee, Viki, who after six years only succeeded in saying the words 'up', 'cup', 'mama' and 'papa', and these words were somewhat unclear. It seemed that the chimpanzee lacked the vocal equipment to enable it to make human vocalisations, even if it were so inclined.

Despite failing to teach Viki to speak, the Hayes' study did spark an idea for a method of teaching language to a chimpanzee that might be more likely to succeed. When she 'spoke' her words, Viki always accompanied the word with the same gesture, such as covering her nose as she said the word.

A further study by Allan and Trixi Gardner noted that chimps beg and make similar gestures spontaneously, and therefore they might be able to learn a language if it were based on gesture rather than vocalisation. In other words, could a chimpanzee be taught sign language, the language used by deaf humans? The language the Gardners selected was American Sign Language (ASL). In order to use this, the Gardners, and those research assistants who would be Washoe the chimp's human companions, had to learn to sign. This was the first in a series of studies that attempted to teach apes ASL.

Capitalising on chimpanzees' natural propensity to copy, imitation of gestures and signs was encouraged. The Hayes had trained Viki to produce her 'words' with the prompt 'Do this'; and a similar game was developed in order to encourage

Washoe to imitate signs. She would happily imitate actions, but not always when asked or in the appropriate situation. The trainers would tickle her as a reward (or reinforcement) for that behaviour. However, she was not always cooperative, and even when she was she would sometimes become angry, sometimes aggressive, and would not take part any more. The Gardners remind us that this is one of the drawbacks of working with a wild animal: 'Pressed too hard, Washoe can become completely diverted from her original object; she may ask for something entirely different, run away, go into a tantrum, or even bite her tutor'.

With Washoe, as in the subsequent studies which attempted to train apes to produce language, instrumental conditioning was used. The Gardners used operant conditioning techniques. If she made a sign that was not totally accurate, the trainers would aim to get her to produce a better sign by shaping her fingers. This 'shaping' of the sign was progressive, and eventually she could be expected to produce a clear sign before it was accepted, acknowledged or rewarded. In this respect, Washoe's language learning was not like the acquisition of children's language. Children do not need to be instrumentally conditioned to acquire language; both vocabulary and syntax are acquired spontaneously in children, with no need for training.

Nonetheless, at the end of the study, the Gardners were convinced that Washoe had acquired signs and was using signs to stand for objects, as well as combining signs to create novel utterances, such as 'listen dog' or 'go sweet'. They suggested that work with other species should be carried out extensively before 'theories of language that depend upon the identification of aspects that are exclusively human' are accepted. They also believed that with refinements to their training process, work with other chimpanzees would exceed what they had achieved with Washoe in this first attempt at teaching sign language to a chimpanzee.

In 1972, three years after the Gardners published their results on Project Washoe, Duane Rumbaugh was working with another chimpanzee, Lana, at the Yerkes Regional Primate Research Centre in Atlanta, Georgia (USA). Rumbaugh did not use ASL, but instead employed a system of symbols, or lexigrams, to represent words. These symbols were arbitrary, that is, they did not look like the objects they stood for. Unlike Washoe, Lana lived in a laboratory and interacted with a machine. She could ask the machine for food, ask the machine to open a blind, play music, and so on. To do this, she had to press a sequence of signs, in the right order.

Teaching chimpanzees grammar

In 1973, another researcher, Herbert Terrace, began his project with a chimpanzee called Nim Chimpsky (after the famous linguist Noam Chomsky, who was of the opinion that chimpanzees could not be taught language). Terrace had ambitious aims and set his sights high, aiming to achieve what other researchers had only hinted was possible, by reporting the way chimpanzees combined words or symbols, to demonstrate that Nim knew grammar. Sue Savage-Rumbaugh, the lead researcher in our core study (below), pointed out in another study that 'the demonstration of syntax' was the 'holy grail of linguists, and, by default, ape-language researchers' (Savage-Rumbaugh and Lewin 1994: 53).

Working with 60 sign language teachers over four years, Nim learned much the same as the other chimps trained in ASL, and eventually had a vocabulary of 125 signs. He made many double word combinations, as other chimps had done (Washoe began spontaneously combining signs once she had learned eight to ten signs).

Terrace and his team were initially convinced that Nim was displaying grammar, and after Nim went back to the Institute of Primate Studies in Oklahoma, Terrace eagerly reviewed his extensive video footage of Nim's interactions. The more he watched, the more his initial belief in Nim's 'grammar' changed to doubt. He noted that by the age of four, three-quarters of Nim's signing was in imitation of his teachers, and much of it focused on requests for food or play activities. The language-like utterances of apes were a form of the clever Hans effect (see below), Terrace concluded. Savage-Rumbaugh points out that Terrace's conclusion was that 'Nim fooled me'. The research paper he and his team presented in 1979 concluded that the 'utterances' of apes were best described as imitations of their teachers, or were unconsciously cued by their researchers, and were not examples of sentences using grammar.

Criticism of ape language studies

The criticism of ape language studies was further compounded in May 1980, when a conference was held by a researcher called Seboek, whose negative opinion was clear six months before the conference, as Savage-Rumbaugh and Lewin (1994: 50) later reported: 'Ape-language is prey to the clever Hans effect, or worse, opined Seboek. The results of research are to be explained as a result of "unconscious bias, self-deception, magic and circus performance"'.

At the beginning of the twentieth century, an amazing demonstration of animal intelligence was being taken from town to town by his owner Willhelm Von Osten. A horse, called clever Hans, appeared to be able to do arithmetic. A maths problem would be written on a blackboard and clever Hans would stomp out the answer using his hoof. He was so rarely wrong that it was assumed that Hans was a very clever Hans indeed.

However, all is not always as it seems. Hans *was* a clever horse, but not for his ability to do mathematical functions. He could read his owner very well, and Hans was able to sense the right answer, as his owner gave involuntary and unconscious cues when Hans had reached it and therefore should stop. This was pointed out to Von Osten, and proved by showing that Hans could not get any answers right if Von Osten was not present, or if Von Osten did not know the answer himself. Von Osten was very disappointed when this was revealed to him, as he had not intentionally defrauded his audiences and believed himself that Hans was getting the answers right on his own.

The clever Hans effect, then, means that the ape language researchers were misinterpreting the behaviour of the chimps as 'language' because they did not realise, like Von Osten, that they were unconsciously cuing the responses from the chimps, or were priming the chimps, whose responses were mere imitation of the signs made to them by their human companions. Examination of footage of both Washoe and Nim, for example, confirmed that imitation accounted for a large part of the chimps' signs.

This is an example of unconscious experimenter bias.

Figure 3.10 Clever Hans

Seboek's conference was given the title 'The Clever Hans Phenomenon: Communication with Horses, Whales, Apes and People'. Three ape language researchers attended: Duane Rumbaugh, who had worked on the Lana Project; Sue Savage-Rumbaugh, who between 1975 and 1980 worked with two chimpanzees, Sherman and Austin; and Herbert Terrace. The first two attempted to support their findings with what they believed were scientific data which countered the arguments that cueing and priming by researchers accounted for ape language, but this was not what the conference concluded.

Herbert Terrace, on the other hand, reiterated his negative views on ape language after working with Nim. Seboek concurred with his view, ending the conference saying, 'In my opinion, the alleged language experiments with apes can be divided into three groups; one: outright fraud, two: self-deception, and three: those conducted by Terrace'. As a result of Terrace's own research paper in 1979 and this conference in 1980, ape language research was viewed with scepticism by academics. It became difficult to publish research in the field.

In between the Terrace paper and the clever Hans conference, Sue Savage-Rumbaugh and her fellow researchers had published their work on Sherman and Austin, and believed they had scientific evidence to suggest that apes are capable of some aspects of language. Sue Savage-Rumbaugh had worked with Washoe after she left the Gardners, and had married Duane Rumbaugh, the researcher responsible for the Lana project. She had wide experience with apes who had been claimed to have language, but had doubts about how much imitation, cueing and wishful thinking might account for claims that apes could understand language, especially spoken language. She had witnessed first-hand Washoe's limited ability to respond to spoken instructions, and in her work with Lana had also found that the chimp could not respond accurately to spoken requests.

Although she went to work with Rumbaugh in 1974, two years into the Lana project, Sue Savage-Rumbaugh chose to focus first on studying and comparing the behaviour of the great apes at the research centre. She was gradually drawn into the Lana project, however, and this was the start of her career as an ape language researcher.

In 1975, she began her work with two chimpanzees, Sherman and Austin. Sceptical about the language abilities which had been claimed for other chimps, and aware of the criticism that the researchers might just be cuing the animal's responses, the emphasis with Sherman and Austin was on getting them to communicate with each other. It was also an aim of the study to demonstrate that their 'language' could go beyond using symbols associatively to trigger outcomes such as getting food, and to show that chimpanzees could use symbols referentially, indicating an understanding that a particular symbol *means* a particular thing. This put the emphasis on trying to demonstrate not what symbols the chimps could use, but what their use revealed about what they *understood* by the symbol.

Language comprehension develops before language production in children, and comprehension outstrips production throughout our lives. (For example, you are capable of *reading* this book — language comprehension — but would you be capable of *writing* it — language production?) Savage-Rumbaugh theorised that it is not only production which can signal that an ape has language. Surely if the ape understands language, he could be said to have language? This represented a turnaround in studies of ape language, no longer focusing on language production and getting apes to demonstrate as many signs as possible, but turning the focus to language comprehension and trying to work out whether the ape could understand that symbols (or signs or words) stand for something.

Table 3.7

Examples of attempts to teach common chimpanzees language (language production studies)

Chimpanzee	Study	Method and results
Viki Figure 3.11	Hayes and Hayes (1951)	Tried to reinforce Viki for spoken language. After six years this was shown to be unsuccessful as she was able to 'say' only four words.
Washoe Figure 3.12	Gardner and Gardner (1969)	Used ASL to try to encourage Washoe to use signs. The signs were taught in a naturalistic environment, based at the Gardners' home in Nevada, by imitation, instrumental conditioning and shaping. Washoe acquired signs and appeared to use them semantically.
Lana Figure 3.13	Rumbaugh (1977)	Lana was taught to use a symbolic system to produce language. Here, a lexigram, or symbol, was used to represent words. Lana communicated by pushing the symbols on a machine, and had to press the right symbols in the right order for her requests to be granted.
Nim Figure 3.14	Terrace (1979)	Terrace focused his study on trying to get Nim to demonstrate grammar. He was initially optimistic and thought that Nim's chaining of signs indicated word order and grammar. On reflection, he noticed that the videotapes of the chimp suggested that the majority of the utterances were simply imitations and did not represent a chimpanzee using sentences.
Sherman and Austin Figure 3.15	Savage-Rumbaugh (1979)	Using the lexigram system, the focus of this study was to see if the chimpanzees understood that words mean something (that they stand for something). The emphasis was on communication between the chimps to avoid the problem of researchers priming or cueing the chimps.

Taking all things into account, in 1980 the general belief among academics – even Herbert Terrace, who had invested a great deal of time and work trying to teach language to a chimpanzee – was that apes were not capable of acquiring language, and that anyone who said they were, was either deluding themselves, succumbing to the clever Hans effect, or, worse still, deliberately defrauding the public.

Based on her work with Sherman and Austin, Sue Savage-Rumbaugh did not agree. Sherman and Austin showed that chimps could be trained to use symbols as referents, but could not acquire this ability spontaneously, and, like other studies, showed that their language production was highly contingent on being fed as a result. Although they did not seem to understand spoken language, this study suggested to Savage-Rumbaugh that if the focus was on comprehension rather than production of language, then apes did have the capacity to demonstrate some aspects of language. An ape she was to meet in 1980, and with whom she is still working today, was to convince her that not only was she right about this, but that she had underestimated what apes might be capable of in terms of language comprehension.

So can an ape learn language? We said earlier that first it depends on what we mean by language. We have seen that studies which focused on language production and the use of grammar by chimpanzees were unsuccessful, or the claimed successes were subject to the criticism that researchers were cuing or priming the chimps' responses. Savage-Rumbaugh changed the focus to language comprehension, and began, with Sherman and Austin, to tease out the aspects of chimps' understanding that are language-like. So if by language we mean 'language comprehension', then it may be that our answer will be yes, apes can learn language.

Figure 3.16 Kanzi with Sue Savage-Rumbaugh

Next we said that whether an ape can learn language depends on what we mean by ape. Kanzi is the main subject in our core study (below). Kanzi is a male bonobo, not a common chimpanzee, whom Sue Savage-Rumbaugh saw born in captivity and has worked with since he was six months old.

The Study

S. Savage-Rumbaugh, K. McDonald, R.A. Sevcik, W.D. Hopkins and E. Rubert (1986) 'Spontaneous symbol acquisition and communicative use by pygmy chimpanzees (*Pan paniscus*)', *Journal of Experimental Psychology*, 115(3): 211–35

Background

Work with common chimpanzees showed that they could not understand spoken English. Critics argued that much of what was claimed to be 'language' used in language production studies in common chimpanzees could be attributed to the animals responding to the cues and prompts given by their human companions, and therefore was not really language at all.

The focus of this study, however, was language comprehension, rather than language production. The authors considered that if an ape:

- began to understand spoken English without being trained to do so;
- could do more than just respond on cue;

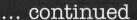
... continued

then this would suggest that the ape would possess language abilities similar to those of humans, and 'even if the ape were unable to speak, an ability to comprehend language would be the cognitive equivalent of having acquired language' (p.214).

Was Kanzi, a bonobo, such an ape?

Key concept

Bonobo

Bonobos were the last of the great apes to be identified. Having been discovered in the Congo (called Zaire from 1971 to 1997) in 1922, they were first called 'pygmy chimpanzees', as they are very like common chimpanzees (*Pan trogladytes*), but smaller. However, they were identified as a separate species in 1922 and called bonobos (*Pan paniscus*).

It is believed that humans and chimpanzees had a common ancestor. Five million years ago, the lineage split into two, with one line leading to man (*Homo sapiens*), and the other leading to both bonobos and chimpanzees.

Bonobos' natural environment is in a remote region of Africa. In the 1970s, an American researcher, Randall Sussman, led a team observing them in the wild:

> 'to reach the region from the USA [you] must first fly to Brussels for a connection to Kinshasa, Zaire's capital city. From there to the Lamako forest requires an eight-day riverboat ride, a two-day trip by Land Rover, and a day's hike through swamp to the research station's base camp … The remoteness of the region explains the world's long ignorance of the bonobo, and until recently protected the animals from danger by human exploitation.' (Savage-Rumbaugh and Lewin 1994: 114)

In this study, the researchers point out that there are marked differences between the bonobo and the chimpanzee. As early as 1925, a researcher called Robert Yerkes had compared a bonobo (Chim) with a common chimpanzee (Panzee), although at the time he believed they were both chimpanzees, as bonobos had not yet been classified separately. Chim seemed an extraordinary animal, much brighter than Panzee and more humanlike in behaviour.

Further research has confirmed the following in comparison with common chimpanzees:

- Bonobos make more frequent eye contact, gestures and vocalisations.
- Bonobos' vocalisations are more frequent and elaborate.
- Bonobos' male–female ties are very close, whereas in chimpanzees they are weak.
- Male bonobos take part in infant care, while male chimpanzees do not.
- In the wild there is a balance of males and females in bonobo groups, whereas there are more females than males in groups of chimpanzees.
- Food sharing is common between adult bonobos, whereas food sharing is limited to mother and offspring in common chimpanzees.

The differences in gestures, eye contact and vocalisations suggested to the authors that bonobos might be better prepared to learn language than other apes. Studies of bonobos showed that they were brighter than chimpanzees, and this again suggested they might be better subjects than chimpanzees for an animal language study.

The authors also explain why no bonobos had been used in ape language studies before: 'this is primarily attributable to the difficulty in obtaining these animals. They are rare, both in captivity and in the wild, and it is presently illegal to export them from their severely threatened native habitat.' (p.214)

... continued

Aims

The aim of this study was to report on the language acquisition of Kanzi, a bonobo, and his younger sister, Mulika. The report covers a 17-month period, beginning when Kanzi was two years and six months old.

The language acquisition in the bonobos was compared, where appropriate, with that of two common chimpanzees, Sherman and Austin, studied earlier (1975–80).

Method

A case study was carried out, focusing primarily on one bonobo, Kanzi, but also including early data of his younger sister, Mulika's, language acquisition. The data were gathered by observation.

It is important to point out, as the authors did, that the findings of the study were 'serendipitous', a lucky accident. They tell us that the study is 'not an experiment, rather a description of events that lead us to the conclusion that Kanzi … was acquiring symbols spontaneously at two and a half years of age … followed by a developmental account of this phenomenon across the subsequent 17 months'. (p.214)

A longitudinal design was used in this study, reporting over a 17-month period of Kanzi's language acquisition. (Comparisons with the common chimpanzees reflected data gathered over a ten-year span.)

Key concept

Longitudinal versus snapshot designs

In a **snapshot** design, different groups of people are tested at the same point in time and their performances are compared. Examples from the core studies include the subway Samaritan study by Piliavin *et al.* (Chapter 2), and Samuel and Bryant's study on conservation (Chapter 4).

The advantages of snapshot studies over longitudinal studies are that they are relatively quick and inexpensive to carry out, can easily be replicated to test the reliability of findings, and are relatively easy to modify. This final point means that if design faults become apparent, the study can be repeated with modifications to eliminate them. It also means that variations of the study can be carried out easily to investigate fully the variables which may affect behaviour.

In a **longitudinal** study, one subject or one group of individuals is studied over a long period of time, taking regular samples of behaviour. This design means we can track development and monitor changes over time. In the Savage-Rumbaugh *et al.* study, for example, it allows us to see the development of Kanzi's language. The longitudinal approach also enabled the researchers to make comparisons between Kanzi and common chimpanzees.

Subjects

Four great apes are reported on in this study: Kanzi, Mulika, Sherman and Austin.

The main focus of this study is a bonobo, Kanzi. He was born in captivity at the Yerkes Regional Primate Centre in Atlanta, Georgia (USA) on 28 October 1980. Kanzi was assigned to the Language Research Centre at six months of age, accompanying his mother, Matata, a wild-caught female bonobo, who was the intended subject for the language study. Matata was not Kanzi's biological mother, but had kidnapped him from his mother, Lorel, when he was just a few hours old.

On 22 December 1983, Matata gave birth to Mulika, the second bonobo subject in this study.

Both Kanzi and Mulika had experienced separations from Matata as infants (for Kanzi, this was when Matata was removed for breeding purposes, and for Mulika, there was a four-month separation due

... continued

to an eye infection). Both bonobos built up a strong bond with their human carers, and although they spent time with their mother each day during this study, both bonobos chose to spend most of their time with people.

The language acquisition of the two bonobos was compared with the language acquisition of two common chimpanzees, Sherman and Austin, previously studied at the Language Research Centre by Sue Savage-Rumbaugh.

Procedure

Kanzi was different from other apes in ape language studies because he was the first to acquire symbols spontaneously, without training. Kanzi acquired symbols while his mother was being trained, and he was never trained or directly reinforced to acquire symbols. He seemed to have learned to use lexigrams spontaneously.

In a longitudinal study where a great deal of data is gathered, the procedure and reporting of data can be very thorough and complicated, and this study is no exception! The procedure is broken down into sections, which we will consider in turn, as follows:

1. Description of the environment where the apes were living

2. The communication system used with the apes

3. The exposure of Kanzi and Mulika to lexigrams – how the bonobos learned

4. Data recording and criteria for language acquisition in the apes

5. Formal testing carried out with the apes

1. Description of the environment where the apes were living

The apes all lived at the Language Research Centre. There were two sides to this centre: 'chimpside', where the ape language studies were carried out, and 'childside', where work was done with children and teenagers with special educational needs to help them develop language.

In the chimpside, the apes could either be outdoors or indoors, depending on the weather.

The naturalistic outdoor environment had the following characteristics:

* The centre was set in a 55-acre forest.

* Every day, food was put at 17 sites in the woods, with the same foods always in the same place. In warmer weather, the chimps would not be fed indoors, so they would have to go out, with their human companions, and gather food in the woods, therefore creating the most natural behaviours possible. Most of their day was taken up doing this.

* Having foods placed in the same locations each day gave an opportunity for teaching Kanzi, and once he had acquired a few symbols he was shown photos of some of the foods, from which he selected what he wanted to eat and was then taken there. He quickly learned the location of all 17 foods and could guide others to each location, often holding the photo all the way. Later, when he had acquired more symbols, he used lexigrams to indicate his food choices. Mulika learned to do this in the same way as Kanzi as she got older.

* Once at the location selected by Kanzi, if the food selected was not eaten, he would be asked if he wanted to put it in the backpack. If he indicated yes (e.g. by pushing the food towards the backpack), the food would be taken. If he did not indicate in this way, the food would be left at the location. Having food from different locations in the backpack gave the opportunity for further communication. If Kanzi indicated 'juice', he would be asked if he wanted the juice in the backpack or if he wanted to go to the location for juice. If he wanted the backpack juice he would touch the backpack; if he wanted to go to the location he would gesture in that direction. (When Kanzi was three years old, a blind test was run with an experimenter who had never been in the woods with Kanzi. A description of this is included in the Results section.)

... continued

The indoor environment had the following characteristics:

- During the day, Kanzi and Mulika were asked to help with activities such as laundry and food preparation. They always wanted to play games (e.g. hide, chase, tickle, playbite). They often helped spontaneously in simple jobs like wiping up spills, washing up, spraying the hose, and so on.

- They were allowed to travel from place to place at the centre (with their human companions), for example to visit their mother, Matata, or to go to the childside.

- They played with toys in their free time (e.g. clay, bubbles, dolls). Kanzi was very fond of balls and often carried more than one at a time. They watched videos of people and animals they knew at the centre. At night, Kanzi asked to watch TV and was shown films with lexigram overlays that were interesting to chimps.

Key concept

Lexigrams

Figure 3.17

Lexigrams are pictures or symbols that are used to stand for words. They are arbitrary, that is, they do not look like the word or object they are being used to describe.

2. The communication system used with the apes

The following table outlines the communication systems used with the apes in this study.

Table 3.8

Visual symbol system	Based on the system developed by Duane Rumbaugh with a common chimpanzee (Lana).
	It consisted of a keyboard of symbols, which lit up when they were pressed. A lit symbol was the equivalent of uttering a word.
	Each symbol, or lexigram, was arbitrary, that is, it did not look like the object or word it stood for.
No. of symbols	Initially eight lexigrams
	At the end of this study, 256 lexigrams
Sound	Kanzi's keyboards were connected to an electronic voice synthesiser, so that words were spoken when the symbols were pressed. This was added after it was discovered that Kanzi understood spoken English.

... continued

Mobility indoors	Lana used only a stationary keyboard, in one place in the room.
	Sherman and Austin used three keyboards connected to the computer by extension cords, allowing the chimpanzees to move the keyboards from room to room with them.
	Kanzi used similar keyboards to Sherman and Austin.
Mobility outdoors	Kanzi used a number of battery-powered keyboards, attached to a portable computer and portable voice synthesiser (limited battery life).
	Kanzi also used 'pointing boards', consisting of laminated cards showing photos of all the lexigrams. Kanzi and Mulika would communicate by pointing to the photo of the lexigram they wanted to use.
	Note: The pointing boards had not worked with Sherman, Austin and Lana, as the common chimpanzees tended to make sweeping gestures towards the card and it was not clear which lexigram they were trying to indicate.
Other means of communication	When communicating through lexigrams, the human researchers also used spoken English and gestures, including approximately 100 ASL (sign language) gestures. The aim was to communicate with the chimpanzees in whatever way worked, and any form of response from the chimpanzees was accepted.

3. The exposure of Kanzi and Mulika to lexigrams – how the bonobos learned

The humans working with the bonobos used lexigrams and spoken English to communicate a wide variety of things. Kanzi and Mulika were taught in a similar environment to that in which Sherman and Austin had been taught, and the same humans who had taught Sherman, Austin and Lana were teachers to Kanzi and Mulika. However, there were important differences in the way Kanzi and Mulika learned language:

- Sherman and Austin were trained to use lexigrams and did not acquire them in an observational setting.
- There was no speech synthesiser on Sherman and Austin's keyboard, as they did not understand spoken language.
- Sherman and Austin did not use a keyboard outside the laboratory, as it was not clear what they were pointing to on the pointing card. It appeared that the common chimpanzees could only use the lexigrams where they pressed the keyboard to light them up.

Similarities between the environment for Sherman and Austin and the environment for Kanzi and Mulika included:

- attachment to caretakers
- the opportunity to observe and interact with people
- exposure to human language
- exposure to gestures, lexigrams and photographs
- formal testing
- opportunities to play, watch TV, and so on.

... continued

Table 3.9

How the common chimpanzees and bonobos learned language

Name:	Kanzi	Mulika	Sherman	Austin
Same trainers	X	X	X	X
Trained to use lexigrams (did not acquire them in observational setting)			X	X
Learned by observation	X	X		
Speech synthesiser	X	X		
Pointing card	X	X		
Lexigrams with lit-up symbols	X	X	X	X
Attachment to caretakers	X	X	X	X
Opportunities to observe and interact with people	X	X	X	X
Exposure to human language	X	X	X	X
Exposure to gestures, lexigrams and photographs	X	X	X	X
Formal testing	X	X	X	X
Opportunities to play (e.g. watch TV)	X	X	X	X

Kanzi and Mulika did not need to be trained to use symbols; they learned by observation. They used symbols spontaneously, understood spoken language, did not mix up symbols once learned (e.g. they did not use the symbol for apple when they meant orange), and could identify symbols regardless of location.

So instead of a training programme, as had been used with Sherman and Austin, the people around Kanzi and Mulika modelled language use, by using the lexigrams and commenting vocally on their daily activities. Sometimes Kanzi and Mulika would observe the usage of the keyboard, and sometimes they would ignore it.

4. Data recording and criteria for language acquisition in the apes

From the age of two years and six months, Kanzi's utterances were *all* recorded and coded for 17 months. Those utterances on the computerised keyboard were automatically recorded. Outdoors, codings and recordings were done by hand and were entered into the computer at the end of the day.

In this study, every one of Kanzi's utterances between the ages of 30 and 47 months, and Mulika's between 11 and 21 months, were included. Their utterances were coded as follows:

- either correct or incorrect
- either spontaneous (initiated by Kanzi and Mulika, with no prior prompt or query or behaviour by their human companions), or imitated (utterances that included any part of a companion's prior keyboard utterance), or structured (those initiated by questions, requests or object-showing by human companions, to see if Kanzi and Mulika could give a right answer).

Data recording was done on the spot in real time. There can be problems with the accuracy of such recordings, so a test of reliability was carried out to establish the accuracy of the observations. (This is described in the Commentary at the end of the study.)

In order to decide whether Kanzi or Mulika had acquired a symbol and added it to their vocabulary, it was important to set up criteria, or rules, for deciding if a symbol had been learned. Earlier studies,

... continued

such as the Gardners' work with Washoe, had set criteria that insisted on the use of signs on consecutive days, and in the correct context. However, the authors of this study considered these criteria to be faulty, as, with prompting and cues, chimps could give a correct sign in the right context without really understanding it. Also, looking for the sign every day often meant setting up a context for it to be used, and again, this might lead to a cued rather than a real use of the sign/symbol.

The criteria established for Kanzi and Mulika was called a **behavioural concordance measure**. Only spontaneous utterances could be scored, and the symbol would be considered as being used properly only if the behaviour of the ape immediately after the symbol was used was consistent (in concordance with) the symbol. For example, 'if Kanzi requested a trip to the treehouse he would be told "Yes, we can go to the treehouse". However, only if he then led the experimenter to this location could a correct behavioural concordance be scored for the word treehouse'. (p.216)

In other words, what Kanzi said had to match up with what Kanzi did. If he asked for a banana and was offered an orange, an apple and a banana, the utterance 'banana' could only be accepted if he selected a banana from the offered selection of fruits; or if he was told he could go and get a banana from a particular location, he would have to lead the researcher to the right place in order for 'banana' to be counted as an utterance. Another way for concordance to be established would be if Kanzi asked for a banana from the backpack and then selected a banana from it (although this was not counted if there were only bananas in the backpack!).

The productive vocabulary of Kanzi and Mulika was scored if they used the utterance correctly on nine out of ten occasions (although these did not need to be on consecutive days, as the bonobos did not use the same symbols every day).

5. Formal testing carried out with the apes

The types of tests used and the results from the tests are described in the Results section, below.

Results

Summarising qualitative and quantitative data from a longitudinal study of this kind can be difficult, given the sheer amount of data collected to be reported. In the research paper, the results section makes up the bulk of the report, and the results are presented under the following headings, which we will follow here:

1. Untutored gestures

2. First appearance of lexigram use for communication purposes

3. Kanzi's progress during the 17 months after his initial separation from Matata

4. Receptive language comprehension

5. Combinations

6. Imitation versus spontaneous utterances

7. Formal tests of productive and receptive language capacity

8. The blind test in the forest

1. Untutored gestures

Aged six to 16 months, both Kanzi and Mulika used gestures spontaneously to get what they wanted. Matata had done this too, but not so much as her offspring did. Sherman and Austin had also done this, but in the common chimpanzees it developed later, and gestures were not as specific as the bonobos' gestures. For example, if Kanzi wanted a nut cracked he would give the nut to a human companion and bang his hand to signal what he wanted. If the human did not seem to understand, he would further gesture by getting a small rock and hitting the nut with it, to show clearly what he wanted to happen.

... continued

2. First appearance of lexigram use for communication purposes

Immediately after Kanzi's mother, Matata, left for breeding purposes, Kanzi started to be more interested in the lexigram keyboard. He had already pressed the lexigram keyboard before she left, and the researchers assumed he was just pressing any key and running to the fridge, associating the keyboard with food. However, to the surprise of the researchers, it became clear that he had begun searching for specific lexigrams. It was still assumed that this was not an indication of his using the lexigrams to request things, but it was treated as if it were, much as human children's accidental utterances are often interpreted as intentional and responded to.

Unexpectedly, and again, much to the surprise of his human companions, it seemed that Kanzi had learned that particular lexigrams stood for particular things. For example, if he pressed 'apple' and was offered, say, an orange, a banana and an apple, he would take the apple and ignore the others. The same was true if he pressed 'banana'. This suggested that he was using the lexigrams referentially, to stand for the items requested. His referential use of the symbols was demonstrated even more clearly when he was shown three fruits, gave the right lexigrams for them and was not interested in eating any of them.

Similar examples of this use of the symbols was reported in the daily notes made soon after Matata left: 'After eating an apple and drinking some juice, both of which he had requested on the keyboard, Kanzi again touched 'juice', then picked up the juice, poured it out and began stomping the apple and juice together while displaying a play face.' (p.219)

Mulika, who had not observed Matata being trained, but had observed Kanzi and humans using the keyboard, began using symbols at 12 months, earlier than Kanzi. Not observed in Kanzi, Mulika went through a stage of using one lexigram, 'milk', as a general request, then pointing to the object she wanted. The use of the lexigram as a request signal is important here, as she could get what she wanted just by pointing, as she had been doing since she was very young.

She generalised 'milk' in this way for two months, then added a second lexigram, 'surprise', which was just what she got: a food she had never had before. She acquired about a dozen more symbols over the next few months, and 'milk' came to refer only to milk itself.

To suggest how the use of symbols might move from associative use to referential use, the authors describe how Kanzi learned the symbol 'strawberries'.

In children and in apes, new words often only reappear in the context in which they were first encountered, only later being generalised and becoming referential in their use. Kanzi was being taken on the mushroom trail when the word 'strawberries' was first introduced, and the group went off to find some. For a while, Kanzi only used 'strawberries' spontaneously while on the mushroom trail. He could only respond accurately to tests of the strawberry symbol once he began to use the symbol beyond the original context. How might this happen? The authors suggest the following:

'As a symbol's usage becomes expanded to an increasing number of contexts it probably becomes more efficient to abstract some commonalities from all these different situations. It is these commonalities that then become the meaning of this symbol. For example, if Kanzi learns to touch the symbol for strawberries when he wants to travel to the place where they can be found, when he is asking for one to eat, and when shown a photograph of strawberries, he will probably extract the one common referent (red sweet berries) from all those circumstances, and assign to that referent the symbol "strawberries".' (p.220)

3. Kanzi's progress during the 17 months after his initial separation from Matata

Kanzi made rapid progress in his acquisition of symbols in this time. Using the behavioural concordance measure, his single-word utterances aged 30–46 months comprised 44 lexigrams.

... continued

Table 3.10

Cumulative list of Kanzi's symbol acquisition

Age acquired (months)	Symbols
30	Orange, Peanut, Banana, Apple, Bedroom[a], Chase, Austin
31	Sweet potato, Raisin, Ball, Cherry[b], Peaches, Coke, Site
32	Melon, Jelly, Tomato, Orange drink
33	Trailer, Milk
34	Key, Tickle[c]
35	Coffee, Juice[d], Bread
37	Groom
40	Egg
41	Hamburger, Water, M&M, Surprise
42	Clover, Matata, TV, Orange juice
43	Mulika, Carrot
44	Grab, Treehouse, Blanket, Blackberry[e]
45	Mushroom trail
46	Refrigerator, Hot dog

Note: Words with superscripts dropped below criterion for the month(s) indicated. a: 33–46; b: 32–34; c: 44–45; d: 43, 45–46; e: 45.

Source: adapted from Savage-Rumbaugh *et al.* 1986: 221

Mulika began to acquire symbols earlier, but more slowly than Kanzi had. It may be that Kanzi learned more than was realised in the time when he was able to observe his mother being trained to use lexigrams, although when Kanzi was first learning he had a keyboard with eight lexigrams. Mulika always had a harder task, learning from Kanzi's keyboard with 256 lexigrams.

Mulika's language use met the behavioural concordance requirements on 85 out of 86 occasions within the latter two-thirds of the period covered by this study. Using the criterion of nine out of ten correct consecutive uses (see below), her vocabulary was 37 words:

milk, surprise, juice, bubbles, t-room, jelly, toothpaste, key, go, coke, blackberry, grape, staff office, jello, water, strawberry, cherry, sour cream, ice, banana, blueberry, orange drink, melon, coffee, Kool-Aid, M&M, orange juice, orange, peanut, food, can opener, apple, peaches, bite, Matata, balloon and lemonade. (p.221)

4. Receptive language comprehension

Children understand language before they produce it, and so did Kanzi. To examine his receptive language, a criterion was established to test what he understood. He had to give nine out of ten correct responses when a symbol was used by a person. For example, Kanzi might be asked to fetch his ball (with the human being careful not to glance at the ball or indicate it in any way).

Kanzi's receptive symbol use exceeded his productive use. Mulika's formal test scores (described below) also showed that what she understood outstripped her productive language use (as measured by the behavioural concordance criterion).

5. Combinations

Kanzi started to use multiple symbols, or combinations, early – within one month of his first spontaneous symbol usage on the keyboard. He used them much less frequently than single-word utterances, accounting for about 6 per cent of his utterances.

Kanzi's use of combinations in the 17 months covered by this study can be broken down as follows:

- Kanzi made 2,805 combined symbol utterances.

- Of the 2,805 combined symbol utterances, 2,540 were non-imitated, and of these non-imitated utterances, 764 were unique, used only once.

- Partially imitated or prompted combinations accounted for 265 of the 2,805 total, with all but ten of these judged to be in the appropriate context.

... continued

The authors compared Kanzi's combinations with those of Nim, the common chimpanzee studied by Herbert Terrace. This showed that Kanzi's combinations tended to add symbols to provide more information (e.g. 'ice water go', to get someone to fetch him ice water). Nim's combinations had often just included meaningless repetitions (e.g. 'play me Nim play').

Most of Kanzi's two-word utterances, however, were best described as joint requests (e.g. 'hotdog coke' was a request for both items at once), or sometimes for both items to be mixed together.

In his three-item utterances, however, he often specified individuals other than himself as the actor and the person to be acted on (e.g. he invented games where he suggested 'A chase B', where A and B were human companions). This is interesting in that his human companions never made such suggestions, so he was not imitating them, and they had not engaged in such games with each other until Kanzi showed an interest in them doing so.

Table 3.11

Examples of Kanzi and Nim's three-word utterances

Kanzi	Nim
Person (g) chase Kanzi	Grape eat Nim
Person 1 (g) tickle person 2 (g)	Finish hug Nim
Chase bite person (g)	Tickle me tickle

(g) indicates a gesture used rather than a lexigram in Kanzi's utterance.

Source: Savage-Rumbaugh *et al.* (1986)

6. Imitation versus spontaneous utterances

Spontaneous utterances accounted for about 80 per cent of Kanzi's single-word and combinatorial (two- and three-symbol) utterances. Prompted, imitated or partially imitated responses accounted for only 11 per cent.

Comparisons were made between imitative utterances in Kanzi, Mulika, Sherman, Austin, Nim and a comparable human child acquiring language. Only Nim's level of imitation was significantly higher than the child's. (He differed from the other common chimpanzees here as he did not receive extra training in using symbols as referents.)

Nim also showed a lower proportion of spontaneous utterances. However, the spontaneous utterances by Sherman and Austin often occurred after a teacher had carried out some behaviour (e.g. introducing food to a situation), suggesting that their utterances depended more on situational cues than the spontaneous utterances from Kanzi and Mulika: 'a large proportion of Kanzi and Mulika's utterances were truly spontaneous and were not elicited by the teacher creating situations that required an utterance.' (p.224)

7. Formal tests of productive and receptive language capacity

In addition to informal testing of lexigrams which Kanzi and Mulika were believed to know already (e.g. when tidying up, Kanzi might be asked to pick up specific items in order), formal testing was also carried out. This was to test for all the items in Kanzi and Mulika's vocabulary. Kanzi was tested in the 17th month of this study, then aged 46–47 months, and Mulika was tested aged 18–21 months.

Earlier ape language studies were open to the criticism that the animal's 'language' was only in response to being cued 'by the contextual setting, inadvertent glances and so forth'. (p.217) The formal tests, therefore, were designed to avoid the possibility of cueing or prompting responses. The tests took the following form:

* They were conducted in the afternoon.
* 20–40 test items were used in each session.

... continued

- The time the test took depended on the amount of time spent playing between test trials.
- No test item was repeated in a session, and no two trials were ever the same.
- The test required a correct response where three or four alternatives were presented to choose from (e.g. 'Kanzi might be presented with the lexigrams green bean, apple and tomato, and asked in spoken English to "show me the tomato lexigram"' (p.217); Kanzi might also be shown a lexigram and asked to pick the item it referred to from three photographs).
- Different alternatives were presented for each item, and the same target item was never presented more than once in a test.
- Photos were in colour, 3½" x 5", and different versions of each target item were included. Lexigrams used were 1" x 1" replicas of those on the keyboard.

Table 3.12

The four types of test

Type of test	How test was conducted
Matching photograph to lexigram	Shown a photo, the task was to select the correct lexigram to match what was shown in the photograph from a choice of three photos. The photo was shown by a first experimenter, and the lexigrams were placed behind a blind by a second experimenter, without the first experimenter seeing them. This stopped inadvertent glances by the first researcher cueing the response. The second experimenter did not observe the response made by the ape, as this was recorded by the first experimenter, raising the blind and recording the response.
Matching spoken English to photograph	Three photos were shown, behind a blind again to prevent cueing, and Kanzi was asked: 'Kanzi, can you show me X? X' (thus the target word was said twice).
Matching spoken English to lexigram	As above, but using lexigrams, not photographs.
Matching synthesised language to lexigram	As above, but instead of a researcher speaking the target word, this was generated by the voice synthesiser speaking the target word twice, and Kanzi selecting from four given lexigrams. This test was used to show that Kanzi was not just responding to the tone of voice or other cue from human speech, and was in fact recognising and responding to the word spoken. The machine produced machine-like language which was in a flat tone. This test was used only with Kanzi.

The performances of Kanzi and Mulika were compared with those of Sherman and Austin on the formal tests. However, Sherman and Austin were found not to be able to match photos to spoken English, so the test matching spoken English to lexigrams, a harder task, was not attempted with the common chimpanzees.

The researchers presented the results of the formal tests in detail, indicating every item tested and the performance of each ape on each test used. Here we will simply summarise the number of correct items from each test.

... continued

Table 3.13
Results of the vocabulary tests for Kanzi

	Match symbol to English	Match photo to English	Match photo to symbol	Match symbol to Votrax speech
Correct	65	56	55	51
Incorrect	1	3	4	15
Total number of items	66	59★	59★	66

* Not all words and symbols could be tested on all trials, as a good photograph to represent them could not be sourced.

Source: adapted from Savage-Rumbaugh *et al.* (1986)

Items were scored as correct if the ape got them right on three out of three trials, and incorrect if the ape got them wrong on two or three out of three trials.

Table 3.14
Results of the vocabulary tests for Mulika

	Match symbol to English	Match photo to English	Match photo to symbol
Correct	41	36	41
Incorrect	1	5	1
Total number of items	42	41★	42

* Not all symbols could be tested on all trials, as a good photograph to represent a symbol could not be sourced.

Source: adapted from Savage-Rumbaugh *et al.* (1986)

Table 3.15
Results of the vocabulary tests for Sherman and Austin

	Match photograph to English		Match photograph to symbol	
	Sherman	Austin	Sherman	Austin
Correct	2	3	30	30
Incorrect	28	27	0	0
Total number of items	30	30	30	30

Source: adapted from Savage-Rumbaugh *et al.* (1986)

These results show that the bonobos could understand spoken English, whereas the common chimpanzees could not. The researchers also describe differences between the two types of ape while being tested. Although not part of their daily routine, Kanzi and Mulika seemed to understand that the tests were not about something that was going to happen: that is, if they pressed the symbol for juice, they seemed to know that this did not mean they would get juice. In comparison, Sherman and Austin did expect to get juice and were confused by the testing procedure.

Kanzi and Mulika could match lexigrams to photos, English words to lexigrams, and English words to photographs. The results showed that they 'associated various referents with lexigrams … these associations were bidirectional, and … spoken English words were as closely linked to lexigrams as were the items that the lexigrams represented'. (p.225)

The tests also revealed that Mulika understood a lot more than the researchers had previously realised. She understood 42 symbols, more than the 37 she had produced herself at that time.

... continued

Sherman and Austin did well on the photo to lexigram tests, but did no better than guessing when it came to tests using the spoken English word. Moreover, during the spoken English tests, the common chimpanzees did not seem comfortable; they 'attempted to avoid them by requesting to go elsewhere; and at times they refused to respond'. (p.225) Sherman and Austin both showed a sign of frustration typical in common chimpanzees during the English tests, scratching themselves all over.

On the synthesised language to lexigram test, only carried out with Kanzi, he did make some errors, but this may be because the machine-like language of the synthesiser makes it hard to understand what the machine is saying. His human carers had similar difficulties identifying the words he failed to match to lexigrams on this test.

8. The blind test in the forest

Four months after the 17 food sites were set up in the forest, when Kanzi was aged three years, a blind test was carried out in the woods, with an experimenter who had never been in the woods with Kanzi. The experimenter did not know her way round the woods, or the way to the locations where the food was placed, or the way back from the woods to the centre.

If Kanzi could communicate his intention to her using lexigrams and photos, and could lead her to the right locations, this would be evidence that Kanzi was using the symbols referentially, that his behaviour in the woods was not simply being cued, and that he was not being inadvertently guided to the right sites by his usual human companions.

'To test Kanzi's capacity to state his intentions to travel to various locations, we enlisted the aid of Mary Ann Romski, who works with children at the Language Research Center. Mary Ann and Kanzi had developed a close relationship during Kanzi's frequent visits to the "childside", but as Mary Ann was somewhat afraid of the snakes and creatures in the forest, she had never accompanied Kanzi into the woods … Mary Ann would be completely lost in the woods without Kanzi's help. If Kanzi said he was going to the treehouse, for example, and then led Mary Ann there, his behavior could not be explained on the basis of subtle cues from Mary Ann…

Mary Ann recorded Kanzi's utterances and the route he led her along in going from one food site to another. During the test, Kanzi used photographs on five occasions and lexigrams on seven to announce a proposed destination, with 100% accuracy. Moreover, on all but one journey between two sites, Kanzi chose the most direct route possible. On that one occasion, he exploited the opportunity of being accompanied by someone who did not know that where they were to go was a part of the forest where he normally is not allowed to go. Kanzi therefore demonstrated not only what he knew about himself, but also what he knew about Mary Ann.' (Savage-Rumbaugh and Lewin 1994:142)

Discussion

While acknowledging that the sample of each species used in this study is small, and suggesting that further studies raising common chimps and bonobos together might reveal more, the authors suggest that there is no need to consider the subjects in this study as atypical of their species; and as a result they offer four comparisons between the common chimpanzees and pygmy chimpanzees (bonobos)' language in their discussion:

1. Common chimpanzees like Sherman and Austin needed to be trained to use symbols, using instrumental conditioning, whereas the pygmy chimpanzees acquired their symbol use spontaneously through observation.

2. Pygmy chimpanzees understand spoken English, whereas common chimpanzees do not. No one trained Kanzi and Mulika to do this, and no one said single words to them over and over again. They only ever heard normal language and extracted words from this. This was an unforeseen outcome of this study, and was integrated into the study as it became apparent (e.g. by adding the voice synthesiser to Kanzi's keyboard).

... continued

3. The pygmy chimpanzees and the common chimpanzees differed in the way they used general symbols and specific symbols. Common chimpanzees easily generalise symbols but do not easily learn to specify. For example, they may use 'juice' and 'coke' interchangeably. Pygmy chimpanzees, however, do specify, and once the difference between symbols has been acquired, they do not make such mistakes. For example, Kanzi might call coke 'juice' only if coke is a novel item and no symbol for coke has been used before. Once a symbol for coke is assigned, the mistake is not made again.

4. Sherman and Austin never formed requests where they were neither the actor nor the beneficiary of the request. Nim did not do this either. Kanzi, however, was able to request that A act on B, where neither A nor B was Kanzi himself. The authors suggest (tentatively) that this particular use of symbols by Kanzi might suggest he was following rules: 'The ability to conceptualize and then to symbolically initiate complex forms of interaction between others would seem to be a precursor of syntactical structure, if not the basis itself for the occurrence of syntax.' (p.230)

Conclusion

The authors end with two conclusions:

- That the work with pygmy chimpanzees supports the view that culture plays a large part in the acquisition and use of symbols to communicate. Is it possible that just one ape, whose capacity for language has been tapped into, could go on to spread this behaviour, to 'push the behaviour of a feral group of apes toward the path of language?'. (p.231)

- In order to truly answer the questions raised by this study and other studies of animal language, the authors emphasise the need for stringent scientific data and comparative studies between species, without which our understanding of language may never be complete.

Commentary: Methods and issues

Research method, design and data gathering

This was a case study using a longitudinal design, with data gathered by observation. The strength of the longitudinal design is that it allows the development of language use by Kanzi and Mulika to be documented over time, and comparisons to be made between the way common chimps and bonobos learn symbol use.

The case study method allows the in-depth study of the subjects, and the fact that every utterance made by Kanzi in the 17-month period of this study was included in the data analysis shows the amount and depth of detailed data that can be gathered when one subject or small group of subjects is studied over time.

Does the study raise any ethical concerns?

Have the ethical implications as to the rights of primates been considered by this study? Is it acceptable to bring them up in an environment which is so totally different from their natural lifestyle? What happens to such animals after the study is finished? Is it acceptable to remove the primate from the humanised environment it has grown up in, and relocate it to a primate organisation or other holding area?

Validity and reliability of the study

The authors themselves were concerned about the accuracy (validity) of their on-the-spot, real-time observations of Kanzi's utterances. They were especially keen to ensure that his utterances should not be misread and that they were not just caused by the experimenter cueing the ape's response. In order to make sure that their observations were valid and accurate, a test of inter-observer reliability was carried out. First, a 4.5 hour video recording was made of one of the researcher's normal sessions with the apes, doing the usual real-time coding. The researcher who was taped was not aware at the time that the recording would be used for a reliability test, so would not have been able to deliberately influence the results of the reliability check. What was found showed that the real-time recording was very good. The real-time recorder recorded 37 utterances, the video observer 46, suggesting that on-the-spot recordings might miss some of the ape's utterances. In the 37 utterances recorded by both observers, there was 100 per cent agreement on which lexigrams Kanzi used and if they were used correctly in context. There was one disagreement about whether a lexigram use was spontaneous or structured. Of the nine utterances recorded by only the video observer, eight were spontaneous and one was structured. Kanzi tended to get attention by repeating himself when an utterance was not seen.

This reliability check provides support for the validity of the interpretations made of Kanzi's symbol use.

In terms of ecological validity, the study tests a species of ape in a humanised environment that it would not encounter in the wild, and therefore the study lacks ecological validity. In comparison with how children acquire language spontaneously, however, this study is more ecologically valid, providing the bonobo with a model of language use to acquire, than the earlier studies with common chimpanzees, where the instrumental conditioning of symbol use, unnecessary in children's language learning, was essential.

The depth of the data recorded and included in the study also supports the validity of this study's findings. Earlier ape language studies had been criticised for selecting utterances that suggested a level of linguistic competence that could not be established as typical for the ape concerned. This is not a criticism that can be made here, as all of Kanzi's utterances over 17 months were recorded and reported in this study.

Is the study useful?

In that it helps us to understand some of our closest evolutionary cousins, this study has great scientific value. This, and subsequent work in the field of ape language should make apparent for everyone the importance of these animals in understanding our own origins. It should also be clear that conservation of such important species should be of concern to us all.

The applications of the studies carried out with apes such as Lana, Sherman, Austin, Kanzi, Mulika and many that followed them have been used to help children with special needs who are unable to speak to develop ways of communicating, based on the lexigram system and on the methods used to help to teach apes symbol use. Because of this application, the work at the Language Research Centre is very useful.

4 Developmental psychology

In this chapter we are going to consider the developmental approach to understanding human behaviour by focusing on the three core studies, all of which contribute to the nature–nurture debate. We are also going to explore two major perspectives in psychology: the Behaviourist Perspective (in the study by Bandura *et al.*) and the Psychodynamic Perspective (in the study by Freud).

Our acknowledgement of how important childhood experiences are has come from the accepted belief that much of what happens to us as children helps shape who we become as adults. Each study takes a very different view of the development of children and provides an excellent introduction to how nature and nurture interact to make us who we are and do what we do.

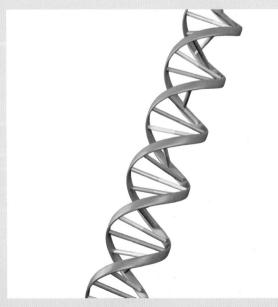

Figure 4.1 Is it nature that determines who we are?

Figure 4.2 Or is it nurture?

Samuel and Bryant study: Conservation

Cognitive development in children

If you were told that you would have to entertain a child for the afternoon, one of the things you would probably want to know is how old the child is. Without being an authority on children's development, you would still be aware that small children have very different abilities to older children, and this will influence what they enjoy doing. This is because children's cognitive abilities, especially their thinking and reasoning, differ with age, just as they differ from the thinking of an adult. Therefore, the things that would amuse a small child would be very different from the things that would amuse a 16-year-old. This way of thinking has changed dramatically from a few hundred years ago. In the seventeenth century it was believed that children's minds were a *tabula rasa* (blank slate), as they entered the world without any knowledge or skills. This view implies that *everything* we know is learned (which is really the argument of pure behaviourists – that is, that *all* behaviour is learned). At that time, most people believed that children were simply miniature adults, with the same thinking and reasoning skills. This was why many children were punished for behaviours which to us would seem quite normal for a child, and why they were expected to accept the behaviour of the adults in their lives without question or explanation.

Nowadays we consider childhood to be a special time for learning, demonstrated by a strong focus on nursery schools and educational toys. We no longer believe that children think in the same way as adults. Much of this knowledge is thanks to a man called Jean Piaget (1896–1980), who developed a theory of children's development which is not only one of the most comprehensive, but also one of the most influential theories of our time. Piaget's theory focuses on the idea that development is maturational (to do with the increasing maturity of the child), age-related and universal across cultures.

Piaget's theory

Jean Piaget was not actually a psychologist, which is quite surprising when you consider how important he is in the world of developmental psychology. He was born in Switzerland and trained initially as a biologist and zoologist. He became interested in the relationship between biology and psychology in the early 1920s, especially in how animals adapt to their environment.

Piaget went to Paris to work for Alfred Binet, who was responsible for developing the first intelligence tests for the French Education Department, as a way of testing children to identify those who had learning difficulties. The idea behind the intelligence tests was to compare children on what was believed to be a fixed ability – their innate intelligence, that is, the level of intelligence they were born with.

Piaget noticed that different children often gave the same wrong answer to certain questions and that these wrong answers depended on their age. It was as if the children went through different stages of reasoning according to their age.

This led Piaget to formulate a theory about intelligence which suggested that it was a kind of biological adaptation which allowed children to develop more efficient interactions with the world around them. Even now there are debates and little consensus about what is meant by the concept of intelligence, and whether it really is fixed at birth or if it can change according to learning and experience. For the moment it is enough that you have an idea of what is meant by the term 'intelligence' in order to understand the nature of the debate.

The needs of small children are taken care of by parents or caregivers, so initially they do not need to have complex skills. Once they are able to interact (and operate) in the world by doing things and making things happen, they need to develop greater understanding of how things work. This requires more complicated thought processes, so the child develops these as necessary.

Piaget realised that the development of mental abilities was not simply the result of a child maturing. He believed that children also need to gain experiences by interacting with their environment. He was of the opinion that children are self-motivated to discover the world – almost to the point that if you put a child in a room with lots of stimulating and interesting toys and games, for example, they would find out for themselves about the properties of those objects and the universal rules that apply to them. Teachers are therefore seen as facilitators rather than directors of children's education, providing opportunities in a stimulating environment to allow children to learn for themselves. This fuelled a massive change in education, with children no longer sitting passively in rows of desks, but becoming active learners, working in small groups to seek out information.

Piaget also recognised that the development of a child's knowledge and understanding seemed to involve a number of stages. To begin with their understanding was quite primitive, and often slightly incorrect, but this would transform as they got older, into an increasingly sophisticated understanding of the nature of the world, brought about by interaction with their environment. He also noticed that this transformation often occurred almost instantly, as if they suddenly gained insight into what they were doing wrong. Once this insight was achieved, the children were unable to return to a previous stage of more basic understanding.

Piaget claimed that each step up the developmental ladder was like a building block and was dependent on having reached the previous stage. He held that these stages were age-related and their sequence was invariant.

In his theory of cognitive development, Piaget identified four major stages in the development of a child's thought, and claimed that all children progress through these stages in this fixed order, although not everyone reaches the final stage:

1. The sensorimotor stage (0–2 years)

2. The pre-operational stage (2–7 years)

3. The concrete operational stage (7–11 years)

4. The formal operational stage (11+ years)

He suggested ages for each stage, although he was aware that the ages were averages rather than actual ages. He also said that children move through the stages at slightly different speeds, depending on their experiences.

Piaget's belief was that children are internally driven to find out about their world, to develop a mastery of their environment. This implies that if children are provided with a stimulating and well-equipped environment, they will explore the environment themselves and find out about the properties of the objects within that environment with little or no guidance.

The stage that concerns us in our core study is the long pre-operational stage from age about two to age about seven.

The pre-operational stage (2–7 years)

During this stage, Piaget suggested that children become more able to represent the world using mental images and symbols. Words are really just sound symbols for objects, and it is at this stage that a child's linguistic skills develop. We all use mental images, or pictures 'in our mind's eye', and even speak to ourselves 'inside our heads'. It is at this age that this kind of skill develops in a child. If we have access to very few symbols it would follow that our thoughts may also be limited, but the more they increase, the more sophisticated our thoughts become. Children of this age also demonstrate symbolism in their play, for example, using a banana as a telephone.

It is important not to imagine that the pre-operational child's thoughts are anywhere near as sophisticated as the thoughts of an adult. Their world is still very concrete – things are what they seem, so the child is more influenced by appearance than anything else. However, sometimes their thoughts may be intuitive, that is, based on what they feel or sense is true, without being able to explain the underlying principles. This may be why children sometimes seem very intelligent, when in fact they have made an intuitive guess without any logical reasoning to back it up.

Piaget's descriptions of children with pre-operational intelligence tended to focus on their limitations, because he believed that they could not yet apply logical mental rules to actual objects in the world. He described these logical mental rules as 'operations'. For example, addition and subtraction are reversible operations because adding three to a number can be reversed by taking three away again. Piaget suggested that children are not able to apply logical operations until they are about seven years old.

The main limitations of pre-operational thought

1. Egocentrism

According to Piaget, pre-operational children are egocentric. This means that they see the world from their own point of view and are unaware that others see it differently. Piaget thought this was the most serious deficiency in pre-operational children's thinking.

Piaget and Inhelder (1956) tested egocentrism with their famous study known as the 'three mountains task'. They asked children to look at a three-dimensional model of a mountain scene, which was based on a large mountain called Le Salève, across the lake from the city of Geneva. The mountains were placed so that one had snow on the top, one had a cross and one had a small house. The child would have a good look at the model and then sit down at one of the chairs placed round a table. The child would then have a doll seated opposite them and would have to choose a picture showing what the doll could see from the other side of the table.

Piaget found that children under five years always picked out the view of what they could see from their own position, and seemed to be unaware that the

Figure 4.3 Piaget's three mountains task

doll would see something different. He also found that between the ages of five and seven years they knew there would be a difference, but they were not sure what it was. When they reached seven years, they seemed to be able to cope with the 'in front' and 'behind' perspectives, but not the 'left' and 'right' perspectives. By the age of eight or nine years, they would be able to choose the right pictures for all the positions round the table. According to Piaget, these findings clearly demonstrated that children are unable to see things from someone else's point of view until they are at least seven years old.

2. Conservation

Piaget developed a number of tests to show whether children had the ability to conserve or not.

Probably the best-known example of Piaget's conservation experiments is the conservation of volume, or liquid. In fact, Piaget demonstrated this in exactly the same way with three beakers – two short beakers and one tall one. Both short beakers had the same amount of liquid in them and the tall one was empty. Piaget would ask which of the two beakers had more liquid, and the child would respond that they were both the same. He then poured the liquid from one of the short beakers into the tall beaker and again asked the child 'Which has more?' Preoperational children would now say the tall thin beaker had more, because they were unable to mentally reverse the transformation they had seen to get the correct answer that both beakers hold the same amount. The preoperational child is fooled by the higher liquid level in the tall thin beaker and assumes it now has more liquid than the other beaker. A child in the concrete operational stage can conserve, and they indicate this by telling you that just because the tall beaker has a higher level of liquid, it is also thinner, and that if you poured it back into the short fat beaker both beakers would have the same level of liquid, so there is still the same amount in both beakers.

When investigating number, Piaget used two rows of counters, equally spaced, and asked the child if there was the same number of counters in each row. The child would dutifully say 'Yes'. Piaget would then spread the second row of counters out and ask the child again if there was the same number of counters. At this point the preoperational child would say 'No'.

Piaget used a similar method to investigate children's ability to conserve weight with balls of plasticine. Below is a diagram of the tests he used to investigate the conservation of volume, matter, length volume and area.

In each of his conservation tests Piaget followed a standard format:

* The child was tested alone.

* The child was shown the two identical objects and asked the pre transformation question, 'Which has more?'

* One of the objects was then transformed – its appearance was changed – in front of the child.

* The child was asked the same question again, 'Which has more?', known as the post-transformation question.

Table 4.1

Type of conservation	Initial Presentation	Manipulation	Preoperational child's answer
Volume	Two identical beakers are filled with equal amounts of liquid. The child agrees that there is the same amount in each beaker.	The content of one beaker are poured into a beaker of a different shape. The child is asked if there is the same amount of liquid in each beaker.	The child says there is more liquid in the taller beaker.
Number	Two rows of objects (e.g. buttons) are shown to the child. The child agrees that there are the same number in each row.	One row is reorganised by spreading the objects out. The child is asking if there are the same amount of buttons in each row.	The child says the 'longer' row has more buttons.
Weight	Two identical balls of plasticine are shown to the child. The child agrees there is the same amount of plasticine in each ball.	One ball is rolled out. The child is asked if there is the same amount of plasticine in each shape.	The child says the longer shape has more plasticine.

3. Irreversibility

Piaget also demonstrated another limitation in pre-operational children's thought using these experiments. If we use the liquid experiment as an example, when the water from the tall thin beaker was poured back into the short beaker, the child would be quite satisfied that there was the same amount of water in both of them once more. The problem was that the child could not understand why this was and was unable to work it out. They were unable to 'reverse' the operation in their heads.

Reversibility is the ability to reverse the logic of a train of thought. According to Piaget, a three-year-old girl would be unable to do this. For example:

Adult: Do you have an older brother?
Child: Yes.
Adult: Does he have a younger sister?
Child: No.

4. Centration

This refers to the way a child will focus or centre attention on only one aspect of a task and ignore all the other aspects. This is when they rely on their intuition about what they can see rather than what they can reason. An example would be to put three sticks of equal length on the table in front of a child. The child would then be asked if the three sticks are the same length or if one is longer than the others. The centre stick would then be moved slightly so the three sticks are no longer in line. It is very likely that the child would then say that the sticks are not the same length (the centre stick will possibly be seen as either longer or shorter), because they will tend to focus on only one end of the stick, rather than both ends.

Evaluation of Piaget's theory

A number of studies have been conducted in order to evaluate Piaget's theory of cognitive development. There is little dispute that children go through the sequence of Piaget's cognitive developmental stages, and that these stages do seem to be cumulative and age-related. However, the ages specified are not as defined by Piaget. Much of the criticism of Piaget's theory is based on the idea that children are far more competent at certain ages than Piaget stated. It has been suggested that the language and methodology used by Piaget in his questioning was responsible for many of the children's supposed inabilities. The focus of studies criticising his work has been on evaluating the methodology he used. In our core study, for example, the authors, Judith Samuel and Peter Bryant test to see if Piaget forced errors in younger children by asking them the same question twice in his standard two–question conservation task, leading to Piaget underestimating the cognitive abilities of children under seven.

The Study

J. Samuel and P. Bryant (1984) 'Asking only one question in the conservation experiment', *Journal of Child Psychology and Psychiatry*, **25: 315–18**

Background

Margaret Donaldson suggested that Piaget actually underestimated the cognitive abilities of young children because he did not appreciate that their cognitive and social understanding are very closely related. In other words, young children fail to demonstrate their cognitive capabilities in Piaget's tests because of their social understanding of the situation. For example, if someone asks you the same question twice, you might think it is because you got the answer wrong the first time.

'What are two and two?'
'Five.'
'What are two and two?'
'Sorry – four.'

This is exactly what happens in Piaget's standard conservation tasks. The methodology he used involved asking the children, after presenting them with two rows of counters, if there was the same number of counters in each row. He would then widen the spaces between the counters on one of the rows and ask the children the same question. As we saw, Piaget found that children under seven years would generally answer the second question incorrectly, and from this he deduced that they had failed to conserve. From his studies, he set the progression from the pre-operational stage to the concrete operational stage at about seven years.

Rose and Blank (1974), however, suggested that the child's error was actually a result of them demonstrating a very sophisticated social strategy, by interpreting that the reason the second question was being asked was because they had given an incorrect answer to the first question. Rose and Blank devised a study to test this where they dropped the pre-transformation question (the question asked before the change in appearance had been made). Their study showed that if children were shown the two rows evenly spaced, and then shown one row being changed and asked if there was the same amount of counters in each row, more six-year-olds would get the answer right.

... continued

Samuel and Bryant were interested in these findings, which seemed to suggest that the younger children made errors in Piaget's traditional two-question task not because they could not conserve (understanding that a change in shape or form does not necessarily mean a change in quantity), but because they were misinterpreting what the experimenter wanted to hear.

The current study by Samuel and Bryant was designed to establish the reliability of Rose and Blank's findings and to extend this study. Rose and Blank had tested only six-year-olds, so Samuel and Bryant tested children aged 5–8½, to see if older and younger children were affected in the same way by the one-question task. Whereas Rose and Blank had only tested the conservation of number (counters task), Samuel and Bryant extended the study to include the two other versions of Piaget's conservation tasks: mass (using Play-Doh cylinders) and volume (pouring liquid into taller, narrower glasses or into shorter wider ones).

Aims

The aim of the study was to test whether the methodology used in Piaget's conservation experiments was the reason why children under eight years made errors, rather than a true lack of understanding of conservation. The study was designed to use Rose and Blank's one-question method.

Method and design

This was a laboratory experiment using an independent groups design.

Subjects

The sample was made up of 252 children from schools in and around Crediton, Devon, UK. Their ages ranged from five to 8½ years. The children were divided first according to age. This gave four groups, each consisting of 63 children. The first group had a mean age of five years and three months, the second, six years and three months, the third, seven years and three months, and the final group, eight years and three months. Each age group was then further subdivided into three more groups consisting of 21 children, to provide the three experimental conditions.

Table 4.2

Mean age in years	Number of children		
	Standard (two-question) condition	One-judgement condition	Fixed-array condition
5¼	21	21	21
6¼	21	21	21
7¼	21	21	21
8¼	21	21	21

Source: adapted from Samuel and Bryant (1984)

Within each age group, 21 children were tested using the traditional two-question method, as used by Piaget; 21 were tested using Rose and Blank's one-question method, asking only the post-transformation question; and a further 21 were tested in a control condition called the fixed-array condition. In the fixed-array condition, children were only shown the materials after they had been changed, and therefore they did not witness the transformation. This condition would show that the other children were using the information about how the materials looked in the first place to inform their answers to the post-transformation question.

Materials

The materials used were the same as those used in the Piagetian experiments: two cylinders of Play-Doh of equal size (for conservation of mass), two rows of counters, with a maximum of six in a row (for conservation of number), and three beakers of liquid, two beakers of the same size and another beaker which was taller and thinner (for conservation of volume).

... continued

Variables

A number of independent variables were being tested:

1. The age of the child – would the older children do better than the younger children?
2. The way the task was carried out – would children do better on the one-question task than the traditional two-question task and the fixed-array condition?
3. The materials used: Piaget suggested that children find the numbers task easier than the mass and volume tasks – would this be shown in the study?

The dependent variable was always whether or not the child got the answer to the post-transformation question right, and was measured as the mean number of errors out of 12 per age group per condition.

Procedure

Children were tested individually under laboratory conditions.

1. The standard group was tested using the standard Piagetian task, which involved asking a pre- and post-transformation question, and witnessing the transformation process.
2. The one-judgement group was tested using only the post-transformation question, after the children had witnessed the transformation process.
3. The fixed-array group was tested by being shown the post-transformation array (not having seen the transformation take place).

The procedure for the standard task to demonstrate conservation of number was as follows. Counters were spread out in two identical rows and the child was asked the pre-transformation question: 'Is there the same number of counters in each row?' The counters in one of the rows were then spread out and the child was asked the post-transformation question: 'Is there the same number of counters in each row?'

The procedure was the same for the mass and liquid experiments, with the mass (Play-Doh) involving flattening (into a pancake) or rolling (into a sausage) one cylinder of Play-Doh, and the liquid condition involving tipping the liquid from one beaker into another of different height and width.

Each child was tested four times on number, mass and volume tasks.

Controls

To ensure that the children really understood, there were four trials in each situation. The order in which the children undertook the tasks was varied systematically to prevent order effects.

Table 4.3

First child	number	mass	volume
Second child	mass	volume	number
Third child	volume	number	mass
Fourth child	number	mass	volume

Source: adapted from Samuel and Bryant (1984)

Results

The children were each tested 12 times (four times on each task), so they had 12 opportunities to get the answer right or wrong. Samuel and Bryant presented their data as the mean number of errors per age group and per condition.

The table below shows that the number of errors made in the one-judgement condition was lower than for the other two conditions in every case. It also indicates that the number of errors made by the children as they got older decreased in every condition. The children in the fixed-array condition made the most errors, showing that they did indeed use their witnessing of the transformation to inform their answer to the post-transformation question.

... continued

Table 4.4

Mean age	Standard (two-question) condition	One-judgement condition	Fixed-array condition
5¼	8.5	7.3	8.6
6¼	5.7	4.3	6.4
7¼	3.2	2.6	4.9
8¼	1.7	1.3	3.3

Source: adapted from Samuel and Bryant (1984)

The table below shows that the mean number of errors in the 'number' test were lower than the mean number of errors in the mass and volume tests in the one-judgement and fixed-array conditions.

Table 4.5

Type of task	Standard (two-question) condition	One-judgement condition	Fixed-array condition
Number	1.476	1.024	1.536
Mass	1.512	1.190	1.714
Volume	1.810	1.595	2.500

Source: adapted from Samuel and Bryant (1984)

After being subjected to a number of statistical analyses, the summary of the results was as follows:

- Children were significantly more able to conserve in the one-judgement condition than in the other two conditions, with children in the fixed-array condition making the most errors. These results establish the reliability of findings in the Rose and Blank study.

- The older children were significantly more able to conserve than the younger children, with each age group doing better than all the children younger than themselves.

- The number task produced significantly fewer errors than the mass and volume tasks.

Discussion

It seems that Piaget was right to suggest that changes in a child's understanding take place over time. As children get older, they understand better that simply changing the appearance of something does not mean that the quantity changes. This was shown by the fact that the children who only saw the fixed array were less able to appreciate this because they could not carry over previous information into the new situation. In fact, adults may well have the same problem. If you were to show an adult two glasses of different sizes containing liquid and ask them if there is the same amount of liquid in each, it is very likely they would either say 'Possibly' or 'No', but they could not be certain.

Piaget also suggested that the number task would be the easiest, and Samuel and Bryant's study clearly shows that he was right in this regard.

However, the findings from the earlier study by Rose and Blank, and the present study by Samuel and Bryant, both suggest that Piaget's method of asking the child the same question twice led children to give the wrong answer when in fact they *could* conserve. This was a result of the children believing that because they were being asked the same question again, a different response was required. The fact that children were better able to conserve on the one-judgement task suggests that Piaget's methodology led him to underestimate the cognitive capabilities of younger children.

The study provides some evidence to support Piaget's theory of cognitive development, and also some findings suggesting that his theory needs to be refined, particularly in relation to the age at which children can conserve.

Commentary: Methods and issues

Research method, design and data gathering

The study was an experiment carried out under controlled conditions. This means that extraneous variables could be strictly controlled, for example, standardisation of the tasks, including the procedure of testing and test materials, helps to support the validity of the study by isolating the IVs as the variables causing any observed difference in the children's ability to conserve. Using an independent design was useful as a control so that the children could each be tested in one condition, e.g. standard or one-question or fixed array, so the other conditions would not contaminate their results. The data was gathered by self report, using the conservation tasks and the children verbally gave their answers. This is the only way to measure the child's ability to conserve as this is a cognitive process that can only be revealed by self report.

The data gathered was quantitative and this is an advantage here as it meant that the data for each age group and condition could be easily summarised as mean number of errors out of 12 making the findings from each condition, and trends across the conditions, easy to present in table form and observe and compare.

When a study uses children as subjects there are some specific methodological and ethical issues that arise. These are explored below.

Key concept

Children as subjects/participants
This study illustrates both practical and ethical issues concerning the testing of children.
1. Practical issues: Children are often tested individually, under laboratory conditions, sometimes by an adult they are not familiar with. This set-up is designed to ensure that children do not contaminate each other's results, and that they do not simply copy a friend's answers or respond to peer pressure. However, it is not usual for children to be out of their social environment and in a laboratory with a stranger. Therefore, we have to question the ecological validity of this method of testing children.
2. Ethical issues: Can informed consent be obtained from children? Parental consent is usually sought. At what age do you think a child should be asked to give their own consent? If a parent gives consent but a child does not, should the child be tested? Do you think that children have the right to withdraw? What about debriefing? Could the children in this study be debriefed?

Does the study raise any ethical concerns?

Where minors (under 16s) are being studied it is always difficult to get informed consent from the subjects themselves, and where tests are carried out by adults on children in a school setting, it is highly unlikely that a child would feel able to refuse to participate or withdraw from the study. However, in this case, the test itself was not stressful or harmful and only took a few minutes. In such tests, the child would not be told they were wrong, but just 'Well done and thank you' at the end of the procedure.

Is the study useful?

Piaget's work has been very influential in education. His theory helped to describe the child for teachers and to establish a curriculum (especially in maths and science), which encouraged active participation in the early years and allowed children to learn at their own pace, depending on the stage of cognitive development they had reached. (You can thank Piaget for hours of fun at the sand tray and water tray with beakers when you were in infant school!)

This particular study highlighted two factors which are useful when considering the practice of teaching. It supports Piagetian theory of progressive stages of cognitive development (although it identified that Piaget's focus on specific ages needs to be more flexible, especially with different types of conservation tasks). It also highlighted how important it is to use appropriate methodology in order to identify the level of children's understanding; otherwise the results can be quite inaccurate.

The implications of this study for education are that teachers need to take into account where each child is in relation to known stages, rather than teaching groups of children the same topic in the same way. We are now very much aware that if a child continues to fail in school, they will become demotivated and may ultimately drop out of education altogether. On the other hand, if each child's strengths and weaknesses are identified, their individual needs can be met more effectively in a mainstream classroom.

It might be worth considering whether teaching children according to their level of development, rather than having age-focused classes, would be more beneficial. You might also consider the impact on teacher's workloads when they have to identify the strengths and weaknesses of each child when faced with classes of 30 or more.

Studies such as Samuel and Bryant's further our understanding of how children think, and demonstrate that their cognitive development and social understanding are very closely related. Often it is the social situation that influences whether or not a child will show what they know!

Validity and reliability of the study

Are there any problems with the methodology that lead us to question the internal validity of the findings? The study itself was well designed and accounted for many of the extraneous variables that could have interfered with the validity of the results. The possibility that the answers were given by chance was addressed by the children having four attempts at each conservation test, and order effects were accounted for by varying the order in which tasks were given. One criticism of the number test was that the children may simply have counted the number of counters used, which might explain the level of accuracy with the number task. All the children used as subjects would have been capable of counting to six, and it would take a very short space of time to add up the numbers on the table.

Validity could be questioned on the basis that children often get nervous in laboratory settings and they also have a limited attention span, which may have resulted in their answers being instantaneous rather than considered. On the other hand, the number of trials should have prevented these factors from influencing the results. However, as with all research, we can never be absolutely certain that subjects are not simply responding to even the most carefully designed experimental situation, and it is possible that demand characteristics may have affected the validity of the findings.

Testing children individually and under laboratory conditions is low in ecological validity (see the key concept above).

Figure 4.4 A 1950s classroom

Figure 4.5 A classroom in the 2000s

Bandura *et al.* study: Imitating aggression

How do we learn?

One of the central debates in psychology focuses on whether behaviour is innate or learned. This next section concentrates primarily on the influence of learning on behaviour, although the core study looks at the way in which children learn aggressive behaviour by observation. The main purpose of choosing this as one of the core studies is that it allows us to focus on the topic of learning and to consider the different ways that children learn. The study also adds fuel to the nature–nurture debate, in so far as most people believe that we have an innate capacity for aggression, but that the way in which it is demonstrated is learned.

Theories of learning

Figure 4.6

In order to consider any of the theories about learning, we ought to look briefly at what we mean by 'learning'. Often the idea that we have learned something comes from observing a change in behaviour, such as being able to solve complicated maths problems or riding a bike. The problem here is that often we learn something but do not demonstrate that skill to others, and therefore they may assume that we have not actually learned anything. Imagine that you have learned to knit at school by watching the teacher following a complicated knitting pattern and then having a brief attempt yourself. At the end of the afternoon, you have learned how to do it, but you may choose not to because you think knitting does not look particularly cool!

Generally speaking, psychologists suggest that learning is 'a relatively permanent change in behaviour due to past experience'. We could argue that you have not actually learned to knit because it is not changing your behaviour, as you are not knitting your own jumpers! On the other hand, you have actually acquired the knowledge of how to knit and this is likely to remain with you for some time (and we cannot be sure that it will not affect your behaviour for ever, because you may wish to start knitting at some point in the future). Hopefully you are beginning to get the idea that defining learning is more complicated than being able to provide a simple definition.

One very useful definition of learning, however, comes from Anderson (1995), who explained that learning is the process whereby reasonably permanent changes occur in potential behaviours as a result of past experiences (which would have been learning situations), but what we must remember is that they may not *actually* change. This seems to be a pretty good explanation of what really happens when we learn. On the other hand, if we are trying to investigate learning, how is it possible to measure 'potential' behaviours? This is the difficulty that has faced psychologists when researching learning, and devising theories as to how it occurs.

Past research into learning has approached the problem by looking at the outcome, because at least that is measurable: has behaviour changed from point A to point B after the teaching has taken place?

This was a focus in the investigations in the Behaviourist perspective. The Behaviourist school was originally established by J.B. Watson in 1913. Watson argued that in order for psychology to be scientific, it must focus on the things which could be assessed objectively rather than inferred.

Human beings respond to a specific stimulus. We talk if someone talks to us; we eat if we are hungry; we get angry if someone provokes us. Each behaviour has an antecedent (a stimulus, or something which provokes that behaviour). Although we might think about our response to a stimulus, we may act simply on instinct. Therefore, anyone trying to analyse human behaviour would find it very difficult to work out the 'thought' part because it may vary for each person, or may be absent, and ultimately, unless we develop telepathic powers, we have no way of knowing whether we are correct!

Consider the following example. Your response to a cat biting your knee could be either instinctive (i.e. kick the cat away) or calculated, which involves thought and maybe a bucket of water and a wet cat! How would an observer actually know your thoughts? They may make inferences, but could not be totally sure. Therefore, the behaviourists suggested that the only answer would be to ignore the thought and simply consider the stimulus and the response, both of which are known (it was the thought part which later interested cognitive psychologists).

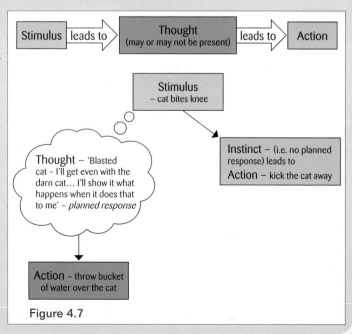

Figure 4.7

Watson also believed that all behaviour consisted of learned responses to different stimuli (which is really a reductionist approach, where all behaviours are broken down to their basic components).

Operant and classical conditioning

B.F. Skinner's theory of learning is known as operant conditioning.

Skinner, who was a behaviourist, claimed that all behaviours are learned. He explained that when an adult praises a child for a specific behaviour, this praise will act as a reinforcement, making it more likely that the behaviour will be repeated. The child learns that their action has produced a positive result, so they will repeat the action. The idea behind this kind of learning is that we learn by making an association between what we are doing and a positive result – we are conditioned to make that association. This illustrates how positive reinforcement works. In addition we also respond to negative reinforcement. For example imagine you kept your bedroom looking like a pigsty and your parents moaned and moaned at you and eventually refused to take you to your friend's house on Saturday night because you hadn't tidied up. After a boring night in you will tidy your room before next Saturday to avoid the punishment of not being able to get to your friend's house without your parents' taxi service! So reinforcement can be either positive, where we carry out an action to bring about an outcome from which we will gain, or negative, where we do the action in order to avoid an unpleasant outcome.

Conditioning theory actually helps to explain much of our behaviour, and is also extremely useful when trying to understand the behaviour of animals.

Imagine that you live in a huge house, with four floors. In fact, it is so big that in order for you to hear whether or not dinner is ready, the butler has to sound a huge gong, which vibrates through the whole house. As you grow up, you always associate that sound with food, and it seems that the minute you hear it you can feel your mouth watering in anticipation of the delicious meal that awaits you.

When you leave home, you move into a flat and become responsible for feeding yourself. One day you are walking past some antique shops when you hear the sound of a gong being hit. It instantly makes you think of dinner and you can feel your mouth watering, so you have to go off to the nearest cake shop to get some food.

What you have not realised is that you have become conditioned to associate the sound of a gong with food. Although you know that a gong does not indicate food when you are away from home, you cannot help the reflex response of your mouth watering when you hear the gong being hit. Where a reflex such as salivation has become the response to a stimulus that does not directly cause the action (a gong does not make your mouth water on its own!) this is known as classical conditioning.

Pavlov and classical conditioning

Classical conditioning was demonstrated by Ivan Pavlov in 1927, after he discovered that it was possible to teach dogs to salivate at the sound of a bell, rather than at the sight or smell of food. The reason was that the dogs did not consciously salivate to the sound of the bell in the first place, just as you did not consciously make your mouth water to the sound of the gong in the example above. The salivation was a reflex response to an unusual stimulus.

Pavlov discovered that the dogs he was using for experiments started to drool before they were given any food. In fact, they drooled when the keeper approached the cage, or when they saw the bucket the food was carried in or even the white coats of the keepers. Pavlov was actually interested in the digestion of dogs and was undertaking research which involved collecting dogs' saliva in a tube attached to the outside of their cheeks. He decided to investigate this further, and wondered if he could teach the dogs to salivate at the sound of a bell, which, as we have said, was a stimulus that would not produce salivation under normal circumstances.

For a while, Pavlov arranged for a bell to be rung every time the dogs were fed. They learned to associate the sound of the bell with the fact that dinner was on its way, and soon they were slobbering the minute the bell was rung. He had taught them to make the association between a stimulus (the bell) which does not normally suggest food, and a reflex response (slobbering). It is important to remember that classical conditioning involves training someone to produce a reflex response to something.

Figure 4.8 Ivan Pavlov is seen here with one of his dogs during a demonstration

Pavlov's experiments in 1889 on the mechanism of digestion in dogs established the role of the autonomic nervous system (ANS) and won him a Nobel prize in 1904. He is best remembered for subsequent work on conditioned reflexes, conditioning a dog to salivate in anticipation of food by ringing a bell each mealtime, until eventually the bell alone provoked salivation – these experiments founded behaviourist psychology.

The process of classical conditioning is often referred to by a series of simple equations.

Before learning:

Food (unconditioned stimulus) = Slobbering (unconditioned response)

The learning process:

Food (unconditioned stimulus) + Bell (conditioned stimulus) = Slobbering (conditioned response)

After learning has taken place:

Bell (conditioned stimulus) = Slobbering (conditioned response)

The most important part of this concept is that it is possible to teach someone to respond with a reflex action to a certain stimulus. If we accept the idea that aggression might be innate, and is a reflex response to certain stimuli, we can see how some people can learn to be aggressive in specific situations.

Operant conditioning and reinforcement

Of course, there are only so many reflexes to retrain. It is possible to learn other things that have nothing to do with reflexes, such as teaching dogs to beg, fetch, roll over, play dead etc.

> Mrs Evans had an old English sheepdog called Josephine. When Josephine was little, Mrs Evans decided to teach her to shake hands. She did this by saying 'Shake hands' to her, and holding her front paw and making her shake hands, and every time she did it, she gave Josephine a doggie chocolate as a reward. The dog soon learned that by 'shaking hands', she would be rewarded, but the trouble was when she had come in from the muddy garden, she would walk up to Mrs Evans and hit her with her front paw, leaving dirty marks all over whatever she was wearing.

What Mrs Evans had done in the example above was to use the process of conditioning to train Josephine to do something which was not a reflex response. This process is called operant conditioning, and involves increasing the likelihood that a behaviour will happen again by reinforcing that behaviour. Mrs Evans paired Josephine's behaviour of giving a paw with receiving a treat (a reinforcement), until the dog could forget the reinforcement because the behaviour would happen anyway.

The difference between this and Pavlov's theory about how we learn is that Pavlov's learned responses would be triggered automatically by a stimulus, without any sort of conscious awareness. B.F. Skinner pointed out that there was a difference between 'automatic responses' (where the response or action happens without conscious thought) and 'operants', where responses happen initially as a result of voluntary choice. Josephine could have chosen not to shake hands when the process of training started, although after a while the response became almost automatic.

Figure 4.9 Skinner with a Skinner box, the equipment used by him to train rats and explore the ways that reinforcement affects learning

Skinner (1938) described how he taught rats to gain food by pressing a lever. He would allow the release of a food pellet every time a rat approached the lever. Each time, the rat would have to get a little bit closer in order to get the food pellet. This would continue until the rat stepped on the lever, possibly by chance, and this released the food pellet. Finally, the rat would only get the pellet when pressing the lever. The rat learned by having its behaviour reinforced. Skinner shaped the rat's behaviour until the rat learned what was required. Sooner or later, the rat would not have to make the conscious decision, 'Mmmm, I'm hungry. I think I will go and press the lever.' It would simply do it without having to think through the process, having made an automatic association between the behaviour and the result.

Humans also make automatic associations, which we had to learn originally. In fact, you are doing exactly that now: you are reading without thinking about what each letter sounds like or what each word means. You learned to read by a process of operant conditioning, because each time you read a word, either your parents or your teachers would praise you, or you would feel so pleased with yourself that this would be sufficient reinforcement for you to continue. It is often the case that when you teach an animal something, and then take away the reinforcement or reward, they stop doing it.

This theory can also be used to explain why some small children have screaming fits or behave badly. Their parents are preoccupied with other things, and the child wants attention. The obvious way to get it, they have learned, is to start having a tantrum. That way, parents have to stop what they are doing and pay attention to the small child. In fact, many child guidance clinics specialise in dealing with children with behavioural problems. Frequently, children who seem uncontrollable are referred to such clinics, where the parents' 'parenting skills' are assessed. The reason why the children are so badly behaved is often because they have learned that bad behaviour pays – they get the reward or reinforcement of their mum or dad's attention.

Think about certain types of behaviour that you have learned will get rewards – being nice to granny, working hard for exams or even washing up. All these have reinforcements that you have learned about, which will make it more likely that you will repeat them. Being paid for working is also a reinforcement – the harder you work, the more money you earn, and the more likely your chances of promotion. You may even find that you self-reinforce by feeling good about what you are doing!

Social learning theory – learning by imitation

Social learning theorists, such as Albert Bandura, are interested specifically in the way humans learn the rules of social behaviour. They agree that all behaviour is learned and that the principles outlined by the behaviourists can also apply to social learning (e.g. the concepts of reinforcement and punishment). They explain that people learn by observing the behaviour of others by an almost unconscious method. The model, or actor, is frequently unaware of being observed, and the observer, or learner, is often unaware that they are actually learning. The behaviour is learned without any reinforcement and may only appear in the future if the reward for that behaviour is worth having. Learning by imitation does not depend on reinforcement, but the *performance* of any learned behaviour will be influenced by reinforcement.

Observation

We are sometimes instructed or subtly cajoled by our parents, our teachers and our peers, but more often we simply observe the way that others behave. We learn what is good and what is not acceptable within our culture by seeing who does well and who gets the rewards. Social learning theory suggests that we are more likely to learn these rules (which will vary between cultures) by observing the behaviour of others, and we are therefore more likely to repeat or avoid the behaviours if they are followed by the addition of rewards and reinforcements, or by punishments such as social isolation or exclusion.

Consider the kind of things you might have learned by observation. You could probably list a dozen different ways of killing someone. Now imagine you have been told to disembowel them. In your mind, can you picture what you would have to do and what the person's innards would look like? It is quite likely that you will be able to conjure up a very gruesome picture, which is messy and bloody and probably quite lifelike. But how do you know all these things? Most likely, you will have seen it on TV or at the cinema. You have learned by observing and have stored that information, to be used if and when necessary. However, you have not been rewarded for learning these kinds of behaviours and you are extremely unlikely ever to demonstrate them (we hope!), which suggests that there is a difference between traditional theories of learning and social learning theory.

The Study

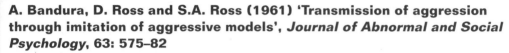

A. Bandura, D. Ross and S.A. Ross (1961) 'Transmission of aggression through imitation of aggressive models', *Journal of Abnormal and Social Psychology*, **63: 575–82**

Background

In order to demonstrate the power of social learning theory, Bandura designed a study to explore whether children would imitate the actions of different role models when given the opportunity. If they did produce the same aggressive actions, this would show two things. First, it would demonstrate that learning can take place with immediate effect, rather than by the step-by-step process which would involve reinforcement of all the component parts of a behaviour. This was the process advocated by Skinner, and Bandura criticised Skinner's approach as it would take too long for all behaviours to be acquired in this way. Second, direct reinforcement is not necessary for a behaviour to be learned. The original model need not be present. The behaviour can be stored up and demonstrated when the appropriate opportunity arises.

Aims and hypotheses

The aim of the study was to see whether children would imitate aggressive behaviour when given the opportunity, even if they saw these behaviours in a different environment and the original model they observed performing the aggressive act was no longer present.

Bandura's study aimed to test four hypotheses:

1. Children exposed to an aggressive model would produce more imitative aggressive acts than children exposed to a non-aggressive model and children not exposed to a model at all (the control group).

2. Exposing children to a non-aggressive model would have an inhibiting effect on their aggressive behaviours and they would show significantly less aggression than the control group who saw no model.

3. It was assumed that pre-school children would have been reinforced for appropriate sex-role behaviour by their parents: that girls would have been positively reinforced for behaving in certain ways (e.g. cooking, being maternal), while boys would have been negatively reinforced for these behaviours, as they were not deemed appropriate for boys. Therefore, Bandura *et al.* predicted that the sex of the model would have an effect: children would be more likely to copy a same-sex model (girls would copy a woman more and boys would copy a man more).

4. Since aggression is stereotypically a male behaviour, boys would have been positively reinforced for this behaviour and girls negatively reinforced. Therefore, Bandura *et al.* expected boys to imitate more aggressive acts than girls, especially with a same-sex (male) model.

Method and design

A laboratory experiment was carried out. The independent variables were:

- whether there was an adult model present or not
- whether the model was male or female
- whether the model behaved aggressively or non-aggressively.

... continued

This meant that different children were tested in the following conditions:

- observing an aggressive male model
- observing an aggressive female model
- observing a non-aggressive male model
- observing a non-aggressive female model
- no model (control condition).

This was a matched groups design, where the overall performance of each group was compared with each of the other groups.

The dependent variable was the amount of aggression demonstrated by the child in a later situation (both imitative and non-imitative).

Subjects

In total, 72 children were tested: 36 boys and 36 girls from Stanford University Nursery School (USA), aged between 37 and 69 months (mean age 52 months), that is, between the ages of three years and one month, and five years and nine months.

The children were allocated to conditions as follows. The control group was made up of 24 children, 12 boys and 12 girls, who would see no role model. The two experimental groups were then sub-divided into two groups of 24 subjects each: aggressive model observers (six female and six male children to see a female role model, and six female and six male children to see a male role model), and non-aggressive model observers (six female and six male children to see a female role model, and six female and six male children to see a male role model).

Controlling extraneous variables

Matching was carried out in order to prevent subject variables from influencing the results. Since some children are generally more aggressive than others anyway, the children were rated for aggression before being allocated to their groups. This was done by one of the female experimenters and the children's nursery school teacher, both of whom knew the children well prior to the study. The children were rated on a five-point scale for previous displays of physical and verbal aggression, aggression towards objects, and their ability to control their behaviour when they were angry (aggressive inhibition).

The results of the two raters were considered to be reliable because there was significant correlation between them. The groups of six children were then established to ensure that the level of aggression shown previously by the children was matched across the groups, so that no one group was generally more aggressive than another at the outset.

Key concept

Reliability and inter-observer reliability

This study establishes the inter-observer reliability between observers/raters.

If a test or measure is reliable, this means that it gives significantly similar results on retesting. For a study or test to be established as reliable, it must be carried out using the same procedure on similar subjects under similar circumstances, to give similar results. The way the results are tested to see if they are similar is to apply correlational statistics. If a significant positive correlation is established, this supports the reliability of the study's findings. This is important because if the findings are not reliable, they will not be valid.

In order to avoid observer bias (i.e. an observer applying ratings or counting categories in a subjective rather than objective fashion), inter-observer reliability needs to be established. This means that two observers rate or observe the same behaviour, and the two sets of ratings are correlated. If a significant positive correlation is seen, inter-observer reliability has been established and the objectivity of the results is confirmed.

In the Bandura study, this stops any conscious or unconscious bias occurring on the part of the teacher or experimenter in their assessment of the children's general aggression.

... continued

Models, materials and location

- **Role models:** One male and one female role model were briefed to behave in a standardised way. The same male and female models were used throughout, and therefore played both the aggressive and non-aggressive roles.

- **Location:** The study took place at the Stanford University Nursery School. There were three rooms used for the study, one in the children's nursery building, and two located away from the children's main nursery building.

- **Room one:** The experimental room had a table and chair in one corner, with potato prints and picture stickers (selected because children like playing with them). In the other corner was another table and chair, with a Tinkertoy set (a kind of construction set consisting of dowels and discs with holes in them to fit them together), a mallet and a five-foot inflatable Bobo doll (which, when you punch it, rocks back up again). This room was located in the main nursery school building and was therefore familiar to the children.

- **Room two:** This room, which was away from the main nursery building, contained a number of very attractive toys, including a fire engine, a train, a plane and a doll with lots of clothes and a cot. The idea here was to try to arouse aggression in all the children by letting them start to play with the toys and then taking them away, saying that these toys were being saved for another group of children.

- **Room three:** This room was next door to room two, away from the main nursery building, ensuring that the setting was separate from where the observation of the models took place. Many children thought they were no longer in the nursery school. Room three was also connected to an observation room with a one-way mirror, through which observers could monitor the behaviour of the children. It contained a number of toys, which were always placed in exactly the same position for each child. This standardisation was done to ensure that one toy was not nearer to or more prominent for one child than for another, as this could have influenced their choice of which toys to play with. The toys were considered either aggressive or non-aggressive. Non-aggressive toys were dolls, bears, construction toys, crayons, cars and plastic farm animals. Aggressive toys were a three-foot Bobo doll, a mallet and peg board, and dart guns.

Procedure

Each child was tested individually in a three-step procedure. The same female experimenter led each child through the three stages.

Stage one (approximately ten minutes): The children in the aggressive and non-aggressive conditions were tested in this step. The experimenter took them into the first room, where they were seated at the child's table and encouraged to play with the potato prints and stickers. The model was then escorted into the opposite corner of the room and told that the Tinkertoy set, mallet and Bobo doll were for him or her to play with. Then the experimenter left the room.

In the aggressive condition the model started by playing with the Tinkertoy set, but after a minute turned to the Bobo doll and started to act aggressively towards it. The aggressive acts were deliberately stylised so that imitation of them would be clear and not just examples of how children would play with the Bobo doll anyway. The physically aggressive acts were repeated about three times in the ten-minute period the child stayed in this room, and they were interspersed with the verbally aggressive responses and non-aggressive phrases.

The physically aggressive acts were:

- Laid the Bobo doll on its side, sat on it and punched it on the nose.
- Raised the Bobo doll up and hit it on the head with the mallet.
- Threw the Bobo doll in the air and kicked it around the room.

... continued

The verbally aggressive responses were:

- 'Pow'
- 'Throw him in the air'
- 'Kick him'
- 'Sock him on the nose'
- 'Hit him down'

The non-aggressive phrases were:

- 'He keeps coming back for more'
- 'He sure is a tough fella'

In the non-aggressive condition, the procedure was the same except that, once seated at the table, the adult assembled the Tinkertoy set in a quiet, subdued way, and ignored the Bobo doll for the ten minutes the child was in the room. After ten minutes, the experimenter came to collect the child, saying they were going to another room now, and said goodbye to the model.

Stage two (approximately two minutes): Each child, including those from the control group, was then taken into room two, where they were subjected to mild aggression arousal. Having been allowed to play with the very attractive toys for two minutes, the experimenter stopped the child and told them that these were her very best toys and she did not let just anyone play with them, but had decided to save them for the other boys and girls to play with. She then told each child that they could play with any of the toys in the next room, and took the child to room three.

- The reason why this mild aggression arousal was induced for the aggression condition was that previous studies had shown that observing the aggression of others often inhibits (suppresses) a person's own aggressiveness. This might mean that the children in this condition were less inclined to be aggressive in room three than the other two groups, which would confound the study.
- For the non-aggressive condition, the presence of the non-aggressive model was supposed to inhibit their aggressiveness, and this could be seen most clearly if the children were less aggressive in circumstances where they had good reason to be aggressive, which is why their aggression was aroused in this stage.
- The control group was exposed to this stage to ensure that fair comparisons could be made with the other two groups of children.

Stage three (approximately 20 minutes): The experimenter then took each child to room three and stayed with them, as some of the children refused to go into this room on their own or tried to leave before the end of the allotted time (this was presumably because they had been upset by stage two). To avoid affecting the children's behaviour, the experimenter worked discreetly at the other end of the room. The child was able to play with the toys and their behaviour was observed for 20 minutes through the one-way mirror. Two observers scored the subjects' behaviour at five-second intervals, which gave 240 observations for each subject. The level of inter-observer reliability was highly significant.

The children were observed for the following categories of behaviour.

Three measures of direct imitation:

- imitation of aggressive acts
- imitation of aggressive phrases
- imitation of non-aggressive phrases.

Two measures of indirect imitation:

- The child hit other things with the mallet (remember, the child had only seen the model hitting the Bobo doll with the mallet).
- The child laid the Bobo doll on its side and sat on it, but was not aggressive towards it.

... continued

Four further types of aggressive behaviour, which were not imitations of the adult role model (this would tell the researchers whether the general aggression of the children was inhibited or increased as a result of seeing one of the two models):

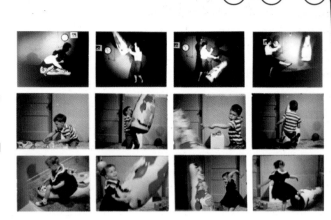

Figure 4.10 Stills from one of Bandura *et al.*'s studies of adults modelling aggression towards a Bobo doll, showing the female adult in the aggressive condition (top row), a male child in the aggressive model condition (middle row) and a female child in the aggressive model condition (bottom row)

- striking, slapping or pushing the doll aggressively
- behaving aggressively towards any other objects
- producing novel hostile remarks aimed at the Bobo doll or other objects (e.g. 'Cut him', 'Shoot the Bobo', 'Knock over people', 'Horses fighting, biting')
- shooting darts or aiming the gun and pretending to shoot at various objects in the room.

Results

The results have been broken down here to make them easier to digest, but at the end of this section you will find the entire table for the mean aggression scores for all subjects. What do the results tell us in relation to Bandura's four hypotheses?

Table 4.6

Hypothesis	What the results showed
Subjects exposed to an aggressive model would produce more imitative aggressive acts than subjects not exposed to any model (the control group) and subjects exposed to a non-aggressive model.	The results showed that this was true for all behaviours.
Exposure to a non-aggressive model would have an inhibiting effect on the subjects' aggressive behaviours and they would show significantly less aggression than the control group who saw no model.	The researchers observed no significant general inhibiting effect, but when the results are looked at by sex of model, the male non-aggressive model can be seen to have a significant inhibiting effect on the children.
The sex of the model would have an effect: children would be more likely to copy a same-sex model (girls would copy a woman more and boys would copy a man more).	Boys showed more aggression if the model was male than if the model was female. Girls showed more *physical* aggression if the model was male, and more *verbal* aggression if the model was female. Subjects who saw the same-sex role model only imitated their behaviour in some categories.
Boys would imitate more aggressive acts than girls, especially with a same-sex (male) model.	Boys did display more *physical* aggression than girls if the model was male, but girls displayed more *verbal* aggression than boys if the model was female.

... continued

Table 4.7 The mean totals of aggressive behaviours and the gender of the role model.

Aggressive behaviours	Female model (mean total)	Male model (mean total)
Imitative physical aggression		
Female subjects	5.5	7.2
Male subjects	12.4	25.8
Imitative verbal aggression		
Female subjects	13.7	4.3
Male subjects	2.0	12.7
Non-imitative aggression		
Female subjects	21.3	8.4
Male subjects	16.2	36.7
Aggressive gun play		
Female subjects	1.8	7.3
Male subjects	4.5	15.9

Source: adapted from Bandura *et al.* (1961)

Table 4.8 The mean totals of behaviour for all conditions.

Response category	Experimental groups				Control
	Aggressive		Non-aggressive		
	F model	M model	F model	M model	
Imitative physical aggression					
Female subjects	5.5	7.2	2.5	0.0	1.2
Male subjects	12.4	25.8	0.2	1.5	2.0
Imitative verbal aggression					
Female subjects	13.7	2.0	0.3	0.0	1.7
Male subjects	4.3	12.7	1.1	0.0	1.7
Mallet aggression					
Female subjects	17.2	18.7	0.5	0.5	13.1
Male subjects	15.5	28.8	18.7	6.7	13.5
Punches Bobo doll					
Female subjects	6.3	16.5	5.8	4.3	11.7
Male subjects	18.9	11.9	15.6	14.8	15.7
Non-imitative aggression					
Female subjects	21.3	8.4	7.2	1.4	6.1
Male subjects	16.2	36.7	26.1	22.3	24.6
Aggressive gun play					
Female subjects	1.8	4.5	2.6	2.5	3.7
Male subjects	7.3	15.9	8.9	16.7	14.3

Source: adapted from Bandura *et al.* (1961)

... continued

Discussion

It appears that although the children who saw the aggressive models were far more aggressive than the other two groups, the gender of the role model had a significant impact on their behaviour.

The female role model seemed to cause confusion in the children, because she was not behaving in a way that they would expect. They made comments like, 'Who is that lady? That's not the way for a lady to behave.' 'You should have seen what that girl did in there. She was just acting like a man. I never saw a girl act like that before. She was punching and fighting but not swearing.' (p.581)

The male role model's aggressive behaviour, on the other hand, was more likely to be seen as normal. The children made comments like, 'Al's a good socker, he beat up Bobo', 'I want to sock like Al', and so on. Bandura points out that this may be due, in part, to the children's expectations of behaviour: they already had ideas about what was sex-appropriate behaviour for men and women. For example, one girl said, 'That man is a strong fighter, he punched Bobo right down to the floor and if Bobo got up he said, "Punch your nose." He's a good fighter like Daddy.' The children's comments show that they had clear ideas that fighting is acceptable, even desirable, for males, but unacceptable for females.

Since girls are more likely to have been discouraged from behaving aggressively as this is male-typical behaviour, and boys will have been encouraged to behave in this way, this explains Bandura *et al.*'s findings that the boys were more aggressive than the girls, and that the male aggressive model elicited the most imitation. Learned appropriate behaviour also explains why the girls were more verbally aggressive and the boys were more physically aggressive in the male aggression condition.

Physical aggression is clearly a masculine-typed behaviour – therefore the boys' domain and not appropriate for the girls – whereas verbal aggression is not so clearly sex-typed and was therefore available as an aggressive outlet for the girls, who may have been suppressing their desire to behave in a physically aggressive way.

The inhibition of aggressive behaviour by the non-aggressive male model can be explained by the fact that male models have a greater effect due to male dominance in society, and also because by playing quietly with the Tinkertoy set, the male model was behaving in a non sex-typed manner.

Do children learn by imitation? This study certainly shows that children can learn as a result of imitation, and without either the child or the model being reinforced. This suggests that modelling is a form of observational learning.

Bandura went on to investigate how modelling leads to learning, developing his social learning theory, which brings together the behaviourist concept of reinforcement and the Freudian concept of identification (which you will learn more about later in this chapter), since behaviour which is positively reinforced is more likely to be imitated, and the person is more likely to imitate a role model with whom they identify.

Bandura *et al.* showed that learning can occur without the learner receiving reinforcement, but suggested that reinforcement may play an important part in the learner's decision to perform the behaviour at an appropriate point. Therefore, reinforcement, whether direct or vicarious, or self-reinforcement, is one factor which may influence the performance of a learned behaviour.

Remember, just because learning has occurred, it does not mean that the behaviour will be performed. We all know how to stick our heads in the oven, but we do not do it!

Commentary: Methods and issues

Research method, design and data gathering

The study was an experiment carried out under controlled conditions. This means that extraneous variables could be strictly controlled, for example, standardisation of the model's behaviour in room one, and standardisation of the way the children were 'mildly frustrated' in the second room, and standardisation of the types and arrangement of the toys in room three. Standardisaton as an experimental control helps to support the validity of the study as it isolates the IVs as the variables causing any observed difference in the children's displayed aggression in room three.

Using a matched groups design was useful as a control of subject variables as it ensured that the study would not be confounded by the most aggressive children all ending up in one of the small groups of six being tested in one condition. If random allocation had been used instead all the most aggressive boys could have ended up in the aggressive model condition.

The data was gathered by observation using an observation schedule with nine categories of both imitative and non-imitative aggressive acts over 20 minutes in room three. The observation was covert (through a one-way mirror) and this hopefully meant that the children would act normally in the room and not inhibit their aggression as they would if they were aware of being observed closely by an adult. The data gathered was quantitative and this is an advantage here because it meant that the data for each model condition and the control condition could be easily summarised as a mean number of times the six children in each condition carried out an aggressive action or imitative action. The quantitative findings from each condition were easy to present in table form so that the children's behaviour in room three could be easily compared across the conditions.

Does the study raise any ethical concerns?

This study raises a number of ethical issues.

There is no mention of informed consent being sought from parents, and the young children would not have been in a position to give consent on their own behalf to take part in the study. Perhaps consent was not sought because the researchers thought parents might not consent to their child being involved in a study on learning aggression! Remember, this study preceded Milgram's obedience experiments (explored in Chapter 2) by two years, and researchers were not as concerned about strictly adhering to ethical guidelines prior to the debate on ethics in psychological research that followed Milgram's study.

The children were distressed during the study. They were deliberately frustrated in stage two when they were told that the really good toys were to be reserved for other children. We know this was significantly upsetting for some of them because the experimenter had to stay with each child in room three, since some of them were upset and refused to stay on their own or wanted to leave before the allotted time was up. The children were therefore encouraged (coerced?) to continue with the study when they clearly did not want to. This implies that they did not have the right to withdraw.

There is the problem of whether or not the children suffered any long-term consequences as a result of the study. It would have not been possible to debrief the children as they would not have understood what had happened, and it would be very difficult for the researchers to undo any harm that had been caused by the study. Although it is unlikely that taking part in the study made the children significantly more aggressive in the future, we can never be certain. This is one of the major problems with any sort of study which involves looking at the origins of aggressive behaviour.

Is the study useful?

The study is useful to psychology in that it demonstrates observational learning in practice and shows how the different models affected the children.

In terms of applications to real-life settings, Bandura's work has been described as the first in a series of scientific studies into media violence. Later studies used video footage of Bobo-bashing as well as 'live' models. However, Bandura himself warned against interpreting his results as evidence of copycat TV violence, cautioning that learning does not necessarily lead to performance. We must be careful, therefore, not to assume that just because there are violent programmes on TV, these behaviours will be copied in the real world.

The study's results show us that there is a clear difference between the aggressive behaviour of boys and girls. But can this difference be attributed to biology or socialisation? Is it that boys have biological differences, such as higher levels of the male hormone testosterone, which make them more aggressive? Is it that both boys and girls are clearly taught sex-appropriate behaviours by their parents, teachers and the media from an early age, and this accounts for why boys are more aggressive than girls? Bandura *et al.*'s study fails to shed any light on this.

If we are to make any use of studies that look at aggressive behaviour, it is important to answer a key question – is aggression largely learned or largely innate? If it is innate, this is very difficult to change; whereas if aggression is largely learned, then presumably it could be unlearned, or we could address how we socialise our children in order to reduce their aggression or channel their aggressive behaviour into constructive rather than destructive actions.

Validity and reliability of the study

In terms of its internal validity, the study could be said simply to be looking at how children learn to be aggressive towards an inflatable doll, and not at how they acquire general aggressive behaviours. The fact that the object of aggression was not human may also limit the generalisability of the results to aggressive behaviour towards people in the real world. A Bobo doll is supposed to be punched and hit. What if the adult had been aggressive towards a toy that would not usually elicit aggressive play? What if the adult had torn the arms and legs off a cute teddy bear? Would the results have been the same, do you think?

The study introduces the concept of inter-observer reliability (see Results section, above). This is important in establishing objectivity in observational research.

In terms of explaining the acquisition of aggressive behaviour, the study lacks ecological validity. Children are very rarely in a room with a strange adult on their own. If they are, it would be unusual for the adult not to engage the child in conversation, or vice versa. Children tend to learn from adults and peers they know and who can offer their opinions and approval of what is going on; they were isolated from this experience in this study.

Freud study: Little Hans

Phobias and the unconscious mind

The development of a phobia is not as simple as it might first appear. Freud's explanation for the development of a phobia relates directly to his theory of child development. It also links to his belief that much of our behaviour is the result of the unconscious, which, unbeknown to us, affects the way we behave. In order to make sense of this, we need to look in some detail at the weird and wonderful world of Sigmund Freud.

Freud is often described by his critics — and those who do not really understand much about him — as a complete 'nutcase' and 'sex-mad'. He did have some unusual ideas, which can seem very strange, but he must be commended for being the first person to make the point that things which we are not consciously aware of can have quite a strong influence on our behaviour.

Figure 4.11 Sigmund Freud

Imagine you are a small boy of three years who is regularly beaten with a large cane. It does not matter what you do, you always seem to be in trouble, and every time you are in trouble, your father beats you. He keeps the cane in a cupboard in the dining room, and just before he actually beats you, he whips the air a couple of times with the cane, just to make the point that it is going to hurt. One day, on his way home from work, your father has an accident in his car and dies. Never again are you beaten, and over the course of the next few years the memory fades, until you can hardly remember your father, let alone the caning.

You are now 20, and are at a mate's house, where you have somehow been roped into helping him to sort out his shed. In the corner are some canes which have been used to support plants, although you have not noticed these. Your mate gets one of them and whips the air with it behind your back. Suddenly you feel this horrific feeling of coldness coming over you and all the hairs on the back of your neck stand on end. You are not aware of why the noise provoked such an extreme response because you have no recollection of being beaten when you were small. But the repressed memory has remained in your unconscious and is triggered by the sound.

Repression

The story above is an example of how Freud theorised that the memories we have of painful or embarrassing incidents are pushed into our unconscious as our body's way of making it possible for us to cope with them. This can also happen with frightening experiences, or when we are so ashamed of something we have done that in order to prevent ourselves from continual suffering, we push the memory into the deep recesses of our mind. Freud claimed that memories which are painful or damaging are often repressed, rather than forgotten, and therefore they can continue to have an effect on our behaviour without us having any conscious awareness of why.

Key concept

The psychodynamic perspective
The psychodynamic perspective comes from the theories of Freud and focuses on the importance of the unconscious mind. The psychodynamic (or psychoanalytical) perspective holds that behaviour is determined by our past experiences, which have been stored in our unconscious mind.

Freud believed that the mind is made up of three different levels: the conscious, the preconscious and the unconscious.

- The conscious consists of the thoughts that we are attending to which are currently in the mind.

- The preconscious consists of information and ideas which can be retrieved easily from memory and brought into our conscious awareness.

- The unconscious consists of information which is very hard (or even impossible) to bring into conscious awareness.

It is important to remember that Freud lived in a time of Victorian morality, where many aspects of our natural drives were considered base and crude. Consequently, people had far more reason to feel guilty than they would today. Perhaps some of his theories were a way of trying to explain these instincts as natural and normal. On the other hand, he was an unusual man and had many strange aspects to his personality, including the unerring belief that he was right in his ideas (a trait which often accompanies an innate lack of confidence – if you have confidence in yourself, you do not mind being wrong from time to time). He was also obsessive in his interests, very neat, tidy and controlled in his behaviour, and perhaps these traits gave him a sort of security.

Freud's background

Freud was born in Freiberg, Moravia in 1856, but lived for most of his life in Vienna. His father was a Jewish wool merchant who had been trading in Moravia, but on account of a failing business he moved his family, first to

Leipzig and then to Vienna. Life was not easy for the family as there was a great deal of anti-Jewish feeling, yet they managed to survive on a meagre income. In 1873, at the age of 17, Freud attended the University of Vienna, where he studied medicine, although he did not graduate until March 1881.

Freud spent three years gaining experience as a clinical neurologist at the Vienna General Hospital and the Salpêtrière Hospital in Paris. It was in Paris that he worked for the neurologist Jean Charcot, who had a keen interest in hysterical illnesses. In April 1886 Freud opened his own medical practice in Vienna and married Martha Bernays later that year. They were extremely poor in the early years, but the marriage lasted for 53 years and Martha bore him six children, the youngest of whom was Anna Freud, born in 1895.

While treating his patients, Freud realised that some of them had what appeared to be real symptoms which had no physical basis (known as hysteria or hysterical illnesses). He became interested in what it was that caused these illnesses, which seemed to be more common in women. As part of his search to find an explanation, he was influenced by Charcot's ideas. Charcot taught that in order to understand hysteria he should look at psychology rather than physiology, and he demonstrated the use of hypnosis as a way of gaining access to the underlying psychological causes for these symptoms. It seemed that many of the 'hysterical' patients had something troubling them which they had repressed, such as a painful memory. Once they admitted their concerns, the symptoms seemed to disappear.

Freud also met and became friends with Josef Breuer, who used a different method of treating hysterical illness, which simply involved allowing the patient, in a totally safe and non-judgemental situation, to talk freely about his or her thoughts and feelings. Breuer believed that through this process, the problems would ultimately surface and, once expressed, would provide a kind of catharsis, or release, which would ultimately 'cure' the patient of his or her symptoms. Freud started to use Breuer's methods, as he thought this was a way for his patients to gain access to the things they did not want to talk about, the things they had buried in the deepest recesses of their minds.

Freud was totally committed to his work, practising as a therapist during the day and writing well into the night. Despite the unpopularity of his theories, his contributions to the world of psychoanalysis comprised 24 volumes. He was obviously an extremely intelligent man, although he was obsessive about his work and his private life, and he could be quite obstinate and very self-opinionated. He believed that his ideas were right and he was very intolerant of those who disagreed with him, which resulted in him losing many of his friends. Freud finally fled Austria for London after the Nazi invasion in 1937 and, despite a long battle, died of cancer in 1939.

The structure of the mind

As we have seen, Freud believed that the mind is comprised of three parts: the area we are consciously aware of; the preconscious; and the unconscious mind. He believed that there was no point attempting to gain direct access to the unconscious mind because not only were people unable to do this, but they were probably not even aware of its existence. However, he did believe that when people were not thinking, they often gave away information, for example, when they made slips of the tongue. This is what happens when you call your teacher 'Mum', or call a recent boy/girlfriend by the name of the person you were dating previously.

Freud started to use different techniques, such as dream analysis, as a way of gaining access to the unconscious mind with the patients he saw with hysterical symptoms. Remember, many of these were young women. Freud unexpectedly discovered that some of them had suffered from sexual abuse as children. What you must remember was that when Freud was practising, 'sex' as we know it today did not exist. It was not considered proper for women to enjoy sex, for example. Sex was only for making babies as far as women were concerned. Men, on the other hand, had carnal desires, and if these were not met by their wife, they would have to take cold showers or seek some kind of solace elsewhere – often with 'ladies of the night'.

Can you imagine the predicament Freud found himself in? He could not blatantly admit that these eminent gentlemen, the fathers or brothers of his female patients, had abused them, and yet this was what he had discovered. He decided to present his findings in 1896, when he gave a lecture on the aetiology of hysteria. He explained that during therapy with patients who had suffered previously unexplained hysteria, it had emerged that they had been sexually abused in childhood, either by an adult or an older sibling, and that until they had had therapy they had been unaware of this. The trouble was that the people Freud was speaking to, who were very influential, responded to his finding with horror and disbelief (or even denial). Freud had to try to rectify the situation he now found himself in and return to a position of favour, so he replaced his theory the following year with what he called the 'Oedipus complex'. What happened, he claimed, was that the abuse was in the mind of the child – a fantasy rather than a reality, and if there was physical evidence of abuse, for example, a pregnancy, he explained this away by saying that the fantasy must have become so powerful that the child had initiated the sexual contact themselves.

The id, ego and superego – the tripartite personality

Returning to Freud's idea that a large part of the mind is unavailable to our conscious awareness, we can see how this links up with his theory of the adult personality, which has three basic parts: the **id**, the **ego** and the **superego**. The ego is the only part that we are actually aware of, although the other two try their best to influence our conscious awareness.

Freud tried to explain the workings of the mind in a purely physiological way, although he realised it was not that simple and that the workings of the mind change and evolve over time. He believed that when we are born, we are driven by what he called the **pleasure principle**, which means that we want to have lots of pleasure and avoid anything nasty. This pleasure principle, or id, consists of primitive desires and primeval urges, which are often reflexes, so contain no logical or rational thought. Imagine a small child in the supermarket. He wants sweeties and he wants them now, no matter what state his mother is in. He does not care about how she feels because he is totally egocentric and driven by his

own desires. We all retain these desires and urges, and, ideally, we would all like our desires to be met *now*, not next week or next year. Most of us, however, find ways of dealing with our id.

How do we do this? The next part of the personality to develop is what Freud called the ego. This operates according to what is known as the **reality principle**. As we start to operate in the real world, we begin to realise that we cannot always have what we want when we want it. So we work out ways of achieving what we want, by waiting for an appropriate moment for example; this comes from our experiences and interactions with others. The ego has no moral basis; it does not consider the moral rights and wrongs of behaving in certain ways, although it does take into account what is and is not acceptable to other people. It realises that if we do follow our desires, we may be excluded by others and this would be pretty awful too (and might make matters worse in the long run). So it tries to satisfy the 'child' within us, in a realistic and acceptable way.

Have you considered where our morals come from? Perhaps Bandura would argue that we learn our moral code of behaviour by observing the behaviour of others, although Freud would disagree. He claimed that the little voice like a parent, which comes to most of us when we are about to do something wrong, is the part of the personality called the superego. It develops as we start to internalise the rules and regulations of our parents and the society in which we live, so it becomes a kind of 'internal parent'. We will look at how this happens in the next section, when we will consider the moral development of the child in slightly more detail. For the moment, it is sufficient to realise that in many ways the superego is as unrealistic as the id. If we always behaved according to a strict set of moral rules, we would become rigid and inflexible.

Freud says that the ego's job is to maintain a state of 'dynamic equilibrium' between these three parts. It has the position of trying to balance them out and satisfy the demands of both the id and the superego. One of the best descriptions of Freud's construct of the personality comes from Nicky Hayes (1994), who claims that the relationship between the three parts is like 'A battle between a sex-crazed monkey and a maiden aunt, being refereed by a rather nervous bank clerk!'

Freud's developmental theory

Freud's theory is called a psychodynamic theory because he claimed that there are psychological forces (psycho) that move or drive us forwards (dynamic) to do things. These are innate instincts. Freud identified two instinctive driving forces. The first is known as Eros, the life instinct, whose main active component is the sexual drive or libido. The second is Thanatos, the death instinct, and its main active component is aggression, towards ourselves and others. Freud initially ignored the aggressive instinct, but found it hard to explain the dreadful loss of life and carnage of the First World War, so he later incorporated Thanatos as a representation of our innate destructiveness and aggression.

Freud believed that the development of a child's personality is based on these biological drives, which evolve through a number of biologically determined stages. He believed that the strongest drive was the libido or sexual instinct, and he maintained that babies and young children are capable of sexual pleasure. (Perhaps the word 'sexual' is too strong here. It might be more appropriate to substitute 'sensual', because Freud was referring to physical pleasure from any area of the body, rather than simply the genitals, which is what adults tend to think of as sexual pleasure.)

Oral stage (0–15 months)

The first stage is the oral stage because the main areas of sensitivity and pleasure are the lips and mouth. The baby gets great pleasure in two ways from putting things in its mouth, even when it is not feeding. One is by sucking and swallowing, and the other is by biting and chewing. According to Freud, if the child's desires are satisfied, they are not left to cry for hours on end without food, and they are weaned at the right time, they will be fine. If, however, they are weaned at the wrong time, they will become 'orally fixated', which means that as adults they will have an excessive interest in oral gratification. They will either become compulsive eaters, drinkers or smokers, or constantly chew things like gum, pens and fingernails. If they get excessive amounts of pleasure from sucking and swallowing, they will become too trusting and gullible and easily fooled, whereas if they enjoyed biting and chewing more they would become sarcastic and verbally aggressive. In fact, Freud believed that these people even become incapable of personal love for others, with a tendency to treat people as objects to be used to fulfil their needs.

Figure 4.12 Freud believed children weaned at the wrong time would become 'orally fixated'

The evidence to support this stage is somewhat sparse. Kline and Storey (1977) found evidence for two different types of oral characters. The first group showed a cluster of traits which could be called oral optimism: sociability, dependability and a relaxed nature. The other group showed a different cluster called oral pessimism: independence, verbal aggression, envy, hostility, ambition and impatience. What we have to remember here is that we can never be sure whether these were a result of their oral experiences or something completely different!

Anal stage (1–3 years)

In this second stage, the sensitive area shifts from the mouth to the anus. According to Freud, the child now derives great pleasure from either expelling or retaining faeces. Although this seems rather weird, many children do have a fascination with their faeces, and when they first manage to go in a potty, they will often express interest and pleasure in what they have done.

During this stage the child is potty-trained, whereas before they could go when they liked, discreetly protected by the gentle comfort of clean nappies! Now the child learns that in order to get praise from its parents it has to behave in a certain way. No longer can it do as it pleases. This may well be the first type of condition that has been put on the child's behaviour, and it learns that there is a huge significance to defecating. Therefore, if the parents are very strict and overanxious about their child's bowel habits, the child will become excessively worried and frightened about going, and therefore will be an 'anal retentive'. The child will associate the normal functioning with messiness and dirt, and may become preoccupied with orderliness and cleanliness as a reaction to this. Freud claims that this trait will continue as the child gets older, becoming an adult who, instead of holding on to its faeces, will hold on to its possessions instead – in effect, a miser, hoarder or collector of some kind.

On the other hand, if the parents are extremely laid back and even overly lenient about the child's ability to use the potty, the child will go anywhere! This child will become an 'anal expulsive', who will grow up to be overgenerous, untidy and completely indifferent to material possessions. Again, these collections of traits are often found together and provide some support for his analysis, but the explanations he gives as to why they cluster together have received very little support.

Phallic stage (3–5 years)

Freud claimed that the area of sensuality shifts from the anus to the genitals when the child reaches the age of about three years. This is the time when children play with their genitals and become inquisitive as to the differences between little boys and little girls. It is also quite normal to see small boys with their hands tucked down the front of their trousers at this age, which you could say lends support to Freud's ideas. The thing is, fascination and comfort (which is the main reason why most little boys hold on to their genitals) are not necessarily the same as sexual interest.

The Oedipus complex and the Electra complex

It is during the Phallic stage that Freud believed the awareness of sex differences forms the basis of what he calls the Oedipus complex. He claimed that girls feel inferior to or jealous of boys because they have a penis, and that boys believe that because girls do not have a penis, they must have been castrated. During this stage, children also have intense emotions, usually directed at the parent of the opposite sex. (How many males actually believe that girls are really castrated boys? Most will say that the thought has never entered their heads, although Freud would say that they were repressing their memories, so of course they would not be able to recollect the idea!)

Before we talk about the Oedipus complex, it might be useful to explain who Oedipus was, for those of you who are not familiar with Greek mythology. Oedipus was the son of the King of Thebes, but an oracle prophesied that Oedipus would kill his father. In order to prevent this happening, his father ordered him to be put to death. He was rescued by a shepherd and was brought up unaware of his identity. One day, when he was on the road to Thebes, he quarrelled with a man and accidentally killed him, not realising that this man was his father. He was made King of Thebes as a result of an act of bravery against a mythical creature called the Sphinx, and subsequently married Jocasta, not realising that she was his mother. When he found out who she was, he gouged out his eyes.

As a result of this relationship between Oedipus and his mother, Freud coined the term 'Oedipus complex' to describe the situation which occurs when boys develop an intense attachment to their mothers.

It is often the case that little boys become quite clingy to their mothers at this age (and often the same is true of girls with their fathers, but we will stick with small boys for the moment). Freud believed that this attachment becomes increasingly intense and causes the boy to regard his father as a rival, especially as the father sleeps with the mother and has the closeness and familiarity with her that the boy would like. However, the boy also sees his father as a powerful and threatening figure who has the ultimate power to deal with this rivalry – namely to castrate him. The small boy is caught at this point between desire for his mother and fear of his father's power.

What we must remember here is that the boy does not have real sexual feelings that we recognise as adults. Most of these feelings are unconscious and cause a kind of internal conflict or anxiety which the small boy has to deal with. Anxiety is an unpleasant state, and we strive for much of our lives to find ways to reduce our feelings of anxiety, no matter how they are caused. Freud claimed that the boy deals with the situation by using a defensive process called sex-role identification. The boy will start to identify with his father and repress any further feelings he has for his mother into his unconscious. He will begin to spend more time with his father, wanting to be like daddy, and this in turn will reduce any further chance of being castrated, as his father will no longer see him as a rival. Through this process he will internalise his father's moral standards and this is the core of the child's superego.

The Electra complex

So what about girls? The Electra complex is the supposed female equivalent, occurring in girls between the ages of three and six years, and manifested by the excessive attachment of little girls to their fathers and corresponding hostility to their mothers. The term 'Electra complex' also comes from Greek mythology. Electra, daughter of the Greek leader Agamemnon, was famous for her devotion and loyalty to her father, who was murdered by her mother and her mother's lover. In order to avenge the death of her beloved father, Electra, with her younger brother's help, murdered the mother she detested, as well as her mother's lover.

The problem was that Freud had not clearly worked out the female side of this developmental process – probably because he found women puzzling throughout his life. The course of the Electra complex goes something like this: the girl will be very close to her mother when she is little, until she discovers that she does not have a penis. This makes her feel inferior and she blames her mother for allowing her to be castrated. She does realise that one way she can feel equal to men is by producing a baby (and this is all from the age of three years!), and she sees her father as a potential impregnator, allowing her to have a child of her own as a substitute for the missing penis. She will therefore transfer her affections from the mother to the father.

Why this happens is the main problem with the Electra complex. Boys renounce their feelings for their mother because of the fear of castration by their father, but this cannot be the case with girls, who have already been 'castrated' by their mothers. Freud suggested that males feel that their penis is the thing they value most in the world, but the thing that girls value is loss of love. If the girl continues with her desire to have a relationship with her father she is likely to lose the love of her mother, so she will renounce her feelings for her father and do her best to make her mother love her by being a good girl. The problem is, the fear on the girl's part would be far less (according to Freud) than the boys' fear, and this led him to suggest that girls have a much less developed superego.

Latency stage (around five years to puberty)

The sexual drives seem to be removed from consciousness during the latency stage, although they are still there. According to Freud, the child has repressed its memories of the earlier sexual impulses by a phenomenon called infantile amnesia. The child redirects the drives into intellectual development and social activities as it learns about the world beyond the family. The friendships it makes tend to be with children of the same sex, which helps the child to deal with any possible sexual thoughts. The problem with this idea is that children from other cultures, where sexual activity is seen as acceptable, show interest in sexual matters throughout the whole of their childhood.

Genital stage (puberty onwards)

With puberty, there is a re-emergence of the earlier drives and the centre of attention is once again the genitals, although this time an adult expression of sexuality is shown through relationships with members of the opposite sex.

Evaluation of Freud's theory of child development

Freud's developmental theory has been challenged and criticised by many researchers, who claim that the theory is untestable. The theory itself was proposed in 1905, when Freud wrote 'Three essays on the theory of sexuality'. This was actually three years before writing about Little Hans (see core study, below), which suggests that his reporting was biased in order to back up his previously formed theory (that is, it was subject to demand characteristics). Freud only met Little Hans twice, and the rest of the information about the boy was reported to him by Little Hans's father, who was a supporter of Freud's ideas. This whole scenario could not be described as objective in any way, and it would be interesting to know how much information Little Hans's father actually missed out when reporting to Freud, as he may only have conveyed what he considered to be important.

If Freud was right, having a father (if you are a boy) is a prerequisite to developing morals, superego, appropriate sex-role behaviour, and so on. What happens to orphans and boys from single-parent families? Is it the case that every young boy without a father fails to develop any morals or an appropriate sex-role? There is considerable evidence from cross-cultural studies that children who are brought up in family groupings which are either extended or different to the two-parent family described by Freud show no problems with either moral or sex-role development.

Freud also claimed that the first five years of life are the most critical, but this almost implies that the rest of your life is irrelevant from a developmental viewpoint. Surely we go on learning from the experiences we have through the rest of our childhood and as adults? As we will see in Chapter 5, the plasticity of the brain's cortex means that new learning can take place over time – so is it not possible to rethink and relearn many of the misperceptions we had as children? We would not dispute that early childhood experiences can shape our lives as adults, but unless the experiences are very traumatic, most of us are a product of *all* our experiences, not just those which take place in the first five years of life.

The Study

S. Freud (1909) 'Analysis of a phobia in a five-year-old boy', in *The Pelican Freud Library, vol. 8, Case Histories 1* (1977) pp.169–306

Background

In the introduction which formed the background to the study, Freud talked about Little Hans and the origins of this particular case study. He acknowledged that Hans was not a normal child and had a predisposition to neurosis, so he realised that it might not be valid to generalise from him to all children. He also said that the argument that children are untrustworthy was unfair. Adults are untrustworthy because they are prejudiced and this might influence what they say. Children, on the other hand, may lie, but they lie for a reason, and this reason may well be one of the most important things to consider.

Hans was described as being a cheerful and straightforward child, but when he became 'ill' (by this Freud meant that he developed his phobia), it was obvious that there was a difference between what he said and what he actually thought. Freud suggested that this was because of things that were going on in his unconscious of which he was unaware. In order to put this right, Freud decided that Hans's behaviour had to be interpreted, and the boy had to be told why he was thinking and acting as he was. Freud was emphatic that this was not putting suggestions into the boy's mind, but was only a way of helping him to understand what already existed. This is the process of psychoanalysis, a form of talking cure used by Freud. The idea was for the client to talk freely, and the analyst would then be able to interpret the client's unconscious desires and anxieties, which would reveal themselves to the analyst in symbolic form, for example, in the client's fantasies and dreams.

Aim

The aim of this case study is to document the case of Little Hans, who developed a phobia of horses. It was used by Freud to support his ideas about the origins of phobias and his belief that they are often influenced by unconscious forces. He also used it to support his ideas on psychosexual development and the Oedipus complex, and the effectiveness of psychoanalytical therapy.

The study reports the analysis of the boy's phobia, a process which was intended to cure him of this 'illness'. It also shows how Freud explained Little Hans's behaviour in terms of an unconscious Oedipal conflict.

Method and design

A case study was carried out longitudinally over a period of months.

Procedure

This case study and the analysis was actually conducted by Little Hans's father, a friend and supporter of Freud. Freud met the boy only twice, on one occasion for a therapeutic session and on another when he paid a social visit to deliver a birthday present to the boy.

The father reported on the boy's behaviour via correspondence (including his own interpretations), and Freud gave directions as to how to deal with the situation, based on his interpretations of the father's written reports and conversations. Freud believed that the reason the analysis could progress

... continued

Key concept

Case study method

A case study is an in-depth study of one participant or a small group of participants, often carried out over an extended period of time (longitudinally). Within the case study method a number of different data-gathering techniques can be used. For example, recorded interviews, case notes (of therapeutic interviews, for example), observation (as in the Savage-Rumbaugh study on Kanzi in Chapter 3) and psychometric tests (which you will see in the study of multiple personality disorder in Chapter 6).

One of the strengths of the case study is its usefulness in describing atypical, abnormal or rare behaviour. In abnormal psychology the case study is seen as a useful way of exploring a participant's past experiences to help them deal with current difficulties. Freud's work derives predominantly from the case studies of his patients.

Another strength is that the data gathered is usually qualitative and rich in detail, so data from case studies can be highly valid. The bond of trust that can be built up between researcher and participant also means that the data is more likely to be valid than if the researcher were a stranger having only one interview with the participant.

However, this close bond between researcher and participant can be a weakness too, as the researcher may lose their objectivity because of their personal relationship with the participant. Their interpretations of data may also be affected by biases formed as a result of their long-term investment in the project. Another weakness of this method is the fact that replication is not usually possible, particularly where a therapeutic approach has been taken. This makes it difficult to establish the reliability of findings from a case study.

Generalising from the findings of case studies can also be difficult, as the cases selected for study are often unusual or even unique. Case studies can be costly in terms of both time and money.

using this kind of method was because the father and son had a very special and close relationship.

It is important to note that Hans's father had been making notes on the boy's behaviour and sending these to Freud for a number of years. Freud had asked all his friends with young children to observe and record their behaviour in order to confirm his theory of psychosexual development.

It is also pertinent to point out that Hans's mother had been a patient of Freud's and had met Hans's father through Freud.

The first information that Freud thought was interesting was Hans's interest in his 'widdler' (penis) when he was three years old. Hans thought everyone had a widdler, males and females alike, and that the only things that did not have widdlers were inanimate objects. He even thought his baby sister, Hanna, who he was told had been brought by a stork when Hans was 3½, had simply not grown hers yet. Hans liked playing with his widdler, which is quite normal for small boys. However, as this behaviour is often frowned upon, parents tried to discourage their children from masturbating, and Hans's mother was no different.

When he was 3½, Hans's mother found him with his hand on his penis. She threatened him with these words: 'If you do that, I shall send for Dr A. to cut off your widdler. And then what'll you widdle with?' Hans's reply, 'With my bottom', suggests that he was none too perturbed by his mother's threat!

His interest in widdlers was quite extensive; he tried to see other people's widdlers and liked showing his off. He even said to his parents that he wanted to see theirs, and Freud explained that this was probably because he wanted to see how theirs compared to his. Hans thought his mother must have a widdler 'like a horse' and presumably thought that as he got bigger, his would grow too. In fact, much of the focus of his dreams and fantasies during this time concerned widdlers and what they do.

Hans wanted his father 'out of the way' so he could have his mother to himself and sleep with her. This idea had come from spending

... continued

lots of time with her when his father was away one summer. He had become apprehensive and nervous about things and had been comforted by his mother, who cuddled him in bed. He enjoyed her attention and probably resented having to share her again on his father's return. In fact, Freud believed that he attempted to seduce his mother when he was 4½, by asking her why she would not put her finger on his penis when she was putting talcum powder on him after a bath. She answered that it was not proper, but according to Freud he had 'found an incidental channel of discharge' for his sexual feelings towards her and this resulted in his 'masturbating every evening, and in that way obtaining gratification'.

Freud claimed that Hans feared that another baby might come (more competition?), but suppressed this anxiety, only to have it surface in another form – a fear of the bath. Hans had said he was worried about drowning in the big bath, having previously been bathed in a baby bath. Freud suggested that this fear came from being frightened that if he was naughty his mother would not love him anymore and therefore might let him drown. Hans also expressed jealousy towards his sister and was asked the following question: 'When you were watching Mummy giving Hanna her bath, perhaps you wished she would let go of her so that Hanna should fall in?' Hans answered 'Yes' to this question, which confirmed Freud's idea that this was evidence of his death wish towards Hanna.

Hans's father wrote to Freud, describing the fact that Hans had developed an irrational fear that a horse would bite him in the street, and that the fear was in some way connected to being frightened by a large penis. His father believed that this was the onset of the illness, and that there was a motive for being ill – he wanted to stay with his mother and never be separated from her, which was the result of a dream where his mother had gone away.

Figure 4.13 Hans had an irrational fear of horses

This irrational fear probably developed from two events: overhearing a father say to his child, 'Don't put your finger to the white horse or it will bite you', and seeing a horse which was pulling a carriage, fall down and flail about in the road. It affected Hans sufficiently to make him fear that a horse would come into the room. Freud suggested that there was a connection between putting a finger towards the horse that may actually be bitten and the event when his mother would not touch his penis with her finger after giving him a bath. This connection had something to do with Hans's knowledge that his parents thought masturbation was not a very good behaviour to indulge in. In fact, Hans's father said to him, 'If you don't put your hand to your widdler anymore, this nonsense of yours will soon get better.'

Freud also suggested that Hans's desire to see his mother's widdler was increasing. At this point, his father told him that women did not have widdlers. Hans may have made the association between his mother's threat to castrate him if he did not stop playing with himself and her lack of widdler. Perhaps she was in fact a castrated man who had played with hers too much in the past and had suffered the consequences!

Freud began to make the connection between Hans's father and Hans's fear of horses, and he started to think that this was a symbolic representation of the boy's fear of his father punishing him as a result of his longing for his mother. This connection was made after Freud was informed about a daydream the boy had had: the fantasy of the two giraffes.

... continued

The fantasy of the two giraffes

Hans: In the night there was a big giraffe in the room and a crumpled one, and the big one called out because I took the crumpled one away from it. Then it stopped calling out, and then I sat down on top of the crumpled one …

Hans demonstrated what he meant by crumpling up a piece of paper. Hans also explained that he had not dreamed about the giraffe.

Hans: No, I didn't dream. I thought it. I thought it all. I'd woken up earlier.

He then went on to explain that he knew you can't really squash a giraffe with your hands, but explained that he had picked

Figure 4.14

up the crumpled giraffe and held it in his hands until the big one had stopped calling out. Once that had happened, he again explained that he sat down on the small crumpled giraffe.

Father: Why did the big one call out?

Hans: Because I'd taken the little one away from it.

This fantasy was recognised by the father as a re-enactment of what happened in the morning when Hans climbed into bed with his parents. Often his father objected and Freud believed that he was represented by the big giraffe, who was calling out because Hans had taken the little giraffe (mother) away. There was also some discussion about whether the long neck of the giraffe represented a penis, but this was denied by Hans.

It was at this point that Freud himself chose to see Hans and asked him about his fear of horses. Freud suggested to the boy that the horse must represent Hans's father. Hans must be frightened of his father because he was jealous of him and felt hostile towards him (as outlined in Freud's Oedipus complex). The reason why Freud made this analogy between the horse and Hans's father was because Hans mentioned the black on horses' mouths and the things in front of their eyes (blinkers). Hans's father had a black moustache and wore glasses.

Hans explained that he was also frightened of horses biting him, as well as being afraid of loaded carts and buses, which was interpreted as having some kind of analogy with pregnancy, a 'loaded' body which would deliver a competitor for his mother's affections. He then told Freud about seeing the horse fall down and kick about with its feet, which terrified him because he thought the horse was dead and this led him to think that all horses would fall down. Hans's father suggested that when Hans saw the horse fall down he must have wished that his father would fall down and die in the same way. According to Freud, Hans's behaviour towards his father after this 'confession' became much less fearful, and he was much more boisterous and overbearing. He did, however, retain his fear of horses.

Hans then developed a preoccupation with his bowels and *lumf* (German for 'faeces'). He had been in the habit of accompanying his mother or the maid to the toilet until he was forbidden to do so. His father identified another analogy, between a heavily loaded cart and a body loaded with faeces. Then Hans started to talk about Hanna, and his father concluded that the reason for the train of thought was because he thought his sister was *lumf* and was born in the same way as we produce *lumf*. This led to the analogy between loaded carts and pregnancy, horses falling over and giving birth: 'the falling horse was not only his dying father but also his mother in childbirth'. He then described

... continued

an imaginary friend called Lodi, who was called after *saffalodi*, a German sausage. This time, Hans's father pointed out that the sausage looked like *lumf*.

The final fantasies Hans produced at the end of his conflicts focused on plumbers and being a parent himself. The first fantasy involved a plumber who 'took away my behind with a pair of pincers and then gave me another, and then the same with my widdler'. Hans's father's interpretation of this was that the body parts were replaced with bigger ones, like his, which meant that Hans wanted to be like his father.

The second fantasy was that Hans was the father of his own children (his mother was now his wife), and his father was their grandfather, in other words, no longer a threat to the boy as a result of his affection for his mother.

This was the final piece of 'evidence' which showed that the Oedipus conflict was the cause of Hans's problems, and that once he had acknowledged his desires towards his mother (which he did symbolically in his fantasies), his problems would be resolved.

Discussion

The discussion focuses on the fact that this study offers support for Freud's theory of sexuality – the Oedipus complex:

* Hans was jealous of his father's relationship with his mother and frightened of him (castration fear), symbolised by a fear of fingers being bitten by horses.
* Hans fantasised about taking his mother away from his father (giraffe fantasy).
* Hans tried to seduce his mother by asking her why she didn't touch his widdler when she was powdering him after a bath.
* Hans finally admitted he wanted to marry his mother, and played a game where he was father to her children.
* Resolution came with wanting to be like his father (the plumber removing his widdler and behind and giving him bigger ones).

Commentary: Methods and issues

Research method, design and data gathering

The case study method was used, with the child being interviewed and a great deal of emphasis being placed on his self-reporting of dreams and fantasies. It was a longitudinal design.

One of the biggest weaknesses of case studies is that contact with the participant over time may well lead to extreme subjectivity. This case study was even more subjective because the child was being 'treated' by his father (emotional involvement), who was a strong Freud supporter (biased), and his mother had been treated by Freud before her marriage (it would be interesting to know why she was treated).

Perhaps some of the interpretations made were because the father was preoccupied with matters sexual or physical. After all, it was Hans's father who suggested that a German sausage looked like *lumf* (faeces). Maybe a sausage is just a sausage if you have never heard of Freud's psychosexual theory of development! Hans's mother and father eventually divorced and both remarried. Between the ages of six and 19 years, Hans lived with his father, while his sister went with their mother. Perhaps the relationship between the father and mother was somewhat strained during the time when Hans became phobic, and in fact the father was projecting his own preoccupations on to his son.

Is the study useful?

Little Hans was the only child studied by Freud. When he met Hans, Freud had already formulated his theory of the Oedipus complex, which supports the idea that his report on Hans was extremely biased. Hans was probably quite normal, but became 'phobic' about horses because of a traumatic event which might well have frightened any small boy. It is quite likely that his fear of horses had absolutely nothing to do with his father, but that this idea was introduced and stuck in Hans's memory.

Freud believed that phobias are the result of hidden conflicts in the unconscious mind, and he interpreted everything on that basis. His questioning of Hans can therefore be understood as a way of getting at the unconscious mind and trying to resolve what he saw as a potential cause of trouble for the boy as he got older. Hans's agreement with many of the interpretations offered to him indicated to his father and Freud that they were correct in their beliefs about the origin of his phobia and the Oedipus complex. Hans's final fantasies about wanting to marry and have children with his mother was the final confirmation they needed.

Another way we could interpret the findings of this study would be to suggest that the boy was suffering from what John Bowlby (a famous child psychoanalyst) called 'separation anxiety'. Bowlby was interested in the effects of early experiences on the emotional development of children. He identified the extreme adverse effects on a child of separation from the mother figure, claiming that 'mother love in infancy and childhood is as important for mental health as are vitamins and proteins for physical health' (Bowlby, 1951). He suggested that if a child had been parted from its mother at some time, the child would experience extreme separation anxiety in case the situation happened again, and this intense anxiety would affect their ability to function effectively.

Hans's mother frequently made alarming threats to Hans to make him behave, such as beating him with a carpet beater. His fear of castration was founded on firm ground – after all, his mother had threatened him with castration when he would not stop fiddling with his penis. She also threatened to leave the family, which would have made him quite insecure, and consequently he may have become very possessive and clingy. Hans was actually kept away from his mother when Hanna was born, and this must have made the situation worse. Because he was frightened that his mother might leave him, he would have felt very angry and unhappy with regard to his mother. However, knowing that it is not right to be fearful or angry with your mother, he may have projected those feelings on to something else – horses. This idea is illustrated in the following conversation, when Hans talked about a fantasy he had that he had taken a horse out of the stable:

> **Father:** You took it out of the stables?
> **Hans:** I took it out because I wanted to whip it.
> **Father:** Which would you really like to beat – Mummy, Hanna or me?
> **Hans:** Mummy.
> **Father:** Why?

Hans: I should just like to beat her.
Father: When did you ever see someone beating their Mummy?
Hans: I've never seen anyone do it, never in all my life.
Father: And yet you'd just like to do it?
Hans: With a carpet beater.

As there are other explanations for the cause of Hans's phobia, we have to question the validity of Freud's interpretation, and this affects its usefulness. In fact, Freud's theory of psychosexual development is considered to be a nice story, but not an accurate description of personality development.

Despite the fact that Freud's theory of child development is without supporters today, very few people question the major contribution that Freud made to our understanding of behaviour, by describing the influence of unconscious motivation on behaviour and interpreting the purpose and meaning of dreams. In this way, Freud's theories have been highly generative and there is no doubt that he should be numbered among the great minds of the twentieth century. Whether we can count the case of Little Hans among his greatest works, however, is unlikely.

Does the study raise any ethical issues?

Whether you think this case study was good or bad, Hans actually came out of it seemingly unscathed, although we cannot be sure that he would not have been fine anyway (i.e. without any psychoanalysis). When he was 19, Hans met Freud and told him that he was well and that he had no troubles or inhibitions. He also claimed to have no memory of the discussions with his father or Freud which took place during his childhood, and that he got on well with both parents, despite their break-up, but missed his younger sister. However, we can never be sure whether this was really true, or because he was repressing the memory.

We must remember that this case study was intended to support the Oedipus complex which replaced Freud's earlier 'seduction theory'. The change from believing that the parent was responsible for child sexual abuse, to suggesting that it was a fantasy in the mind of the child, however, was responsible for society's reluctance to acknowledge how widespread such abuse really was. Even if there was some overt physical evidence of abuse, such as a pregnancy, the child would be blamed. In this respect, it would have been better if Freud had stuck to his original ideas. This suggests that Freud's work may have done more harm than good.

Validity and reliability of the study

As with all self-report data, there can be problems with validity. On the one hand, Freud suggested that children's memories were in fact quite accurate, but the next minute he was making some fairly stunning leaps by reinterpreting what Hans said to give it a different meaning. Perhaps Hans's memory was originally quite accurate, but the introduction of new interpretations by his father (and Freud) may have affected his subsequent memory of events, or clouded his interpretation of them. In fact, the whole study brings new meaning to the idea of leading questions.

Key concept

Leading questions

We came across leading questions in the Loftus and Palmer study on eyewitness testimony in Chapter 3. Their definition is as follows: 'A leading question is simply one that, by its form or content, suggests to the witness what answer is desired or leads him to the desired answer.'

In Freud's study of Little Hans, Hans's father uses leading questions in his analysis of the boy. (e.g. 'When the horse fell over, did you think of your daddy?' Hans replies, 'Perhaps. Yes. It is possible.')

This is a problem, as it means that the child is being influenced by his father's expectations, which in this instance are very much in tune with Freud's theory of child development, and this means that the findings are not objective.

Psychoanalysts claim that they cannot be judged by anyone except a psychoanalyst, because no one else would understand the procedures and would therefore be biased in some way. In effect, this makes their beliefs and profession unquestionable – perhaps we should simply accept that the case history of Little Hans is true, because until we are psychoanalysts ourselves, we cannot judge it!

5 Physiological psychology

You need to have some understanding of the structure of the nervous system because psychology also involves an understanding of physiology. If you are a biologist, you will have already some insight into how our bodies work and you will be familiar with the information in the next section (which is very basic). However, for those of you who have spent your time trying to ignore biology, hopefully this simplistic overview of the physiology of the nervous system will inspire you to go and find out more about the cutting edge of modern psychology: cognitive neuroscience.

In many ways it is very easy to forget the physical basis of all human behaviour – our bodies. Our bodies are the most amazing organisms, which are so complicated that it is likely we will never understand absolutely everything there is to know about them. There have also been many heated debates about whether our bodies are all there is to us, or whether we also have a spirit (or soul). If our bodies are all there is, when we die, we must cease to exist. On the other hand, if we also have a spirit, does that die with us or does it go on existing? This is known as the mind–body problem, which questions the basis of consciousness and existence itself. There seems to be no easy answer to this conundrum.

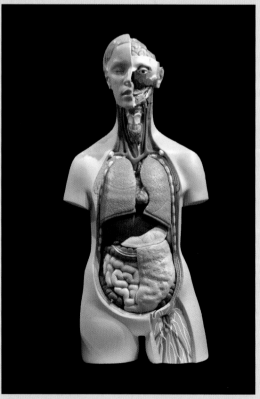

Figure 5.1 To understand psychology we must understand physiology

The physiology of the nervous system

The way the nervous system is structured is absolutely fascinating. It is so complex and each component is so tiny. With all the technological knowledge in the world, we have not yet been able to mimic much more than the most basic of human abilities. Humans can make assumptions that are correct on the basis of very little information; computers are far more likely to make errors. They cannot use information that is not clear, whereas we process the past, the present and what we know about the future, at the same time. That is not to say that we do not make errors; we just make far fewer than computers.

Cognitive psychology uses the information-processing approach, which makes the analogy between humans and computers to explain behaviour. This analogy is relevant not only because of the way both humans and computers process information, but also because both use electricity. Obviously we do not have to plug ourselves in to the mains, but we do work by a system of electrochemical changes, caused by external stimuli and by changes in our bodies.

The structure of the nervous system

The nervous system includes the central nervous system (CNS), which is the brain and spinal cord. This is the central control for all the activities of the body, where information received is processed and there is coordination of actions and reactions, both conscious and unconscious. The nervous system also includes the peripheral nervous system (PNS), which consists of a network of neurones which are located around the whole body and are responsible for carrying information from the world to the CNS, and from the CNS back to the different parts of the body. The PNS can also be subdivided into the somatic nervous system and the autonomic nervous system (ANS).

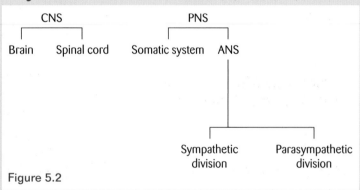

Figure 5.2

The somatic nervous system is the part that is generally conscious of the responses it is making. For example, the sensory nerves of the somatic system carry information about external stimulation from the different receptors to the CNS. The information is 'decoded', and messages are carried back from the CNS to the muscles of the body, where action is then taken in response. Therefore, the somatic part of the nervous system is responsible for all the muscles we use to make voluntary movements, as well as involuntary adjustments to posture and balance.

The nerves of the ANS run to and from the internal organs and are affected generally by information from inside the body (although occasionally they may respond to external information). The messages transmitted by the ANS regulate the function of these internal organs, such as heart rate, speed of respiration and digestion. It is called the autonomic nervous system because many of the activities it controls are autonomous and self-regulating, and these continue to take place even if a person is asleep or unconscious.

The ANS can be further subdivided into the sympathetic division and the parasympathetic division:

- The sympathetic division is the mechanism that speeds bodily systems up and prepares the organism for activity – it has an excitatory function. It is the fight/ flight mechanism which prepares the body for a response, for example, by speeding up the heart, dilating the arteries of the essential organs and constricting the arteries of the less essential organs, such as the skin and digestive organs. (We need more blood to the vital organs in order to survive. We do not need to digest things if we are running away – that can be done later.)

- The parasympathetic division is responsible for returning the body to normal by slowing it down again and allowing bodily functions to return to their original state – it is inhibitory.

In order for these actions to occur, neuronal fibres from both the sympathetic and parasympathetic divisions supply most organs, and the normal state of the body is maintained by a balance between these two systems.

What are neurones?

Neurones are the cells of the nervous system and are responsible for carrying messages from one part of the body to another. We have three types of neurone:

- sensory neurones

- motor neurones

- inter-neurones.

There are between ten and twelve billion neurones in the nervous system, which will give you an idea of how tiny they are. A nerve is actually a bundle of neurones (like a telephone cable), which are held together by glial cells. Glial cells are smaller cells than neurones and provide the neurones with nutrients and structural support.

The three different types of neurones all have different functions:

- Sensory neurones transmit impulses received by receptors to the central nervous system.

- Inter-neurones receive the signals from the sensory neurones and send impulses to other inter-neurones or to motor neurones. They are found only in the brain or the spinal cord.

- Motor neurones carry outgoing signals from the brain or spinal cord to the effector organs, such as the muscles or the heart and lungs.

All these neurones form connections with each other in order to carry information around the body by way of impulses, or electric messages. The messages or impulses that travel along our neurones can be thought of as bursts of electrical energy. We talk about these

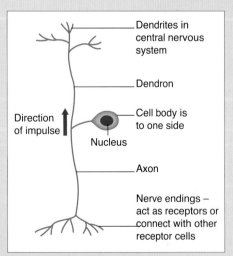

Figure 5.3 A simple diagram of an unbranched sensory motor neurone e.g. skin

Dendrites in central nervous system

Dendron

Cell body is to one side

Direction of impulse

Nucleus

Axon

Nerve endings – act as receptors or connect with other receptor cells bursts of electricity as bursts of fire. A single neurone 'fires' when the stimulation reaching it from other neurones exceeds a certain threshold. Imagine a number of drips falling from various branches of a tree into a large bath underneath – when the bath is full, a final drip will make it overflow. The firing of a neurone is just like this – the sum of lots of stimulation makes it reach a certain level, causing it to fire.

Some of these impulses are messages to do something (excitatory messages), and some are messages to remain inactive (inhibitory messages). The messages are passed from one neurone to another across what is known as a synaptic gap (a synapse is the junction between two nerve cells) by neurotransmitters which are actually chemical messengers. The whole process is extremely complex and it is not necessary for our purposes to go into the way synapses work. Sufficient to say, increases or decreases in the levels of neurotransmitters can affect the speed of message transmission, which, in turn, will affect the way a person thinks, reacts or responds physically to different situations. Many of the drugs that are used to change mood, such as antidepressants, affect the quantity or actions of neurotransmitters in the brain.

What sets these cells apart from other cells is their shape. From the central body of the neurone come lots of small, thin fibres called dendrites. Some are very short and others extend over long distances, with lots of branches. Consequently, the shape of a neurone can vary enormously, and it is the shape which dictates both the number of excitatory or inhibitory connections they make with other neurones, and how each one will contribute to the overall functioning of the organism, even though they all work in the same way. There are also different types of nerves: myelinated and non-myelinated. Some nerves need to transmit their messages over longer distances very quickly. This is when you would find myelinated nerves, which are nerves surrounded by a myelin sheath. The myelin allows the impulse to 'hop' along the neurone rather than running as a kind of wave, thus speeding up the transmission of the impulse. If the myelin breaks down, the impulse goes very slowly, or is lost altogether, which is what happens in conditions such as multiple sclerosis.

This should begin to give you an idea of the flexibility of the nervous system in terms of the number of connections that can be made between the many different components of the body. In fact, each neurone can make up to 10,000 connections with its neighbours.

If you imagine a set of roads converging, with roundabouts and junctions and flyovers, giving you unlimited choices as to where you can go, this should give you an idea of the range of connections that can be made with the increasing number of junctions between neurones. No single neurone creates thoughts or behaviours; it is the different patterns of activity that arise from the firing of millions of different neurones which result in different activities. In fact, even when a person thinks they are at rest (and neurones should be relatively quiet), if we were to scan the activity of the brain, we would see that the neurones still seem to be alive, with constantly changing interconnections. If you think how these patterns must increase and interconnect when we are engaged in any sort of task, from complex mental thought to physical activities, it will give you some idea of how active our brains must be. Every time we experience a sensation this will result in new neuronal connections being made, and this pattern will fade away unless the information relating to this experience is stored in our brains for a particular reason.

The brain

The area of the body where most of our neurones are located is the brain. In fact, the brain consists of nothing but millions of neurones. It is the most amazing wiring network, and different areas seem to be responsible for different things. It looks rather like a walnut, with lots of furrows or crevices, which are known as sulci. Just like a walnut, it is divided into two halves, called hemispheres. The left hemisphere controls most of the right-hand side of the body, and the right hemisphere controls the left-hand side.

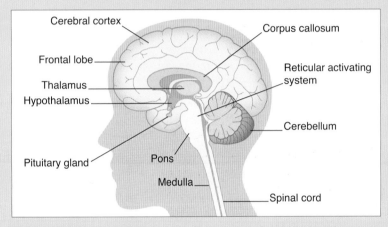

Figure 5.4 The main structure of the brain

Much of the evidence we have about which part of the brain is responsible for particular responses or activities, commonly known as 'localisation of function', comes from the investigation of individuals who have suffered some form of brain damage. If a certain area is damaged and results in a person being unable to perform a certain action, this would suggest that the damaged area is responsible for the non-function.

Each hemisphere has the equivalent of three layers: the hindbrain at the core, the midbrain and the forebrain (which contains the cerebral cortex). Although the cerebral cortex is the area most relevant to us, it is useful to have an overview of how the other structures of the brain assist in our day-to-day activities.

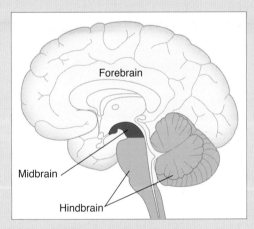

Figure 5.5 The three parts of the brain: the hindbrain, midbrain and forebrain

The hindbrain

The hindbrain consists of the cerebellum, the pons and the medulla. The cerebellum plays an important part in movement. It is where memories for automatic sequences of actions are stored and any damage to it will cause problems in movement, such as walking or the coordination of fine movements. The pons is a kind of bridge, or connection, between the two halves of the cerebellum. The medulla oblongata is the crossover point between the fibres from the brain and the spinal cord. The medulla also contains lots of vital reflex centres that control and regulate many of our basic bodily functions, such as the cardiovascular system and respiration.

The midbrain

The midbrain is smaller in humans and other mammals than in birds and reptiles. It is the top of the brainstem and connects the cerebral cortex (or forebrain) to the spinal cord and hindbrain. At its core is the reticular activating system (RAS), which brings sensory information from the spinal cord to the cerebral cortex and takes back motor information. It plays a very important part in maintaining or controlling levels of arousal and may even have an influence on personality. According to Eysenck (1970), people who fit the category of introverts have a high level of arousal in their RAS and therefore seek to reduce it, whereas extroverts have a low level of arousal and constantly seek to raise it, by choosing external situations which are 'busier' than their introvert counterparts. It is the RAS which influences our ability to pay attention selectively to different stimuli, as well as the way we become used to stimuli which are continuous and therefore not necessarily important. It also has a role in sleeping and waking, because it is when the level of activity in the RAS falls below a certain level that we fall asleep.

The brainstem

The brainstem, made up of the midbrain, pons and medulla, is the most primitive part of the brain and is estimated to have evolved more than 500 million years ago. It is often referred to as the reptilian brain because it controls the basic elements of life, with no higher-order thought processes. You cannot form a close, loving relationship with a reptile because it is incapable of thinking and feeling in the same way as even lower-order mammals such as rats and mice. It simply functions from day to day, with a heart that beats, lungs that inflate and deflate, and a maintained blood pressure level; it can move, fight, mate and produce other stereotypical behaviours which give it the ability to survive. Beyond that, none of the characteristics we associate with intelligent life exist, simply instinctive behaviours.

The forebrain

The forebrain is the largest and most obvious part of a mammal's brain. The outer layer is called the cerebral cortex and is made up of the cerebral hemispheres. Under the cortex are a number of other structures, including the thalamus, the hypothalamus, the pituitary gland, the basal ganglia, hippocampus and amygdala, some of which form what is known as the limbic system (involved in emotional behaviour, motivation and learning). The limbic system is a kind of centre where the more primitive parts of the brain join with the 'newer' cortex and integrate information from the outside world and the internal functioning of the body.

Although these individual structures do not concern us directly, they all have an influence on our behaviour and, for that reason, they are briefly described below.

- The thalamus works as a kind of relay station, linking sensory signals between the cerebral cortex and the sense organs.

- The hypothalamus helps to control the body's internal environment, such as temperature regulation, appetite and thirst. It also influences other motivated behaviours, such as sexual behaviour and emotional arousal levels. Eating disorders can be triggered by a disorder of the hypothalamus; if it is damaged, a person's internal temperature regulation may well be affected, making them overheat or feel extremely cold. The hypothalamus is also involved in the regulation of levels of hormones in the body and controls pituitary gland activity.

- The pituitary gland is actually an endocrine gland (producing hormones). It is attached to the base of the hypothalamus and responds to information from the hypothalamus to release hormones into the bloodstream. The secretions of the pituitary gland control the timing and amount of secretion by other endocrine glands.

- The basal ganglia play a part in voluntary movements.

- The hippocampus plays an important role in the laying down of new memories, so any damage seems to result in a lack of ability to store new information. According to Colin Blakemore (1988), it is the 'printing press' for our stored memories. The hippocampus is also linked to spatial memory, and recent research has indicated that lesions to the hippocampus affect our ability to remember the location of different things.

- The amygdala is important for feeding, drinking, sexual behaviour and aggression. If it is electrically stimulated in non-human animals, such as cats, they will either attack another individual or become very placid. What seems to happen is that it changes how animals interpret information and therefore affects their responses.

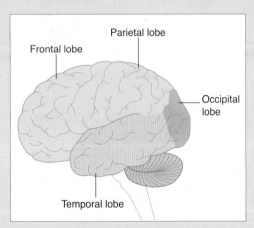

Figure 5.6 Lobes of the cerebral cortex

The cerebral cortex

The cerebral cortex itself, as we have seen, consists of two hemispheres, each receiving information from the opposite side of the body. The two sides, which are almost mirror images of each other, communicate via a tract of fibres called the corpus callosum. Each hemisphere is divided into four lobes, which are defined by major sulci.

The lobes of the cerebral cortex are:

- The **occipital lobes**, located at the back of the head, are the areas which receive the main input from the visual pathways. The rear of the lobe contains the primary visual cortex; if this is destroyed the person loses their sight.

- The **parietal lobes** are located between the occipital lobe and the central sulcus (which divides the parietal lobe from the frontal lobe). They are specialised to deal with information from the body such as touch and temperature, and help to interpret body position. They also play a part in vision; it has been found that damage in this area does not result in a failure of vision or touch, but produces disturbances in the integration and analysis of sensory information. A good example of this is the case of a man who had a tumour in his parietal lobe, and could recognise a clock as a clock, but could not tell the time from the position of the hands on the clock face.

- The **temporal lobes**, located on either side of the head, near the ears, receive information from the ears about sounds and balance. They also contribute to the more complex aspects of vision, such as face recognition. They play a part in emotion and motivation, and if they are damaged this may lead to extremes of emotional response. Wernicke's area is located in the temporal lobe on the left-hand side, and plays a critical role in language comprehension.

- Finally, the **frontal lobes** seem to be responsible for all the higher-order and more complicated functions, such as thinking, planning and forming ideas. They also play a part in memory formation and retention. Frontal lobes are said to contain our personalities; they contribute to our emotional responses and control our social inhibitions. This area is the last part of the brain to stop growing, and it continues to change even after birth, since the neuronal connections that are located here seem to continue forming. Broca's area is found in the left frontal lobe in humans and is critical for the production of language. People who have left-sided strokes (burst blood vessels in the left-hand side of the brain) often lose their ability to speak, and this would indicate that Broca's area has been affected.

The area directly to the rear of the central sulcus is known as the **sensory cortex** and is responsible for receiving any sensory information, such as touch, pressure, pain, smell and temperature. The area at the back of the frontal cortex, directly in front of the central sulcus, is the **primary motor cortex**. This area is responsible for movement, especially fine movement.

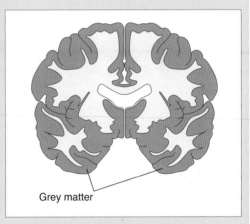

Grey matter

Finally, it will be useful for you to be familiar with the term 'grey matter', which you may have heard used when referring to the brain. Grey matter really does exist in the brain. It is a general term given to the regions of the brain and spinal cord that are made up mainly of cell bodies and dendrites of nerve cells, rather than myelinated axons, which look white. Grey matter includes the cerebral cortex, the central part of the spinal cord and the cerebellum and hippocampus.

Figure 5.7 This coronal section through the brain illustrates the areas of grey matter and white matter (appears as light grey). Coronal sections are sections that are made through the brain from top to bottom, just like looking face on at another person. The white areas in the middle are the ventricles of the brain.

Methods of investigating brain function

Much of what was learned about brain function in the early exploration of the brain was discovered either through anatomy (post mortem dissection of the brain and comparative studies with animal brains) or through the study of people who had suffered brain damage through disease, stroke or accident and inferring about the function of the normal brain from the activities that people with brain damage could and could not do. Technology has advanced, however, and there are today a number of ways of recording and observing the activity of the live human brain. It is possible to use a number of brain-imaging techniques, or brain scans, in order to assess the functioning of our brains, and both the normal and abnormal brain can be investigated using these techniques.

EEG machines

Electroencephalograph (EEG) machines have been in use since the early 1950s in psychological investigations. EEGs measure brain activity by tracing the electrical impulses under the surface of the skull by sticking electrodes to the scalp. The electrical impulses from each of the electrodes were amplified and traced (or drawn) onto a roll of paper (these days they appear on a computer screen and we can make a computer printout). They are often used in the investigation of sleep, to pick up activity from different areas of the brain, and to detect epilepsy.

MRI scans

Which of the brain structures you have read about so far can you identify in this scan?

MRI (magnetic resonance imaging) is a scanning technique used in medical and research settings. In medical settings it advanced beyond what can be shown on x-rays, as it shows far more detail in soft tissue, and this makes it a suitable method for imaging the brain. It works using a strong magnetic field and radio pulses. Patients lie in a round tunnel, surrounded by a large magnet which generates a powerful magnetic field. The required part of the anatomy is 'magnetised' and exposed to radio pulses which cause the tissues to give off radio signals that can be measured. Hundreds of measurements are taken which are converted by computer into a two-dimensional picture of the area.

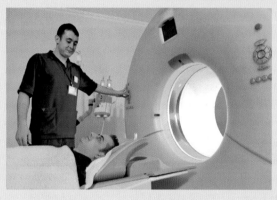

Figure 5.8 A person having an MRI scan

Maguire *et al.* study: Taxi drivers' brains

Brain plasticity: How flexible are our brains?

Our brains, or parts of them, can actually change size (or rather shape or structure) in order to accommodate new information.

Jacobs *et al.* (1993) looked at the portion of the human cerebral cortex responsible for understanding words (Wernicke's area), using deceased individuals who had given their consent prior to death. They compared the effects of enrichment in tissue from individuals who had received a college education with others who had left education after secondary school. The results demonstrated that the nerve cells in the college-educated participants showed more dendrites than those in the secondary school population. Further experiments on human tissue have supported the findings of the animal research and the conclusion that the brain does change in response to enrichment, in both animals and humans.

It is likely that you have been told at some time that you only have the brain cells you were born with, and as you get older they begin to die off, with alcohol and other damaging substances causing you to lose them more quickly. More recent research indicates that brain cells can actually regenerate. For example, Eriksson *et al.* (1998) identified the fact that the human hippocampus retains its ability to generate new neuronal cells throughout life, through a process known as neurogenesis.

Studies have established the neuroplasticity of the brain: brains can change in response to external stimuli. Imagine a piece of plasticine. It changes in response to the pressure or moulding that is applied to it. This is what happens with the brain; it changes and responds to the demands placed on it by increasing the cell dendrites and therefore the number of synapses available, in order to meet increased processing demands. These changes can be both functional (e.g. changes in neurotransmitters) and structural (changes in the size and number of synaptic connections between neurones).

Our core study investigates neuroplasticity in one structure of the brain, the hippocampus.

The hippocampus

The hippocampus is a very important brain structure for all types of memory. The hippocampus is linked to the conversion of information from short-term to more permanent memory. The impact of a damaged hippocampus is that memories of the past are retained, but new memories are not stored (known as anterograde amnesia), although individuals with a damaged hippocampus can learn new skills. This suggests that there may be different types of memory stores for different types of information. Another function of the hippocampus is to connect memories with each other, thus giving them meaning. For example, the hippocampus may connect the memory of a visit to a certain location with the information about where you went and how it looked and sounded.

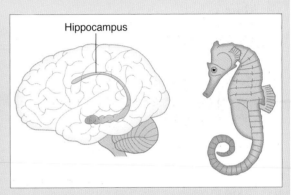

Figure 5.9 The brain structure, the hippocampus, (left) is so-called because anatomists thought it resembled a sea horse, and the greek for seahorse is hippocampus

The hippocampus is also associated with the memory of spatial relationships, the location of places or objects and the distances and routes between them. It is this function of the hippocampus that our core study focuses on. If we have to learn a great deal of information to help us find our way around a complex environment, what happens to our hippocampus?

The Study

E.A. Maguire, D.G. Gadian, I.S. Johnsrude, C.D. Good, J. Ashburner, R.S. Frackowiak and C.D. Frith (2000) 'Navigation-related structural changes in the hippocampi of taxi drivers', *Proceedings of the National Academy of Science*, 97: 4398–403

Background

The hippocampus helps us to navigate, that is, to find our way round both familiar and new environments. This means that this area of the brain plays an important part in our spatial memory.

If the needs of our spatial memory change or increase, will the hippocampus change to accommodate this? Maguire *et al.* suggest that it will, and provide evidence to support their theory from animals and birds: 'in some species hippocampal volume [that is, the size of the hippocampus] enlarges … during seasons when demand for spatial ability is greatest.' They also point to reported evidence that brain differences exist between humans with different skills, for example, musicians and non-musicians, who place different demands on their brains. Maguire *et al.* claim that studies

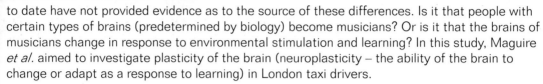

... continued

to date have not provided evidence as to the source of these differences. Is it that people with certain types of brains (predetermined by biology) become musicians? Or is it that the brains of musicians change in response to environmental stimulation and learning? In this study, Maguire *et al.* aimed to investigate plasticity of the brain (neuroplasticity – the ability of the brain to change or adapt as a response to learning) in London taxi drivers.

Someone who wants to be a London taxi driver has to pass examinations set by the police in order to get their taxi driver's licence. This is known as 'being on The Knowledge' and involves approximately two years spent learning how to get around London. This requires them to make increasing demands on their spatial memory. It is for this reason – the increased environmental demands on their spatial memory as they acquired 'The Knowledge' – that they were considered excellent subjects for this study.

Aims

To investigate the differences in the brain, especially in the hippocampus, in London taxi drivers, and to establish whether, compared to controls, differences in hippocampal volume would be observed. The study also aimed to further investigate the functions of the hippocampus in spatial memory.

Method and design

The study was an experiment using an independent groups design, comparing the brains of London taxi drivers with controls who were not taxi drivers.

In addition, correlational analysis was carried out to see if hippocampal changes increased with time as a taxi driver and were therefore likely to be environmentally determined.

Subjects

1. Taxi drivers:

- 16 right-handed male London taxi drivers, aged 32–62 (mean age = 44).
- All had been licensed London taxi drivers for at least 1.5 years (mean time as a taxi driver = 14.3 years, range = 1.5–42 years).
- The average time they had spent 'being on The Knowledge' was two years.
- All had healthy general medical, neurological and physiological profiles.

2. Control group:

- 50 right-handed males aged 32–62, who had been scanned for the MRI database at the Wellcome Department of Cognitive Neurology.
- They were selected so that no females, no left-handers, no under-32s or over-62s and no one with health problems were included.

Procedure and measurement

The taxi drivers' brains were scanned using an MRI scanner. These were structural MRI scans designed to investigate the anatomy of the brain (its structure), as opposed to functional MRI scans which investigate the physiognomy of the brain (how it works).

Their scans were analysed and compared with the scans of the control subjects.

The measurement of brain differences used two techniques:

- VBM (voxel-based morphometry) was used to measure the grey matter volume and indicate general brain differences between the two conditions. A voxel is a three-dimensional measurement of volume that allows a computer program to calculate the volume of area, in this case the grey matter in the brain in structural MRI scans.

- Pixel counting was carried out on the scans of the taxi drivers and 16 age-matched controls taken from the 50 control subjects. Pixel counting was carried out by 'one person experienced in the technique and blinded to the subjects' identity as taxi drivers or controls and the outcome of VBM analysis'. A pixel is a two-dimensional measurement of area. It was possible to calculate

... continued

differences by pixel counting 'slices' of the scan. The scan was separated into 26 slices and 24 of these focused on the hippocampus, as follows:

- posterior (rear/back) hippocampus – six slices
- hippocampus body – 12 slices
- anterior (front) hippocampus – six slices.

Results

What did the VBM analysis of the scans show?

VBM analysis showed that in the taxi drivers there was an increase in grey matter in only two areas of the brain: the left and right hippocampi. There was an *increase* in grey matter bilaterally (that is, on both the left and right sides) of the posterior hippocampi, but a *decrease* in grey matter bilaterally in the anterior hippocampi.

VBM thus confirmed a structural difference in the hippocampi of taxi drivers compared with controls.

What did the pixel-counting analysis of the results show?

Pixel-counting analysis revealed that there was no difference in the overall volume of the hippocampus between taxi drivers and controls. However, it did show a regionally significant difference by side (right and left) of the hippocampus (see the table and figure below).

Table 5.1
Results from the pixel-counting analysis of the MRI scans of taxi drivers and controls

Anterior hippocampus	The non-taxi drivers (controls) had higher hippocampal volume in the right anterior hippocampus than in the left.
Hippocampus body	The taxi drivers showed no difference in overall volume in the hippocampus body compared with controls, but analysis by side showed non-taxi drivers had higher volume in the right side.
Posterior hippocampus	The taxi drivers had a generally higher volume in their posterior hippocampus than the non-taxi drivers.

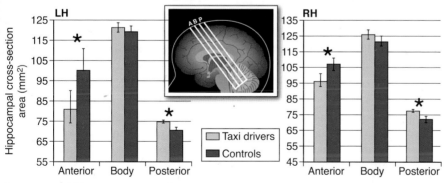

Figure 5.10 Volumetric analysis findings

The orientation of the slices measured in the volumetric analysis in the hippocampus is shown in the inset picture.

(Left) The mean score of the three cross-sectional area measurements from the left hand side of the brain. Taxi drivers had a significantly greater volume relative to controls in the posterior hippocampus.

(Right) The mean score of the three cross-sectional area measurements from the right hand side of the brain. Controls showed greater hippocampal volume in the anterior area. There was no significant difference between the two groups in the hippocampus body.

Source: Maguire *et al.* (2000). Copyright 2000 National Academy of Sciences, USA

... continued

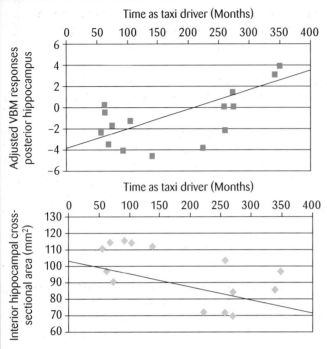

Figure 5.11 Correlation of volume change with time as a taxi driver: in VBM analysis, the volume of grey matter in the right hippocampus was found to correlate significantly with the amount of time spent learning to be and practising as a licensed London taxi driver, positively in the right posterior hippocampus and negatively in the anterior hippocampus

Source: Maguire *et al.* (2000) Copyright 2000 National Academy of Sciences, USA

Correlational analysis of changes to the hippocampus

The authors carried out a correlational analysis to see if there was a correlation between the VBM analysis of hippocampal volume and time spent as a taxi driver ('time spent' included time spent 'being on The Knowledge' and time practising as a taxi driver after qualifying).

The correlational data showed a positive correlation between one brain area only, namely the right posterior hippocampus, with time spent as a taxi driver (see figure 5.11). There was a negative correlation between time spent as a taxi driver and the volume of the anterior hippocampus. (The authors report that data was removed from this analysis for one taxi driver who had been in the job for 42 years. Given that the next highest length of time in the job was 28 years, the subject was removed from the analysis for statistical reasons as an outlier. The authors report that evidence from this subject was nonetheless consistent with their general findings from the taxi drivers.)

Discussion

The authors conclude that 'the data presented in this report provide evidence of regionally specific structural differences between the hippocampi of licensed London taxi drivers and those of control Ss'. Correlational analysis also confirmed that this difference was related to environmental stimulation. Increases/decreases of hippocampal volume in the posterior/anterior hippocampi of taxi drivers with time supports the idea that the brain has changed in response to the demands of being a taxi driver, rather than the idea that people choose to be taxi drivers because they have pre-existing brain differences.

The fact that the hippocampal volume correlated positively with the length of time as a taxi driver suggests that the hippocampal changes occur in line with the demands on spatial memory made by their job. This suggests that the human brain has plasticity, the ability to change (at least locally in the hippocampus) to meet the demands of the environment.

The authors report that their findings are consistent with findings from animal studies of rodents and monkeys, as well as studies of patients with brain damage (lesions). Findings from brain-damaged patients where the posterior hippocampus is not damaged demonstrate that the patients can recall cognitive maps they knew before the lesions were present.

In terms of how the hippocampus contributes generally to our spatial memory, the authors suggest that their findings indicate different roles in spatial memory for the anterior and posterior hippocampi. They suggest that the posterior hippocampus is involved when we are using previously learned information, and the anterior hippocampus (along with the posterior hippocampus) is more involved when we are learning about new environmental layouts.

... continued

The fact that the right and not the left hippocampal volume correlated with years of taxi driving experience suggests that the left and right sides of the hippocampus have separate functions. The authors suggest that the right holds 'mental maps' and the left holds memories and events not dependent on using such cognitive maps.

The authors suggest that the increased tissue volume in the posterior hippocampus in the taxi drivers occurs to accommodate their vast knowledge and mental map of the layout of London and how to find their way round the city.

In evolutionary terms, the authors point out that the hippocampus is an 'old' part of the brain which may have evolved to deal with navigation. Although in humans it is also adapted to be involved in other types of memory, such as episodic memory (memory for events), it 'retains an ability to store large-scale spatial information'. While the hippocampus does not operate alone, but works with other areas of the brain to support navigation, the key role of the hippocampus seems to be 'crucial to the storage and use of mental maps of our environments'.

The authors concede that structural MRI does not reveal exactly what is happening in the hippocampus to lead to the changes they observed in taxi drivers. However, they offer the theory that what happens is an 'overall reorganization of hippocampal circuitry'.

The study has implications for the rehabilitation of people who have suffered brain damage. The findings show that, at least in certain areas, the brain is capable of adaptation in response to environmental stimulation. People who have suffered brain damage or disease might be helped in the future if it could be shown that areas of the brain other than the hippocampus could respond and change.

Commentary: Methods and issues

Methods and measurement

You need to consider the strengths and weaknesses of the experimental method and of using an independent groups design in relation to this study:

- The laboratory setting for the scans enables the use of highly technical equipment (MRI scanning suite) and allows for precise measurement of data. Both the VBM and pixel-counting analysis provided quantitative data (in mm^3) about the volume of grey matter/volume of the hippocampus.

- The use of technical equipment can be costly, both in terms of equipment and the amount of specialists' time it takes to carry out the tests and analyse the results.

- Physiological methods of measurement, such as brain-imaging techniques, are the only method available for this kind of study of the structure of the brain (you cannot self-report about the size of your hippocampus and it is not directly observable to the naked eye in living participants).

- Without quantitative data, statistical analysis of the differences between the two groups, or analysis of the correlation between VBM measurements and time spent as a taxi driver would have been impossible to establish.

Does the study raise any ethical concerns?

The study is carried out according to the British Psychological Society's (1993) ethical guidelines:

- The subjects were not deceived; they gave their informed consent; they had the right to withdraw; and they were not negatively affected by their experience.

- Also, given that the study points towards (albeit probably in the distant future) implications for the rehabilitation of brain-damaged patients, we could describe the study as ethically worthy.

Is the study useful?

The study is useful in that it furthers our understanding of how the brain works, and provides evidence about the plasticity of the brain. As the authors suggest, there are implications for brain-damage sufferers in what this study reveals about neuroplasticity: rehabilitation of individuals who have suffered brain damage might be assisted if it was clear which areas of the brain are capable of adaptation and what environmental cues might stimulate them to change.

The MRI scan is one of a number of brain-imaging techniques that represent relatively new technological advances in science, and are enabling researchers to map the functions and observe the structure of the human brain. As advanced as the technology is, however, it remains limited. As the authors point out, the changes can be observed and quantified, but as yet the underpinning causes of the changes can only be theorised about, and this perhaps limits the usefulness of the study.

Although it may appear that neuroscientists are at present merely scratching the surface of their discipline, studies such as this one are important in leading the way in brain research, and may well be significant stepping stones towards a full understanding of the structure and function of the most complicated phenomena in the universe, the human brain.

Validity and reliability of the findings

The volume differences in the hippocampus were established by two concurrently valid independent measures (VBM and pixel counting), supporting the validity of the findings.

The authors had theorised that the hippocampal changes occurred because of being a taxi driver and not because people who already possessed differences in their hippocampi would choose to become taxi drivers. The validity of this theory is supported by the correlational evidence, which showed that the changes in hippocampal volume correlated with time spent as a taxi driver. Changes in the hippocampus were more marked as time spent as a taxi driver increased.

The validity of the findings is also supported by the fact that evidence from comparative studies with animals and brain-damaged patients are consistent with the findings from the taxi drivers.

A reason to question the validity of this plasticity of the hippocampus being typical of everyone is that the sample is not exactly typical of the general population. It may be that not everyone's brain could or would respond in the same way to the environmental demands of doing 'The Knowledge' and being a taxi driver in London. For a start, there is a clear gender bias in the sample and we cannot assume that female and male brains operate similarly in terms of spatial memory.

In terms of ecological validity, being scanned in an MRI scanner is not something that a person would have to do every day. However, in this case, the variable being measured (hippocampal volume) would not be one that the subjects could actually falsify, so the data is unlikely to be affected by responses to demand characteristics or the artificiality of the laboratory setting. So it does not affect the outcome of the study if the process of being given an MRI scan lacks ecological validity.

Dement and Kleitman study: REM sleep and dreaming

Sleep and dreaming

We spend one-third of our lives asleep. We all know that we cannot do without sleep, yet it seems such a waste of time. Have you noticed that sometimes, during the week when you have to get up, you can't seem to wake up, and at the weekend when you can lie in bed, you wake up really early when you don't have to? This suggests that our feelings of needing sleep seem to relate to our state of mind. If we are enjoying ourselves at a party, we find it easy to stay awake, whereas if we are at home, bored, we feel very sleepy. People suffering from depression feel very tired all the time and sleep more than they would do normally.

We vary in the amount of sleep we need throughout the course of our lives:

- When we are babies, we sleep and wake many times during the course of the day.

- As we get older, many of us sleep only once, at night, although people from very hot countries may well have a siesta during the day when the sun is at its highest in the sky.

- We seem to need less sleep when we are in our teens and twenties, yet with the passing of the years we seem to need more sleep.

- When we are much older, our need for sleep often decreases again.

The reasons for these changes are complex and relate not only to our bodily requirements, but also to the stresses and strains of everyday life. In many ways, the most stressful times appear to require the most sleep, but they seem to be the times when we get the least.

While we are asleep we have periods of relative quiet and periods when we know we dream. One of the most exciting things about sleep can be the dreams we have. You can be anything in dreams, although they are not always about pleasant things. They are sometimes weird, sometimes very enjoyable or erotic, and sometimes they seem to perform the function of providing an insight into our problems. The analysis of dreams was one of Freud's interests, and in some daily newspapers you will occasionally see articles on how to analyse your dreams – although whether this dream analysis actually bears any relationship to reality is another matter! One of the problems with psychoanalytical claims about dream content is that they are unverifiable: untestable in a scientific methodology. The authors of our core study, Dr William Dement and Dr Nathaniel Kleitman were pioneers in the development of methods to investigate sleep and dreaming in a scientific way.

How is sleep investigated?

Most of the work undertaken on sleep has been carried out in sleep laboratories. These consist of small bedrooms next to an observation room where the experimenter spends the night and monitors the sleeper's behaviour, both by observation and also by wiring the sleeper up to a series of recording instruments. The sleeper may also be videoed to record his or her behaviour. Can you imagine how difficult it would be not only to sleep in a strange bed, but also to know you were being watched?

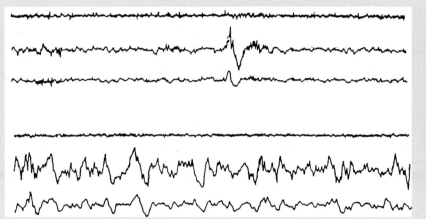

Figure 5.12 Traces from EEG, EMG and EOG machines

In sleep laboratories a range of physiological measurements are used to investigate the activity of the nervous system. Participants can be wired up to three types of machines, which all work in the same way:

- An EEG (electroencephalogram) measures brain activity: the electrodes are placed over the head to record the electrical activity of the underlying neurones.

- An EMG (electromyogram) measures muscle activity: facial and jaw muscle activity is monitored by electrodes placed on the jaw area.

- An EOG (electro-oculogram) measures eye movements: the electrodes are placed around the eye socket.

From investigations using these physiological methods the sleep cycle has been traced.

The sleep cycle

- **Stage one** sleep is the first 'drifting' stage that we go through on our way to deep sleep. It can occur when the natural light fades, as this information is transferred through the eyes to the pineal gland in the brain, which starts to produce a hormone called melatonin. Melatonin indirectly makes us feel sleepy, and therefore, when it gets dark, we may begin to feel drowsy. If we are in bed, this presents no problem, of course, and we start to drift off into stage one sleep. Have you ever noticed that sometimes, just as you are drifting, you jerk violently and it wakes you up? This is when the neurones are discharging randomly before you enter the second stage.

- **Stage two** is deeper than stage one, but we can still be woken easily. The heart rate, breathing and brain activity are slower than at stage one.

- **Stage three** is deeper still, with more long, slow delta waves. We are difficult to wake at this point and the heart rate, blood pressure and temperature are dropping.

- **Stage four** is known as delta or quiet sleep. This is the stage where it is hardest to wake us, unless the stimulus is very relevant, such as the alarm clock or a baby crying. This sleep lasts for approximately 30-minute bursts. During this stage we are able to toss and turn and move our limbs as necessary.

A whole sleep cycle lasts for about 90 minutes and involves us moving 'down' through all four stages and moving 'up' again. This 90-minute cycle is present in infants who are fed on demand, and has also been noticed in adult activities. We can be engaged in something for about 90 minutes, but suddenly have the urge to go and get a drink or have a break.

REM (Rapid Eye Movement) sleep

When we return to where stage one would be, we enter a different kind of sleep known as rapid eye movement sleep (REM sleep), where our eyes dart back and forth beneath closed eyelids. This is observable by the human eye, as the eyes visibly move beneath the eyelids. It is different because it is an active sleep – in terms of our brainwaves and eye movements – but, strangely enough, our bodies are actively inhibited from movement. This means that we are, in effect, 'paralysed', so we do not move during this period of sleep. Because the blood pressure rises, this is the time when males experience erections in their sleep, even though the rest of the body is immobile. Our pulse, respiration rate and blood pressure increase and our brainwave patterns look like they would when we are awake. It is even harder to wake someone from this sleep than during stage four. It is sometimes known as 'paradoxical sleep', a term coined by Michel Jouvet in the late 1950s. Jouvet was carrying out research into insomnia when he noticed how high brain activity occurred that resembled wakefulness, but at the same time the body was in extreme relaxation and was very difficult to rouse. The term paradoxical literally means apparently self-contradictory, as the activity of the brain and body are in complete contrast to each other.

Most of the research carried out on sleep has considered either types of sleep, sleep deprivation or dreaming, although early studies were beset with numerous difficulties in effectively determining and quantifying levels of sleep. The core study in this area is one that was undertaken by Dement and Kleitman and looked at the relationship between REM sleep and dreaming using an EEG machine to measure sleep, which at the time was a new technology.

The Study

W. Dement and N. Kleitman (1957) 'The relation of eye movements during sleep to dream activity: An objective method for the study of dreaming', *Journal of Experimental Psychology*, 53: 339–46

Background

One of the problems researchers in the field of sleep and dreaming faced in the 1950s was the problem of measurement. How could you measure objectively if someone was dreaming or not? Prior to this study, researchers had had to rely on the self-report of subjects.

Dement and Kleitman theorised that it might be possible to find an objective way to tell whether someone was dreaming or not by investigating whether physiological phenomena correlated significantly with dreaming. You could then measure these physiological reactions and assume that the person was dreaming. This would reduce the problems of forgetting, falsification and responses to demand characteristics that occur with the self-report method of measurement. A study by Aserinsky and Kleitman (1955) had shown that when subjects were in REM sleep they recorded dream activity more than when they were in NREM (non-rapid eye movement) sleep. Moreover, it was possible to measure REM sleep objectively using an EEG machine. REM sleep is characterised by a low-voltage, relatively fast pattern in the EEG. From this, Dement and Kleitman theorised that it might be possible to find an objective way of measuring whether someone was dreaming or not by investigating whether REM sleep correlated significantly with dreaming.

Aims and hypotheses

The aim of the study was to see if the physiological aspects of REM sleep related to the subjects' experience of dreaming. The study aimed to investigate a number of factors:

- First, it was intended to observe and record the length, frequency and patterns of the subjects' REM sleep.

- Second, three hypotheses were to be tested:

1. There is a significant association between REM and reported dreaming. This would establish that measuring REM sleep would be a valid and objective measure of dream activity for future researchers to employ.

2. There is a significant positive correlation between the estimate of time spent dreaming and the measurement of REM sleep.

3. There is a relationship between the pattern of eye movement and the reported content of the dream.

Method and design

A controlled investigation was carried out in a sleep laboratory.

- For hypothesis one, the purpose was to compare dream recall in REM and NREM sleep. Dement and Kleitman measured whether the subject was in REM or NREM sleep, as identified by the EEG pattern being recorded, and whether the subjects reported that they had been dreaming or not on being awoken. This data was then analysed to see if there were differences between REM and NREM sleep as regards dream recall.

- For hypothesis two, quantitative data was collected for correlational analysis, to establish whether there was a positive correlation between REM time and estimated time of dreaming.

- For hypothesis three, qualitative data was gathered regarding the content of subjects' dreams and this was compared with observations of the way the subjects' eyes were moving (REM movements can be observed with the naked eye).

Subjects

Seven adult males and two adult females were studied, with five studied intensively and the other four used to confirm the findings.

... continued

Apparatus

Subjects were tested in a sleep laboratory, using an EEG machine to measure sleep objectively. Electrodes were attached to subjects' eyes to measure eye movement, and to their scalps to measure brain activity. A doorbell was used to wake subjects and a tape recorder was used to record subjects' recollections of what they had been dreaming.

Procedure

Subjects were tested individually. They were instructed to report to the laboratory a little before their usual bedtime. Subjects were also told to avoid alcohol and caffeine, but to eat normally on the day of the experiment. This was done as a control to prevent the effects of caffeine or alcohol from affecting the findings.

Electrodes were applied to the subjects' heads and faces. To avoid entanglement and to allow the subjects free movement, all wires were gathered at the top of their heads and then led in a single cord to the lead box. Subjects slept on their own, in a quiet, dark laboratory. Their brainwave patterns were recorded constantly throughout their period of sleep.

Testing hypothesis one

At various times during the night, some of which were during REM and some during NREM, subjects were wakened by a doorbell. They had been instructed to record immediately into a tape recorder whether or not they had been dreaming. Return to sleep usually occurred in less than five minutes. To further control extraneous variables, there was no contact with the experimenter before dream reports, in order to avoid experimenter bias. Subjects were not told whether they had been in REM or NREM sleep, and the pattern of awakenings for each subject was varied to avoid bias:

* Two subjects (initials PM and KC) were woken according to a random numbers table, to remove any likely pattern.
* One subject (IR) was woken at the whim of the experimenter.
* One subject (DN) was woken during three REM periods and three NREM periods.
* One subject (WD) was told he would only be woken in REM sleep, but was actually woken in NREM sleep periods too.

Testing hypothesis two

Subjects were woken either five or 15 minutes after REM sleep began and were asked to estimate the length of their dream by choosing from either five or 15 minutes. These findings were then correlated with the length of time in REM sleep. Subjects were also asked to relate the content of their dream, and the length of the narrative was correlated with the duration of REM sleep before they were woken.

Testing hypothesis three

Subjects were woken one minute after one of four patterns of eye movement had occurred:

* mainly vertical (eyes moving up and down)
* mainly horizontal (eyes moving from side to side)
* both vertical and horizontal
* little/no eye movement.

They were asked what they had just been dreaming about, and the data was analysed to see if the pattern related to the content of the dream.

The total number of awakenings (for all nine subjects) was 351 times over 61 nights, which averaged at 5.7 awakenings per subject per night. Awakenings were spread out over the night as follows:

* 21 per cent in the first two hours
* 29 per cent in hours three and four
* 28 per cent in hours five and six
* 22 per cent in hours seven and eight.

... continued

Results

Dement and Kleitman observed the following about REM sleep:

- All subjects showed periods of REM every night that they slept in the laboratory, as shown by low-voltage, fast EEG patterns.
- The average occurrence of REM was one period every 92 minutes for the whole group, with variations between 70 and 104 minutes.
- The length of REM was between three minutes and 50 minutes, and tended to increase in length as the night progressed.

Hypothesis one: Eye movement periods and dream recall

(Note that for all hypotheses, dreaming was deemed to have occurred if the subject could give a relatively coherent and detailed description of the dream.)

- As shown in the following table, more dreams were reported in REM than in NREM sleep.

Table 5.2   Showing instances of dream recall after awakenings during periods of REM or NREM

Subject	REM sleep		NREM sleep	
	Dream recall	No recall	Dream recall	No recall
DN	17	9	3	21
IR	26	8	2	29
KC	36	4	3	31
WD	37	5	1	34
PM	24	6	2	23
KK	4	1	0	5
SM	2	2	0	2
DM	2	1	0	1
MG	4	3	0	3
Total	152	39	11	149

Source: adapted from Dement and Kleitman (1957:341)

- Where no dream recall was recorded, this tended to be in the earlier period of the night (19 of the 39 no-recalls in REM sleep were in hours one and two).
- Subjects were woken 132 times when they had ceased REM by more than eight minutes, and, of these, only six subjects recalled dreams. However, when woken within eight minutes of ceasing REM, five out of 17 reported dreaming. This indicates that the closer subjects were to REM, the more likely they were to be able to recall their dreams. When subjects were awoken from deep sleep (stage four sleep – a period of NREM sleep characterised by high-voltage, slow waves in the EEG), they were often bewildered and reported that they must have been dreaming, although they could not recall the dream content, or they said that they had not been asleep at all. Sometimes they described experiencing feelings such as pleasantness or anxiety, but could not relate these to dream content.

Hypothesis two: Length of rapid eye movement periods and subjective dream duration estimates

- As shown in the table below, there was a significant relationship between subjects' estimate of dream length and the amount of time spent in REM for both the five- and 15-minute periods. The table also shows that there were significantly more correct estimates of length of REM than incorrect estimates. There were more wrong estimates after 15 minutes, so the longer the subject had been in REM sleep, the less accurate they were at estimating dream length.

... continued

Table 5.3   Results of dream duration estimates after five or 15 minutes of rapid eye movements

Subject	Right	Wrong	Right	Wrong
DN	8	2	5	5
IR	11	1	7	3
KC	7	0	12	1
WD	13	1	15	1
PM	6	2	8	3
Total	45	6	47	13

Source: adapted from Dement and Kleitman (1957:343)

- There was also a significant relationship between length of narrative and REM period.

Hypothesis three: Specific eye movement patterns and visual imagery of the dream

The study suggests that the subjects' eye movements related to dream content, indicating that the eyes move as if seeing what the subject was dreaming about.

There was a strong association between the pattern of REMs and the content of the dream, with horizontal and vertical movements relating to dream reports of looking up and down or left and right. The kinds of situations reported by subjects were such events as looking up at cliff faces or throwing tomatoes at each other.

Periods where movements were mixed were associated with looking at close objects, and the periods where there was little or no movement were associated with dreams of looking at stationary or distant objects.

Discussion

The results obtained by waking subjects strongly support the connection between REM sleep and dreaming. Dement and Kleitman point out that, on the basis of their findings, 'it cannot be stated with complete certainty that some sort of dream activity did not occur at other times' (p.345), that is, in NREM periods, although they considered this unlikely since their results had shown low recall of dreams in NREM sleep, and because REM sleep occurs in the lightest level of sleep.

Dement and Kleitman recorded that when woken within eight minutes of ceasing REM, five out of 17 subjects in NREM sleep reported dreaming. This may account for some of the recordings of dream recall in NREM, as it may be that those awoken within eight minutes were still recalling dreams they had been having while in REM sleep.

They suggested that their findings on the correlation between dream recall and length of time in REM sleep indicated that dreams are not instantaneous or happen very rapidly, but rather 'seemed to progress at a rate comparable to a real experience of the same sort'. (p.346) In other words, dreams occur in real time.

Dement and Kleitman considered their findings in relation to other studies of REM sleep and of dreaming, and considered that any inconsistencies between findings were due to methodological issues. For example, while Dement and Kleitman recorded periods of REM sleep in their subjects for every night they had been tested, earlier work had not shown this. They put this down to earlier studies recording only samples of behaviour and therefore missing REM periods, or not amplifying the EEG high enough to make accurate recordings of when REM was occurring.

Dement and Kleitman concluded that the measurement of REM during sleep can be used as an objective measure of dreaming. They say that this enables further research to study objectively the effect of other factors on dreaming, such as environmental change, drugs and stress.

Commentary: Methods and issues

Research method, design and data gathering

The use of self-report measures for dream recall and dream content presents a problem. As well as general concerns about falsification of data by subjects and responses to demand characteristics, a number of factors suggest that the data collected by self-report from subjects in this study may not be accurate.

- Even though there were far more reports of dreaming during REM and no dreaming during NREM, the reason for the lack of reports of dreaming during NREM may have been something to do with the depth of sleep and the lack of ability of subjects to remember the dream as they awoke from such a deep level of sleep.

- The length of dream narrative was probably influenced by the talkativeness of the subjects, with subjects who were naturally more talkative giving a much longer description of their dreams. This, in turn, might have influenced how quickly they went back to sleep.

- The nature of the method of waking subjects (by doorbell) may have affected their ability to recall the dream.

There are also problems with correlational evidence. We must remember that this study was looking for a relationship between REM and dreaming. Even though a significant relationship was found, we still cannot confirm that one causes the other. Correlation does not mean causation. It may be that their co-occurrence was caused by another variable.

Does the study raise any ethical concerns?

Given the complicated instructions for data recording and the fact that the subject had to agree to sleep wired to an EEG machine in the laboratory, and to be woken in the night, we should assume that their informed consent was obtained for taking part in the study. Neither harm nor significant stress was caused to the subjects in the study, so we can conclude that it was carried out ethically.

Is the study useful?

This study was the first to attempt to study dream activity scientifically. It was highly generative, that is, it led to a great deal of further research in the area of sleep and dreaming. This means it was very useful to psychologists working in this field. On the other hand, issues such as low validity and low generalisability may mean that the findings are not very useful in describing real sleeping behaviour.

Validity and reliability of the study

- Sample biases are present. The disproportionate number of males to females may have influenced the study. We cannot be sure that the results of the study were not simply biased towards the dream patterns of men rather than women.

- The sample size was also extremely small, and this makes it difficult to generalise to all people. Also, since this study used subjects who were able to report to the university laboratory just before bedtime and were people for whom periods of disturbed sleep were not going to cause problems, it may well be that the individuals who were studied were students, although this is not specified in the study.

- The study was carried out at one university in the USA and therefore has an ethnocentric bias, which means that we have to be careful in making any attempt to generalise the findings to a broader population. This leads us to question the validity of the findings. As discussed above, there is also the possibility that the study might have been affected by individual differences between subjects or by demand characteristics, as well as the use of correlational analysis. These factors all pose a threat to the validity of the findings.

- The situation may have affected the type of sleep shown by subjects; after all, sleeping wired up in a laboratory is not conducive to getting a good night's sleep. Therefore, we could criticise the study for a lack of ecological validity. This again limits its generalisability to real sleeping behaviour, and this means we have to question both the validity and the usefulness of the findings.

- The relationship between patterns of eye movements and dream content has not been supported by later studies. For example, babies in the womb and people blind from birth have periods of REM, yet they must be unable to recall images of objects and events as they have had no experience of these.

- Later studies have also indicated that not everyone follows the pattern of REM sleep being associated with dream recall. For example, some subjects who claim they rarely dream report a low level of dreaming during REM sleep. It seems likely, therefore, that there are individual differences between subjects.

Postscript

It was believed that we only dream during REM sleep. However, it has now been shown that we do dream during stage four sleep, though the dreams are not stories like the ones we are used to. If people are awakened from stage four sleep, they are more likely to report a situation or some kind of feeling or awareness, although some of the most terrifying nightmares occur during stage four sleep.

We still do not know the function of dreaming. Some researchers suggest that it is simply a way of putting the events of the day in some kind of order. Some, like Freud, believe that it is our unconscious finally having free rein, and our id running away with itself. Others say it is simply random neuronal firings, which trigger some distant memory or thought that we try to make sense of and therefore turn into part of a story. Whatever the reason, it seems that REM sleep is far more important to us than NREM sleep.

If we deprive someone of sleep for a night, they will spend more of the next night in REM sleep than normal, but will not necessarily increase the amount of NREM sleep they have missed. This is called the REM rebound, where we seem to compensate for the amount of REM sleep lost. This explains why people are not too bad at having their sleeping hours slowly reduced. What they do is to maintain the amount of REM sleep and reduce the amount of NREM sleep. There have been a number of reports as to what happens to humans if they are deprived of REM sleep. Although the findings are contradictory, it seems that people may develop a kind of paranoia where they are very suspicious of other people's motives. They may also have what are often called hallucinations but are really visual illusions or distortions, that is, they are based on some external stimulus, but this is interpreted wrongly (Dement 1960).

Sperry study: Split brains

Hemisphere de-connection (split brains)

As we have already discussed, the brain is divided into two relatively symmetrical halves, known as the left and right hemispheres. We also know that in right-handed people the left-hand side of the brain largely controls the right-hand side of the body, and vice versa, but it is not known why this crossover occurs. The two hemispheres are joined by what are known as commissural fibres, and the corpus callosum is by far the largest commissure (cross-hemisphere connection), responsible for carrying the majority of information between the two hemispheres. It is often misconstrued that the two hemispheres are totally different and have entirely different functions. It is true that they do differ in some ways, but they are nowhere near as different as we are led to believe by some books, which seem to suggest that the function of the left-hand side of the brain is to be clever, rational and reasoning, and that the right-hand side is purely the spiritual, artistic part.

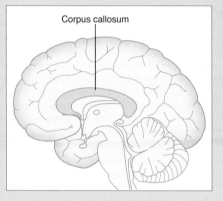

Figure 5.13 The corpus callosum

Lateralisation of function

In most people there is some 'lateralisation of function', which means that one side has a different role to the other. In the majority of people the language centres are on the left-hand side – Broca's area is responsible for speech production and Wernicke's area is responsible for speech comprehension. This is the case for the majority of right-handed people, although people who are left-handed may well have their language centres on the right-hand side of their brain. However, it is virtually impossible to give exact percentages, so it is best to accept the fact that the majority of people, left- and right-handed, have their speech centres located in the left hemisphere. This would mean that any damage to the left side of your head would probably leave you either unable to speak or understand, or neither speak nor understand.

Much of the evidence that has been gathered about hemisphere function has come from people who have suffered strokes (or cerebrovascular accidents, to give them their correct name). This is the most common source of brain damage in old age and is caused by a blood clot or other obstruction closing off an artery, or by an artery rupturing. This will result in the area around the site being deprived of oxygen or nutrients and the relevant neurones dying. Because the left-hand side of the brain controls the right-hand side of the body, a left-sided stroke will result in right-sided lack of function. This can be quite mild, such as a non-mobile side of the face, or more severe, as with hemiplegia, where the whole of the right side of the body ceases to function. What makes it worse is the fact that the person often loses the ability to either comprehend or produce words, so not only are they non-mobile, but they are also isolated in their own little world. It is often very frustrating for a stroke victim who is recovering from damage that has affected Broca's area, as they know exactly what they want to say, but just cannot say it.

Severing the connection

The two symmetrical hemispheres are only slightly different in the tasks they carry out. In order for us to function adequately, these two parts need to communicate with each other, which they do by means of the corpus callosum. This gives the side of the brain without speech centres access to words and descriptions which it would be without if there was no bridge between the two. It is easy to imagine what would happen if that bridge was not there. Such a thought gives new meaning to the phrase, 'the left hand does not know what the right hand is doing!'

There are rare instances of people having the connections between their two hemispheres severed, either as a result of an accident or, more likely, as one of the surgical treatments for epilepsy. Epileptic seizures are a result of abnormal electrical discharges of groups of brain neurones, described by Carlson (1986) as the 'wild sustained firing of cerebral neurons'. The source of the hyperactivity is usually in the temporal lobe and results in the person briefly losing contact with reality, and even experiencing hallucinations. Sometimes the seizures can be more sustained, and these are known as grand mal seizures. During one of these, the person becomes unconscious for a few minutes and experiences muscle spasms which may result in them breaking their bones or damaging themselves; they may also lose bowel and bladder control. When the seizure is over, the muscles relax and the person will wake up, but they are often extremely disoriented and embarrassed. A seizure like this would obviously be quite debilitating and would put the person in some danger, so any attempt to reduce the severity or frequency of such seizures would clearly be of great benefit.

One surgical way of preventing the spread of the wildly excited neuronal firings was to sever the corpus callosum, preventing the other side of the brain from becoming involved and thus reducing the severity of the effects. This method was very successful and it was found that not only did it stop the discharges from spreading, but it also reduced the epileptic seizures to negligible proportions. This surgical procedure is known as a commissurotomy and was used in life-threatening and severe cases of epilepsy, known as status epilepticus, to treat patients and end the threat to their life of them experiencing a seizure which would not stop but would lead to heart failure and death.

You would think that an operation of this severity would result in lots of side effects, but, extraordinarily, most of the people who underwent the surgery suffered very few side effects that were noticeable in their everyday lives. In effect, they were living with two brains in a single head, each one functioning adequately. There *were* side effects, however, and it is these effects that form the focus of the core study undertaken by Roger Sperry in 1968. It also gave Sperry a unique opportunity to map lateralisation of brain function.

The Study

R.W. Sperry (1968) 'Hemisphere deconnection and unity in conscious awareness', *American Psychologist*, **23: 723–33**

Background

Before we look at the study itself, you need to know a little about Sperry and his work. Sperry was a neuropsychologist who conducted a number of studies on split-brain patients while working at the California Institute of Technology. In the early 1950s he undertook research which involved splitting the brains of cats and monkeys. By training the animals he discovered that you could teach one hemisphere a task, while the other hemisphere remained unaware of the information learned. This supported his idea that the brain consisted of two separate modules rather than one unified whole. The importance of his work was recognised when he shared the Nobel prize for physiology and medicine with David Hubel and Torsten Wiesel in 1981. (Hubel and Wiesel pioneered a method of studying the physiology of vision by inserting very thin wire electrodes into the columns of neurones in the optic cortex and recording their response to different stimuli.)

Many of the effects of splitting brains were investigated in the laboratory with relatively simplistic tasks. They involved presenting information to one or other eye so that the information went to the opposite side of the brain. If the information was presented to the far right visual field, it would go to the left-hand side of the brain, which contains the speech centres. Therefore the person would be able to say what they had just seen. If the information was presented to the far left visual field, it would go to the right-hand side of the brain, which has no speech production centre. Therefore the person would know what it was, but would not be able to say what they had just seen. However, if this person was then asked to draw the object with their left hand (with their eyes closed), they could do so.

Each eye has information that goes to the opposite side of the brain, crossing over at a point called the optic chiasma. (If this crossover point were also severed, this would result in information from one eye going to one side of the brain only, and this has actually happened in a few cases.)

The subjects were asked to fixate on a spot in the centre of a screen. The image was projected for one-tenth of a second, which was insufficient time for them to move their eyes enough to send information to the opposite side of the brain. Therefore, for any of the split-brain studies which involve projecting objects for someone to look at, we accept the fact that the information projected on one side of the fixation point (that is, in the far left or far right visual field) is only seen by the corresponding eye and only goes to the opposite side of the brain.

These studies are not really ecologically valid because in the real world the situation would not occur, unless someone had only one eye. However, a later set of studies on split-brain patients, conducted by Gazzaniga *et al.* (1977), although also lacking ecological validity, showed how important it is for the two hemispheres to connect.

Gazzaniga *et al.* developed a contact lens which allowed the presentation of sophisticated images to only one side of the retina, and therefore to only one side of the cortex. In one study they presented a female subject, V.P., with a short film showing one person throwing another into a fire. The image was presented to the right hemisphere (with no language), and although the woman was fully alert throughout the course of the film she was only aware of having seen some kind of light. She reported that she felt scared and jumpy but was not sure why, so she explained her feelings by saying that she felt scared of Gazzaniga, although she knew she liked him. It seems she labelled her state of arousal by the situation she was in, namely having contact with her surgeon. She transferred the fear the film had created into a fear of Dr Gazzaniga.

Beneath the corpus callosum is another tract of fibres that connect the more primitive part of the brain – the limbic system. The limbic system is found under the cortex, and forms the junction between the older, more primitive parts of the brain with their unsophisticated emotional responses, and the more logical, reasoning cortex. Here there is another tract of fibres which connects the two

... continued

hemispheres – the anterior commissure. Very basic information about emotional responses such as anger or fear are passed from this area to both sides of the cortex, but the more sophisticated responses of the cortex are missing.

The article by Sperry describes the results of a series of experiments undertaken on people who had already had their corpus callosum severed as a treatment for severe epilepsy.

Aim

The aim was to investigate the effects of this de-connection and show that each hemisphere has different functions; in other words, to map lateralisation of brain function and show that information in one side of the brain is not accessible to the other side.

Method and design

The design was a quasi-experiment which compared split-brain subjects with 'normal' subjects in laboratory tests, and compared case studies of all the individual patients.

Subjects

The split-brain subjects were 11 patients who had already experienced a commissurotomy prior to the study. The sample type is therefore an opportunity sample. All subjects had a history of severe epilepsy which had not responded to drug therapy. Two of the patients had been operated on successfully to sever their corpus callosum some time before the experiments took place. The remaining nine had only recently undergone surgery.

Procedure

The equipment used allowed for various types of sensory information to be presented to one or other hemisphere, in different combinations. Visual information was presented by projecting images on a screen in front of the subject. Tactile information would be presented to either the left or the right hand, or to both hands, without the patients being able to see what the object was. A representation of the apparatus is given in the figure below.

Subjects had to remain in silence during the studies unless they were asked questions by the experimenter. This was to prevent them passing information from the left side of the brain to the right side, as sound can be taken in by both ears simultaneously. For example, if the subject identified an object and then said what it was, this information would be available to both hemispheres.

Visual investigations

Visual investigations involved showing one stimulus at a time to one visual field, or showing two stimuli simultaneously to the two different visual fields.

- One visual field (targeting only one side of the brain at once): These tests required the subject to cover one eye. They were told to look at a fixation point in the centre of the screen. The image was projected for one-tenth of a second on either the left or the right of the fixation point, which would send the image to either the far right or far left visual field respectively. It was projected for that short space of time to prevent the information going to the wrong half of the visual field if the subject moved their eye, which would send the information to both sides of the brain. This is because there is an overlap in the centre of the visual field (at the fixation point), which means that the right and left brain

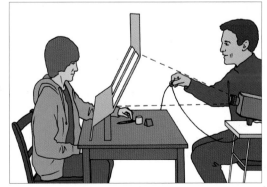

Figure 5.14 Apparatus used for study.
Source: adapted from Sperry (1968)

... continued

both get information about objects viewed at that point. For example, the first screen shown below would send the image of a key to the right side of the brain as it is projected in the far left visual field, picked up only by the left eye. The next screen would send the image of the key to the left side of the brain as it is projected in the far right visual field, picked up only by the right eye.

- Both visual fields: The subject would look at the fixation point on the screen while two images were flashed simultaneously either side of the fixation point. This screen would send the image of a key to the left side of the brain (because it would be seen by the right eye in the far right visual field) and the image of an apple to the right side of the brain (because it would be seen by the left eye in the far left visual field).

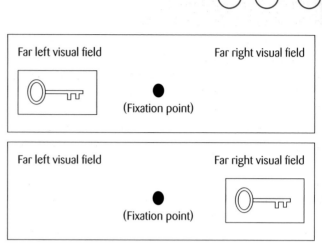

Figure 5.15 Testing each hemisphere separately

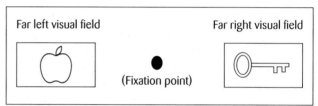

Figure 5.16 Testing both hemispheres at once

The subjects would then be asked to say what they had seen. Typically, they would say 'key', although they would have no conscious awareness of having seen anything else. They would then be given a pen with the left hand and be asked to draw what they had just seen (although they would have to do this with their eyes closed or with their hand out of sight, because if they could see what they were doing, the dominant hemisphere would interfere with their recall). Typically, they would draw an apple. If they were then shown the picture, they would not know why they had drawn it, as the information about the apple had *not* gone into the dominant left hemisphere, which is the hemisphere containing language (speech).

Tactile investigations

- One hand:
- The subject's hands are hidden from their view behind the screen. The subject is then asked to find an object corresponding to what they have seen on the screen.
- The object is placed in one hand, without the subject being able to see what they are holding, and they are then asked to say what they have been given.
- The object is placed in one hand, without the subject being able to see what they are holding, and they are then asked to point to what they have been given.
- Both hands at the same time:
- The subject works with their hands out of sight. The subject is given two different objects, one in each hand, and then the objects are taken away.
- The subject is asked to find the objects by touch from a pile of items.
- The subject is asked to say what they have just held.

... continued

Tests of the right hemisphere

Because the right hemisphere does not produce language, in order to test if it has any ability to make mental associations, work logically or experience separate emotions from the left hemisphere, the following tests were undertaken:

* The left eye (therefore right hemisphere) is presented with an object on the screen. The subject is asked to pick out similar objects by touch from an array of objects.
* Simple mathematical problems are presented to the left eye. The subject is asked to sort objects by shape, size or texture, using their left hand.
* An array of geometric shapes is projected to both visual fields on the screen. In the middle of this selection is the picture of a nude, which is presented to the left eye only. The subject is later asked if they saw anything other than the geometric shapes. The right hemisphere may respond non-verbally and this may reveal what has been seen.

Results

Visual stimuli presented to one visual field

* When subjects were shown an image in one visual field, they would only recognise the image as one they had already seen if it was shown again to the same visual field. The reason for this is that information would have gone only to one side of the brain and not the other.
* If an image was shown in the right visual field (left hemisphere), the subject was able to say what they had seen, could identify what it was from an array of pictures shown to the right eye by pointing to it, and could find it with their right hand from an array of objects.
* If it was shown to the left eye (right hemisphere), the subject was unable to name it, but could draw it (with eyes closed) with their left hand, could identify what it was from an array of pictures shown to the left eye by pointing to it, and could find it with the left hand from an array of objects.

Visual stimuli presented to both visual fields

The subject would be able to say what they had seen presented in the right visual field, but would be unaware that they had seen anything else. If they were given a pen in the left hand and asked to draw with their eyes closed, they would be able to draw what they had seen with the left eye, although they would seemingly have no conscious knowledge of having seen anything else and would be very surprised when they discovered what they had drawn. They would be able to name the object once they had seen the drawing with the right eye.

Tactile investigations

The results of the tactile investigations were the same, irrespective of whether the object was held by one hand at a time or by both hands simultaneously.

* The subject would have no problems identifying an object by name if it was put in the right hand, but if it was put in the left hand they would have no conscious awareness of it. However, they would be able to find it by touch with the left hand in a bag full of objects.
* When the objects were placed in one hand, subjects could point to what the object was with the same hand which had held the object.

Tests of the right hemisphere

* Subjects were able to pick out semantically similar objects. For example, if they saw on the screen a picture of a wall clock with the left eye (therefore right hemisphere) and the only related item in a tactile array was a toy wristwatch, this would be the object chosen.
* Right hemispheres were able to carry out simple mathematical problems.
* Left hands were able to sort objects by shape, size and texture.

... continued

- When subjects saw the array of geometric shapes, they would giggle or look embarrassed when the picture of the nude appeared, even though they could not say what they were responding to. This non-verbal response suggests that the right hemisphere has a second conscious entity.

Discussion

The study gave considerable support to the idea that the brain consists of two seemingly independent hemispheres, each with its own consciousness, and that there is no transfer of information between the two sides. For the subjects studied, the dominant hemisphere was the left-hand side, which contains the speech centres. This explained why, when information was presented to the right hemisphere (via the left eye), they were unable to say what they had experienced. The final tests of the right hemisphere give further support to the idea that the two hemispheres have their own consciousness, whereby one responds in a typically human way, by giggling at the nude, while the other has no idea what is going on.

Commentary: Methods and issues

Research method, design and data gathering

In order to demonstrate the effects of the surgical severing of the corpus callosum, Sperry tested the subjects under strictly controlled conditions. Using this method he was able to show evidence for brain lateralisation and work out what functions the two hemispheres of the brain perform. The strengths of carrying out research under highly controlled conditions are apparent in this study. For example, without the controls of using the screen to hide their hands from view, flashing the images only briefly and instructing the subjects not to talk unless spoken to, the functions of the two hemispheres would not have been revealed.

The findings of the study would be unlikely to be reproduced in a real-life situation or to have any impact in real life, because a person with a severed corpus callosum who had both eyes open would be able to compensate. This would be possible either because the information would be received by both sides of the brain at the same time, or because the information would be carried to the minor hemisphere by speech. (This indicates that the minor hemisphere – the right hemisphere in right-handed people – must have some speech abilities or it would not understand.) Therefore, the study lacks ecological validity. However, this is not a problem here as Sperry was fully aware that the split brain patients led normal lives. What he was trying to do here was to eke out what they could not do under controlled scientific setting, and not generalise his findings to explain any real-life behaviours of the split brain patients.

Does the study raise any ethical concerns?

The study is ethical as the subjects consented to be studied, no deception was used and they were neither harmed nor unduly stressed by the experimental tests.

Is the study useful?

Sperry's work was ground-breaking in beginning to understand the physiognomy of the brain, that is, how the brain works. It revealed the importance of the corpus callosum as a pathway for internal communication between the two sides of the brain.

Validity and reliability of the study

There are two problems with the findings that make us question their validity.

• The sample was extremely small as the condition is quite rare. We have to question whether studies of the 'abnormal' brain can really be generalised to the 'normal' brain. It may be that the experiences of the subjects prior to the surgery made their brains very different from normal brains anyway. These differences could have been caused by the epilepsy, the life-threatening nature of their disorder or the medication used to try to treat it. Add to this the fact that the subjects have undergone major brain surgery and you can see that there are significant problems with the generalisability of the findings from these subjects.

• Sperry emphasises in his conclusion to the study that even within this small sample of 11 subjects, there were 'with respect to the deconnection symptoms mentioned, striking modifications and even outright exceptions' among the split-brain patients. If there are individual differences in brain lateralisation in a sample so small, imagine the extent of individual differences we might find in the human brain in the general population.

6 The psychology of individual differences

In this last section on the core studies we will look at individual differences, a term often used in psychology. What are individual differences? Put simply, they are the differences between individuals which make it very difficult to group people together as one bunch or 'type'. Of course, we can find things that people have in common, such as their cultural backgrounds, their gender or their age. We may even be able to identify things about their personality or how clever they are, which puts them in a group with others who share similar characteristics. What we must always remember is that although we may share characteristics or abilities with others, this is only part of the story. Each of us has also had a unique set of life experiences, which has contributed towards making us what we are, and this individuality must be acknowledged, irrespective of our opinions about the differences between us.

You will have realised that our lives are enriched by the huge diversity in the human race – for example, the artistic, literary, scientific, rich, poor, old, young, blonde, brunette, male and female. After all, what a boring life we would lead if we were all the same. The difficulties with considering the wide variations in human beings, however, arise when those variations become so extreme that they make certain individuals stand out from the crowd. Take, for example, the physical characteristic of height. What is a 'normal' height? If someone is very short or very tall, are they then abnormal? If that person is 'abnormal', should he or she be treated differently or have allowances made for them, like taller doors or longer beds? Once we start to categorise or quantify people, that automatically suggests that there is a normal and an abnormal, and this is fraught with problems. Surely it depends on who is doing the judging? The first section in the chapter considers how some of these issues relate to the behaviour and characteristics of individuals, rather than their physical appearance.

Figure 6.1

Rosenhan study: On being sane in insane places

What is abnormality?

Has it ever worried you how psychiatrists and psychologists determine whether someone is abnormal? After all, most of us, at some time or other, go through stages of being a bit weird, don't we? But where do we draw the line between weird and actually 'abnormal'? And if we are abnormal, does that mean we are mentally ill?

One thing that can change our behaviour quite dramatically is the run-up to impending exams. Have you suddenly discovered how housework takes on new meaning? Bedrooms suddenly get tidied, and even the washing-up seems a better prospect than getting your head down to some really serious work. Isn't this sudden fascination with housework some kind of weird, abnormal behaviour? Then, as the exam gets closer, you feel more and more stressed and unhappy, and instead of being your normal, happy-go-lucky self, you become totally antisocial and very quiet. We could say that your behaviour has showed 'substantial change', but does that mean you have actually become 'abnormal'? Well, maybe it is abnormal for you, but there is a reason for it, and surely that makes a difference? It is no more than a kind of temporary abnormality, because as soon as the exams are over, you will revert to your normal self.

You can see that the label 'abnormal' is not quite as clear-cut as it seemed earlier, and cannot simply be assessed by looking at the way someone is behaving at a given moment. We have to take into account how the person has been over a period of time. We need to consider the situation they are in and whether there is a reason for the way they are behaving.

Defining abnormality

There have been a number of attempts to try to find a way of differentiating the normal from the abnormal. The problem is that none of them is really satisfactory. This is a problem because if we are to decide that someone is abnormal, or 'mentally ill', and needs 'treatment' then it is very important for us to know exactly what this 'abnormality' is. Otherwise how is a person to get a valid diagnosis, if they need one, and access to the right level of treatment and care, if any is needed?

The following story was written by a patient at a psychiatric hospital. If you read it, it will make you realise that labelling someone as abnormal, just because they do not behave in the same way as everyone else, has enormous ethical implications.

> Once upon a time, there was a happy man called Joe Odd. He lived in a little hut on the side of a hill with his dog, and from his window he could see right into the distance. Around the hut was a beautiful garden where he grew flowers and vegetables and lots of lupins, because lupins were his favourite flowers.

On weekdays he went to work in the valley where all the people lived in little boxes which all looked just the same, but afterwards he could go home to his little hut and watch the sunset. The people who lived in the boxes thought Joe was very strange because they all watched television. At first they said, 'Why don't you live in a box like us?' So they broke his windows and made up bad stories about him and the police said he was causing a breach of the peace.

'Ain't Joe weird – I bet he's queer … or maybe into little boys … yeah, a child molester.'

'And he hates everyone … he's dangerous … let's get him.'

So Joe locked his door and barred his windows and was afraid to go out. The garden became overgrown with weeds. Only his dog stayed by his side. One day a man came to the hut and said, 'Mr Odd, this hut is unhealthy because there is no bathroom, so we are going to pull it down, but we cannot rehouse you because you do not meet the requirements.'

Joe wandered from place to place and stole bottles of milk from doorsteps. One day the police caught him and a social worker came to take his dog to the RSPCA. Joe was so upset that he hit the social worker, so she said he could not be in his right mind and would have to be assessed. They sent Joe to a mental hospital where the doctor examined him and asked him lots of questions about his childhood and his bowel movements, then wrote on some labels and hung them round his neck. Then another social worker wrote a report about how Joe had lived in a hut with the doors and windows barred. So the doctor hung another label round his neck saying 'PERSECUTION COMPLEX', and gave him some pills to make him feel better. Joe did not like the pills because they made him feel strange and he refused to take them, so the doctor hung an 'UNCOOPERATIVE' label round his neck and gave him an injection instead.

Every week the doctor asked him lots of questions to find out what was wrong with him, but Joe refused to answer anymore, so the doctor hung an 'UNCOMMUNICATIVE' label round his neck as well. After a long time they told Joe he was better and they found him a regulation box to live in under the rehabilitation scheme. Joe lived in his little box and from his window he could see lots of other boxes, all looking just the same.

The welfare workers told him he was coping very well, but sometimes Joe still had a feeling he wanted to hit people, only he could not remember why he felt like that, because the pills made his head feel sleepy. The social worker looked at Joe's labels and told him that this was all part of his illness and that it might take a long time before he felt really better. One night he thought he heard a voice in his head saying, 'Come with me … I know a beautiful place … Come with me.'

'I can't. I am very ill. Can't you see all those labels round my neck?'

'Take them off, Joe,' said the voice again and again and again.

At last Joe lifted the labels from round his neck and threw them away. He was surprised how easy it was, and his head felt so much lighter. He opened the door and followed the voice. He walked for miles and miles and came to a beautiful place with lots of other odd people. He grew some more lupins and played music and painted pictures and flew in balloons, and he bought a cat who followed him everywhere, and everybody there loved Joe. Then one day the people in the boxes found out where he was and said he would have to come back because he was very ill.

A fleet of police cars and ambulances came after him with sirens screaming, and Joe ran along the beach into the waves to escape the noise for ever and ever and ever …

Figure 6.2

Can you see how abnormality is actually quite a frightening concept, because it implies that there is some kind of 'normal' way of behaving, and if we do not fit into that, we can be removed rather than cause our society any sort of discomfort? Although this is a story, the situation can actually become more serious when people who are not willing to conform to the behaviour that society expects, like political objectors, are made to conform by being removed and locked up under the pretext that they are abnormal and therefore mentally ill.

Abnormality as a useful concept

There are times when labelling someone as 'abnormal' can be positive. If we have a person who is extremely distressed and unhappy, and their pattern of behaviour is similar to that of others who are also distressed and unhappy, we can put them in some kind of category which means that we might have a better idea of how to support them. To take an example, this sometimes happens with children who present with difficulties with social interactions and social communication, who become distressed by changes in routine and who may find themselves isolated and anxious. If we look at the nature of the difficulty they are experiencing, we might find it helpful to consider whether they have an autistic spectrum disorder. If this is the case, they will receive specific support both within school and at home, which will make life much more acceptable for them.

Taking a less extreme example, someone who has learning difficulties with literacy, who is diagnosed as dyslexic, may feel a tremendous sense of relief, because that 'label' will have explained their difficulty, without suggesting that it is just because they are not very clever, for example.

Figure 6.3 Children with social difficulties often become isolated and anxious

It has been recognised that there are lots of different types of abnormality, and each one seems to have a number of common features. Although there is a danger in trying to put people into categories and labelling them accordingly, if they are categorised as carefully and accurately as possible, it means that medical professionals do not have to spend ages trying to work out what is going on for each individual person and can perhaps help them that much more quickly. After all, we know that someone with depression, for example, will have a whole list of symptoms which are likely to follow on, such as problems with sleeping. These problems could be addressed without having to wait to see how the disorder progresses.

What happens when the categorisation is wrong, though, especially when the person may well have been labelled and treated accordingly by medical professionals? Unfortunately, many of the labels of mental disorders automatically mean that an individual will be stereotyped, and this will impact on the way they are treated. Take the case of schizophrenia. Many people would describe a schizophrenic as someone who has a split personality, and they would come up with all sorts of behaviours that they might expect to be associated with that categorisation. Well, they would be wrong, because schizophrenia is a kind of *disorganised* personality, not a split personality. Split personality is known as *multiple personality disorder* (MPD), and is also referred to as dissociative identity disorder (DID), which you will read about in the next section. Many diagnosed schizophrenics who are receiving treatment have no symptoms at all. So what is the answer?

Classifying and diagnosing mental disorders

What American psychiatry has provided as the answer is a classification system that lists all currently accepted diagnoses of mental disorders and their symptoms and is used by psychiatrists in their work. This system is known as the Diagnostic and Statistical Manual of Mental Disorders (DSM) and was introduced in 1952 by the American Psychiatric Association.

The current version is the DSM-IV-TR, and the latest version, DSM V is due to be published shortly. The system has been revised over the years as problems were found with the accuracy of diagnoses and the revisions have aimed to improve both the validity and diagnosis of mental health problems.

The DSM consists of five axes or dimensions, which are not only used as a diagnostic tool, but also help with the planning of treatment and prediction of outcomes. Each person is assessed on every axis to give a much broader picture of what is going on in their lives, which is extremely important if we are to give a fair and valid diagnosis.

Diagnosing someone with a mental illness is a serious matter. There are so many issues that need to be considered before we risk planting some kind of label on a person, which may well be with them for the rest of their lives. Schizophrenia, for example, is an incurable illness. If someone is diagnosed, they will only ever become a schizophrenic in remission. Therefore, we cannot risk making a mistake.

The key study in this area emphasises just how easy it was to make mistakes when diagnosing mental illness, and how, once someone had been labelled as mentally ill, all their behaviours were seen in a different perspective.

You will be pleased to know that the diagnostic criteria used today are far more sophisticated than they were at the time of the core study, which was carried out in 1973. The DSM-II was in use at the time, and this second version did not have the five axes, but much more simplistic diagnostic labels. The system we now use for categorisation, we hope, is much less likely to lead to misdiagnosis than it was in the past.

The Study

D.L. Rosenhan (1973) 'On being sane in insane places', *Science*, **179: 250–8**

Background

David Rosenhan was one of a number of academics in the 1970s who were concerned about the validity and reliability of psychiatric diagnoses. The system being used by psychiatrists at the time of this study was DSM-II. Rosenhan was concerned that the diagnosis was not objective: 'it is commonplace … to read about murder trials where eminent psychiatrists for the defense are contradicted by equally eminent psychiatrists for the prosecution on the matter of the defendant's sanity.' (p.250) In other words, the same symptoms reported by a patient could be interpreted in different ways by different psychiatrists. This, of course, brings the reliability of the diagnostic system into question.

Rosenhan also points out that 'what is viewed as normal in one culture may be seen as quite aberrant in another' (p.250), and again, this challenges the idea that there is an objective and universal notion of what normality and abnormality actually are.

Rosenhan was not suggesting that odd and deviant behaviour, and the distress it brings to those experiencing it or to those around them, does not exist. He did, however, take issue with the way

... continued

such behaviour was described and categorised by the system. He wanted to investigate whether the diagnoses given to patients came from symptoms being displayed by the patient themselves, or whether their behaviours were being described as abnormal because they were in a psychiatric setting.

Haney, Banks and Zimbardo's Stanford prison experiment (1973) (see Chapter 2) aimed to test the dispositional hypothesis, in other words, to test whether it was the dispositions or character traits of the individuals who were in prison, or who worked in prisons, which made prisons brutal places, or whether the brutality was created by the way prisons were organised. The researchers came to the conclusion in their study that the best explanation of prison brutality was a situational one, that the brutality was caused by the way prison life was structured, including social roles, and the consequent psychological effects on those working in and being held in prisons.

Rosenhan's study considers a similar question. Is all the behaviour of patients on psychiatric wards described as abnormal because it is seen as a symptom of the individual's illness? Do the hospital staff identify behaviour which is a normal response to being in a psychiatric unit as 'abnormal' and evidence of the person's illness? He asks, 'Do the salient characteristics that lead to diagnoses reside in patients themselves or in the environments in which observers find them?' (p.251)

In other words, is the diagnosis of mental illness flawed because, once on the ward, the person is seen as abnormal and all their behaviours are judged in this context? Rosenhan's study suggests that the descriptions of patients' behaviour were individual when they should be situational.

Aims

The aim of Rosenhan's study was twofold. First, he aimed to test the diagnostic system to see if it was valid and reliable. He decided to do this by getting himself and seven others admitted to psychiatric hospitals to see if and how they would be discovered to be 'sane'.

Once on the ward, would the behaviour of these 'pseudopatients' be considered normal, and not lead to a psychiatric diagnosis, or would their behaviour be considered 'abnormal' because of the context they were in? If the former were true, there would be evidence that the diagnostic system was valid and reliable. If, however, the latter were true, and the pseudopatients were not detected, then, given that:

- the hospital staff were not incompetent
- the pseudopatient behaved as normally in the hospital as outside it
- it had never been suggested previously that the pseudopatient belonged in a psychiatric hospital

the fact that the pseudopatients were not detected would 'support the view that psychiatric diagnosis betrays little about the patient but much about the environment in which an observer finds him'. (p.251)

The second aim of the study was to observe and report on the experience of being a patient in a psychiatric hospital. There was little objective evidence on this as doctors did not follow up patients who were discharged, and even if they did, such data might be too subjective (and Rosenhan suggests it might be considered unreliable, as the person was previously considered insane). Researchers had acted as patients in previous studies, but the findings of these may not be valid, since the hospital staff were aware of their presence and may not have treated them like real patients. What would the pseudopatients experience and observe on the psychiatric ward?

Investigating the first aim: Could hospital staff identify the pseudopatients as being 'normal'?

Method and design

The admission of the pseudopatients to the hospitals was studied as a field experiment, and data regarding the experience of being a patient in a mental institution were gathered by covert participant observation.

... continued

Subjects

The subjects were the hospital staff and patients in psychiatric wards in 12 hospitals in the USA.

To get a representative sample, the hospitals were in five different states, from the east and west coasts; some were old and shabby, some were quite new; some had good staff–patient ratios, some did not; one was private, the others were federal or state-funded, with one university-funded; some carried out research, some did not.

Figure 6.4

Procedure

The pseudopatients were eight 'normal' people (five men and three women), and Rosenhan himself was one of them, and the first to gain admission to a hospital. Apart from a psychology graduate in his twenties, all were older and 'established' in their jobs or roles: three psychologists, a paediatrician, a psychiatrist, a painter and a housewife. All used fake names to protect their health records in the future, and the subjects who were working in the health service pretended they were in other occupations, to avoid the 'special attentions' that might be given to people from the health professions.

To gain admission, the pseudopatients were to self-present or self-refer. They phoned the hospitals for an appointment, and on arrival complained that they had been hearing voices which were unfamiliar, of the same sex and said 'empty', 'hollow' and 'thud'. Any other information given by the subjects was completely honest, including details of their family and personal background and recent life experiences. (Note: There had originally been nine pseudopatients, but data from one was omitted from the results because he falsified his personal history.)

These symptoms were chosen because they simulated existential symptoms which come from the realisation that life is really meaningless and so, as moral free agents, we have to create our own values through our actions and accept the responsibility for those actions – we cannot blame our lives on anyone else. This 'What's it all for?' experience is often distressing. Also, there are no reports of existential psychosis in any literature on mental illness, and therefore, it was thought that, although auditory hallucinations are a classic feature of schizophrenia, this would make the diagnosis harder to recognise.

(Schizophrenia = a psychiatric disorder which results in the patient suffering from a disorganised personality. They are likely to experience hallucinations, usually auditory, and delusions of grandeur or delusions of persecution.)

As soon as they were admitted to the ward, the pseudopatients ceased simulating any symptoms and aimed to behave as normally as possible, which they were able to do after the 'short-lived nervousness' they had experienced on admission faded away. This nervousness was caused either by the fact that they were admitted so easily and were fearful of being spotted as frauds straightaway and embarrassed, or, for those who had never been on a psychiatric ward, the novelty of the setting.

Results

All the pseudopatients were admitted to the hospitals, where they remained for between seven and 52 days (mean length of stay 19 days). Of the 12 admissions (some pseudopatients sought admission to more than one hospital), 11 were diagnosed with schizophrenia and one, with identical symptoms, of course, with manic-depressive psychosis. This has a more favourable prognosis (more likely to get better), and it is interesting that this was the diagnosis from the only private hospital in

... continued

the sample! When those diagnosed as schizophrenic were finally discharged, it was with the diagnosis of schizophrenia in remission. Therefore, none of the pseudopatients was detected as a fake. This was a clear failure in the diagnostic system and it was observed in all 12 hospitals in the sample.

To say they were not detected means that they were not detected by the *staff* in the hospitals. The patients, however, had their suspicions. In the first three hospitalisations, clear records of patient responses were made, with 35 of a total of 118 patients voicing their suspicions. They said things such as, 'You're not crazy. You're a journalist, or a professor [referring to the continual note-taking]. You're checking up on the hospital.' Most patients, however, were reassured by the pseudopatients' claims to have been sick before admission and fine now, but some held the view throughout that the pseudopatients were not 'real' patients. Why did the psychiatrists misdiagnose the pseudopatients? In general medicine, Rosenhan points out, it is better to err on the side of caution and risk diagnosing a healthy person as sick rather than to 'miss' an illness.

This may have been why the pseudopatients were given the misdiagnosis in the study – the doctors were being cautious. In this case, they may have decided that it was better to assume the pseudopatients were ill than to risk the possibility of failing to diagnose someone who was in fact ill.

In cases where the diagnosis is not clear, being cautious and risking the error of diagnosing a well person as sick makes sense in general medicine. However, in psychiatry this is altogether a different issue. If a healthy person is diagnosed as having a psychiatric disorder, this leaves them permanently stigmatised.

If staff mistook fake patients for real ones, would it also be possible that the opposite would occur, and that they would identify real patients as fake ones? A follow-up study was carried out to test this.

Follow-up study

Rosenhan told the staff at a large hospital, who had heard about the first part of the study and doubted that they would not be able to spot pseudopatients, that some time during the next three months, one or more pseudopatients would attempt to gain admittance to the hospital.

Each member of staff was asked to rate on a ten-point scale the likelihood of the patients who appeared being pseudopatients. Out of 193 patients who attended for psychiatric treatment, 41 were confidently judged to be pseudopatients by at least one member of staff; 23 patients were suspected by at least one psychiatrist; and 19 were thought to be acting by one psychiatrist and one other member of staff. In fact, the 193 patients were all genuine patients, as Rosenhan had sent along no pseudopatients. The hospital staff had been judging regular patients.

Rosenhan's conclusions

The fact that the pseudopatients were not detected and were each given a psychiatric diagnosis indicates that psychiatric diagnosis is not always valid. Rosenhan's claim that 'we cannot distinguish the sane from the insane in psychiatric hospitals' is actually given considerable support.

In the follow-up study, the finding that approximately 10 per cent of their normal clients were judged as pseudopatients by two staff members, including a psychiatrist, led Rosenhan to conclude that 'any diagnostic process that lends itself so readily to massive errors of this sort cannot be a very reliable one'. (p.252)

Rosenhan describes what he calls 'the stickiness of psychodiagnostic labels'. He says, 'Having once been labelled schizophrenic, there is nothing the pseudopatient can do to overcome the tag. The tag profoundly colours others' perceptions of him and his behaviour.' (p.253)

In the next section, we shall see how the behaviours demonstrated by and information given by the pseudopatients was interpreted according to their diagnoses.

... continued

Investigating the second aim: The experience of psychiatric hospitalisation

Method and design

Participant observation was used to observe the behaviour of real patients and the hospital staff, and to record the experiences of psychiatric patients. Pseudopatients also kept a diary and made notes to record their experiences and observations. This was a field study.

Subjects

The subjects were the hospital staff, the real patients and the pseudopatients themselves.

Procedure

Once admitted, the task of the pseudopatients was to behave as normally as they did outside the hospital (where no one had ever suggested that they needed to be in a psychiatric hospital!).

The pseudopatients observed and made notes about their experiences quite openly in front of staff and other patients.

Results

What was the pseudopatients' reaction to their experience?

The pseudopatients found the whole experience extremely unpleasant, not from associating with the patients, but because of their experiences with staff. It was found that there were instances of serious physical abuse to patients. Rosenhan reports having watched a patient being beaten by an attendant for going up to him and saying, 'I like you'.

Figure 6.5 The pseudopatients made notes about their experience

Acts of violence tended to go unchallenged. Verbal abuse was also recorded. Morning attendants would often wake patients with, 'Come on, you m—f—s, out of bed!' (p.256) Patients' privacy was minimal and the patients suffered loss of power and depersonalisation. They felt as if they were invisible, or unworthy of account, and this threatened their sense of identity.

The pseudopatients' note-taking behaviour

Although they had been concerned that their constant note-taking would be challenged or prevented, and had made elaborate arrangements to remove their notes from the wards each day for fear of confiscation, these precautions proved needless.

None of the staff asked them what the notes were, but simply assumed the behaviour was part of their illness. For example, in one case, the comment, 'Patient engages in writing behaviour' was inserted in the daily case notes, as if this were some bizarre and inexplicable symptom of the patient's 'illness'. On another occasion, a patient making notes was told gently by the doctor, 'You needn't write it … If you have trouble remembering, just ask me again.' This shows us how the label given to the patient – their diagnosis – affected the way the doctors and staff perceived their behaviour.

That the note-taking was observably 'normal' for someone studying the hospital was expressed by the real patients, many of whom suspected that the pseudopatients were checking up on the hospital. This did not seem to have occurred to any of the members of staff.

Further examples of how labelling affected the staff's description of the patients and pseudopatients

Anyone who has been in hospital will know that it can be very boring. You soon adapt yourself to getting through the day by moving from one routine activity to another, and mealtimes provide a way to structure the day. You find yourself looking forward to the three o'clock tea trolley for your cup of tea and custard cream. On one occasion, patients waiting outside the cafeteria for lunch were observed by a doctor in the case notes to be displaying the 'oral-acquisitive nature of the syndrome'.

... continued

Rosenhan comments, 'It seemed not to occur to him [the doctor] that there are very few things to anticipate in a psychiatric hospital besides eating.' (p.253)

Another example of the staff failing to recognise the situational impact on behaviour was noted when one of the pseudopatients was pacing the long hospital corridors. A kindly nurse approached him and asked, 'Nervous, Mr X?' 'No, bored,' he said. The nurse assumed that his pacing was a symptom of his disorder rather than his response to the unstimulating and monotonous environment in which she was observing him.

One pseudopatient talked about his upbringing and family, which seemed a typical example of how we experience changes in relationships with our parents as we get older. Sometimes we are closer to one parent at a young age, but when we reach adolescence, we find that we have become closer to the other. This may be due to one of our parents finding it harder to relate to small children, but enjoying a new-found closeness as the child matures. It is similar with marital relationships, which do not always run smoothly. Occasionally, minor rows had developed in the marriage of this pseudopatient, which were relatively meaningless. He also reported that his children had rarely been spanked. There seems nothing unusual about this history. However, the case notes talked about him having 'a long history of considerable ambivalence in close relationships, which begins in early childhood'. The notes continue by saying that his relationship with his father changes from being distant to 'becoming very intense. Affective stability is absent'. This last sentence means that his feelings have no stability – implying that he has emotional swings. The report goes on to describe the fact that his efforts to 'control emotionality with his wife and children are punctuated by angry outbursts and, in the case of the children, spankings.' The report has clearly been distorted by the diagnosis to fit in 'with a popular theory of a schizophrenic reaction'. (p.253)

If a patient went 'berserk' because he had been intentionally or unintentionally mistreated by an attendant, a nurse coming along would not inquire as to what had happened to lead to the outburst. It seemed not to be an option that the behaviour was a result of immediate environmental factors impacting on the patient, or anything to do with the staff or the hospital. Instead, his behaviour was seen as being due to his illness or perhaps his having been upset by a family visit (especially if they had visited recently).

Medication

Rosenhan reports that 2,100 pills were handed out to the pseudopatients during their stays in the hospitals, although all but two were pocketed or flushed down the toilet. The pseudopatients often found the medication of other patients down the toilet before flushing their own. As long as the behaviour of the patients was acceptable while on the wards, such actions were not noticed.

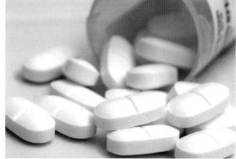

Figure 6.6

Staff contact

The staff tended to keep themselves away from the patients except for administrative or practical duties. The doctors were even more remote than the nurses, and seemed to maintain the greatest distance, only seen by patients when they came on to the ward to start their shift and again when they departed, with the time they were on duty being spent in the 'staff cage' or in their offices. Patients spent, on average, less than seven minutes a day with senior members of staff over the course of their stay. Surely it should have been the other way round, with these senior members of staff who wield the most power being the most familiar with the patients' case histories and behaviours?

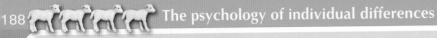

... continued

The physicians acted as models for those lower down the staff hierarchy. The attendants were the staff on the ward who had least power and while they were the ones likely to have the most contact with the patients, even they were inclined to take their lead from the physicians and avoid contact with patients by spending most of their time in the staff cage.

Powerlessness and depersonalisation

These two key psychological factors were observed to be affecting the patients (and the pseudopatients).

The pseudopatients reported on the patients' complete lack of power in the psychiatric wards. Their movements were watched and restricted, they had virtually no contact with staff, and their medical files were available to all members of staff, even volunteers.

Acts of violence against patients were observed by other patients, some of whom were pseudopatients writing it all down. The abusive behaviour immediately stopped when another member of staff appeared. The fact that staff were considered credible witnesses and patients were not is an indication of the patients' lack of power.

We have already noted that those with the most power (the physicians) spent least time with the patients, and that attendants spent most of their time in the cage, where the power within the ward was based. The fact that staff went about their business as if the patients were not there, and that the ward staff spent as little time on the ward with the patients as possible, added to the invisibility felt by the pseudopatients.

The patients also suffered from a minimum of personal privacy. For example, physical examinations carried out prior to admission were conducted in semi-public rooms where 'staff went about their own business as if we were not there'. (p.256) Once on the ward it was not unusual for toilet cubicles to have no doors and for the 'personal hygiene and waste evacuation' of the patient to be 'monitored'. (p.256)

Evidence from the study shows that patients could not initiate contact with staff, that they were expected to be passive and to respond only to any overtures initiated by staff members. Rosenhan illustrates this point clearly with the findings of a study on responses to patient-initiated contact carried out at four of the hospitals. The nature of this study involved recording responses by staff to a courteous and relevant request made by the pseudopatient. This was adapted to fit the target person and the setting, but followed along the lines of, 'Pardon, me, Mr [or Dr or Mrs] X, could you tell me when I will be eligible for grounds privileges?' (or 'When will I be presented at the staff meeting?'). The request was never asked of the same staff member on any one day, to avoid irritating them or raising their suspicions, and it was neither bizarre nor disruptive. It was the initiation of a perfectly reasonable conversation.

Table 6.1

The responses to patient-initiated contact

Contact	Psychiatrists in Rosenhan's study	Nurses and attendants in Rosenhan's study
Moves on, head averted	71%	88%
Makes eye contact	23%	10%
Pauses and chats	2%	2%
Stops and talks	4%	0.5%
Number of respondents	13	47
Number of attempts	185	1,283

Source: Adapted from Rosenhan (1973:255)

... continued

As you can see from the table, the patients were pretty ineffective when it came to initiating a conversation with a staff member with a polite and relevant question. The response rate for psychiatrists was only about 7 per cent, with the other staff being even worse, responding only about 4 per cent of the time.

As Rosenhan points out, the time a person spends with you can be a measure of your importance to them. Lack of eye contact and lack of verbal contact indicate avoidance and depersonalisation. Given this fact, it is not surprising that the pseudopatients felt deindividuated and unworthy of account. The fact that the majority of reactions were in the 'Moves on, head averted' category shows how they may have come to believe that they were 'invisible' to staff.

Rosenhan compared these findings with a similar study carried out at Stanford University. A female student asked six similar questions (for directions, about college admission and if there was financial aid) of tutors in the university faculty and the university medical centre. In the university medical centre she added a comment after her first question. To some respondents she said, 'I'm looking for an internist', and to others she said, 'I'm looking for a psychiatrist', and to yet a third group she made no additional comment; otherwise the questioning was the same. The results were as follows:

Table 6.2

Responses to questions asked by a female student in the university medical centre

Contact	'Looking for a psychiatrist'	'Looking for an internist'	No additional comment
Moves on, head averted	0%	0%	0%
Makes eye contact	11%	0%	0%
Pauses and chats	11%	0%	10%
Stops and talks	78%	100%	90%
Mean number of questions answered (out of six)	3.8	4.8	4.5
Number of respondents	18	15	10
Number of attempts	18	15	10

Source: Adapted from Rosenhan (1973:255)

The response rate was generally much higher in the university medical centre than it was for the pseudopatients on the ward. It is interesting that when the female student indicated she was 'looking for a psychiatrist', the percentage response decreased to 78 per cent. This may indicate that people find mental illness quite hard to deal with, and were reluctant to help someone 'looking for a psychiatrist' because of the social stigma associated with mental illness.

What were the consequences of depersonalisation for the pseudopatients? Rosenhan reports that the pseudopatients were sufficiently distressed by their experience of depersonalisation to instigate a number of attempts to re-establish and assert their identity. The graduate student in psychology asked his wife to bring in his books so he could catch up on his studies, even though this was likely to give away his true profession. Another pseudopatient tried to initiate a romantic involvement with a nurse. He then told staff he was applying to be a psychology graduate and then engaged in psychotherapy with other patients. It is clear from these examples that the pseudopatients were greatly affected by their experience, and these could be seen as attempts to reassert their individuality.

... continued

What were the sources of depersonalisation?

Rosenhan considers two sources of depersonalisation in psychiatric hospitals. First, he sees depersonalisation as a product of generally held prejudices towards the mentally ill. 'The mentally ill', he tells us, 'are society's lepers.' We avoid contact with them at all costs. This is ingrained in the history of institutionalised care for the mentally ill, who were often locked up indefinitely and subjected to brutal treatment. Society's response was not only out of sight, out of mind, but 'if you are out of your mind it is best if you are out of our sight'. Rosenhan points out that the staff in psychiatric wards are not immune from this prejudice, and that it influences them in the hospital setting, just as it does outside the hospital on people in society at large.

The second source of depersonalisation, according to Rosenhan, was a result of the hierarchical structure where, as we have seen, doctors have all the power, patients have none, and those staff in between follow the doctors' model of avoidance of contact with patients. Rosenhan says that this does not mean that the staff were uncaring, in fact, he states, 'our overwhelming impression of them was of people who really cared, who were committed and who were uncommonly intelligent'. However, 'where they failed, as they sometimes did painfully, it would be more accurate to attribute those failures to the environment in which they, too, found themselves than to personal callousness'. In other words, the behaviour of both the staff and the patients can be attributed to situational rather than individual factors.

Other sources of depersonalisation may also be at work; where money is tight, patient contact may be first to suffer. This is facilitated by the extensive use of psychotropic drugs, which control the patients and keep them passive.

Rosenhan's conclusions

Rosenhan describes how psychiatric hospitals create environments where behaviour gets easily distorted to fit in with diagnostic labels and social prejudices. Consequently, patients are treated in such a way as to perpetuate any problems they may have. Rosenhan suggests the need for further research into social psychology of institutions, both to facilitate treatment and to deepen understanding. After all, would it not be better to work at changing the way we think about people in distress and try to provide the kind of social environment which would help and support them?

If patients were powerful rather than powerless, if they were viewed as interesting individuals rather than diagnostic entities, if they were socially significant rather than social lepers, if their anguish truly and wholly compelled our sympathies and concerns, would we not *seek* contact with them, despite the availability of medications? (p.257)

Commentary: Methods and issues

Is the study ecologically valid?

To the extent that the real behaviour of real patients and real staff was observed, the study is high in ecological validity. However, can we consider the reports of the pseudopatients' own feelings and responses as being the same as those of real patients? For example, the experience of the pseudopatients was different from the real patients' experience in that the pseudopatients knew that their diagnosis was false and that they were not really mentally ill. Their experience was comparable to real patients' experience in that staff were unaware of the false diagnosis of the pseudopatients and treated them the same way as they treated the other patients, and in this way their experience is a valid one.

As to whether the conclusion that there were problems with diagnosis is genuine, there are some concerns that need to be addressed. Although, once they had been admitted, the pseudopatients believed they had stopped showing any signs of abnormality, we cannot be sure that this was the case. If they were anxious and nervous, this might well have influenced their behaviour, both prior to diagnosis and after they had been admitted to the wards. This, and the novel experience of being institutionalised, or being separated from loved ones, may have meant that their behaviour appeared more unusual than they might have thought.

The study highlights the ease with which the pseudopatients were misdiagnosed. However, the doctors were not completely wrong in their diagnoses, because after a period of observation they did diagnose the pseudopatients as having schizophrenia in remission, in other words, their absence of symptoms was noted and they were discharged. Nonetheless, this does not account for their misdiagnosis in the first place.

Does the study raise any ethical considerations?

The ethical considerations of the study involve deception, whereby the medical practitioners were deceived by the pseudopatients in the symptoms they claimed to be experiencing. The follow-up study also raises some ethical concerns. It involved real patients being treated with undue suspicion and perhaps not receiving the care they felt they needed. This could have added to the anguish they were already experiencing, as they would not, presumably, have self-referred for psychiatric care if they were not experiencing a considerable amount of distress.

The covert observation of staff and patients on the wards raises the issue that informed consent was not obtained from the subjects. They were not given the right to withdraw and they could not be debriefed. Rosenhan justifies this by pointing out that without concealment of the identities of the pseudopatients, the findings would not be valid. He says that to counteract any effects of this concealment, he ensured that the anonymity of particular hospitals and their staff would be maintained.

What about the ethics surrounding the safety of the pseudopatients? At the outset, Rosenhan says he did not realise how difficult it was to get discharged at short notice from a psychiatric ward. However, with legal advice, a writ of *habeus corpus* was prepared for each of the pseudopatients on entry and an attorney was kept on call. (Although usually used to compel the police to justify the continued detention of a suspect, a writ of *habeus corpus*, issued by a judge, would require that a person who is detaining another present the detainee in court.)

The pseudopatients reported that they did not like the experience and wanted to be discharged straight after admission. However, they did as they had been instructed and Rosenhan was able to report their findings.

At least the pseudopatients had the advantage of knowing that they were not mentally ill, and, unlike the real patients, would leave behind them the powerlessness and depersonalisation of the institution when they left the hospital. For the real patients who needed care, however, powerlessness and depersonalisation were part of the package. Even if they did get well enough to be discharged, the stigma of mental illness would be with them forever.

Studies that are highly useful and which lead to change for the better can be described as ethically worthy. It is important to point out that although this study raises some ethical issues, the findings it generated and its purpose in testing and establishing the reliability of psychiatric diagnosis mean that it had a worthy purpose. In this case we can conclude that the end justified the means.

Is the study useful?

At the time it was reported, the study highlighted problems with the diagnosis of mental illness that needed to be addressed. The current diagnostic criteria, DSM-IV-TR, is a great deal more reliable and valid than DSM-II. However, that DSM V is due to be published as this book is written suggests there is still room for improvement.

To gain admission to an institution now in the USA is much more difficult than at the time of Rosenhan's study. Now the patient must:

* be diagnosed as having a mental disorder (and diagnosis now takes longer to confirm, e.g. continuous symptoms for one to six months for schizophrenia)

* be suffering from a disorder which could not be treated in a less restrictive environment

* be a danger either to themselves or to others.

Because of this, Rosenhan's study would not be possible to replicate. This is a strength and not a weakness, and demonstrates the impact of studies such as this one on the diagnostic system.

The study also provided evidence of the powerlessness and depersonalisation that was experienced by the patients, the lack of contact with staff, the abusive behaviour that went unchecked and the reliance on medication rather than contact with caring and supportive staff in the treatment of psychiatric patients. Nowadays, the 'total institution' approach to the care of psychiatric patients is considered the exception rather than the norm. Where possible, people are cared for in the community. However, this does not mean that there are not problems associated with such provision. Financial pressures mean that the care that is needed may not be provided. Staff may be overstretched and serve large geographical areas.

Most depressing is that the social stigma associated with psychiatric illness is no less in evidence now than it was in 1973, and integrating people with mental illness into a community that both fears and shuns them can be difficult. Education is a key factor in successful integration.

Thigpen and Cleckley study: The three faces of Eve (multiple personality disorder)

What is personality?

Personality can be defined as 'the distinctive and characteristic patterns of thought, emotion and behaviour that define an individual's personal style and influence his or her interactions with the environment' (Atkinson *et al.* 1993: 525). This definition really captures the fact that each of us has distinctive patterns of thought, emotion and behaviour, and it is how these patterns interact that makes us what we are. It also suggests that if each one of us has these patterns, the component parts of each can be compared to those of other people. In other words, our common understanding is that we have one personality that makes us unique and individual.

But is it possible to have more than one personality?

Multiple personality disorder

One of the most fascinating mental disorders is multiple personality disorder (MPD), or dissociative identity disorder (DID), as it is now known. It is fascinating, partly because it is so rare and causes such bizarre behaviour, and partly because it is a disorder which has a purely psychological basis.

People who suffer from DID appear to have all the different aspects of their personality, but each part is contained in a separate unit. Pervin suggested that in a 'normal' person all these processes act together to form an integrated whole, which is what our personalities are, but it seems that with DID they do not form an integrated whole. Instead they stay as individual units, each one taking on aspects of an individual personality, so it is as if one body contains lots of different people.

Someone who suffers from DID can therefore have any number of different personalities and each split is locked into its own personal role. Each personality has its own characteristics, likes and dislikes. Each may even live its own life alongside the others, while being contained within one body: the childlike part, the sensible part, the jealous part, the fun-loving part, and so on, which all exist as individual units, are often given different names.

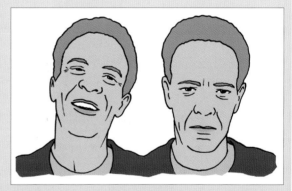

Figure 6.7 Multiple personalities are often very different from one another

In order to be diagnosed as having dissociative identity disorder, the DSM-IV-TR says the person must have at least two separate 'personalities', which are called ego states or alters, and each one must have its own way of feeling and acting that is totally independent from any of the other alters. Each of these alters has to come forward and take control at different times. Their existence cannot be temporary; they must exist for some time and should cause the person quite a lot of disruption, rather than simply being the result of taking drugs or drinking too much, for example.

People who suffer with DID are extremely likely to have gaps in their memories. If they are aware of one alter, but there are actually three, for example, they will not know what is going on when the other two take turns at being in control. It will be as if they keep having blackouts or lapses in memory, which must be really frightening. What must be even worse is if one unrecognised alter does something that the person is unaware of. When the second alter arrives, it will have to deal with the consequences. In fact, it could be quite embarrassing if one alter went out partying and the next day left the other to account for the disapproval they might face after their alter's drunken antics!

Some alters may know about some of the others, but not all of them, and some may be unaware of the existence of any other personality. There are often primary alters and subordinate alters. The primary alters are the main personalities, which manifest most often. The subordinate alters have less relevance and are rarely present, or may even be undetected for some time after the disorder is recognised. Often the subordinate alters may hear the voices of the others but not be aware of who they belong to; in other instances, some of the alters may even talk to each other. Each alter will usually be very different, possibly even of the opposite sex. Some may be older than others, some may be extrovert and some introvert. Each one will have its own patterns of behaviour, its own experiences, its own memories and its own relationships with other people. It is literally like having a number of different people living in the same body, each one making their own decisions and acting out their own roles. They may even have different physical characteristics, for example, one may be left-handed, another right-handed. One may even like one type of food while the next finds it disgusting.

Although DID was recognised in the nineteenth century, it seems that there was a fall in reported cases between 1920 and 1970, but then it increased again. This may well have been due to the popularity of schizophrenia as a diagnosis in the intervening years. One thing that was quite interesting was that there was a rise in the number of alters of diagnosed patients that seemed to coincide with the publication of a book called *Sybil* (Schreiber, 1973), which told the story of a woman with 16 personalities. Before Sybil, the number of alters was two or three, but after the book the average rose to ten.

Possibly the most accepted theory to explain DID is that it occurs in early childhood as a way of coping with traumatic or disturbing events. Learning theorists suggest that the child learns how to deal with the stressful memories by adopting an avoidance technique. The child 'hypnotises' or fools itself into believing that the events have not happened to them, but to someone else, and this someone else becomes another alter. Bliss (1983) discovered that people suffering from DID are easier to hypnotise than controls, and suggested that this might support the idea.

Not surprisingly, women are more likely to develop DID than men. This may well be affected by the fact that the number of girls who become victims of sexual abuse is higher than for boys. A study of 796 college students found that 19 per cent of the women and 8.6 per cent of the men had been sexually abused as children (Finkelhor, 1979). The women often present other symptoms, such as depression or headaches, before the DID is acknowledged. It seems that DID is frequently accompanied by substance abuse, self-abuse or suicide attempts – all of which go along with low self-esteem or guilt arising from abuse.

It is not surprising, then, that children who have been through such traumatic relationships find it hard to deal with what has happened. Of course, they would need to protect themselves from any further hurt, and perhaps this fragmentation is a way of doing so. If this is the case, the treatment must involve trying to convince the person that it is not necessary to split their personality in order to deal with their earlier traumas, and helping them to reintegrate. However, before this can happen, they have to acknowledge the actual split. It seems that hypnosis is a good technique to use as it gives the person access to hidden portions of their personality.

A landmark case of multiple personality disorder was that of Eve White, the subject of our core study. This was the most carefully documented report of MPD/DID at the time and, as such, deserves a place within the core studies.

The Study

Corbett H. Thigpen and Hervey Cleckley (1954) 'A case of multiple personality', *Journal of Abnormal and Social Psychology*, **49: 135–51**

Background

Is the diagnosis of dual-personality or multiple personality disorder (the precursors of the diagnosis DID) a valid one? Is it really possible for more than one 'personality' to reside in one body, each with experiences, memories and wills separate and distinct from each other?

Thigpen and Cleckley described the scepticism with which psychiatry regarded such a diagnosis; that the MPD sufferer was to psychiatry what the unicorn or centaur was to natural history – simply a myth. Although cases had been reported in the past, notably that of Mrs Beauchamp, reported by Morton Prince in 1909, modern psychiatry in the 1950s tended to gloss over or ignore MPD. The authors suggest that this is probably because of a lack of contemporary and objective evidence. The diagnosis relies heavily on the patient's subjective reporting of experience, and may therefore be the product of the patient's deceit or the observer's wishful thinking, and was (and still is) treated with a great deal of scepticism.

Thigpen and Cleckley, however, believed they might have discovered such a case, and this study is a report of their findings. They too had viewed MPD with scepticism, but now reported that 'our direct experience with a patient has forced us to review the subject of multiple personality. It has also provoked in us the reaction of wonder, sometimes of awe'. (p.136)

Had the psychiatrists really encountered the psychiatric equivalent in myth and rarity to the unicorn? Was this a true case of MPD?

Aim

The aim of this case study was to document the psychotherapeutic treatment of a 25-year-old woman, who had a history of severe headaches and blackouts, and whom therapy had revealed appeared to have multiple personality disorder. The purpose was to review the evidence and consider the validity of the diagnosis.

Method

The case study method was used, with the subject (patient) attending for regular therapeutic sessions over a 14-month period. Using notes from over 100 hours of therapy, the researchers documented the evidence for the diagnosis of MPD.

The data, therefore, was heavily reliant on the patient's self-report of her subjective experiences. The therapists also interviewed the patient's husband and family.

As well as the evidence from interviews, tests were carried out in an attempt to distinguish the personalities from each other. Psychometric measures were taken of memory function and IQ, the Rorschach ink-blot test was used, and EEG patterns were recorded and compared. A handwriting expert also compared the handwriting of the personalities.

The subject and the beginnings of the evidence of MPD

The patient in the study, given the name Eve White by the researchers to protect her identity, was, on referral, a fairly run-of-the-mill case. She had been referred because of 'severe and blinding headaches'. At the first interview she told of 'blackouts' following the headaches, where she suffered memory loss.

Eve White's marriage was disintegrating and this caused her a great deal of concern and distress. She had a four-year-old daughter, to whom she was devoted, and this compounded her distress about her failing marriage. At first she was only able to attend for consultation irregularly, as she was travelling quite a distance. After some months of therapy, the authors noted that 'encouraging symptomatic improvement occurred, but it was plain that this girl's major problem had not been settled'.

... continued

Figure 6.8 Photograph of Joanne Woodward as Eve White, Eve Black and Jane in the film Three faces of Eve which won her an Oscar for best actress

Her case seemed ordinary, with Eve White being described at that time as a client presenting with 'commonplace symptoms and a relatively complex but familiar constellation of marital conflicts and personal frustrations'.

The loss of memory for a recent trip puzzled the psychiatrists, but they hypnotised her and this seemed to be cleared up. However, it was at this point in her treatment that an event occurred which was to be a key factor in the emergence of 'another' personality in the therapy room. They received a letter from Eve White which appeared to have been finished off by someone else, the writing described as a 'child-like hand'.

Questioned on her next visit, Eve White denied sending the letter, but did remember starting one.

She was then agitated and distressed and asked whether it meant she was insane if she was hearing an imaginary voice. This question surprised the therapists, because Eve White had shown no other symptoms of 'schizoid' behaviour, and also because she was able to report the voice with a concern about the experience which was atypical of those patients experiencing auditory hallucinations.

Before the therapists could reply, however:

> 'as if seized by a sudden pain she put both hands to her head. After a tense moment of silence, her hands dropped. There was a quick restless smile, and in a bright voice that sparkled she said "Hi there, Doc …"' (p.137)

> 'She then crossed her legs and the therapists noticed for the first time that they were attractive. It seemed as if someone else, someone other than Eve White, was now present in Eve White's body:

> Instead of that retiring and gently conventional figure, there was in the newcomer a childishly daredevil air, an erotically mischievous glance, a face marvellously free from the habitual signs of care, seriousness and underlying distress, so long familiar in her predecessor. This new and apparently carefree girl spoke casually of Eve White and her problems, always using she or her in every sentence, always respecting the strict bounds of a separate identity. When asked her own name she immediately replied "Oh, I'm Eve Black".' (p.137)

The therapists were so convinced that this was a 'newcomer', different from Eve White in every respect, that they believed this might be a case of MPD, a major 'find' in the world of psychiatry. From this point on, their interest in and therapy with this client increased.

Differences between and experiences of Eve White and Eve Black

Over the 14 months of therapy, the therapists found out a lot about the personality they called Eve Black (EB):

- EB had 'enjoyed an independent life since Mrs White's early childhood', so had appeared long ago in Mrs White's life.

- Eve White (EW) was not consciously aware of EB, and although told of the existence of EB in therapy, she remained unable to access EB or her memories or experiences. EW was 'in abeyance' or 'unconscious' when EB was 'out' (one 'personality' at a time is supposedly dominant in such cases, and the dominance of the other personality was described as her coming 'out').

... continued

- EB, on the other hand, was aware of EW and was able to follow the thoughts and actions of EW as a 'spectator'. Although an onlooker in EW's home life and aware of EW's feelings, EB did not participate in or share them. She dismissed as 'silly' EW's concerns about her failing marriage, and spoke of the devotion of EW to her four-year-old daughter as 'something pretty corny'.

- EB could at first only be 'brought out' by the therapists while EW was under hypnosis. However, she could 'pop out' at any time in EW's life. The therapists did not know how she did this, but she would not come out at their request without hypnotising EW. However, after a few sessions using hypnosis it was possible to study the two personalities simply by asking one to allow the other to come out to speak to the therapists. This helped the therapists, but it made life difficult for EW, as now EB found she could get out more and take over. EB being in control often made for unpleasant consequences for EW.

- EB was neither compassionate nor cruel to EW; she seemed unaffected by human emotions. EB was 'shallowly hedonistic', intent only on pleasure-seeking and fun in the present moment. Unfortunately for EW, 'fun' for EB had often meant 'mischief' as a child, and she reported having got EW into trouble with her parents at six years old. They had forbidden her from walking through the woods to play with children who lived on the other side, as they felt it was not safe. EB had done this, however, and had only let EW 'come out' to receive the 'whipping' for disobeying her parents.

- It soon became clear that EB was prone to lying. Her 'evidence' in therapy was therefore considered by the authors to be less reliable than that given by EW, who seemed honest and open. EW could substantiate some of EB's stories, however, agreeing that there were times as a child when she had received punishments from her parents without knowing the reason why. Some of EB's claims about her adult behaviour were substantiated by EW's husband and family.

- Until she agreed to be 'introduced' to them by the therapists, EB had managed to conceal herself from EW's family when she was out. She had done this by pretending to be Eve White (imitating her voice and mannerisms and behaviours). When EB's true character had been shown, EW's family considered the 'wayward behaviour, ill will, harshness and occasional acts of violence' as being 'unaccountable fits of temper in a woman [EW] habitually gentle and considerate'. (p.139)

- On one occasion, EB 'recklessly bought several expensive and unneeded new dresses and two luxurious coats'. This caused EW's husband to go into a rage for 'wantonly plunging him into debt'. EW tried to protest her innocence, but of course, her husband did not accept this. He did calm down, however, when she agreed it would be a disaster for them to be in such debt and took the clothes back to the shop. EW told the therapists she thought her husband had planted the clothes to make her look as if she had gone mad. This fitted in with the problems they were having in their marriage. EB had not only been extravagant in her shopping, but also 'revels in cheap night clubs, flirting with men on the make'. She also told the therapists, 'When I go out and get drunk … she wakes up with the hangover. She wonders what in the hell's made her so sick'. Although EB had not been the cause of the marital problems between EW and her husband, it was clear that her behaviours when she was out did little to help overcome them, if indeed any sort of reconciliation were possible.

- Although usually indifferent to EW's four-year-old daughter, EB did once hurt her, although she denied this (even though there was evidence to the contrary from EW's husband). She did confess to it later, saying flippantly, 'The little brat got on my nerves.'

With all this evidence, the therapists came to believe that EW and EB were indeed two separate personalities, taking turns in the same body. However, they recognised that it was difficult for them to explain to anyone else exactly *what* it was that made them believe that EB was different from

... continued

EW, drawing the parallel that a man could pick out his wife from 100 other women looking and dressing similarly, but could not give the instructions to a stranger to do the same. They did, however, draw up a comparison between the two to try to catalogue the qualitative differences between them that, for Thigpen and Cleckley, marked out EW and EB as distinctly separate from each other.

Table 6.3

Summary of differences between Eve White and Eve Black

Feature	Eve White	Eve Black
Summary of character	Demure, 'almost saintly'	Party girl, childishly vain, egocentric
Face	Sweet and sad	Pixie-like eyes dance with mischief
Dress and behaviour	Dresses sensibly (conservatively); has a stooped posture, is dignified; reads poetry; is well-liked, industrious and capable	Dresses provocatively, is witty, coarse and rowdy; likes to play pranks: her intent is fun, but the consequences are often cruel for others
Attitude	Serious, and distressed by her current problems; did not blame her husband, loved her daughter deeply	Never serious, unaffected by human emotions, grief and tragedy
Allergy to nylon	Reported no such allergy	Claimed to be allergic to nylon and did not wear stockings when she was out for long periods

Source: Adapted from Thigpen and Cleckley (1954:141–2)

Of course, this evidence is subjective, and in an attempt to satisfy scientific readers, Thigpen and Cleckley arranged for tests to be carried out to try to establish the two personalities as distinct from each another. Two types of tests were used: psychometric tests, where IQ and memory function were tested, and two projective tests, the Rorschach ink-blot test and a test drawing human figures.

Key concept

Projective tests

In a projective test, the subject is asked to draw something or look at something. The way they draw the figure, or what they 'see' in the ink blot, is supposed to reveal their personality; in other words, they 'project' themselves on to the test and this can supposedly be summarised by a person trained in administering the tests. Whether such tests provide a valid description of the person is affected by the fact that the respondent may lie, manipulating their responses to try to give a good (or perhaps, bad) account of themselves. The test interpretation will also be affected by the prevailing beliefs of the psychiatric profession at the time of testing, or indeed the personal beliefs held by the tester.

Figure 6.9

... continued

The tests were carried out by a well-qualified expert. The findings are summarised in the table below.

Table 6.4

Test	Eve White	Eve Black
Wechsler intelligence test (IQ)	110	104
Wechsler memory test	Superior	Inferior
Projective tests (human figure drawing and Rorschach test)	Indication of: R repression conflict and anxiety in her role as mother hostility to her mother	Indication of: regression (the name she used was in fact the patient's maiden name), indicating a desire to return to an earlier period of life, before marriage

Source: adapted from Thigpen and Cleckley (1954)

The findings from the tests are not conclusive and do not provide evidence that the two 'personalities' are separate from each other.

Attempts at therapy and the emergence of a third personality, Jane

Although a fascinating case for both the therapists and the reader, the purpose for the patient of being in consultation with the therapists was to get relief from her difficulties and distress. The therapists noted that in previously reported cases, the secondary personality 'helped' the other. There appeared to be no evidence of EB helping EW; in fact, all the evidence appeared to the contrary – EB's behaviour when she was out simply made matters worse for EW.

As a therapeutic intervention, Thigpen and Cleckley tried to encourage EB to help. She would, however, only help if it interested her to do so. She would lie and pretend to be helping when she was not, when in fact she was doing the opposite, and 'her behaviour was particularly detrimental to Eve White's progress'. (p.142) They did, however, manage to encourage her to cooperate by bargaining with her. It became clear that now she was aware of her existence, EW could block EB out and prevent her from taking over (although EW was still not wholly successful at this). The therapists bargained with EB for good behaviour in return for more time out.

Further revelations came from EB at this point. She could influence EW even when she was not out. It was she, she claimed, who had been the voice EW had heard, and she who was responsible for giving EW headaches. She also claimed to be able to wipe out memories from Eve White, and she used this as an explanation for EW having no memory of beatings she was made to receive at the hands of a man with whom EB had cohabited prior to EW's own marriage. While there were no records of the 'marriage', a distant relative had described to the therapists that there was good evidence that she had lived with a man at this time, although EW denied this ever happened.

After about eight months, it appeared that EW was indeed getting better. She was no longer with her husband, and her daughter was living with her parents. This latter point caused her great distress, but she was comforted by the fact that she was able to hold down a job and provide for her daughter. She was doing well in her job and was hopeful of a reunion with her husband. EB had been causing less trouble, and rarely 'came out' at work, which she found boring, because she did not want to interfere with the 'breadwinner' when she was earning her keep. However, in leisure hours she often 'got in bad company, picked up dates, and indulged in cheap and idle flirtations', but EW, unaware of this, was spared the embarrassment of this conduct.

... continued

However, at this point, when things seemed to be going so well, EW took a turn for the worse. The headaches and blackouts returned, and this time a room-mate found her unconscious twice as a result of the blackouts. What was different was that EB claimed not to be causing the headaches, and, although she did not get headaches, she claimed she was also experiencing the blackouts this time. She told the therapists, 'I don't know where we go, but go we do.'

EW found it hard to work and her new-found confidence waned. It looked as if she would have to be hospitalised, as the therapists thought 'a psychosis was impending'. Although they kept this from EW, they told EB about it by way of warning her off mischief: if EW was put in an institution, so would she be, and this would greatly curtail her activities!

Thigpen and Cleckley also attempted to fuse the two personalities together, on the assumption that they had somehow started off as integrated and later fractured. They did this by trying to call both personalities out at the same time, but this caused the patient more distress and they stopped attempting it.

They then approached this aim by trying to work back into childhood with the two personalities, presumably to take them back to the point where EB emerged. They were able to do this with EW through hypnosis, but never managed to hypnotise EB.

Soon after the headaches and blackouts had returned, EW was in such a session, recalling a painful experience when she had been scalded by hot water as a child, when:

> *'As she spoke her eyes shut sleepily. Her head dropped back on the chair. After remaining in this sleep or trance perhaps two minutes her eyes opened. Blankly she stared about the room, looking at the furniture and the pictures as if trying to orient herself. Continuing their apparently bewildered survey, her eyes finally met those of the therapist, and stopped. Slowly, with an unknown husky voice, and with immeasurable poise, she spoke. "Who are you?"' (p.144)*

Thigpen and Cleckley say it was apparent that this was neither EB nor EW. A third personality had 'come out', and the therapists called her Jane. They studied this 'other woman' and described her as follows:

> *'she apparently lacks EB's obvious faults and inadequacies. She also impresses us as far more mature, more vivid, more boldly capable and more interesting than EW ... in her [Jane] are indications of initiative and powerful resources never shown by the other [EW].' (p.145)*

The differences between Eve White, Eve Black and Jane

By their descriptions, it is clear that Thigpen and Cleckley could identify EW, EB and Jane by their demeanour and behaviour. But again, this is subjective evidence.

Two more experts were brought in to study the now three personalities for evidence of observable distinctions between them that would support the diagnosis of multiple personality disorder. The handwriting of each was analysed by an expert who concluded that 'beyond any doubt they have been written by one and the same individual'. An EEG was used to record and compare their brainwave activity. The results were as follows.

Table 6.5

Eve White	Jane	Eve Black
11 cycles per second (normal)	11 cycles per second (normal)	12.5 cycles per second, a slightly fast EEG reading that is sometimes associated with psychopathic personality

Source: adapted from Thigpen and Cleckley (1954)

... continued

Jane and EW could not be distinguished from each other; they were both described as 'normal'. EB, however, was borderline-normal and was distinguishable from Jane and EW.

The way forward for the patient?

Having studied the three personalities for some time, the therapists came to see Jane taking over as a possible answer to EW's problems:

> 'As time passes, Jane stays "out" more and more. She emerges only through EW, never yet having found a way to displace EB or to communicate through her.' (p.146)

They describe Jane as compassionate for EW's distress and able to come out and help EW at work. They say:

> 'Could Jane remain in full possession of that integrated human functioning we call personality our patient would probably, we believe, regain full health, eventually adjust satisfactorily, perhaps at a distinctly superior level and find her way to a happy life.' (p.146)

However, they claim that it was neither their intent, nor was it in their power, to bring about such an outcome. They ask: 'Would any physician order euthanasia of the heedlessly merry and amoral but nevertheless unique EB?'

Although Jane would be a good mother to EW's daughter, and probably would not return to EW's husband and the problems of the marriage, would 'killing off' EW, or allowing her to 'leave forever' for her child's sake be the right answer? Jane thought not. She wrote to the therapists, having 'seen' EW apparently saving a child from being knocked down in the street: 'She [EW] must not die yet. There is so much I must know, and so very much I must learn from her … '; and on the saving of the child: 'I have never been thus affected by anything in my four months of life.'

Jane had shared knowledge of both Eves' behaviours after her own emergence, but had no access to experiences or memories of either Eve before she had first emerged, knowing only what she had been told. EW was conscious of neither Jane nor EB, although she was aware of their existence through the reports of the therapists. EB was aware of EW but not of Jane.

Discussion

Thigpen and Cleckley considered that they may not have observed a true case of MPD, but may have been 'thoroughly hoodwinked by a skilful actress'. (p.147) However, given that the therapy went on for an extended period of time, during which they noted nothing that would suggest the patient was faking, they state: 'we do not think that any person could over months avoid even one tell-tale error or imperfection'.

Was Eve White's disintegration of personality due to schizophrenia? Thigpen and Cleckley considered this to be unlikely, since none of the personalities showed any symptoms of that disorder.

In moving towards the diagnosis of MPD, Thigpen and Cleckley concede that they may have lost their objectivity because of their involvement with the patient, and therefore their judgement was affected by their relationship with her. They point out that while the three personalities appeared distinct and separate to the therapists, the evidence from objective testing was 'not particularly impressive', and could not provide clear evidence of distinctions between EW, EB and Jane.

The therapists were careful not to make the claim that the case was indeed one of MPD, but suggest that the experiences of their client raised a number of important questions for both psychology and psychiatry. What do we mean by 'personality'? How are we to describe it?

They discuss the case of Mrs Beauchamp, presented by Morton Prince in 1909, and suggest that a review of his work and further study of patients with MPD in the future might give psychiatrists the necessary insight to explain that which could not be explained scientifically at the time of writing up the case of Eve White.

Commentary: Methods and issues

What are the strengths and weaknesses of the case study method?

The strengths include the large amount of detailed and qualitative data gathered about the patient in over 100 hours of therapy. The longitudinal nature of the study made it harder for the patient, if she was faking, to keep up any pretence.

The weaknesses include the possibility that the researchers' relationship with the patient may have affected their judgement of the case and led to them being unwittingly 'fooled' by the patient, or indeed overlooking any evidence that might have suggested she was 'play-acting', or evidence of any other explanation for the behaviour they observed.

Does the study raise any ethical concerns?

The study was governed by medical ethics at the time, rather than the ethical guidelines for research with human participants in use today. The use of a pseudonym was an ethical consideration to protect the patient and her family on publication of the case. The researchers also raise the point of whether it is ethical to 'kill off' one of the personalities (if the disappearance of one of them was akin to their 'death') in therapy.

Is the study useful?

As it presented an intriguing case and asks thought-provoking questions about our use of the term 'personality', the study is useful in encouraging us to further our understanding of human behaviour and experience. However, whether the findings in this unique case can be useful, even to a particular client group, is questionable. The number of people with such a disorder is very small, and it is possible that their differences would so greatly outweigh their similarities as to make the experience of one such case bear little resemblance to any other.

Is the study valid and reliable?

If Eve White was just a 'skilful actress' then the study is not valid. The dependence of the diagnosis on self-report of the patient's experiences contributes still to the debate surrounding DID. The study is quite low in ecological validity, since the data were gathered by self-report in therapy sessions, and therefore may not be a true representation of Eve's everyday behaviour.

It is very difficult, if not impossible, to establish the reliability of abnormal cases such as that of Eve White, which are very rare, if not unique. Replication of case studies in general is difficult because of the extent and detail of the investigations carried out, and in any case we would be unlikely to find someone equivalent to Eve White to investigate.

Postscript

The real name of the subject for this key study was Chris Sizemore. She wrote a book called *I'm Eve* (Sizemore and Pittillo, 1977), where she maintained that Thigpen and Cleckley's case study was just the tip of the iceberg. She reported that her personality continued to fragment after the end of the therapy, until 21 separate alters inhabited her body. She stated that there were nine before the time of her therapy and that Thigpen and Cleckley never managed to make contact with them. There were a number of traumatic events in her childhood which may have caused this fragmentation, although none of them was sexual in nature. She had seen a man drown when she was about two years of age, and had witnessed another cut into pieces by a saw at a timber yard. One event which left her traumatised, and may well have been at the root of the fragmentation, was when she was held high off the floor by her mother and made to touch the face of her dead grandmother. She was five years old at the time, but even as an adult she could remember the clammy cold cheek. Sizemore believes that the reason she developed these separate personalities was as a way of coping with the harshness of life.

Figure 6.10 Chris Sizemore – the real Eve

In 2006, Chris Sizemore and her son Bobby, who is a school guidance counsellor, spoke to students at Stetson University in the USA. They had decided to speak to the university because some of the students at the university had been counselled by Bobby when they were still at school. The university provided a report of the event and the information here is taken and adapted slightly from the Stetson University website.

The focus of the discussion enabled Chris to talk of her struggles with DID. She explained that she had now been 'healed' for 30 years. Her son also talked about what it was like growing up with a mother who had the condition, and said that he could tell, by looking at her eyes, whenever a role-change had taken place.

During the discussion, Bobby explained that his favourite alter was known as the Retrace Lady: She was 'the one I considered my truest mother as I was growing up. She went away during the integration (of the personalities into a whole).' He also talked about his least favourite, known as Strawberry Girl. He explained that he was shopping on one occasion with the Retrace Lady, when he briefly left the store to go to a nearby drugstore. When he returned, he found the Retrace Lady had disappeared and Strawberry Girl had taken her place. 'She had filled more than three shopping carts with every strawberry-flavoured food item she could find in the store.'

Bobby also explained that the only sacrifice he made growing up was the inability to invite friends to his house. He felt safe among all the personalities he met, although he favoured some more than others. He said his older sister Taffy and his father provided family stability. 'I give my sister and father all the credit in dealing with the situation,' he said. 'My sister raised me many times and deserves the majority of the credit for the way the family dealt with (the situation).' His father as breadwinner assumed a burden of expensive medical treatment. Together, they coped as a family in an era when people facing mental challenges were routinely placed in asylums.

Chris explained that she had received more than 40 years of psychotherapy under the care of Dr Tony Tsitos. One questioner asked her why the personality changes stopped. She explained that 'I think of it as a healing.' Tsitos helped her to heal herself by letting 'each personality solve her own problems and let the others know'. In the past, severe headaches accompanied the personality changes. Chris said that when she gets a headache now, the doctor tells her to take an aspirin.

One student asked how Chris deals with people who challenge that MPD is not a real disorder. 'That's their problem,' she joked, before saying that Duke University researchers analysed the brushstrokes of paintings created by her seven artist personalities. Each had a distinct brushstroke.

Chris said her many personalities arose in response to 'hurtful events' during childhood. Today, 'I don't need them,' she said of the personalities. 'As a whole person, I can face my realities and deal with them.'

Griffiths study: Cognitive bias in gamblers

Some people like nothing better than to sit down and watch a really good film in the warm, while others may prefer to surf in an icy-cold sea in November, or leap out of an aeroplane with only a piece of silk to stop them from crashing to the earth. Some people are interested in art, history or ballet, while others could imagine nothing more boring than walking round an art gallery, and would rather climb into underground caverns, often full of water, with only a torch to light their way. Some people like to go on holiday to hot countries and laze about by the pool all day, reading a book, while others would rather hike across the countryside, camp on the side of a mountain and battle against the elements. Some people are willing to gamble large sums of money when the outcome is uncertain, while others would rather save their money and ensure it is safe.

What is it that makes some people more adventurous or more willing to take risks than others? Is it something fundamental about their physical make-up or personality that makes them behave as they do, or is it simply that some people think very differently to others due to their past experiences?

Interestingly, the reason that risks exist is because things that we consider valuable, such as our money or our life, are placed in a precarious situation. Some risks are the result of choice – for example, parachuting, when we are putting our lives at risk – while others are not within our control. When we think about risks, we also think about gains – for example, a large win at the bookie's or the adrenaline high from flying in the air – and this makes us realise that risky situations may also provide opportunities and experiences that would be unavailable to us if we did not put ourselves in that situation.

In an attempt to answer our earlier question about what it is that makes some people more adventurous or more willing to take risks than others, we are now going to look at gambling. Although gambling is not typical of all risk-taking behaviours, when you consider the levels of losses and gains, it can involve enormous risk. It can also be studied more easily in controlled laboratory situations, in order to help us understand the cognitive processes that gamblers (and therefore other risk takers) may use.

Gambling as an addiction

Perhaps the reason why some people want to gamble is because it has become a kind of addiction – this would mean that rational decision making is not possible. If we accept the Canadian Mental Health Education Resource Centre's definition, which describes an addiction as 'A behavioural pattern characterized by compulsion, loss of control, and continued repetition of a behaviour or activity in spite of adverse consequences', we can see that this might be the case.

Figure 6.11 Some people are more prone to risk-taking than others

When we consider what we mean by an addiction, we usually assume that the addiction is to something like drugs or alcohol, which, when withdrawn, will produce unpleasant physical and psychological symptoms. Mark Griffiths is leading the way in broadening the definition of addiction to include other activities, such as gambling, overeating, exercise, sex, computer games, and using mobile phones, to name just a few, and he believes that we need to view addiction in its broadest sense. He has studied what he calls 'pathological gamblers' for more than 20 years, and in 1996 he argued that there is a set of features which are common to all addictions:

- Salience: the activity becomes the most important thing in their lives and dominates their thinking, making them crave the activity and effectively taking over their social lives.

- Mood modification: they become highly aroused when engaging in the behaviour.

- Tolerance: they need to keep increasing the activity in order to achieve the same level of enjoyment.

- Withdrawal symptoms: if they stop the behaviour they feel physical and psychological discomfort.

- Conflict: the activity conflicts with the rest of the person's life and may put them in a state of conflict and discomfort.

- Relapse: even if the person gives up the activity, it is very likely that they will relapse.

The decision as to whether gambling can be considered an addiction is left to you to decide, but for the purpose of this discussion we will accept that there are such people as 'gambling addicts'. If this is the case, perhaps their addiction can explain the risky behaviours they become involved in. They may become totally obsessed with the activity so that it dominates their thoughts. They become excited and elated when they do gamble, and as time goes on they have to take more and more risks in order to achieve the same level of enjoyment. As we know, high levels of arousal do not go hand in hand with clarity of thought, so their thinking may become distorted, which explains why their behaviour might be irrational.

Gambling and cognitive bias

When trying to understand the reasons for the huge differences in human behaviour, ranging from one extreme to the other, we can only hypothesise. There is a wide range of possible explanations as to why some people gamble and others do not and it may be we have to conclude that there is no single, definite cause, and instead try to identify what the features are that people who engage in gambling share in common. The answer to that seems to be their cognitive style.

If we consider how we would make decisions in an ideal world, these would be based on gathering all the information in front of us and being able to look at every possible answer until the correct answer was found – very similar to the solving of algorithms in mathematics. This way of processing information is very time-consuming and laborious, and often we do not have all the information available, so we may need to refer to past experiences that have led to a 'correct' conclusion, or look at what is available and use our intuition to help us make the appropriate choice. The second strategy, known as heuristics, is described by Kahney (1993) as 'rule of thumb, problem solving methods which often succeed but do not guarantee a solution to a problem'. Both these strategies have been studied by psychologists investigating problem solving and decision making in humans.

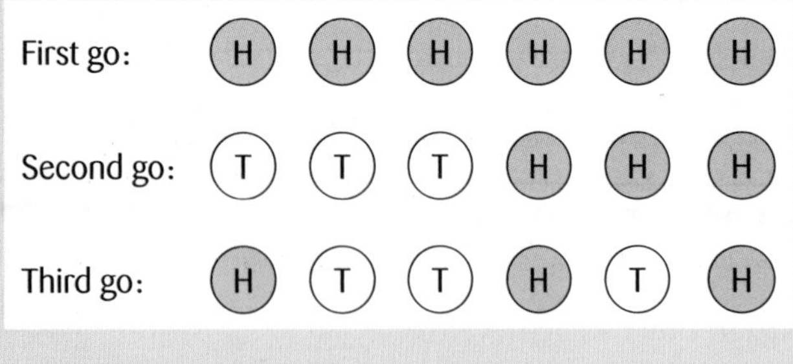

First go: H H H H H H

Second go: T T T H H H

Third go: H T T H T H

Which of these is the least and which is the most likely?

Figure 6.12

The rules of thumb used by gamblers are frequently based on stereotypical or preconceived ideas. Gamblers may intuitively compare the situation with their preconceived ideas or limited knowledge, believing that their knowledge represents how things really are. Gross (2005: 446) described the gambler's fallacy very effectively in figure 6.12.

Most people believe the first outcome is the least likely of the three and the third the most likely. In fact, the probability of the three sequences is identical. Our assumption that coin tossing produces a random sequence of heads and tails leads us to decide that the third is the most likely (because it looks the most random). Such a belief will affect the way that gamblers behave. If they had tried to solve the puzzle using an algorithm, they would have found the correct answer, but may well have spent all day trying to figure it out.

Attributional bias

There are other cognitive biases that are used by gamblers which affect the way they make decisions. One such bias relates to a social psychological concept known as the fundamental attribution error. When we attribute causes to someone's behaviour, we are biased towards the view that they are doing something 'because they are like that'. We believe that what we are seeing them do is what they would always do in a similar situation. We are actually making two mistakes here: we are ignoring the situational factors which influence their behaviour, and we are assuming that people are consistent in their behaviour, which often they are not. Now imagine this in terms of gambling. We sometimes attribute causes to the behaviour of inanimate objects, for example suggesting that the roulette wheel never gives a certain number, or that the row of pears never appears on a fruit machine.

Another related attributional bias is the actor–observer effect. This suggests that the fundamental attribution error occurs when we are describing the behaviour of someone else (when we are the observer), but when we are describing our own behaviour (when we are the actor), we tend to describe it in terms of the situation we were in at the time, rather than in terms of our persistent characteristics. This leads to a further bias, called the self-serving bias. Here we tend to attribute the cause which presents us in the best light and allows us to preserve our self-esteem. For example, if you got an A in your AS Psychology, you might say: 'I am a hard-working, fantastic student and my success is evidence of my brilliance' (an internal attribution); but if you got a U, you might say: 'The textbook was rubbish, so how could I have been expected to pass?' (a situational attribution). Again, in terms of gambling, when the gambler wins, it is because they are skilful; whereas when they lose it is because the fruit machine has been tampered with or rigged. These false beliefs can often explain the irrationality of gamblers.

Do gamblers think differently from non-gamblers? Are their cognitive biases irrational, and can these biases explain why some people continue to gamble, or become regular gamblers or gambling addicts, and others do not?

The Study

M.D. Griffiths (1994) 'The role of cognitive bias and skill in fruit machine gambling', *British Journal of Psychology*, 85: 351–69

Background

Griffiths begins by explaining that Corney and Cummings (1985) have identified the fact that humans show a number of consistent cognitive biases when processing information. Previous studies of gambling have focused mainly on the illusion of control, which was described by Langer (1975), and explained by Griffiths as 'an expectancy of success higher than the objective probability would warrant'. (p.352)

Consider the following situations:

- When you are selecting your own lottery numbers and choice is a factor.
- When you are playing your favourite fruit machine.

Do you think the outcome is under your control in some way? In reality, you have no control, even though you may falsely assume that you do. The outcome is actually a matter of chance.

Wagenaar (1988: 30) considered current and past research into gambling and compared 'normative decision theory' and 'heuristics and biases' (see below). He concluded that gambling is influenced by cognitive thought processes, and it is these processes which serve to motivate gamblers, rather than 'defects of personality, education or social environment'.

Wagenaar suggests that gamblers actually use a range of cognitive distortions, and that although they do not use heuristics more than non-gamblers, they do 'select heuristics at the wrong occasion'. He indicates that when gamblers use heuristics, they feel they have reduced the overall uncertainty of their bet (although this is not really the case).

... continued

Key concept

Normative decision theory/descriptive decision theory

In an ideal world, when we make a decision we would like that decision to be the best decision. If the person making the decision is rational, able to think clearly and aware of all the facts, it is likely that the decision will be the correct one. The theory of how this would work is called normative decision theory. The trouble is, how often does this actually happen?

Normative decision theory is a theory about how decisions should be made in a rational world (like using algorithms). Descriptive decision theory, on the other hand, deals with how people actually make decisions.

Normative decision theory would make it possible to predict what sort of choices a gambler would make. The problem is that because gambling is an irrational activity, the theory would predict that people would not gamble in the first place (Wagenaar 1988).

Griffiths indicates that the most significant distortions used by gamblers are as follows:

- Illusion of control: When gamblers have a higher expectation of winning than is probable because there is an illusion of being able to control what is going on (see above).

- Hindsight bias: When retrospectively people are not surprised about what has happened and even believe they predicted the outcome (of a chance event); for example, 'I knew I'd land on Mayfair!' in a game of Monopoly, when this depends on a roll of the dice: pure chance (mentioned by Griffiths but not described in the study).

Key concept

Heuristics

Heuristics are simple, efficient rules which have been proposed to explain how people make decisions, come to judgements and solve problems. On the whole, these work well in practice, but they can contain cognitive biases or distortions, such as the fundamental attribution error.

- Flexible attributions: When gamblers see their successes as being due to their own level of skill and their failures as due to external forces.

- Representative bias: When people mistakenly believe that a sample of results are representative of all results. For example, if they win the first few bets, they believe that these wins are going to represent the level of success for the rest of the night.

- Availability bias: When someone uses available information or experience to evaluate the probability of the same thing happening again; for example, if you hear others winning on slot machines, you think this is the norm.

- Illusory correlations: The superstitious belief that events go together even when they do not. For example, Henslin (1967) identified that craps players roll dice slowly if they wanted to get a low number and hard if they want a high number.

- Fixation on absolute frequency: Gamblers measure their success by looking at the number of times they win in a session, rather than considering the relative frequency of wins overall.

These cognitive distortions may explain why some gamblers do not learn by their previous mistakes, and might help to explain their supposedly irrational behaviours. Griffiths does point out, however, that they are not very useful as *predictors* of behaviour, as the same heuristic may not be used in all situations, not even by the same individual.

In this study, Griffiths describes the cognitive psychology of fruit machine players, considering the cognitive variables that are involved in gambling with fruit machines:

... continued

- Regular fruit machine gamblers consider their actions to be due in some part to skill. Griffiths tested whether this skill was real or simply a mistaken perception on the part of the gamblers.

- Some addicted fruit machine gamblers understand fully that in the long run they will lose every penny that they gamble. However, there is still a chance to 'win', in terms of how long they can stay on the machine for their money, with the goal being to stay on the machine for as long as possible using the least money, 'playing with money rather than for it'. (p.354) Gamblers implied that skill would be required in order to be able to do this. Skill is being defined here as 'the ability of the individual to affect the outcome of gambling positively (e.g. more gambles with initial money staked and/or more winnings with initial money staked'. (p.354) Griffiths investigated the level of skill that regular and non-regular gamblers assign to themselves and to playing fruit machines in general.

- Cognitive biases are used by fruit machine gamblers (e.g. specialist features such as 'nudge', 'hold' and 'gamble' buttons give the gambler the illusion of control. Griffiths investigated whether the cognitive biases would be used more by regular than non-regular fruit machine gamblers. Would regular gamblers be more irrational? By 'irrational' Griffiths means 'incompatible or contrary to reason, e.g. personification of the machine'. (p.354) Personification means treating or talking about the machine as if it were a person, with its own thoughts, intentions and emotions (e.g. 'It wants me to win' and 'This machine hates me today').

Aims and hypotheses

- Hypothesis 1: The level of skill that regular gamblers report is perceived, and when objectively observed there would be no differences between regular and non-regular fruit machine gamblers on level of skill.

- Hypothesis 2: Regular fruit machine gamblers would produce more irrational verbalisations when asked to use the talking aloud method than non-regular fruit machine gamblers.

- Hypothesis 3: Regular fruit machine gamblers would describe themselves as more highly skilled at fruit machine gambling, and would be of the opinion that fruit machine gambling requires a higher level of skill than that reported by non-regular fruit machine gamblers.

- Hypothesis 4: Gamblers in the thinking aloud condition would take longer to complete the task than those tested in the non-thinking aloud condition (see Procedure, below).

Method and design

This was a field experiment, carried out in a local amusement arcade, with the owner's full support, using an independent groups design.

A field experiment was used to avoid the possibility that a laboratory setting for a test of fruit machine gambling might be low in ecological validity.

Subjects

A total of 60 subjects were tested: 44 male, 16 female, with a mean age of 23.4 years. All had played fruit machines at least once in their lives. Beyond this, they fell into two groups.

Table 6.6

30 regular fruit machine gamblers who played fruit machines at least once a week	30 non-regular fruit machine gamblers who played fruit machines once a month or less
29 male	15 male
1 female★	15 female
mean age 21.6 years	mean age 25.3 years

* Griffiths acknowledges the gender imbalance, but notes that fruit machine gambling is male-dominated, so regular female gamblers would be relatively rare. *Source:* adapted from Griffiths (1994)

... continued

The sample was made up mostly of volunteers, who responded to a small poster put up at the university and local college campuses in Plymouth. In addition, some of the regular gamblers were recruited by a regular gambler who Griffiths knew.

Procedure

- All subjects were tested individually.
- Each subject was given a £3 stake to gamble on a fruit machine (= 30 'free' gambles).
- All were asked to try to stay on the machine for a minimum of 60 gambles (break even and win back £3 with their stake).
- At 60 gambles, each subject was given the option to stop and keep any winnings or to carry on gambling.
- Griffiths notes that gambling with your own money has been shown in some studies to be a determining factor in the excitement and risk taking associated with gambling. He also noted that gambling with someone else's money has been shown to have a disinhibiting effect (makes you stop, holds you back). However, he quotes evidence from Ladouceur (1991) to justify his choice of giving a £3 stake. Ladouceur had shown that the disinhibiting effect could be counteracted by allowing the subject to keep any winnings that might be made, so this is what Griffiths did.
- All subjects were asked to gamble on a Fruitskill fruit machine unless they objected. Three regular gamblers did object, either because they were not familiar with the Fruitskill machine or because they preferred a different machine. Seven further regular gamblers began on the Fruitskill machine, then changed machines, each changing at least three times.
- Regular and non-regular gamblers were randomly allocated to the thinking aloud (TA) and non-thinking aloud (NTA) conditions. The thinking aloud method was used because 'it is considered probably the best method for a precise evaluation of concurrent cognitive abilities of an individual during a specified activity'. (p.356) Also, evidence shows that although the thinking aloud method slows down performance, there is no other negative effect. To test this, Griffiths included his fourth hypothesis, that those in the thinking aloud condition would take longer to complete the task.

All subjects in the TA condition were given the following additional standardised instructions: 'The Thinking Aloud method consists of verbalising every thought that passes through your mind while you are playing. It is important to remember the following points:

1. Say everything that goes through your mind. Do not censor any of your thoughts even if they seem irrelevant to you.

2. Keep talking as continuously as possible, even if your ideas are not clearly structured.

3. Speak clearly.

4. Do not hesitate to use fragmented sentences if necessary. Do not worry about speaking in complete sentences.

5. Do not try to justify your thoughts.' (p.356)

For each subject, and at all stages of the experiment, Griffiths was nearby. While they played the fruit machine he recorded (by observation):

- total time in minutes subject was on the fruit machine
- total number of gambles
- amount of winnings
- the result of every gamble.

Key concept

Thinking aloud method
This is a method for getting subjects to reveal their cognitive processes by literally thinking aloud, saying what they are thinking while they are doing something, such as playing a fruit machine, as in this case.

... continued

To gather data to answer the question of whether there is a skill difference between regular and non-regular gamblers, seven objective behaviours were observed and recorded for each subject, see figure 6.12.

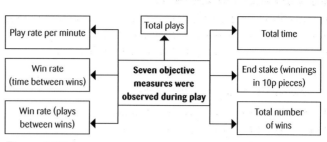

Figure 6.13

To record the verbalisations of subjects in the TA condition they spoke into a lapel microphone which was attached to a portable tape recorder. All tapes were transcribed within 24 hours to ensure that Griffiths was able to remember the context of the comments.

After playing the fruit machine the subjects were interviewed using a semi-structured interview, to gauge their opinions about the level of skill involved in fruit machine playing and their judgement of their own skill level.

Results

These need to be considered in three parts:

1. The differences between the regular and non-regular gamblers on the seven objective behavioural variables. Would there be no differences between the regular and non-regular gamblers on the task?

Hypothesis 1 was generally true, as shown by the fact that there were only two differences between the regular and the non-regular fruit machine gamblers on the seven objective behavioural measures:

* Regular gamblers had a higher playing rate, approximately eight per minute compared to the non-regular gamblers' approximate six plays per minute.

* Regular TA gamblers had a significantly lower win rate in gambles, but not in time (i.e. the number of gambles, but not the amount of time elapsed between each win, was lower than for the other groups).

2. The measure of rational/irrational comments from the content analysis of the verbalisations of those in the TA condition. Would the regular fruit machine gamblers make more irrational comments and show more evidence of cognitive biases?

Hypothesis 2 was that the regular fruit machine gamblers would be more irrational than the non-regular fruit machine gamblers. In order to operationalise this, Griffiths established (by listening to the tapes) a set of 30 categories of utterance. He then performed a content analysis of all the TA recordings, observing for the 30 categories.

The first four of these categories would show irrational behaviour. The regular gamblers were more irrational, giving approximately 14 per cent irrational comments in total, compared to approximately 2.5 per cent for the non-regular gamblers (see table below).

Griffiths noted that some heuristics were used by the regular gamblers, but they 'did not seem to be abundant'. (p 360)

He cites examples of hindsight bias: 'I had a feeling it was going to chew up those tokens fairly rapidly' and flexible attributions: 'I'm losing heavily here … [the machine's] not giving me the numbers I want. I've just taken a quid off it so it wants its money back' and some completely erroneous perceptions: 'I'm only gonna put one quid in to start with because psychologically I think it's very important … it bluffs the machine – it's my own psychology.'

Figure 6.14

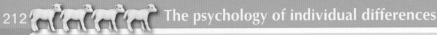

... continued

Griffiths points out that the regular gamblers' comments often have examples of personification: 'The machine that chews tokens; the machine that can be bluffed'. (p.360) He also says that the regular gamblers were often far more direct, and frequently swore at the machine: 'It probably thinks I'm a f**kwit – it's not wrong!

... so harsh, it's really f**king me over ... I had a feature held and then it stopped them ... f**king conned ... b*****d machine.'

Table 6.7

Results for the four irrational categories of verbalisations from the TA condition

Irrational verbalisations categories	Regular gamblers	Non-regular gamblers
1. Personification of the fruit machine e.g. *The machine likes me*	7.54	1.14
2. Explaining away losses e.g. *I lost there because I wasn't concentrating*	3.12	0.14
3. Talking to the fruit machine e.g. *Come on, aren't you going to pay out for me?*	2.64	0.90
4. Swearing at the fruit machine e.g. *You bastard*	0.60	0.08
Total % of irrational verbalisations = highly significant (p<0.001)	14%	2.5%

Source: adapted from Griffiths (1994)

For a discussion of the inter-observer reliability of the coding system, see Commentary, below, under Validity and reliability of the study.

3. A comparison of the regular fruit machine gamblers and non-regular fruit machine gamblers' opinions of the level of skill involved, and their own level of skill, in playing fruit machines (evidence from the interview stage).

Hypothesis 3 was measured by various questions on skill in the semi-structured interview phase of the study.

Table 6.8   Example questions on skill and the responses of the regular and non-regular fruit machine gamblers

Example question on skill	Responses of regular gamblers	Responses of non-regular gamblers

Is there any skill involved in playing a fruit machine?
 	
Is it:
    all chance?
    mostly chance?
    equal chance/skill?
    mostly skill?
    all skill?
	Most regular gamblers said 'equal chance/skill'
	
	= 18/30 responses
		Most non-regular gamblers said 'mostly chance
		
		= 19/30 responses

... continued

Table 6.8 (contd.)

Example question on skill	Responses of regular gamblers	Responses of non-regular gamblers

How skilful do you think you are compared with the average person?
 	
Are you:
   totally unskilled?
   below average skill?
   average skill?
   above average skill?
   totally skilled?
	All regular gamblers reported their skill level as 'average skill' or higher, with 23/30 saying 'above average skill' or higher
	
	('above average' = 18/30, 'totally skilled' = 5/30)
		29/30 of the non-regular gamblers reported their skill level as 'average skill' or lower, with 7/30 saying they had 'below average skill', and 12/30 saying they were 'totally unskilled'

Source: adapted from Griffiths (1994)

The answers to these questions showed that hypothesis 3 was correct. Regular fruit machine gamblers did see fruit machine gambling as relying more on skill than non-regular gamblers, and they also assessed their own skill more highly than non-regular gamblers did.

When asked, 'What skill (if any) is involved in playing fruit machines?', the regular and non-regular gamblers came up with similar ideas. However, four skills were suggested significantly more often by the regular gamblers:

- knowledge of the 'gamble' button
- knowledge of 'feature skills' (skill chances, etc.)
- knowledge of when the machine will pay out
- not playing if the machine has just paid out.

These suggest that regular and non-regular gamblers have different ideas about the skills involved in playing fruit machines.

In terms of hypothesis 4, the TA condition did take longer than the NTA condition, but not significantly longer.

Of the 14 regular gamblers who managed to stay on for 60 gambles, ten of them stayed on until they had lost everything. Interestingly, of the seven non-regular gamblers who reached 60 gambles, only two stayed on until they had lost everything.

Discussion

The results showed that there was no difference between the regular and non-regular fruit machine gamblers (supporting hypothesis 1). However, regular gamblers did stay on the machines for longer, so perhaps they were more skilful, although their skill was shown in the way they were able to make their money last longer. Overall, there was no difference in total winnings, although the skill seemed to be that the regular gambler's wins involved higher payouts. The fact is that regular gamblers play faster and more often, and so have more wins than non-regular gamblers (so probably think they are more skilful), but consequently they will lose more money using this technique.

Gamblers who thought aloud took longer to gamble, although the results were not significant.

Some gamblers objected to being told which machines to use, which suggests that they do have an illusion of control over familiar machines.

Regular fruit machine gamblers seem to know in advance that they will play until they have lost all their money, but seem to enjoy staying on the machine for as long as possible, using the least

... continued

amount of money. This suggests that just playing (rather than winning) is a reward in itself, and supports the idea that the player may be playing for reasons of social involvement, leisure, relaxation or escapism (p.363).

Although regular gamblers made more irrational verbalisations than non-regular gamblers, the number of irrational verbalisations was considerably less than had been found in previous research. Ladouceur *et al.* (1988) had found in their study that 80 per cent of their regular gamblers' verbalisations were irrational, whereas the total was 14 per cent in the current study (compared to 2.5 per cent of non-regular gamblers).

As expected, non-regular gamblers were found to ask more questions and produce more statements of confusion and non-understanding than regular gamblers. Griffiths said that this was a good way to validate the criteria used to differentiate between the two groups.

When being asked to verbalise what they were doing, the regular gamblers often went quiet for periods of up to 30 seconds, possibly because their actions were automatic and they were not thinking about what they were doing.

The study raised questions about the thinking aloud method. The behaviour of the gamblers who thought aloud did not differ from those in the NTA condition, so it seems that by verbalising what they were doing, the gamblers' cognitive processes were not affected. On the other hand, the data did not appear to explain *why* the regular gamblers persisted in their 'losing' behaviour. Griffiths acknowledges that there was a descriptive difference between the two groups, and suggests that the things they said may have been 'symptoms' of a deeper underlying reason, to do 'with the gamblers' psychological and/or physiological constitution' (p.354), although this required further research. On the other hand, Wagenaar (1988) argued that the difference between the two groups of gamblers was just due to the heuristics they used, rather than some deep-seated personality defect.

Griffiths suggests further research into the use of heuristics by employing the thinking aloud method and getting gamblers to use a rigged slot machine to manipulate wins and losses. He is still unsure whether heuristics are affected by the mood of the person gambling or their gambling history, and cites the time when he had a number of wins and how this distorted the reality of the situation.

The hypothesis that regular gamblers would be more skilful than non-regular gamblers was supported by self-comparison ratings and questions about skill factors during play. Griffiths wonders whether the different skills involved such techniques as using the 'nudge' and 'hold' buttons to boost individual wins, thus allowing the gamblers to extend their time playing.

Fisher (1993) said that playing skills are linked with motivations to gamble. She identified three major skills.

Figure 6.15

... continued

Table 6.9

Skill	Description
Choosing which machine to play	Taking into account how much money has been put in and how much the machine has paid out.
Knowing the exact sequence of symbols on the fruit machine's reel	The reels differ on each machine, so this may be why players have favourite machines. This would also explain how players use the nudge facility successfully to move on to the next fruit in order to win.
Gambling	Using the gamble button. This button (according to members of the gaming industry) does not increase the winnings and operates purely by chance. Gamblers believe it involves skill to use it effectively. This is therefore a 'pseudo-skill' feature.

Source: adapted from Griffiths (1994)

In this study, 20 skills were identified by gamblers, and Griffiths suggests that there are a few skills which could be considered more important than others, although he did [at the time of writing about this study] question whether they are *genuinely* skilful.

Table 6.10

Skill	Description
The hold button	If the player wins, they can 'hold' the symbols for another win. Griffiths describes this as an 'idiot skill', saying it would be stupid not to hold the winning symbols.
Knowing the reels	A genuine skill, according to Griffiths.
Light oscillation	Involves the simultaneous pressing of a button when a light shines through particular symbols.
Lighting up	Sometimes the fruit will have another symbol on it which will light up part of a further array. The player plays again (probably a number of times), in order to find other fruits to light up the next part of the array. The problem is that the machines will not keep the other parts lit for more than a few plays, so it is unlikely the player will get to light up a whole array. This can suggest the machine controls the win rate and the gambler is pitching him or herself against the machine.
Knowing the machine	Players suggest intuitive feelings of knowing when the machine will pay out.

Source: adapted from Griffiths (1994)

Griffiths does acknowledge that probably the most technically skilful element in fruit machine gambling is basic familiarity with the machine, and this will be obvious between regular and non-regular gamblers. He suggests that the real difference is probably cognitive, whereby the regular gamblers process information about skill differently and think there is more skill involved in playing the machines than there actually is. They are also more likely to think the machine is like a person, going so far as treating it like an 'electronic friend'. He points out that this is not uncommon for people who spend a lot of time with particular machines (e.g. cars and boats, games consoles and computers).

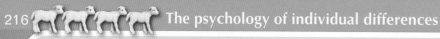
... continued

Finally, Griffiths suggests that gamblers who are undergoing 'rehabilitation' may benefit from knowing about irrational gambling bias. He suggests that cognitive behaviour modification (also known as cognitive behaviour therapy) can help to modify the thought processes of individuals who are habitual gamblers. He suggests using tape recordings of the irrational biases of hardened gamblers to show how irrational they really are (called playback therapy by Griffiths). He cites the case of four of the gamblers in the study who volunteered to hear their verbalisations played back to them. They all commented on how they were surprised at what they had said. One of the gamblers (diagnosed as a pathological gambler according to the DSM-III-R) was re-interviewed at a later date and reported that his gambling had declined as a direct result of hearing himself.

Although there are no actual case studies using this method to promote cognitive restructuring (Walker 1992), Griffiths suggests that knowing in detail about their thoughts and experiences can help to moderate or remove the hardened gambler's motivation to gamble.

Griffiths emphasises that the talking aloud method only allows us to describe the cognitions self-reported by the regular gamblers, and the irrational utterances they make; it does not allow us to predict which cognitive biases lead to or stimulate persistent gambling. However, he suggests that further research might show which heuristics would be used in a given situation, and the talking aloud method might be a helpful method for investigating this. This might also help to explain whether the selection of particular heuristics depends on intrinsic factors (e.g. psychological factors such as mood or desire for escapism) or extrinsic factors (e.g. Griffiths' own experience of fruit machine gambling leads him to believe that big wins while gambling 'stimulate' irrationality). For Griffiths, this is an area that warrants further research.

Commentary: Methods and issues

Research method, design and data gathering

The study uses the experimental method. It is a field experiment, using an independent groups design, comparing regular and non-regular fruit machine gamblers. As a field study using an independent measures design, control of extraneous environmental and personal factors may be a problem, so we cannot rule out the possibility that this study failed to adequately control extraneous variables, which is a threat to the validity of the findings.

Data-gathering methods used while the subjects were playing the fruit machines were overt observation of seven behavioural variables, and self-report of thought processes in the TA condition. All subjects self-reported their responses in the interview stage of the study. Overt observation and self-report methods are subject to falsification by participants, and responses could have been manipulated in order to respond to demand characteristics if the participants could have worked out the purpose of the study.

Data gathered was largely quantitative, and statistical analysis was carried out to establish any differences between conditions. Qualitative data was also presented in terms of examples of how cognitive biases might show themselves; for example, personification of the machine can be seen in the comment: 'Can I win more than 10p this time?... No!! ... Obviously the machine's being a bit of a bastard at the moment.' (p.361)

The use of quantitative data offers a number of advantages, including the fact that comparisons could be made easily between participants and conditions, showing that there were differences in the way the regular and non-regular gamblers were thinking while they were gambling. Qualitative data, however, gave examples of the specific differences in the ways that the regular gamblers were thinking in comparison with the non-regular gamblers, and specifically highlighted the irrational elements of their thought processes, showing not only that they did think differently, but also giving detailed examples.

Does the study raise any ethical concerns?

The study was carried out according to the British Psychological Society (1993) ethical guidelines.

The subjects were not deceived; they gave their fully informed consent; they had the right to withdraw; and generally they were not negatively affected by their experience.

There is a possibility that some of those four regular gamblers who heard their verbalisations played back to them and were surprised by their behaviour and the things they said while gambling might have gained self-knowledge they found embarrassing or even disturbing. However, since this would not have damaged their self-esteem unduly, and in one instance seems to have acted as a wake-up call to a persistent gambler to change his ways, it could be argued that the end justified the means in this case.

Griffiths tries hard to suggest that there might be a way to rehabilitate problem gamblers based on his evidence in this study that regular gamblers have cognitive biases. His intention of trying to help problem gamblers means that this study is ethically worthy.

Is the study useful?

In the discussion of his study, Griffiths considers whether there are implications in his findings that could assist the rehabilitation of problem gamblers. He says his findings suggest that the difference between regular and non-regular gamblers seems to be a cognitive one (although he cautiously proposes that further research might be needed to fully confirm this!). He suggests that this cognitive difference represents an 'irrational gambling bias' (p.367) in regular gamblers, and that this might be helped by using cognitive behaviour modification.

Key concept

Cognitive behaviour modification using CBT
Cognitive behaviour therapy (CBT) is a form of talking therapy that attempts to help the client change or modify their behaviour by changing their cognitions, their thoughts about themselves and the situations they are in.

Griffiths suggests that this might include using the thinking aloud method while the gambler plays, then allowing the gambler to listen to the tape of their verbalisations while they were gambling. Griffiths gives this the name 'audio playback therapy'. He bases his suggestion on anecdotal evidence from the four gamblers who took up the offer to listen to themselves afterwards, and who said they could not believe they had said the things they had said or how they were thinking when they were gambling.

Moreover, Griffiths talks about one subject who was diagnosed according to DSM-III-R criteria as a pathological gambler. On meeting Griffiths at a later date, this subject told him that his gambling behaviour declined and then stopped altogether after the experiment, and that hearing the playback of his tape had played a large part in stopping him gambling, as he had listened in disbelief to his irrational behaviour and comments while gambling. Griffiths says: 'Through this self-introspective process he claimed he realized the futility of his gambling and eventually stopped playing.'

Although Griffiths himself admits there is no evidence that cognitive behaviour therapy has helped pathological gamblers, it might be that it would if the specific behaviours and thought processes, such as those cognitive biases which stimulate the particular persistent gambler, could be addressed, perhaps using his suggested audio playback therapy method.

Validity and reliability of the study

Griffiths refers to validity and reliability a number of times in his study. For example, he justifies his choice of a field setting in the amusement arcade to avoid the problems of low ecological validity which might occur if the fruit machine gambling were observed in a laboratory setting.

Griffiths also considers the inter-observer reliability of the coding system of 30 categories which he designed to perform his content analysis of the verbalisations of subjects in the TA condition.

Key concept

Inter-observer reliability
To establish inter-observer reliability, the observation needs to be repeated by a second observer (either at the same time with the same sample, or at a similar time with a similar sample), using the same categories or coding system.

The two sets of data from the two observers are then correlated, and there must be a significant positive correlation (as a rule of thumb a correlation coefficient of +0.8 should be recorded) between them in order to establish inter-observer reliability.

Inter-observer reliability needs to be established to ensure that observations and categories are objective and not affected by subjective observer bias.

If the observation proves not to be reliable, this leads us to question the validity of the findings, and reduces the scientific value of the study.

Unfortunately, Griffiths has to admit that his attempts to establish inter-observer reliability were not very successful and showed only low reliability. However, he explains why this might be, saying that both the other observers who tried to apply his coding system were disadvantaged. The first observer could not apply the coding system accurately because of their lack of experience of fruit machine gambling. The second observer, a regular fruit machine gambler, had difficulties using the coding system because of poor understanding of the context in which the comments were made. In other words, the coding system could only be applied by someone who had been present at the time of the recording, understood the context and had a good understanding of fruit machine gambling. Since only Griffiths was in this position, he was the only one who could apply the categories, which means that the reliability of the coding system could not be established.

Griffiths suggests that the study as a whole leads us to question the validity of the thinking aloud method as a way of observing cognitive processes in gamblers. For example, he notes that at times the regular gamblers would go blank, or silent, for up to 30 seconds at a time, suggesting they had moved from conscious cognitive processing to a form of 'automatic pilot', where they could play without being conscious of what they were thinking. This was not apparent in the non-regular gamblers, and leads us to question whether we get a valid measure of the cognitive processes of regular gamblers.

Other challenges to the validity of the study include problems with demand characteristics. Subjects may have responded, when verbalising their thoughts, when playing the machine or in the interview stage, in ways which they thought the researcher expected or wanted them to behave. This subject bias might lead us to question the validity of the findings and the conclusions drawn from them.

Generalisability issues may also be a challenge to validity. It may be that gamblers in other areas, or those who gamble in different ways (e.g. bingo, scratch cards or poker), might not behave in similar ways to the gamblers in this study. Also, it may be that *volunteer* gamblers affect the generalisability of the findings to a broader population, as volunteers are always an atypical sample and do not represent their target population fully.

We can also question the validity of Griffith's suggested application for his findings (see above: Is the study useful?). Griffiths himself admits there is no empirical evidence of the effectiveness of cognitive behaviour modification in helping problem gamblers stop gambling, and Griffiths' own suggestion is based only on anecdotal evidence, so we cannot be sure if it would work in practice. More research would need to be undertaken before the validity of this application could be proven.

7 Approaches and perspectives and Section C of the Core Studies examination

In addition to learning about the core studies as individual pieces of research and assessing them in terms of the methods and issues, you also need to consider them as illustrating an approach or and/perspective in psychology.

In the Core Studies examination, Section C focuses on the approaches and perspectives. In this chapter you will look at the structure of Section C with some example questions and answers.

We will look at the approaches and perspectives separately, beginning with the five approaches.

To remind you, on the OCR AS-level specification the fifteen core studies fit into the five approaches as follows.

Table 7.1

Social approach	Milgram – Obedience	Piliavin, Rodin and Piliavin – Subway Samaritan	Reicher and Haslam – BBC prison experiment
Cognitive approach	Loftus and Palmer – Eyewitness testimony	Baron-Cohen *et al.* – Autism in adults	Savage-Rumbaugh *et al.* – Ape language
Developmental approach	Samuel and Bryant – Conservation	Bandura, Ross and Ross – Imitating aggression	Freud – Little Hans
Physiological approach	Maguire *et al.* – Taxi drivers' brains	Dement and Kleitman – Sleep and dreaming	Sperry – Split brains
Individual differences approach	Rosenhan – Being sane in insane places	Thigpen and Cleckley – Multiple personality disorder	Griffiths – Fruit machine gambling

Approaches in psychology

Each of the approaches focuses on a different explanation of human behaviour. Human behaviour is complex, and so different approaches look at different aspects of it and try to offer useful explanations for specific behaviours.

A human being can be seen as a biological system affected by biological factors such as genes or brain structure. Or we can look at the person as a social being who is influenced by the presence and behaviour of others, or as an individual, different from other human beings in certain ways such as having schizophrenia or being intellectually gifted. We can look at the way a person develops, for example, how they develop their problem-solving skills or how they learn and acquire behaviours such as aggression, or we can consider the person in terms of their cognitive function as a processor of incoming information from their senses and consider how these processes work. Each of the five approaches, then, contributes to psychology by focusing on explanations of human behaviour that, when we consider them together, help us to get a good understanding of human psychology.

It is important to note here that the approaches can overlap, for example, we have considered social cognition in the core studies, where the way we think interacts with our social behaviour, apparent in Piliavin *et al.*'s cost-benefits analysis in decision making in emergency situations, and in Baron-Cohen *et al.*'s Theory of mind explanation of the social difficulties experienced by people with autism. You will also have heard of cognitive neuroscience, a multi-disciplinary approach to studying the brain and behaviour, and this incorporates both cognitive and physiological psychology. In addition, many cognitive neuroscientists are interested in brain dysfunction, so the individual differences approach is also incorporated into cognitive neuroscience through the study of patients with brain damage through trauma or accident, or with diseases such as schizophrenia or Alzheimer's disease.

For the purposes of the OCR Core Studies examination, however, we consider the five approaches as separate from one another.

Assumptions of the approaches

Each of the five approaches make different assumptions about the causes of human behaviour. We will look at examples of these in turn:

Assumptions of the social approach

The social approach assumes that our behaviour is not always the result of our own free will. The situation we are in will have a strong influence on how we behave. For example, the presence of a legitimate authority figure can override our individual conscience (e.g. in Milgram's study), or our group identity (e.g. in Reicher and Haslam's study) can have more impact on our behaviour than our individual personalities. An assumption of the social approach is that situational rather than individual explanations of social behaviour are often more accurate as context and culture has a strong influence on how we behave.

Assumptions of the cognitive approach

The cognitive approach focuses on how information received from our senses is processed by our brains. This approach assumes that how we process information, including how we perceive, store and retrieve information, influences how we behave.

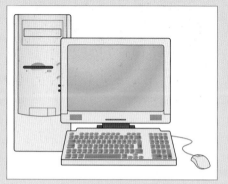

The cognitive approach assumes, unlike the behaviourist perspective, that we can and should study mental processes such as memory, ways of thinking and problem solving in order to further understand human behaviour. It assumes that these mental processes can be studied scientifically, so the experimental method is favoured by cognitive psychologists in their research.

The cognitive approach uses a computer analogy to describe how the brain processes information, assuming that comparisons can be made between how machines process information and how brains process information.

Figure 7.1

Assumptions of the developmental approach

A major assumption of the developmental approach is that children are psychologically different from adults. Samuel and Bryant provide support for Piaget's theory that suggests that children of different ages think differently from each other, for example, children under eight do not conserve as well as children over eight. In addition, some developmental approach theories assume that children's development occurs in stages, whose sequence is invariant and which are universal. Examples of this include Piaget's theory of moral development and Freud's psychosexual stages of personality development.

The developmental approach assumes that children can learn through the behavioural principles of operant and classical conditioning and modelling (Bandura's social learning theory).

Some developmental theories assume that bad early experiences can have a negative effect on us in later life, and that the root cause of adult psychiatric problems lies in problems with their psychiatric development as a child (Freud's psychodynamic theory)

Figure 7.2

Assumptions of the physiological (biological) approach

The physiological approach assumes that behaviour can be largely explained in terms of biology (e.g. genes/hormones): what is psychological is first

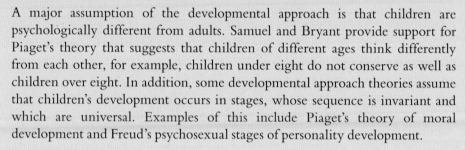

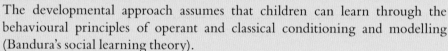

biological. This approach assumes that psychology should study the brain, nervous system and various biological systems in an attempt to explain behaviour. According to the physiological approach, psychology should be seen as a science, to be studied in a scientific manner (usually in a laboratory), measuring variables objectively, for example, using physiological measures such as MRI scans or EEG recordings.

Figure 7.3

Assumptions of the individual differences approach

The individual differences approach assumes that that the differences between people, such as personality, abnormality or intelligence, and not just the factors that people share in common, have an important influence on our behaviour. This approach assumes that it is not only the ways we are the same as one another (the nomothetic approach in psychology, attempting to establish general rules about behaviour), but also the ways in which we differ from others and are individuals that is important for psychology to investigate. This is known as the idiographic approach.

Each of the approaches, then, make different assumptions about human behaviour, and this will have an impact on which aspects of behaviour researchers working within an approach choose to study, and on the methods researchers use to investigate behaviour.

Figure 7.4

Exam focus

Section C part (a)

In part (a) of Section C on the Core Studies examination you will be asked to outline an assumption of one of the approaches (or perspectives). For this you will be able to earn 2 marks out of the 24 available in Section C, so you should learn a two-line assumption for each approach. To help you to do this, copy out and complete this table.

One assumption of the social approach is
One assumption of the cognitive approach is
One assumption of the developmental approach is
One assumption of the physiological approach is
One assumption of the individual differences approach is

Section C part (b)

In the Core Studies examination, Section C part (b) you will be asked to explain a given behaviour in relation to one of the approaches. There are 4 marks available for this question, so you have four minutes to write your answer.
Usually these questions will reflect what you have studied in the Core Studies. Here is an example.

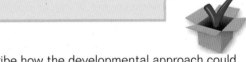

Describe how the developmental approach could explain children's aggression. [4]

Sample Answer

In the developmental approach researchers have considered whether children are born aggressive or learn to be aggressive. Bandura carried out a study to show how children can learn to be aggressive by imitating the aggressive behaviour of an adult model who was aggressive in a stylised way towards a Bobo doll. The study showed that children exposed to the aggressive model imitated what they had seen more than the control condition and Bandura concluded that children learned this aggressive behaviour by imitation of a powerful role model. He also showed that gender matters in the imitation of aggression. Both boys and girls were less likely to imitate a female aggressive model's physical aggression. This suggests that another developmental approach theory, reinforcement and operant conditioning, may have led the children to have expectations of what types of aggression should and should not be done by 'ladies', and therefore what they as children should and should not imitate.

... Continued ▶

Answer questions 1 to 5 below.

1. Describe how the physiological approach could explain dreaming. [4]
2. Describe how the developmental approach could explain children's intellectual development. [4]
3. Describe how the social approach could explain helping behaviour. [4]
4. Describe how the cognitive approach could explain why eyewitness testimony is not always reliable. [4]
5. Describe how the individual differences approach could explain gambling behaviour. [4]

Section C part (c)

In the Core Studies examination, Section C part (c) you will be asked to describe a similarity and a difference between studies within an approach. There are 6 marks available here, 3 for the similarity and 3 for the difference. The two studies you compare for the similarity need not be the same as for the difference. Here is an example taken from June 2010.

Activity

Describe one similarity and one difference between any studies that use the physiological approach. [6]

To ensure that the answers you give are psychological in nature, it is a good idea to use the methods and issues here to make your comparison and contrast against.

Remember: the methods are experiments (lab/field), case study, self-report, observation and issues such as validity and reliability, and the issues are ethics, longitudinal and snapshot studies, qualitative and quantitative data and ecological validity.

Sample Answer

One similarity between the studies by Dement and Kleitman on REM sleep and dreaming and Maguire's study on taxi drivers is that they were both highly controlled studies carried out under laboratory conditions. Dement and Kleitman tested their participants in a sleep lab and Maguire *et al.* tested their participants in an MRI suite. This increases the scientific value of these studies.

A difference between these two studies is related to ethics. Maguire's study was carried out ethically with the fully informed consent of the taxi drivers to being scanned in the MRI scanner and they were not put under undue stress. On the other hand, Dement and Kleitman woke their sleep lab participants often through the night and it could be argued that this might cause them stress or have a knock-on negative effect on them in terms of their ability to function and concentrate the next day. As a result, the Dement and Kleitman study raises ethical concerns and the Maguire study does not.

Activity

Answer the following:

1. Describe one similarity and one difference between any studies that use the social approach. [6]
2. Describe one similarity and one difference between any studies that use the cognitive approach. [6]
3. Describe one similarity and one difference between any studies that use the developmental approach. [6]
4. Describe one similarity and one difference between any studies that use the individual differences approach. [6]

Strengths and weaknesses of the approaches

The five approaches have their strengths and weaknesses. You need to be able to explain strengths and weaknesses of the approaches in the examination, using a core study to illustrate the strength or weakness you are presenting.

Strengths/advantages of the social approach

One strength of the social approach is that it can provide information to explain how other people, such as authority figures or people we see as being in the same group as ourselves, have an effect on our behaviour.

One example of this from the core studies is the study by Milgram. He showed that the relationship the 'Teacher' had entered into with the authority figure, the 'Experimenter', overrode their personal conscience – faced with the conflict to follow their conscience and stop hurting the learner or to carry on obeying the experimenter many chose to obey, even though it was clear that this caused some of them a great deal of personal distress.

Another example of this is in the study by Reicher and Haslam which showed that the way groups are organised can affect behaviour. According to social identity theory, members of subordinate groups behave individually when the group boundaries are permeable and collectively when they are impermeable. This was observed in the prisoners, especially those in Cell 2 in the study.

This means that studies from the social approach are useful as they help to explain the causes of social behaviour and further our understanding of how situational factors and social settings affect or behaviour.

Another strength of the social approach is that it can provide useful information to explain how social cognition influences our social behaviour. This means that how we think about a social situation affects how we behave. For example, Piliavin *et al.* suggested that the reason why the drunk victim received less help than the ill victim was because of the costs–benefits analysis made by the potential helpers who seemed to have decided that the costs of helping the drunk victim were higher than the costs of helping the ill victim.

This clearly shows what we think will affect how we respond in a situation. Such insights into behaviour means that the social approach makes an important contribution to psychology as a discipline.

The social approach often uses field experiments to study social behaviour. This is a strength of this approach as this method enables researchers to study how people behave in naturalistic settings. An example of this from the core studies is the study by Piliavin *et al.* who studied helping behaviour by staging an emergency in a real-life setting on a New York subway train and observing the passengers' behaviour. Seeing someone fall over and needing help is something that people may well experience in everyday life.

This means that this social approach study has high ecological validity and can explain how people behave in real-life settings as opposed to how they behave in the artificial setting of the laboratory.

Weaknesses/limitations of the social approach

One limitation of the social approach is that studying social behaviour under laboratory conditions can be problematic since subjects or participants may not behave in a typical or naturalistic way.

An example of this from the core studies is the study by Milgram. In this study Milgram chose a controlled laboratory set-up to study obedience to an authority figure instructing the 'Teacher' to give electric shocks to the 'Learner'. Basing the study in a laboratory means the study may lack ecological validity and can also be affected by subject reactivity. The findings cannot be generalised to behaviour beyond the laboratory setting: we cannot be sure that those who obeyed the malevolent authority figure in the study did so just to please the experimenter, and we cannot assume that they would obey to the same degree in the real world.

The use of field experiments in the social approach can also make it difficult to study social behaviour because it is difficult to control extraneous variables in a field setting. An example of this from the core studies is the study by Piliavin *et al.* who studied helping behaviour by staging an emergency on a subway train and observing the passengers' behaviour.

This means that the study may lack validity because we cannot be sure that extraneous variables have not confounded the study.

A problem with social approach studies is that they can raise ethical concerns. To try to stop behaviour being affected by subject reactivity, deception (e.g. a cover story) is often needed in social psychological studies. For example, Milgram used the cover story that the aim of his investigation was to see the effects of punishment on learning, when in fact he was studying obedience to authority.

Use of deception raises ethical concerns which means the researcher must carefully weigh up whether the study justifies breaching the ethical guidelines, and social psychologists need to be ready to defend any use of deception in their study.

A limitation of the social approach is that studies can lose validity over time. The problem with evidence from social psychological studies is that because of social or cultural changes, the study's findings may go out of date.

For example, Piliavin *et al.* found a high helping rate for the 'victim' in their 1969 study, but we cannot assume that they would get the same findings if their study was repeated today since people may be more or less helpful now than they used to be.

This means the findings of Piliavin *et al.*'s study may have lost validity over time and cannot easily be generalised today.

A problem for researchers in the social approach is that social behaviour can be difficult to measure. For example, it is hard to find an ecologically valid measure of obedience. In Milgram's study he measured obedience by how far the participants would go on the shock generator when it was clear the 'Learner' did not want to continue, or worse still was unable to continue because he had 'been harmed'. In real life we do not do anything like this.

What this means is that the findings lack ecological validity and cannot easily be generalised to a real life setting, and this problem can limit the usefulness of social approach studies.

Strengths/advantages of the cognitive approach

A major strength of the cognitive approach is that it favours the scientific method, using the laboratory experiment to investigate mental processes. This enables researchers to establish cause and effect between variables.

An example of this from the core studies is the study by Loftus and Palmer. In this study the researchers home in on one variable, the changing of the form of a question, and how it impacts on memory.

This means that the cognitive approach brings academic credibility to psychology as a discipline since it favours a scientific methodology.

The emphasis on controlled scientific study in the cognitive approach provides objective evidence in which we can have confidence. Since quantitative data can be gathered, it is also easier to test such studies for reliability.
An example of this from the core studies is the study by Baron-Cohen *et al.* This study could be quite quickly and easily repeated to see if its findings are replicable, as it would be relatively easy to test the eyes task and other tasks on a similar group of people.

This means that the scientific value of cognitive approach studies can be increased, since replication of findings is an important feature of scientific enquiry.

Studies from the cognitive approach can be useful in helping explain behaviour and have some practical applications in everyday life. An example of this from the core studies is again the study by Baron-Cohen *et al.* In this study it was established that even those with high functioning autism have difficulties reading the mental states of others. This is useful because understanding the problems of people with autism and Asperger's syndrome can be useful to those who care for them at home or interact with them in the community.

Some cognitive approach studies assume that there is continuity between the way animals, particularly primates, process information and the way humans process information. By studying animals we can understand human cognitive processes, for example, the acquisition of language.

An example of this from the core studies is the study by Savage-Rumbaugh *et al.*

In this study the ability of apes, both chimpanzees and bonobos, was studied and by studying what the apes can and cannot do we can infer those aspects of language that are unique to humans, for example, complex grammar (the rules of language)

This means we can find out about human behaviour without the practical and ethical concerns that might be raised by an in-depth study of, for example, the language development of a human child.

Weaknesses/problems/disadvantages of the cognitive approach

The use of laboratory studies in the cognitive approach raises concerns about the ecological validity of the research, and this method also increases the chances of participants responding to demand characteristics in the study.

An example of this from the core studies is the study by Loftus and Palmer. In this study participants were shown film clips (because of the practical and ethical problems with viewing real-life accidents), and were then asked questions about what they had seen, reducing ecological validity and introducing an opportunity for participants to work out the purpose of the study and behave accordingly.

This means that there are a number of challenges to the validity of cognitive studies carried out in the laboratory, and this reduces the scientific value of research in the cognitive approach.

✖ At present, there are limitations to the way data is gathered in the cognitive approach. Cognitive processes can only be studied by inference, that is, we cannot study them directly – we can only gather what is going on in someone's head by recording what they can or cannot tell us (self-report) or can or cannot do (observation), or at best by making and interpreting recordings of the active parts of their brain by, for example, using MRI scans.

Examples of this can be seen in each of the three cognitive core studies. In the studies by Loftus and Palmer and Baron-Cohen *et al.*, the researchers had to rely on the self-report responses of participants in order to measure their memory and ability to 'mindread' others' emotions. In the study by Savage-Rumbaugh *et al.* the researchers could only overtly observe Kanzi's lexigram use and the context in which he used them in order to make inferences about his use of language.

✖ The cognitive approach relies a great deal on self-report and observational methods to gather data, and the biases present in each type of measurement may mean that the findings are not valid.

Strengths/advantages of the developmental approach

✔ One strength of the developmental approach is that it has furthered our understanding of the causes of behaviour.

For example, the behaviourist perspective focuses on how the environment impacts on behaviour. Both reinforcement and observational learning (social learning theory) show that behaviour is shaped by the interaction between the individual and the environment. Bandura's study in particular shows how adults act as powerful role models for children.

Such insights into behaviour means that the developmental approach makes an important contribution to psychology as a discipline.

✔ Another strength is that the developmental approach studies children's psychological development, not just their physical development. An example of this is Piaget's theory of cognitive development, investigated by Samuel and Bryant, focusing on children's performance on the conservation tasks.

✔ The developmental approach has, through such theories, shown that children are cognitively different as well as physically different from adults and this has had a huge impact on the way we teach children in schools. For example, Samuel and Bryant's study confirms Piaget's theory that children's thinking is qualitatively different from adults. This theory has been very useful for teachers, and Piaget's work has contributed greatly to the primary science and maths curriculum and how it is taught.

✔ One strength of the developmental approach is that it often uses the case study method to investigate development. For example, the use of the case study method in the study by Freud gives a great deal of qualitative data and Hans was studied over a period of time to get a full picture of his experiences.

This brings to the developmental approach the advantages associated with longitudinal research, including rich detailed data, and trust in the researcher that can lead to increased validity of the findings.

Weaknesses/limitations of the developmental approach

A problem with the developmental approach is that to study development you often have to study children. This raises ethical concerns because children cannot give their fully informed consent, cannot operate their right to withdraw and cannot be debriefed. It is also unethical to introduce variables that might harm the child.

For example, Bandura *et al.* aimed to encourage aggressive behaviour in the children who observed the aggressive model, and this may have had an impact on their behaviour which meant they did not leave the study in the state they entered it, an important ethical requirement.

Another problem for the developmental approach is that there are also practical problems to be overcome when studying children. For example, studying children in a controlled setting, as in stage 3 of the study by Bandura, may lack ecological validity, as their behaviour in this setting, alone and isolated from their peers, may not be typical of how they would behave in a realistic social setting.

A problem with using case studies and clinical interviews in the developmental approach is illustrated in Freud's study. The close relationship between Hans and his father may mean that the boy was susceptible to leading questions and this reduces the quality of the evidence. For example, when Hans' father asked, 'When the horse fell over, did you think of your daddy?' Hans' response; 'Yes. Perhaps. It is possible', may have been to please his father rather than to truly express what he thought at the time.

This means that the validity of the findings can be challenged and suggests there are limitations of the case study method as it is used in the developmental approach.

Strengths/advantages of the physiological approach

One strength of the physiological approach is that it is leading to a greater understanding of the physiognomy of the brain, in other words, we are learning how the brain works and how it impacts on our behaviour.

For example, Maguire *et al.*'s work on the hippocampi of taxi drivers confirms the role of this structure in the brain in spatial memory and wayfinding (navigation), and also illustrates the plasticity of the brain.

The discipline of cognitive neuroscience is at the cutting edge of scientific enquiry and is making major contributions to our understanding of both normal and abnormal brain function.

A major strength of the physiological approach is that it is highly scientific, grounded in biology and uses a rigorous scientific methodology in research. All of the Core Studies use rigorous scientific methodology:

- Dement and Kleitman studied dreaming in the controlled environment of the sleep lab, using an EEG to record REM and non-REM sleep.

- Maguire *et al.* carried out a controlled study comparing taxi drivers' brains using technical equipment, the MRI scanner, to measure the brain scientifically

- Sperry used specialised apparatus to draw out the differences in the brains of split brain patients.

This means that the physiological approach brings academic credibility to psychology as a discipline since it favours an objective scientific methodology.

Weaknesses/limitations of the physiological approach

Even though the physiological approach tries to be scientific, our limited ability to study brain processes directly and objectively means we often have to rely on self-report data, and here demand characteristics may be a problem.

For example, in Dement and Kleitman's study, the subjects could have falsified reports about whether they were dreaming or not, or about the content of their dreams. This means that studies in the physiological approach that have to rely on self-report may not be entirely valid.

A further problem for physiological approach studies is that studies carried out in the laboratory can be low in ecological validity.

For example, Dement and Kleitman had their participants sleep in their sleep laboratory. We sleep differently when we are not in our own bed, and this must have been more true where participants were not only in a strange bed but also being observed, wired up to an EEG machine and awoken by a doorbell at intervals through the night.

While the laboratory can provide a high level of control for physiological approach studies, there may be some loss of ecological validity as a result.

Strengths/advantages of the individual differences approach

A strength of the individual differences approach is that case studies are often used. Case studies are in depth and often longitudinal studies that focus on one individual or one case. A detailed case history can be useful in describing the experience of unusual or unique cases. For example, Thigpen and Cleckley studied Eve White, carrying out a longitudinal, in-depth case study of her to investigate whether or not she was a true case of multiple personality disorder.

The use of case studies in the individual differences approach may improve our understanding of the experience of such unique individuals as Eve, and help suggest treatments that may help her or anyone else presenting similar symptoms in the future.

Another strength of the individual differences approach is its recognition that individual differences are an important element of people's behaviour which is often overlooked by other approaches. For example, Griffiths shows that individual differences in the cognition of the regular gamblers, such as irrational thinking, help us to explain why some people are regular gamblers and some people are not.

By focusing on the ways people differ from other people rather than how their behaviours fit in with general rules, the individual differences approach makes an important contribution to psychology as an academic discipline.

Another strength of the individual differences approach is that this approach includes the study of abnormal behaviour. This is useful for helping to explain abnormal behaviour and for improving the experience of both those suffering from mental illness and those who work with them and care for them.

For example, Rosenhan's work contributed to the debate over the validity and reliability of the diagnosis of mental illness and exposed some of the negative experiences of being a patient on a psychiatric ward at the time of his study. This study, and others investigating the diagnostic process, led to revisions in the diagnostic system and improvements in psychiatric care.

This illustrates the usefulness of findings from the individual differences approach in explaining abnormal behaviour and improving the diagnosis and care of patients with mental illnesses.

Weaknesses/limitations of the individual differences approach

One problem with the individual differences approach is that often it focuses on unique cases. The rarity of cases, such as the case of MPD reported by Thigpen and Cleckley, may lead to intrusive investigations and excessive study and testing, which may not help the individual and could in fact distress them. This raises ethical concerns about the balance between investigating a case and offering treatment where appropriate and causing possible harm to the person being investigated.

There are problems with the type of data gathered in studies in the individual differences approach. In some studies in this approach large amounts of qualitative data is gathered and this can present problems for researchers. Here are some examples:

- Thigpen and Cleckley's work shows how difficult it is to provide qualitative data that is objective or convincing, especially in the controversial case of MPD. Even after 14 months and over 100 hours of therapy they could not be sure that Eve was not just a really good actress pretending to have MPD.

- Griffiths devised and applied a complicated quantification system for the analysis of the transcripts from the talking aloud method, but failed to establish the reliability of this coding system, again showing the difficulties of providing convincing scientific evidence from qualitative data.

- Rosenhan's work relies on the qualitative reports by participant observers, and it may be that they lacked objectivity in reporting what was for them a negative personal experience entirely from the perspective of a pseudopatient on a psychiatric ward.

While qualitative data can provide a rich and detailed account of behaviour in studies in the individual differences approach, there are difficulties with its interpretation, objectivity and analysis which leads us to question its validity.

Psychologists have to be careful that their findings are not misused. By focusing on the differences between people, the individual differences approach may emphasise these differences and this can lead to discrimination.

For example, Rosenhan's work shows how labels that are used to describe mental illness can become a problem. Once diagnosed with schizophrenia, this label can mean that people may make judgements about the person or even discriminate against them, for example, when selecting for employment where such diagnoses have to be declared.

Researchers in this area must present their data responsibly and be sensitive to the possible implications of highlighting differences between people.

Exam focus   ▶

Section C, part (d)

In part (d) of Section C on the Core Studies examination you will be asked to discuss the strengths and weaknesses of a specified approach using examples from any studies that take this approach. There are 12 marks available for part (d), so in the examination you have about twelve minutes to write your answer. You need to write about two strengths and two weaknesses in detail, explaining each point clearly and illustrating your point with a relevant core study.

How can you make sure you get 12 out of 12 here? One way might be to present each point, that is, each strength or weakness, using the model:

Point + explain, example, comment

You should identify and explain your chosen strength or weakness (point and explain), then use an example from a core study from the relevant approach to illustrate the point you have made. To fully explain your point you should finish off with a comment to show that you understand the implications of the strength or weakness ('This means that …').
Here is an example for a strength of the social approach.

Sample Answer

Point + explain =
The social approach often uses field experiments to study social behaviour. This is a strength of this approach as this method enables researchers to study how people behave in naturalistic settings.

Example
An example of this from the core studies is the study by Piliavin *et al.* who studied helping behaviour by staging an emergency in a real-life setting on a New York subway train and observing the passengers' behaviour. Seeing someone fall over and need help is something that people may well experience in everyday life.

Comment
This means that this social approach study has high ecological validity and can explain how people behave in real-life settings as opposed to how they behave in the artificial setting of the laboratory.

In the examination you get three minutes to write this. You may be thinking right now that you will never be able to do that, but the way to ensure that you can is to PREPARE and PRACTISE.

Activity

1. For each of the approaches, copy and complete the following revision table. The social approach has been started for you.

The social approach

	Point + explain	Example	Comment
Strength 1	The social approach often uses field experiments to study social behaviour. This is a strength of this approach as this method enables researchers to study how people behave in naturalistic settings.	An example of this from the core studies is the study by Piliavin *et al.* who studied helping behaviour by staging an emergency in a real-life setting on a New York subway train and observing the passengers' behaviour. Seeing someone fall over and need help is something that people may well experience in everyday life.	This means that this social approach study has high ecological validity and can explain how people behave in real-life settings as opposed to how they behave in the artificial setting of the laboratory.
Strength 2			
Weakness 1			
Weakness 2			

2. Have a go at the following Section C part (d) questions on approaches.
   a) Discuss strengths and weaknesses of the social approach using examples from any studies that take this approach. [12]
   b) Discuss strengths and weaknesses of the cognitive approach using examples from any studies that take this approach. [12]
   c) Discuss strengths and weaknesses of the developmental approach using examples from any studies that take this approach. [12]
   d) Discuss strengths and weaknesses of the physiological approach using examples from any studies that take this approach. [12]
   e) Discuss strengths and weaknesses of the individual differences approach using examples from any studies that take this approach. [12]

In the examination you will also get a choice of questions in Section C, either question 17 or 18. Each question will focus on one approach or perspective (more on perspectives next). Here is an example.

1. Outline one assumption of the cognitive approach. [2]
2. Describe how the cognitive approach could explain problems with eyewitness testimony. [4]
3. Describe one similarity and one difference between any studies that use the cognitive approach. [6]
4. Discuss strengths and weaknesses of the cognitive approach using examples from any studies that take this approach. [12]

Apart from the second question, the structure of these questions is predictable, which is helpful for you as it means you can prepare and practise these questions as part of your revision.

Perspectives in psychology

Having ended on the approaches with a Section C question, you will start the perspectives by looking at possible Section C questions.

Past Section C question (June 2010) on the behaviourist perspective	Possible Section C question on the psychodynamic perspective
Outline one assumption of the behaviourist perspective. [2]	Outline one assumption of the psychodynamic perspective. [2]
Describe how the behaviourist perspective could explain obedience. [4]	Describe how the psychodynamic perspective could explain phobias. [4]
Describe one similarity and one difference between any studies that could be viewed from the behaviourist perspective. [6]	Describe one similarity and one difference between any studies that could be viewed from the psychodynamic perspective. [6]
Discuss strengths and weaknesses of the behaviourist perspective using examples from any studies that could be viewed from this perspective. [12]	Discuss strengths and weaknesses of the psychodynamic perspective using examples from any studies that could be viewed from this perspective. [12]

These questions should look familiar to you by now, as they follow exactly the same structure as the approaches questions.

You studied the psychodynamic perspective when you were studying Freud's case study of Little Hans and the behaviourist perspective as background to the study on imitating aggression by Bandura *et al.*

For Section C you need to know an assumption of the perspective; how the perspective has described or would describe a given behaviour; similarities and differences between two studies that can be viewed from that perspective, and the strengths and weaknesses of the perspective illustrated by studies that can be viewed from that perspective.

You will now go through these in turn. To simplify this, we will look at the behaviourist perspective first, followed by the psychodynamic perspective.

The behaviourist perspective

Some assumptions of the behaviourist perspective are as follows:

The behaviourist perspective assumes that all behaviour is learned, and that learning happens through the processes of classical conditioning, operant conditioning (reinforcement) or through social learning. This means that the behaviourist perspective is at the extreme nurture end of the nature–nurture debate.

- The behaviourist perspective considers that explanations of behaviour based on internal causes or mental states are generally useless, and to study behaviour psychologists should focus only on what can be overtly observed.

- The behaviourist perspective assumes that both normal and abnormal behaviours are all learned and can be unlearned, and behaviour can be controlled and altered, not just described and quantified.

How would the behaviourist perspective explain behaviour?

The first assumption we looked at is the explanation for all behaviour according to the behaviourist perspective, so whatever behaviour you are asked to write about, the answer is that the behaviourist perspective would assume that you learned the behaviour.

Exam focus

Section C, part (b)
Activity
How would the behaviourist perspective explain obedience?

Sample Answer

The behaviourist perspective begins by assuming that all behaviour is learned, so according to this perspective obedience is a learned behaviour. It may have been taught to us using positive and negative reinforcement when we were children, for example, by being praised for doing as we were told and scolded for not obeying. This would mean that initially we obeyed because of extrinsic reinforcement, but eventually obedience would become internalised so that we would feel bad if we disobeyed, and this means that our need to obey and our need to avoid disobedience has a very strong influence on our behaviour.

Write an answer for the following Section C, part (b) question.
How would the behaviourist perspective explain aggression?

The similarities and differences between studies in the behaviourist perspective

When it comes to making comparisons between studies, this is quite a challenge since it is difficult to identify studies in the 15 core studies that take a behaviourist perspective. The study that does take a behaviourist perspective is Bandura *et al.*'s study that illustrates social learning theory, or modelling, as method for learning. Because of this, it might be wise for you to learn a new study that does take a behaviourist perspective, the case of Little Albert. However, you do not need to learn about this study in a great deal of depth, since you will not be asked detailed questions about it in the examination. You will just use it to compare with Bandura *et al.*'s study and use it to illustrate the strengths and weaknesses of the behaviourist perspective.

The case of Little Albert

This is the classic behaviourist study by John Watson and Rosalie Raynor (1920) who wanted to see if it was possible to induce a fear of a previously unfeared object, a white rat, through the process of classical conditioning. The subject of this study was the 11-month-old child of a wet nurse so he was in a hospital environment. This was a case study carried out over a period of weeks under controlled conditions.

For several weeks, Albert played happily with a white rat showing no fear. When he was 11 months old, the experiments began. While he was playing with the rat, the experimenters struck a steel bar with a hammer close to Albert's head. Albert was very frightened by the noise. This was repeated each time he reached for the rat. The rat and noise were presented to Albert seven times, two on the first day and then five in session two a week later. Each time he showed a fear reaction to the pairing.

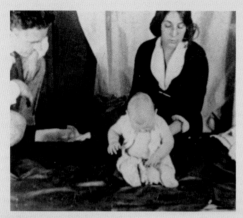

When the rat alone was presented after the five pairings with the fear stimulus Albert responded by immediately crying, turning to the left and crawling away. This suggested that after seven pairings the child had developed a phobia of the rat.

The researchers tested the generalisability of this fear and found Albert was afraid of other furry things too, including a seal fur coat and a Santa Claus mask. He was also conditioned to fear a dog and a rabbit. His fears were shown to stand the test of time and to show themselves in different contexts. After the fifth session Albert's mother left the hospital taking Albert with her, so he was never counter-conditioned.

Figure 7.5 Little Albert

The case of Little Albert has courted much controversy, as you can probably imagine, and been the source of many myths in psychology. You will possibly study this in more depth if you study Health and Clinical psychology in A2, but this is enough detail for our purposes.

We can now compare and contrast the studies by Bandura *et al.* and Watson and Raynor.

Remember we can use the methods and themes to make comparisons between these studies.

Activity

Comparing studies that can be viewed from the behaviourist perspective
Answer the following questions.
1. In terms of the similarities between the studies by Bandura *et al.* on imitating aggression and Watson and Raynor's case study of Little Albert
   a) Explain how both of the studies raise ethical concerns.
   b) Explain how both studies could be argued to lack ecological validity.
   c) Explain how both studies used observation as a data-gathering method.
2. In terms of the similarities between the studies by Bandura *et al.* on imitating aggression and Watson and Raynor's case study of Little Albert
   a) Which of the two studies has the most scientific credibility and why?
   b) Which of the two studies is the most generalisable to a broader population?

Some strengths and weaknesses of the behaviourist perspective

✓ One strength of the behaviourist perspective is that it highlights the role of nurture in learning, and shows the important influence environment has on our behaviour. For example, Bandura *et al.*'s study shows us how we learn by observing those around us in our environment, our role models. This illustrates an important all-at-once method of learning behaviour.

A second strength of the behaviourist perspective is that it assumes that behaviour can be both learned and unlearned, which means we can control and change behaviour using behaviourist techniques. For example, the implication of Watson and Raynor's study on Little Albert was that phobic responses are learned and can be unlearned. The behaviourist perspective therefore offers a hopeful theory about the causes of phobia and there are a number of successful treatments for phobias, such as systematic desensitisation, based on the principles of classical and operant conditioning.

A third strength of the behaviourist perspective is that in its attempt to study behaviour it favours the scientific method and laboratory experiments in particular. For example, Bandura *et al.* carried out a laboratory study to investigate the effect of both aggressive and passive models on children to see if the children would learn by observation, and were able to operate a highly controlled study.

This focus of the behaviourist perspective on studying observable behaviour in laboratory experiments gave psychology as a discipline the scientific credibility it previously lacked.

A weakness of the behaviourist perspective is that by favouring the laboratory experiment as a research method studies in this approach can lack ecological validity and therefore fail to resemble behaviours that people might perform in real life. For example, Bandura *et al.*'s study lacks ecological validity. There is no adult–child interaction in the study (in stage 1), whereas an adult would not usually ignore a child in a room with them. In addition, a child is rarely left alone with a stranger, and adults do not normally play with toys as they did in the study. The study is therefore not representative of situations in which children find themselves in 'real life'. If studies lack ecological validity this reduces our ability to generalise the findings to real-life settings and this in turn reduces the usefulness of the studies.

In terms of Bandura's social learning theory, how are we to control what our children are or are not exposed to? This contributes to a number of important social debates including those concerning censorship of the media.

Another weakness of the behaviourist perspective is that there are moral issues and ethical objections raised against the behaviourist perspective. If the principles of behaviourism can be used to control people and change their behaviour, then who should decide which behaviours should be changed and who controls the controllers?

In addition, we might also question the ethics of the methods used by both Bandura *et al.* and Watson and Raynor in their investigations of the principles of the behaviourist perspective.

You should now be ready to attempt the question at the start of this section on perspectives.

Activity

1. Outline one assumption of the behaviourist perspective. [2]
2. Describe how the behaviourist perspective could explain obedience. [4]
3. Describe one similarity and one difference between any studies that could be viewed from the behaviourist perspective. [6]
4. Discuss strengths and weaknesses of the behaviourist perspective using examples from any studies that could be viewed from this perspective. [12]

The psychodynamic perspective

Some assumptions of the psychodynamic perspective are as follows:

- The psychodynamic perspective assumes that all behaviour has an unconscious cause, even slips of the tongue. Therefore all behaviour is determined. We have no control over our unconscious and therefore have no free will. Behaviour is motivated from the unconscious by two instinctual drives: Eros and Thanatos.

- Another assumption of the psychodynamic perspective is that the personality has three parts which reside in the unconscious called the ego, the id and the superego. The id and superego can create conflict for the ego if the desires of the id (to spend unconscious energy) are disapproved of by the moral conscience, the superego. Failure of the ego to resolve this conflict, for example, by using defence mechanisms such as repression, sublimation or denial, can lead to 'ego anxiety' which, according to the psychodynamic perspective, is the cause of mental health problems.

How would the psychodynamic perspective explain behaviour?

The psychodynamic perspective assumes that behaviours are caused by the ego seeking to spend psychic energies that are generated by the unconscious mind in conscious reality. The psychic energies are either aggressive energies or life energies, such as libidinal energy.

However, if there is a conflict between the demands of the id and the superego, the moral part of the personality, the ego, may have difficulty spending the energy. This causes ego anxiety, and the energy that is not spent builds up in the unconscious. The energy then erupts into consciousness in the form of mental health problems such as phobias.

The defence mechanism of displacement comes into play in Little Hans' phobia: he displaces his unconscious fear of his father's punishing for his feelings towards his mother on to the horse.

The similarities and differences between studies in the psychodynamic perspective

After Freud's case study of Little Hans, it is again quite a challenge to identify other studies from the core studies that can be viewed from the psychodynamic perspective. However, Thigpen and Cleckley's study of Eve can be used as a comparison here. This case study documents the psychiatric treatment of Eve, essentially using a talking cure as pioneered by Freud (although not using psychodynamic principles in the therapy) and makes reference to Freudian defence mechanisms, repression and regression in the Rorschach profiles of Eve White and Eve Black respectively.

Both Freud and Thigpen and Cleckley carried out longitudinal studies of their subjects. Using this method enabled the researchers in both studies to track and document the progress and resolution of the psychological problems being experienced: Hans' phobia and Eve's multiple personality disorder.

Both of these studies are case studies and both used clinical interviews to gather data. The clinical interviews in the case of Thigpen and Cleckley were the therapeutic sessions with their client and for Freud's study the clinical interviews were the interviews that Hans' father had with the boy about his dreams and fantasies. By using clinical interviews both studies were able to gather highly detailed qualitative data. However, a problem with the longitudinal design of the studies meant that the researchers may have lost their objectivity and may have focused on gathering only data that supported the idea that Eve was a true case of MPD or data that Hans really was experiencing Freud's Oedipus complex.

One way in which the studies by Freud and Thigpen and Cleckley differ from each other is that Thigpen and Cleckley were experts in their field, psychiatry, and admirably cautious in making assumptions about whether Eve was a true case of MPD. Freud, on the other hand, considered no other explanation for Hans' phobia other than his interpretation of the boy's phobia of a horse biting his finger being representative of the boy's Oedipal castration anxiety.

Freud gathered and presented only qualitative data, mostly of the boy's dreams and fantasies such as the fantasy of the two giraffes. In comparison, Thigpen and Cleckley used triangulation of methods in their investigation of Eve, including clinical interviews, psychometric tests of memory and IQ, projective tests including the Rorschach ink blot test and EEG tests of Eve White, Eve Black and Jane. It was the fact that these objective tests of the different personalities was 'unimpressive' that made the researchers cautious in claiming that Eve was a true case of MPD, as to make this claim they only had self-report data to rely on and they had to admit she might simply be a good actress, feigning her symptoms.

Activity

Copy and complete the following table.

Similarities between Freud's study of Little Hans and Thigpen and Cleckley's study of Eve White	Differences between Freud's study of Little Hans and Thigpen and Cleckley's study of Eve White

Some strengths and weaknesses of the psychodynamic perspective

✅ One strength of the psychodynamic perspective is that Freud's theory raised for the first time the importance of the unconscious mind as an influence on our feelings and behaviour, making an important contribution to our understanding of the human mind. Freud was the first to stress the importance of psychological factors causing abnormal behaviour. In the case of Little Hans, for example, Freud considered the boy's phobia as resulting from psychological conflict.

✅ Another strength of the psychodynamic perspective is that Freud developed a psychological treatment, or talking cure, for abnormal behaviour. For example, Hans' father was carrying out psychoanalysis of the boy in order to help resolve the boy's phobia. Although most modern therapists do not use

Freudian principles, Freud's legacy is apparent in modern forms of counselling.

✓ Another strength of the psychodynamic perspective is that Freud's work made the case study method popular in psychology. Case studies provide in-depth detail about a person or client's experiences, both current and in the past. The case study method remains popular in the area of abnormal psychology. For example, both the studies by Freud and Thigpen and Cleckley used case studies to investigate clients with abnormal behaviour, Hans' phobia and Eve's possible MPD.

✗ The greatest weakness of the psychodynamic perspective is that it is unscientific in its analysis of human behaviour. Many of the concepts central to Freud's theories are subjective and as such impossible to scientifically test. For example, how is it possible to scientifically study concepts like the unconscious mind or to prove the existence of the Oedipus complex, as in the study of Little Hans? Many psychologists reject the psychodynamic perspective because the theories and concepts cannot be empirically investigated.

✗ Another weakness of the psychodynamic perspective is that the evidence for psychodynamic theory is taken from Freud's case studies. For example, Freud used the case study of Little Hans to provide evidence for the Oedipus complex. The main problem here is that case studies are based on studying one person in detail, and with reference to the case of Little Hans the evidence from the case study is highly subjective and can be affected by researcher bias. This puts the validity of the findings into question and makes generalisations to the wider population difficult. We cannot assume that Hans is in any way a 'typical' little boy.

You should now be ready to attempt the question at the start of this section.

Activity

1. Outline one assumption of the psychodynamic perspective. [2]
2. Describe how the psychodynamic perspective could explain phobias. [4]
3. Describe one similarity and one difference between any studies that could be viewed from the psychodynamic perspective. [6]
4. Discuss strengths and weaknesses of the psychodynamic perspective using examples from any studies that could be viewed from this perspective. [12]

8 The psychological investigations exam: Research methods

When conducting their research, psychologists use a range of research methods, data–gathering methods, designs and sampling methods and take a number of methodological and general issues into account in their research. A range of techniques is also used to present and analyse the data that has been gathered.

The methods and techniques selected depend on what and whom the researcher is investigating, and, as you will see in this chapter, can be influenced by both ethical considerations and practical considerations.

For both the Core Studies examination and the Psychological Investigations examination you need to be able to identify, describe, apply and evaluate psychological research methodology.

One of the difficulties students often have is working out the difference between a research method, a data-gathering method, a design and a methodological issue. Use table 8.1 to help you.

In the OCR AS-level specification the core studies introduce you to a range of methods used in psychological research, including experiments carried out either in the psychology laboratory or under controlled conditions such as Baron-Cohen *et al.*'s eyes task, field experiments carried out in natural settings such as Rosenhan's study on Being sane in insane places, controlled observations such as Milgram's obedience study and case studies such as Thigpen and Cleckley's Three faces of Eve.

In the Core Studies examination (Section B) you may be asked to explain the key features of a chosen research method, e.g. field experiments or case studies, and consider the strengths and weakness of the chosen method in psychological research using the core studies as examples.

In the Psychological Investigations examination you will be expected to know about research methods, designs, data-gathering methods and methodological and general issues and write about these in relation to examples of research given to you in the examination (the 'source material') to show that you understand and can apply the research issues. What you have learned in the core studies will help you in the Psychological Investigations examination, but you will not be asked or expected to write about any of the core studies in the Psychological Investigations examination as the emphasis in this examination is on research methodology in general.

This examination requires that you have learned about four general topics as they are used in psychological research:

- experiments
- observations
- self-reports
- correlations.

Table 8.1

Research methods	Data-gathering methods	Designs	Methodological and general Issues
The experimental method Case study Correlation Observational methods★ Self-report methods★ (e.g. interview, survey)	Self-report methods (e.g. questionnaire, interview, asking questions, psychometric tests) Observations (e.g. using an observation schedule to code and categorise behaviours, content analysis) Physiological measures (e.g. structural MRI scan, EEG) and biochemical measures (e.g. testing saliva for levels of cortisol as a measure of stress)	Experimental designs (repeated measures, matched subjects independent groups) Longitudinal and snapshot (or cross-sectional) designs	Making generalisations: sampling methods Use of qualitative and quantitative data Validity and reliability Ethical considerations

★This may seem confusing, as self-reports and observations appear in two columns, but as you will see, we use these data-gathering methods in experiments, correlations and case studies. So for the method, always work out if it is an experiment, case study or correlation before asking if it is an observational research method or a self-report research method!

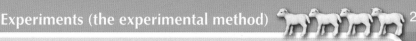
Experiments (the experimental method)

Think about the following questions:

- What are the key features of science?

- What is an experiment?

Once you can answer these questions, you should have a good understanding of what is and is not an experiment in psychology and why we do experiments in psychology.

What are the key features of science? In scientific enquiry there are four key features:

- **Theory:** We start with an idea or hypothesis (prediction) about something, for example, using leading questions will affect people's memory of an event.

- **Empirical evidence:** We need to carry out a study to provide objective evidence for the theory. Loftus and Palmer designed a study to investigate their theory and provide proof for it. A causal relationship between two factors (the independent and dependent variables) is investigated.

Key concept

Independent variables and dependent variables

The variable that is manipulated by the experimenter (E) to see if it has an effect on another variable is called the independent variable (IV).

The variable which is measured to show if the IV has had an effect is called the dependent variable (DV).

The IV is thus the input variable and the DV the output variable. A simple way of saying this is:

IV = Cause   DV = Effect

- **Control:** The study must be conducted under controlled conditions so that we can be sure that we are studying what we intended to study. Loftus and Palmer standardised their study to ensure that the leading questions were the only reason for the change in speed estimate in study 1.

- **Replication:** If a study and the theory it supports is to be true (valid), then it must be shown to be replicable, that is, if we carry out the study under similar circumstances or test the idea in a similar way then the findings are reliable (consistent on replication). In their study 2, Loftus and Palmer repeated a similar test of leading questions and found that the effect on memory was indeed reliable, lending support to the validity of their theory

What is an experiment? The experimental method is a research method that can establish causal relationships between variables. A hypothesis is formulated to predict the effect of one variable, known as the independent variable (IV), on another variable, known as the dependent variable (DV). Usually two conditions are operated, with one testing participants in the experimental condition, where the IV is introduced, and one testing Ss in the control condition, where no IV is introduced. The control condition is used for comparison to see if the IV has affected the DV.

What we are saying here is that experiments are more than just 'investigations' and they have key features that must be present including:

- The effect of independent variable(s) on dependent variable(s) is being tested.

- Controlled conditions are established, e.g. using standardised procedures.

- Replication of the procedures is possible, an important element of science, in order to test the reliability of the findings.

Laboratory and field experiments

Experiments can be carried out under controlled laboratory conditions or in the field in a natural setting. The choice of location reflects a balance between strict control to isolate the IV as a causal variable and the need to ensure that the study has sufficient ecological validity for the results to be generalised to a real-life setting. Laboratory conditions give the highest level of control but field experiments can offer a more realistic setting for a study and therefore can be more ecologically valid when we are studying social behaviour.

Applying experimental controls

How do experimenters isolate the IV as the causal variable in an experiment?

As we have said, control is a very important feature of science. In an experiment there are a range of control features and techniques that we can use in order to be sure that it is the IV, and not any other variable, that has caused any observed change in the DV.

This is known as controlling extraneous variables, or applying experimental controls in an experiment. Extraneous variables are simply any variables other than the IV that could have an effect on the DV in an experiment.

Key concept

Controlling extraneous variables
For an experiment to establish that it is the IV causing any observed change in the DV, all other variables, known as extraneous variables, need to be controlled or kept constant. The experimenter has to make sure the subjects or participants are not too dissimilar from each other to prevent individual differences from affecting the study, and has to control situational variables by, for example, standardising procedures and instructions.

All the extraneous variables that we want to control will fall into one of two categories:

- **Subject variables or personal factors:** These are factors within a person that can vary over time or vary with a situation; for example, I am confused in a physics lesson but not confused in a research methods lesson in psychology, or I am bored when watching football but interested when watching cricket, or I am alert mid-afternoon but tired late at night, or I used to like excitement when I was young but prefer a cup of tea and a biscuit to a roller coaster now I am older. Subject variables can also vary between people, for example, your memory is better than mine, or you are better at texting on your mobile than me, or you like football and cricket but I only like cricket, or your best time of the day for being alert is late at night whereas mine is mid-afternoon, or you are young and like to party and I am old and I no longer do! More obvious differences between people include age, gender and ethnicity.

- **Situational variables or environmental factors:** These are factors which can vary in the environment including level of noise in a room, number of people present in a situation, time of day, the way an experimenter behaves towards the participants and the procedure of a study (the way participants are tested).

It is essential that we control extraneous variables in an experiment because if any extraneous variable is not controlled it will spoil our study by becoming a confounding variable.

Key concept

Confounding variables

A confounding variable is any extraneous variable which has not been controlled but has operated alongside the IV in the experiment, making it impossible to establish whether it was the IV or this second variable which has caused any change in the DV. This uncontrolled extraneous variable has confounded the study, which means that because of this variable we cannot isolate the IV as the cause of any change in the DV. If it is possible that the study has been affected by confounding variables then the validity of the study can be challenged.

Controlling situational variables or environmental factors

There are a number of strategies for controlling extraneous environmental variables. These include standardisation, randomisation and counterbalancing.

Standardisation means keeping the test conditions the same for every subject or participant. It is a method of controlling situational variables or environmental factors which might have an influence on the subject or participant's behaviour. To keep all extraneous variables constant across experimental conditions, researchers use standard apparatus, standard instructions and procedures and standard locations. In fact, as an experienced student you have often been tested in standardised conditions. Think of the test conditions for an examination: you get the same time allowed, same test paper with the same questions and same amount of marks per question as your fellow candidates, same instructions, same amount of space between you and the other candidates (we actually have to measure this!), and you do this at the same time as everyone else in the country doing the same test paper as you. This is all designed to produce fair testing conditions, and this is the same with standardisation in psychological research.

Figure 8.1 Random allocation

If subjects or participants were treated differently, this would mean that fair comparisons between their responses could not be made and this would threaten the validity of the findings.

Randomisation, or random allocation, is where subjects or participants are allocated to experimental conditions on a chance basis, by drawing lots or tossing a coin, for example. This is again done to control extraneous variables. Random allocation can be used to avoid experimenter bias (whether conscious or unconscious) when allocating participants to conditions for a study.

Counterbalancing is a third technique for controlling situational factors such as time of day or location. Imagine that a teacher wants to find out if students can work better from handouts that have pictures and diagrams or from handouts that do not. She has two classes of 20 students, one she can test in the morning in a bright new room in a new block in the school and one she can test in the afternoon whom she teaches in an old dingy room in an old part of the school.

If she tests the morning group with the pictures handout (Condition A) and the afternoon group with the no pictures handout (Condition B) the study could be confounded by time of day and by the location. However, to avoid this, these situational variables can be controlled by counterbalancing their effects on the study using what is called an ABAB design. What this means is that half the morning group is tested with the pictures handout (Condition A) and half the morning group is tested in the no pictures condition (Condition B). The same is done in the afternoon, and this means that any effect of the time or location should affect the groups equally and should no longer confound the study.

Key concept

Counterbalancing to control for order effects

Counterbalancing is a method of controlling variables, especially order effects in repeated measures designs, by systematically varying the order of presentation of tasks to subjects or participants. For example, alternating the test procedure so that half take the control test first and the other half take the experimental test first. This spreads out the effects of order of presentation across the test conditions. Where one half of the subjects or participants do one condition first, Condition A followed by Condition B, and the other half does the opposite, Condition B followed by Condition A, this is known as an ABBA counterbalancing design.

Exam focus

Experimental controls

For the Psychological Investigations examination you need to be able to identify any controls used in the study described in the source material and suggest experimental controls that could be used in the study and why they should be used.

Activity

A researcher wanted to investigate if there was a gender difference between young women and young men in their sensation-seeking and risk-taking behaviour. A questionnaire was devised and administered to all the participants.

All 200 students in a school sixth form assembly at a local school were asked to take part in the study and were each given the questionnaire. They were asked to complete the questionnaire over the next 24 hours and post it into a box in their common room by the end of the next day.

Figure 8.2

(a) Identify one experimental control that was used in this study and explain why it was used.
(b) Suggest one further experimental control that ought to be used in this study and explain why it ought to be used by the experimenter.

Controlling subject variables and personal factors (individual differences)

To control extraneous personal variables experimental designs can be used:

- repeated measures design

- matched subjects design

- independent groups design.

These designs have two functions:

- to provide a way for experimenters to control extraneous subject variables and personal factors

- to provide experimental and control conditions for the experiment.

In a repeated measures design each subject or participant is tested in every condition – thus each subject provides their own comparison (control) scores. A repeated measures design is therefore a related design as each pair of scores is from one participant.

Table 8.2

✔ Strengths of a repeated measures design	✘ Weaknesses of a repeated measures design
By comparing each person with themselves the likelihood that individual differences between subjects will confound the study is reduced. This is the best design therefore for controlling subject variables in an experiment. This design can use fewer participants than a matched subjects or independent groups design so may be more cost- and time-effective.	The repeated measures design can be affected by 'order effects': practice, fatigue and boredom, so requires counterbalancing to control for these. If subjects are tested twice or more they may work out the IV (they do this by picking up on the demand characteristics in the study) and may try to behave according to what they believe is expected.

An alternative to a repeated measures design is to use a matched subjects, or matched pairs, design. Here each participant is paired up with someone on the basis of the variables that matter to the study, for example, gender, age, position in the family, level of aggression, intelligence, level of skill or experience at doing something. One of the pair is tested in the experimental condition and the other one is tested in the control condition. This is also a related design, as each score in the experimental condition must be compared with its related score in the control condition.

Table 8.3

✔ Strengths of a matched subjects design	✖ Weaknesses of a matched subjects design
A matched design avoids some of the problems that a repeated measures design presents, for example, a matched subjects design is not affected by order effects and is less likely to be affected by demand characteristics as each participant is tested only once. A matched design controls subject variables better than an independent groups design as participants are matched on the variables important to the study.	There are some problems with the matched subjects design that means it is not often used. First, it is very time-consuming to match participants, and second it is impossible to match them on enough variables to be sure that there are no possible extraneous individual differences that might confound the study, which means that the design would in fact be best described as an independent groups design.

In an independent groups design an homogenous sample is randomly allocated to the experimental condition(s) and the control condition. Each subject or participant is tested in only one condition. The scores for each group are compared with the scores for the other group. For example, a group of students could be selected to take part in the study, as students are an homogenous group (they share similar characteristics), and they could then be randomly allocated to conditions, as in the Loftus and Palmer study. Random allocation to conditions is assumed to spread out any individual differences across conditions.

Since this method compares the whole experimental condition's scores against the whole control condition's scores this is known as an unrelated design.

Table 8.4

✔ Strengths of an independent groups design	✖ Weaknesses of an independent groups design
An independent groups design is not affected by order effects as each participant is tested only once in one test condition. This design is also less likely to be affected by demand characteristics than a repeated measures design as each person is tested only once and has less opportunity to work out the hypothesis being tested and act accordingly. This design is less time-consuming to conduct than a matched subjects design.	An independent groups design does not control extraneous subject variables effectively, so individual differences between the participants may confound the findings. It is the least effective method of controlling subject variables. It is hard to find a truly homogenous sample which can be randomly allocated to give groups where all possible individual differences are controlled. As a result, large samples are often needed in order to be sure that any effect of the IV is caused by the DV and not by individual differences between the groups being tested.

Exam focus

Experimental designs

For the Psychological Investigations examination you need to be able to offer definitions of the designs, identify designs from source material, evaluate the strengths and weaknesses of the design used in source material and offer an alternative design for a given study and consider its possible effects on the study.

Activity

A researcher wanted to find out if watching a film about teenagers who did charity work in aid of teenagers in need across the world would make teenagers who viewed the film behave more helpfully.

The film was shown to 50 students, 25 male and 25 female, and a questionnaire was given to them immediately afterwards asking them to commit to helping the charity in one or more of the following ways:

- sign-up to an online petition to help the charity get funds from the government
- give a small donation of 50p to the charity
- collect money for charity in the High Street for one hour on a Saturday
- take part in a sponsored walk in aid of the charity lasting three hours on a Sunday, seeking their own sponsors beforehand and collecting the money after the event.

Figure 8.3

A further group of 50 students was asked to complete the charity questionnaire without seeing the film.

(a) Explain what is meant by a repeated measures design. [2]

(b) Explain what is meant by an independent groups design. [2]

(c) Identify the experimental design being used here and give a strength of using this design in this study. [3]

(d) Suggest how an alternative design could be used in this study and explain how your suggested alternative design might improve this study [4]

Longitudinal versus snapshot designs

In a snapshot design, different groups of people are tested at the same point in time and their performances compared. Examples from the core studies include the Subway Samaritan study by Piliavin *et al.* and Samuel and Bryant's study on conservation.

The advantages that snapshot studies have over longitudinal studies is that they are relatively quick and inexpensive to carry out, can be easily replicated to test the reliability of findings and are relatively easy to modify. This final point means that if design faults become apparent, the study can be repeated with modifications to eliminate them. It also means that variations of the study can be easily carried out to investigate fully the variables that may affect behaviour.

In a longitudinal study, one subject or participant or one group of individuals is studied over a long period of time, for example, taking periodic samples of behaviour. This design allows us to track development and enables us to monitor changes over time, for example, in the Savage-Rumbaugh *et al.* study it allows us to see the development of Kanzi's language. The longitudinal approach also enabled the researchers to make comparisons between Kanzi and common chimpanzees.

Quasi design of experiments

Quasi experiment have some, but not all of the features of a 'true' experiment. Natural experiments are an example of this, where the IV occurs naturally or is already established and cannot for either ethical or practical reasons be actually manipulated by the experimenter and can only be observed by them. For example, if the IV is age, or gender or ethnicity, this obviously cannot be changed by the experimenter for the purpose of the experiment. An example of this type of quasi experiment is the Baron-Cohen *et al.* (autism) study, where people already were normal or had autism or Tourette's syndrome. This design can limit the amount of control the experimenter has over the IV, as we obviously cannot use controls such as random allocation to conditions here, but the strength of this design is that it allows us to study the effects of these variables on behaviour using as controlled a method as is available to us.

Hypotheses and experiments

In terms of the main features of science, the hypothesis is the **theory,** and testing the hypothesis is how we get our **proof**. Researchers devise and test hypotheses to lend weight to their theories.

A hypothesis is a prediction about the relationship between two variables and in an experiment the alternate or experimental hypothesis tells us exactly what effect we predict the independent variable will have on the dependent variable.

Key concept

Experimental or alternative hypotheses
The plural of hypothesis is hypotheses. In an experiment the alternate or experimental hypothesis will predict the effect of the IV on the DV, for example, 'Children tested in the one-judgement condition will make fewer errors on the conservation tasks than those in the same age group tested in the two-question condition or the fixed array condition.'
The alternate or experimental hypothesis is also known as the research hypothesis.

Hypotheses can be either one-tailed or two-tailed.

In a one-tailed hypothesis a specific effect is predicted. This is also known as a directional hypothesis. One-tailed hypotheses have only one possible true outcome. For example, 'Students who listen to music while studying will score higher in their end of term test than those who study without music.' Those who listen to music must do better in order for this hypothesis to be true.

- In a two-tailed hypothesis an effect is predicted but not specified. This is also known as a non-directional hypothesis. Two-tailed hypotheses have two possible true outcomes. For example, 'Listening to music while studying will affect a student's performance in their end of term test.' Now those who listen to music can do better or worse to make this hypothesis true.

Activity

1. Explain the difference between a one-tailed and a two- tailed hypothesis.
2. Identify whether the following five alternate (research/experimental) hypotheses are one-tailed or two-tailed:
   - Dog owners are more physically fit than cat owners.
   - Boys score differently on a test of aggressiveness from girls.
   - People given 20 emotionally charged words to learn will remember significantly more words than people given 20 emotionally neutral words to learn.
   - Students who have a computer at home for their own exclusive use do better in their exams than students who do not.
   - Doing more than ten hours' part-time paid work affects students' examination performance.

   Tips for identifying whether a one-or two-tailed hypothesis is being tested in an experiment:
   - One tailed – look for words ending with –er, such as better, faster, healthier, or look for the words more or less.
   - Two tailed – look for words 'affects' or 'influence', where an effect is predicted but not specified; look for the prediction of a 'difference', again unspecified, between conditions.

3. For each of the five examples above, identify the IV and the DV.

   Tips for identifying the IV and the DV:
   - The DV is always the effect, so for the DV look for the results of the study.
   - When explaining an IV or DV state it in a way that can be measured, for example, by saying 'amount of' or 'number of …' or 'level of …'. Where the IV is one of two types, such as gender, state it as categories – 'Whether the participant is male or female …'

The null hypothesis

For statistical purposes, which will become clear to OCR students in the A2 part of the course, it is important to know how to formulate a null hypothesis.

The null hypothesis tells us that the IV will **not** have the predicted effect on the DV. The null hypothesis always states that there will be no difference between conditions, regardless of whether the alternate hypothesis is one- or two-tailed. For example, 'There will be no difference in the number of errors made on the conservation tasks between children tested in the one–judgement condition and those in the same age group tested in the two-question condition or the fixed array condition.' Or 'There will be no difference in the end of term test scores between those students who listen to music while studying and those who study without music.'

Key concept

The null hypothesis

The null hypothesis is the no-effect hypothesis and says that the IV will have no effect on the DV. Why do we need this? Well, this is where science as you *thought* you knew it will surprise you. At the head of this chapter you were asked to think about what we mean by science, and students will often say in response to this question that science is about doing tests and experiments to prove things to be true.

That's only half true. We do tests and experiments in science, but we are not trying to prove them to be true, instead we are trying to see if they can be proved false or not.

Karl Popper proposed the definition that phenomena can be considered scientific if it can be objectively tested and proved (or not proved) to be false. That means that the aim of science is to see if phenomena can be falsified.

Well, this is a problem for us as we have an alternative hypothesis that we do not want to be false. In fact we very much want it to be true. So what we do now is begin our study with the assumption that it is not true, and that is why we need the null hypothesis. We then set about trying to show that the null hypothesis (the no effect version) is not true.

If we can provide evidence that the null hypothesis is not true and can be rejected, this means we have supported the alternate hypothesis and we have in fact got scientific evidence for our theory. You'll probably want to read that again … a few times!

Activity

1. Explain the difference between the alternative hypothesis and the null hypothesis in an experiment.
2. For each of the five hypotheses below write out a suitable null hypothesis.
   (i)   Dog owners are more physically fit than cat owners.
   (ii) Boys score differently on a test of aggressiveness from girls.
   (iii) People given 20 emotionally charged words to learn will remember significantly more words than people given 20 emotionally neutral words to learn.
   (iv) Students who have a computer at home for their own exclusive use do better in their exams than students who do not.
   (v)   Doing more than ten hours' part-time paid work affects students' examination performance.

Operational hypotheses

Hypotheses need to state variables in an operationalised format. Here is an example:

Theory = eating chocolate improves examination performance

But what does the researcher mean by 'eating chocolate' and 'examination performance'?

An operational hypothesis makes it clear exactly how these variables will be measured: 'Participants who eat 200g of 70 per cent cocoa chocolate 20 minutes beforehand will score higher in their mock GCSE maths examination than those who eat no chocolate.'

Figure 8.4

Key concept

Operationalising variables

If a variable is to be studied scientifically (or objectively) then it must be operationalised. Operationalising a variable means defining and measuring the variable in a way which is unambiguous, so anyone using the measurement to measure that variable in a given situation would come up with the same result. For example, for the variable 'memory' we could operationalise this as 'the number of words a person can freely recall from a list of 100 words learned in two minutes'. As long as we have the same list of words we can all be tested and get comparable 'memory' measures on this scale.

Exam focus

Hypotheses

Activity

A researcher wanted to find out if watching a film about teenagers who did charity work in aid of teenagers in need across the world would make teenagers who viewed the film behave more helpfully.

The film was shown to 50 students, 25 male and 25 female, and a questionnaire was given to them immediately afterwards asking them to commit to helping the charity. The questionnaire gave a score of 0 to 50, with 50 being the most helpful. A further group of 50 students was asked to complete the charity questionnaire without seeing the film.

(a) Write a suitable alternate hypothesis for this experiment. [3]

(b) Write a suitable null hypothesis for his experiment. [3]

Tips for writing hypotheses for experiments

It is best to write an alternate hypothesis as a prediction about participants' behaviour:

Model: Participants in condition X will do better at … /score higher on … than participants in condition Y.

Example: Participants who see an ill victim fall on the train will help faster and more often than participants who see a drunk victim fall on the train (this is where the design is independent groups and the hypothesis is one-tailed).

or

Model: Participants will do better in condition X than condition Y (this is where the design is repeated measures and the hypothesis is one-tailed).

The null hypothesis simply states there will be no difference between the two conditions.

Model: There will be no difference in … [the behaviour being tested and observed] … between those tested in condition A and those tested in condition B

Example: There will be no difference in the amount and speed of help offered by participants who see an ill victim fall on the train and participants who see a drunk victim fall on the train.

The procedure of experiments

In the Psychological Investigations examination you may be given as many as ten marks in a 20 mark question for describing the procedure of a proposed study.

What does it mean by 'Describe the procedure of a study' for the Psychological Investigations examination? Here are some clues:

- The procedure of a study tells us exactly how data is collected, what variables are being measured and how they are being measured. This will explain if data is gathered by asking questions, including a description of any questionnaire or other materials to be used, or by observing, including details of what behaviour(s) are observed.

- The procedure includes information about where the study takes place (can be as simple as 'in a quiet room', 'in a laboratory', 'in a classroom' or 'in a field setting in the school dining room').

- The procedure describes who is being tested, including details of the sample type, sample size, how the sample would be obtained (sampling method) and any other details (age or gender of participants).

- The procedure describes the way extraneous variables are controlled (experimental design, standardisation, randomisation, alternating conditions).

- The procedure tells us exactly how participants are treated and exactly what they are asked to do (or are observed doing), and who could or did test them.

- The procedure describes any confederates used in the study and how they behave.

- The procedure explains whether participants are tested individually or all at once in a large group.

- The procedure should include the briefing and debriefing of participants, explaining what is said to them before taking part and when they had finished.

In describing the procedure you should include all the points above. If you have read a psychological study in its original form you should find all these details included. The purpose for including all this is so that the study can be replicated to test for reliability to see if the results prove consistent on replication. If the results are reliable, this lends weight to their scientific credibility.

Exam focus

Testing hypotheses

In the Psychological Investigations examination you may be asked to describe a suitable procedure for testing a given hypothesis for ten marks, or to describe AND evaluate a procedure for ten marks. The latter of these is the hardest task so we will focus on that in this activity.

Activity

Describe and evaluate a possible procedure for testing the hypothesis 'Participants will recall more words if they learn a list of words organised into meaningful categories than if they learn words presented in a random order.'

In your answer you should:
- Include the 'Who? What? Where? When? How?' of the proposed study.
- Use psychological terms and concepts.
- Offer both strengths and weaknesses for at least three points in your procedure.

Here is an example answer.

Sample Answer

Who would you test? 'An opportunity sample of 30 sixth form students, a mix of males and females, would be gathered from the library and private study area at a local school. A strength of this sample is that it is cost-effective and convenient to obtain. A weakness is that students have ethnocentric biases (age, intelligence) that would mean that we would not be able to generalise the findings to people in general.'

... Continued ▶

Sample Answer (contd.)

How would you test them, with what materials, when and where? 'I would test 30 people at once in a quiet classroom in a school at 10a.m., alternating the materials throughout the room so that one person would get 25 words organised into meaningful categories, e.g. tree/bark/branch/leaf/climb to learn and the next would get the same 25 words presented randomly to learn in two minutes. After two minutes they would turn over the sheet and on another sheet of paper write down as many of the words as they can remember out of 25. A strength of testing them in one room at one time is that the location is standardised and extraneous situational variables of time of day and location are controlled. However, by doing this there is the possibility that the participants will be able to see that others have different formats to learn from and may guess the hypothesis and respond to demand characteristics, challenging the validity of the findings.'

What experimental design is this? 'I would be using an independent groups design. The advantage of this in this study is that there would be no order effects of practice at the learning task and that the same words can be standardised across both conditions, improving control over situational variables. A weakness is that individual differences in the students' memory skills cannot be easily controlled and these may confound the study, especially where a small sample of 15 are in each condition.'

Activity

1. A researcher wants to find out if boys have better memory for words associated with sporting activities than girls. Describe and evaluate a suitable procedure for investigating this. [10]
(In addition to describing and evaluating a suitable procedure, the examination may ask about improvements you could make to your proposed procedure and their possible effects on the results of the proposed study.)

2. Suggest two improvements to your proposed procedure and explain how these changes would improve your proposed study. [6]

Tips for improving the procedure of a study

There are a number of ways you could suggest the procedure of the study might be improved. Here are some ideas:

Table 8.5

Current suggestion	Problem this suggestion raises	Proposed change or improvement	Likely effect on results
Test each participant one at once	Raises the possibility of situational variables such as time of day confounding the study	Test the participants together in a group at the same time instead	Prevents the possibility of situational variables such as time of day confounding the study, and increases the level of control so may improve the validity of the results
Test the participants together in a group	Raises the possibility of participants working out that different conditions are being tested (demand characteristics) and increases the chances of participants copying what others do	Test each participant one at once instead	Reduces the likelihood of results being contaminated by participants copying one another's results. Also reduces the chance of demand characteristics threatening the results of the study as participants are less likely to work out the aim of the study.
An independent groups design is suggested	Since an independent groups design may be affected by individual differences between participants, there is a threat to the validity of the results	Use a repeated measures design instead or use a matched subjects design (if repeated measures is not possible)	Reduces the possibility of individual differences contaminating the results, increasing the validity of the results as the study is less likely to be affected by extraneous subject variables

Matching the participants on skills such as memory, intelligence and experience will reduce the effect of individual differences on the study |
| A repeated measures design is suggested | Since a repeated measures design may mean that participants work out the aim of the study by responding to demand characteristics, there is a challenge to the validity of the study | Use an independent groups design instead | Reduces the possibility of demand characteristics affecting the study, so the results may be more valid (trustworthy) |

Quantitative and qualitative data

When we think of measurement, we tend to assume that this means that numbers will be used to tell us how much or how many of something there was. This is precisely what you get with quantitative data. An advantage of using numbers to measure variables is that it allows for easy comparisons to be made between subjects or participants, for example, on a memory test, subject one scored 10 out of 100 and subject two scored 90. We can also summarise quantitative data easily, using averages or percentages. For example, Milgram found that 65 per cent of his Ss went up to 450 volts.

It is easier to establish the reliability of results when quantitative data is collected, as you can repeat the test to see if the findings are replicable or not.

Quantitative data alone can be quite narrow, however, and can also lack ecological validity. For example, if you ask someone, 'How are things with you?', they are more likely to say, 'Pretty good, thanks', than 'On a scale of 0 to 100, where 0 is terrible and 100 is unqualified bliss, I'd say today I was scoring 65.'

In order to increase the level of detail and the validity of findings, qualitative data can be gathered. This usually consists of descriptions in words of what was observed. For example, Milgram tells us subjects were seen 'to sweat, tremble, stutter, bite their lips … [and] these were characteristic rather than exceptional responses to the experiment' (Milgram, 1969, p.375). This tells us a lot more about the experience of subjects in the experiment than just the fact that 65 per cent of subjects went to the end on the shock generator.

Qualitative data can also be reports of interviews, responses to open questions in questionnaires and reports of what subjects or participants said and did during a study. Using this type of information gives a richness and detail to the findings and is more valid. However, it is harder to make comparisons between subjects or participants' responses or to summarise qualitative data.

In experiments, however, researchers tend to measure their variables quantitatively to allow analysis of the findings to be carried out.

Descriptive statistics for experiments

Once we have gathered our data in an experiment we use descriptive statistics to present, summarise and describe our findings.

For the experimental method you need to know about the following descriptive statistics:

- Measures of central tendency – the averages: mode, median and mean

- Measures of dispersion – e.g. the range

- Pictorial representations of data – e.g. bar charts and graphs

Imagine we have carried out a study to see the effects of age on memory. Subjects or participants have learned 30 items in two minutes and then freely recalled the items to give their memory score out of 30. The researcher predicted that a younger age group would do better on the test. The groups are split into 30 to 45 year olds and 55 to 70 year olds with 20 participants in each condition.

A table of the raw data might look like this.

Table 8.6

The number of items recalled out of 30 for the 30–45 year olds and the 55–70 year olds

Age group	Scores out of 30 on the memory test
30–45 year olds	15, 15, 15, 15, 16, 17, 17, 17, 18, 18, 18, 20, 20, 21, 21, 23, 27, 28, 28, 30
55–70 year olds	9, 10, 10, 11, 11, 13, 13, 15, 15, 16, 16, 16, 21, 22, 22, 23, 23, 24, 24, 24

From the raw data we can see some things, for example, the lowest score (9) was in the older age group and the highest score (30) was in the youngest age group, but if we want to compare the groups more easily we may want to use some statistic to summarise the data. This is where we can use the averages to summarise the data so that we can make comparisons between the groups' scores to see if they support the researcher's predictions.

Measures of central tendency: Averages, the mean, the median and the mode

The mean average is calculated by adding up all the scores in the set and dividing by the number of scores. This is the arithmetic average. For example, to calculate the mean for the 30 to 45 year old condition in the memory test you need to add all their scores and divide by 20. If you do this, the answer you will get is 19.95. If you then calculate the mean for the older age group you will get 16.9.

By comparing the mean scores we can see that the results do give evidence for the prediction that the younger group would score higher than the older group, as indicated by the higher mean score of the 30 to 45 year old condition.

The mean, therefore, gives an arithmetically accurate average score for each group which we can compare to see if the alternative hypothesis was supported or not.

If we were measuring things like time, or weight or height or anything where decimal accuracy has real meaning, then the mean average is the best and most accurate measure of central tendency to work with.

However, there is a problem with the mean here, as it can give us what is called 'spurious accuracy'. For example, is it possible to remember 19.95 items. What would the recall of .95 of an item be like? Also, neither of the scores we calculated (19.95 and 16.9) represent even one true score in the set of scores.

Where we are measuring in whole numbers a potentially more useful measure of central tendency is the median. The median gives us the central point of a set of scores.

The median is worked out by putting all the scores in size order (this is done for you in the table) and finding the central point. If there are an even number of scores in the set you take a mean average of the middle two scores to find the median.

To find the median, then for the 30 to 45 year olds' scores, we have to find the central two scores since there is an even number of scores, so we find the tenth and eleventh numbers. These are both 18, so the mean average of these (18+18 divided by 2) is 18, so the median for this set is 18. Now we have a whole number to represent a set made of whole numbers, and it even represents at least three of the actual scores, so in this instance the median is a better average than the mean.

The median of the 55 to 70 year olds scores is 16, again a whole number to represent a set of scores that are whole numbers, and again representing three actual scores from the set. In this case, the median is a better (more representative) measure of central tendency than the mean.

We could also calculate the mode for the sets of scores. This tells us the most typical score since the mode is simply the number that occurs most frequently in the set. For the 30 to 45 year olds the mode is 15, and for the 55 to 70 year olds there are 2 modes, 16 and 24. The mode will always represent at least two scores in the actual set of scores, but loses its meaningfulness if there are more than two modes. Of course, if each score occurs only once in a set then there is no mode, so this measure of central tendency is not useful where all items are different in the set.

Exam focus

Measures of central tendency
Here is a question taken from the January 2010 Psychological Investigations examination.

Activity
Researchers conducted an experiment to investigate the ability of ten males and ten females to recognise emotions displayed on the face. A set of 12 photographs of the same person displaying the six primary emotions (happiness, sadness, anger, surprise fear and disgust) was used. Participants had ten seconds to look at each photograph and had to identify the emotion displayed before moving on to the next. One mark was awarded for each correct response, giving a total out of 12.

(a) Explain what is meant by the descriptive statistic the mean. [2]
(b) Explain how the mean would have been calculated for the males and females in this study. [4]
(c) When would the descriptive statistic called the 'median' be more appropriate and why? [4]

Measures of dispersion – The range

As well as being able to summarise a set of scores by looking at central, average or typical scores, it is also useful to know how widely dispersed or spread out the scores are. To calculate the range of a set of scores you simply subtract the lowest score in the set from the highest score. For our example, the range for the 30 to 45 year olds is calculated by subtracting 15 from 30, so the range for that set of scores is 15.

Activity

Work out the range for the 55 to 70 year olds' scores in Table 8.6 (page 257).

Graphical representations of data – Bar charts

Bar charts are a useful and meaningful way of presenting data from an experiment providing that you keep it simple!

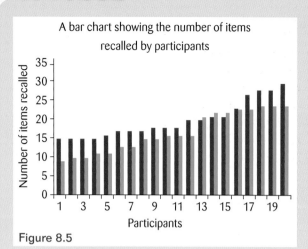

A bar chart showing the number of items recalled by participants

Figure 8.5

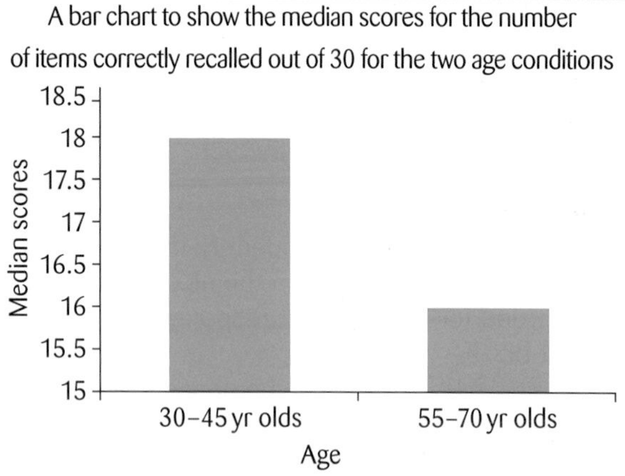

A bar chart to show the median scores for the number of items correctly recalled out of 30 for the two age conditions

Figure 8.6

For example, a useless and meaningless bar chart might look like figure 8.5.

This doesn't tell us anything at a glance, and since we use the graph to clarify our results for the person reading about them, we need a simpler graph to show what we have found.

In order to achieve this simple bar chart, you should draw a bar chart using a measure of central tendency for each condition, such as the mean or median, and use two bars to show any observed difference between the two conditions. It is easy to draw conclusions from a simple two-bar bar graph. We can now see if the data supports the alternative hypothesis or not.

Observations

In psychological research, observational methods can be used on their own as a method in themselves (Milgram carried out a controlled observation in his obedience study) or as a way to gather data within an experimental design, as used by Griffiths in his field experiment on gamblers' thinking errors.

For the Psychological Investigations examination there are a number of issues related to observations that you need to know about:

- Observations can be structured or unstructured.

- Observations can be carried out covertly, that is, undercover and without the knowledge of those being observed, or overtly, where subjects or participants are either aware of or have been informed of the fact that they are being observed.

- Observation can be carried out as participant or non-participant observation. This means that the researcher is either a part of the setting or event he or she is observing (participant), or is outside of the setting (non-participant).

- The way we choose to sample behaviour in a structured observation can be by time sampling and event sampling. An observation schedule is a form of event sampling.

- Sometimes we do not observe people directly at all but instead use audio or video recordings or written material, a technique known as content analysis.

- To ensure that an observation is carried out objectively and without bias in the interpretation and application of the observation criteria, we test for inter-observer reliability.

Unstructured and structured observations

In an unstructured observation the researcher or observer continuously records and reports on behaviour noting everything that happens, and with this 'observe and report everything' method a number of problems can arise. For example, there might be too much going on and so many things to try to record that the observation is not very successful. The data that is gathered may be too dense and detailed to reveal anything to the observer. It would be difficult to summarise and present the data and it would be difficult to make comparisons between different participants or situations being observed.

So in order to focus the observation and increase the usefulness and objectivity of the study, researchers plan and carry out structured observations. This means they impose a structure on their observation to decide on the aim of their observation (what behaviours in particular they are interested in recording), and the observational systems they will use for recording the data. These may include the designing of a coding system or a category checklist against which the observations will be made. The structured approach allows comparisons to be made across trials and for trends in the data to be more easily seen.

For example, in the Piliavin *et al.* Subway Samaritan study, for each trial observer 1 noted race, sex and location of every passenger, seated or standing, in the critical area. He also noted the total number of passengers in the whole compartment and the number who helped including their race, sex and original location.

Structured observations also employ time and event sampling techniques (see below).

Covert and overt observations

Covert observation is where the subject or participant does not know that he or she is being observed. This is useful because it means that 'natural' behaviour can be observed, especially if the study is carried out in the field. However, observing subjects or participants without their consent and therefore possibly invading their privacy raises ethical issues.

In a controlled laboratory-based study observation is often carried out in the psychology laboratory through the use of a one-way mirror.

Overt observation is where the subject or participant knows that he or she is being observed and has either given their consent or is aware of being observed because of the observer's presence. This method makes it possible to carry out ethical research. The problem with this is that the subject or participant may not display 'natural' behaviour if they are aware of being observed, and may respond to demand characteristics or behave differently because of social desirability bias.

The advantage of covert observation is that you are sampling 'real' behaviour, uncontaminated by the subject reactivity. Some researchers believe that the only valid way to sample typical human behaviour is by covert observation in a field setting, the method used by Piliavin *et al.* in their study.

Activity

(a) Explain the difference between covert and overt observation methods.
(b) Draw up a revision table to show the strengths and weaknesses of covert and overt observation methods.
(c) Other than Piliavin *et al.*'s Subway Samaritan study, identify one other study from the core studies that uses covert observation techniques and one other study that uses overt observation techniques. What are the strengths and weaknesses of these observation techniques in these studies?

Participant and non-participant observation

Participant observation is a method of gathering data through observation techniques where the observers are part of, or are pretending to be part of, the setting or situation they are observing. In the core studies, for example, in the Piliavin *et al.* Subway Samaritan study the two female observers were pretending to be normal passengers on the subway train, and in the Rosenhan Sane in insane places study the pseudopatients were pretending to be normal patients while they were making their observations in the hospitals.

In these studies, the participant observation was also covert observation. However, this does not always have to be the case, as an observer can get consent from the group they are observing as a member, so that the ethical guidelines do not have to be broken.

One advantage of being a participant observer, as in the Piliavin *et al.* study, is that you have a good vantage point for your observations. However, your mere presence may change the course of the events you are observing. It could be that the inactivity of some potential helpers in the adjacent area in the trials was because of the inactivity of the two observers; we can't know for sure.

Another advantage of participant observation is that as an 'insider' you can get an insight into the experience yourself, and also gather detailed and valid data about the situation if you are observing over an extended period of time, as in the Rosenhan study. However, it is also possible that if you are observing as a participant observer for a long period of time you may become too involved in the setting to be objective about your observations. Could Rosenhan and his pseudopatients remain truly objective if they were seeing the hospitals only from the point of view of a patient?

The alternative to participant observation is called non-participant observation where the observer is not a member of the group being studied or playing a part of just another person in the situation. The advantage of non-participant observation is that you may remain more objective about what is being observed, but you may not have the same level of insight into the behaviour as you would if you were a participant observer.

Content analysis

An observer can code written material (such as articles in a newspaper) or filmed material (such as television adverts or soap operas), and this kind of observation is called a content analysis. This method eliminates the ethical concerns that arise when studying human participants, as the information being observed is already in the public domain.

Content analysis can also be used to code and observe qualitative data to turn it into quantitative date. Griffiths established 30 categories of utterance to use in order to analyse the content of the thinking aloud recordings.

Time sampling and event sampling, including observation schedules

Time sampling is a way of sampling behaviour during an observation whereby the observers observe according to time. There are two ways of doing this:

- Time point sampling where the observer records what the participant is doing at fixed intervals, for example, every five seconds over twenty minutes, as in the Bandura *et al.* study.

- Time event sampling, where a fixed period of time is set for observation, such as the first ten minutes of every hour to observe the number of people using a café over a working day, for example.

Using time sampling means that the observer has a manageable way of sampling the behaviour they are interested in, but it is possible that in the time periods they are not observing they may miss some behaviours and therefore end up with data that is not valid.

Event sampling is a way of sampling behaviour during an observation whereby an event is recorded each time it happens. For example, an observer may want to find out if more male or female students take up the offer of free fruit at break times at their school. They could observe children at break time and tally how many males and females come and collect fruit. This gives them two 'events' to observe for: 'male student collecting fruit' and 'female student collecting fruit'.

In event sampling, observers use observation schedules, or observation categories.

Key concept

Observation schedules and categories
In structured observations the researcher will devise an observation schedule, so that what is going to be observed and how it is going to be observed is all decided before the observation takes place. This form of event sampling is to establish categories of behaviour to observe:
- 'Punching Bobo', 'imitative verbal aggression' (Bandura study)
- 'Walks on, head averted', 'stops and talks' (Rosenhan study)
- 'Total winnings', 'plays per minute' (Griffiths study)

Advantages of using categories in observations are that they provide quantitative data which can be fairly easily compared between subjects or groups, easily presented and summarised and can also be analysed statistically.

However, observation using categories has a main weakness. It may give a very restricted view of what is actually happening. This is especially true if time-point sampling is also used. The researcher may miss important behaviour and the data is not as in-depth as simply observing and recording all behaviour as it is occurring.

Inter-observer reliability

In order to avoid observer bias, that is, an observer applying ratings or counting categories in a subjective rather than objective fashion, inter-observer reliability needs to be established. This means that two observers rate or observe the same behaviour and the two sets of ratings are correlated. If a significant positive correlation is seen (as a rule of thumb, we would look for a correlation of +0.8 or higher), inter-observer reliability has been established and the objectivity of the results confirmed. This supports the validity of the findings of the observation.

In the Bandura study inter-observer reliability was established to prevent any conscious or unconscious bias occurring on the part of the teacher or experimenter in their assessment of the children's general aggression prior to the children being allocated to the test conditions. A positive correlation of +0.89 was found between the teacher and Miss Ross's ratings of the children's aggressiveness.

Exam focus

Observations

This is a question taken from the January 2009 Psychological Investigations examination. Answer all the questions as on the PI paper they are all compulsory questions. In the examination you would get approximately 20 minutes to plan and write the answer to this question.

Activity

Researchers want to conduct an observation investigating the use of mobile phones by students in their free time in college.

1. Describe and evaluate an appropriate procedure that could be used in this study. [10]
   In order to answer this question, first read the advice on procedures in the section on experiments. In describing the procedure of an observation, be sure to include and explain the use of some observational techniques, e.g. structured observation, participant/ non-participant observation, covert/overt observation, time and event sampling. Include an observation schedule of categories or ratings and explain if this would be a laboratory-based observation or a naturalistic observation. Explain how you would ensure the observation was objective. Make sure that you write about the strengths and weaknesses of three of your suggestions for this observation, relating them directly to this study.
2. Explain the difference between time sampling and event sampling in observational research. [4]
3. Outline one strength and one weakness of conducting observational research in this study. [6]

Self-reports

As with observational methods, self-report methods can be used on their own as a method in themselves. For example, a survey could be carried out to find out why students love psychology so much, or self-report techniques can be used as a data gathering tool to measure variables within an experiment or for a correlation.

Self-report data ranges from subjects or participants' responses to being asked simple questions such as 'Which has more?', as in the Samuel and Bryant study on conservation, to the detailed notes of interviews presented in case studies by Freud (Little Hans) and Thigpen and Cleckley (Three faces of Eve).

The advantages of using self-report data are that we are able to measure cognitive variables such as memory, knowledge and attitudes, which cannot be either observed directly or tested for in any biological test. Without self-report, the study by Loftus and Palmer on memory and language would not be possible, for example.

However, the validity of self-report data can be questioned where subjects or participants are able to deliberately falsify their answers. This can be because they are responding to demand characteristics present in the study or because of evaluation apprehension: they lie to give a socially desirable answer to avoid being judged negatively.

Self-report data-gathering techniques

To gather self-report data a number of techniques are used which each have their own specific strengths and weaknesses:

- questionnaires
- open and closed (free response and fixed/forced response) questions
- rating scales
- interviews
- psychometric tests.

Questionnaires

Questionnaires are sets of questions that are usually completed as pen and paper tests, but can also be done over the internet or telephone.

An advantage of questionnaires is that they enable a great deal of data to be gathered from a large sample very quickly, making this a cost- and time-effective method of data collection. However, the main problem is that the data is open to falsification by respondents, who lie to avoid embarrassment (evaluation apprehension) to give socially desirable answers, or in response to demand characteristics present in the type of questions being asked or the topic they believe is under investigation.

Asking the right question in the right way is very difficult, and researchers have to be careful to frame their questions carefully using language their respondents will understand.

Questionnaires that use closed questions are easier to analyse and compare between subjects or participants since they give us quantitative data. However, closed questions are also likely to frustrate respondents where forced choice responses are the only option (yes/no/don't know rating scales).

Open questions can yield more valid and detailed information (qualitative data), but the disadvantage is that it can be harder to make comparisons between subjects or participants.

Figure 8.7

Key concept

Open and closed questions

Open (-ended) questions, or free response questions, allow the participant freedom to respond and give them the opportunity to explain their answers.

For example: Why do you think some people don't obey the law and continue to use their mobile phone without using a hands-free kit while they are driving?

Open (-ended) questions provide qualitative data, and the advantage of this is that we get rich, detailed information. Here we have increased realism (validity), as respondents are not forced to respond in a particular way and this allows them to qualify their responses rather than just give 'yes/no/don't know' answers. Freedom to respond removes the negative feelings respondents have when forced to choose from a limited range of responses.

However, it is harder to analyse and compare responses to open questions, as the data needs to be coded or quantified in some way to do this and this may not be easy. It is therefore difficult to establish the reliability of qualitative responses.

Closed questions, or fixed response or forced response questions, on the other hand, give the respondent a limited range of responses to choose from.

For example: Do you think that the early experiences people have as children have an effect on them in later life? Yes/No/Don't know

Or: On a scale where 0 means 'Not at all necessary' and 10 means 'Absolutely essential' how important do you think it is to include fruit in your diet every day?

1 2 3 4 5 6 7 8 9 10

Closed questions provide quantitative data, and an advantage of this is that the results can then be easily summarised, presented and compared between participants or conditions. It is also easier to test the reliability of data where quantitative measures have been used.

This type of question can lack ecological validity, however, due to the forced choices of answers available.

The researcher is only gathering limited information, and important information may be missed where respondents are unable to qualify or explain their answers. Respondents may feel frustrated or constrained by the limited number of responses available and this may affect their attitude towards the research.

Exam focus

Open and closed questions

Activity

1. (a) Explain the difference between open and closed questions.
   (b) Draw up a revision table of the strengths and weaknesses of open and closed questions in psychological research.

(This question is taken from the May 2009 Psychological Investigations examination.)

A researcher is interested in finding out why students at a large sixth form college have decided to study psychology. He is going to use a self-report questionnaire.

(a) Suggest one open and one closed question that could be used to investigate subject choice. [4]
(b) Discuss the validity of the question you have suggested to investigate subject choice. [4]

(This question is taken from the January 2010 Psychological Investigations examination.)

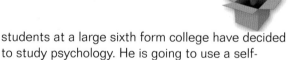

Activity

Researchers conducted an investigation about dreaming using a self-report. Some examples of what participants were asked are presented below:
- On average, how many dreams do you remember having each week?
- Briefly describe the best dream you have ever had.
- Do you appear in your own dreams? Never/Sometimes/Always

(a) Identify one open question and one closed question from this investigation. [2]
(b) Outline one strength and one weakness of the closed question you have identified. [6]
(c) What is qualitative data? [2]
(d) Identify how qualitative data would be obtained from one of the questions used in this investigation. [3]

Rating scales

Variables can be measured on rating scales, providing a quantitative measure. Often this is used in self-report questionnaires and structured interviews.

For example: On a scale of 1 to 10, where 0 is very miserable and 10 is ecstatically happy, circle the number that indicates how happy you are at the moment.

1 2 3 4 5 6 7 8 9 10

Likert scales can also be used. A Likert scale is where people are given a range of answers from which they select the one that represents the extent to which they like/dislike something or agree/disagree with something:

For example: Psychology is a fascinating subject and I am very glad I chose to study it at AS level.

I strongly agree/I agree /Not sure/Don't know/Disagree/Disagree strongly

A Likert scale can increase the ecological validity of a rating scale, since people have a range of verbal options to choose from, and this is not as artificial as, say, choosing from a simple numerical scale of 1 to 10.

By assigning numerical values to the responses – 1 for disagree strongly, 2 for disagree, 3 for don't know, 4 for agree, 5 for agree strongly, it is possible to generate quantitative data from Likert scales.

Because the data from rating scales is quantitative, all the strengths and weaknesses of quantitative data apply. As with all rating scales, Likert scales are basically closed or fixed response questions, and so the strengths and weaknesses of these also apply here.

Exam focus

Rating scales
This question is taken from the June 2010 Psychological Investigations examination.
A researcher has become interested in studying stress associated with driving and wishes to conduct an investigation to assess stress levels of motorists in England using the self-report method.
(a) Suggest an appropriate question using a rating scale, which could be used in his study. [2]
(b) Evaluate the validity of using this question in this study. [4]

Interviews

As the name of this self-report method suggests, this is where participants are interviewed, usually face-to-face, and their responses recorded. They may be written down 'on-the-spot', or recorded on audiotape or videotape and later transcribed.

There are two types of interview, the structured interview and the clinical interview:

Key concept

Structured interviews and clinical interviews

A structured interview is where the same set of questions is asked to each subject or participant in the same order.

An advantage of this is that it is easier to gather quantitative data than in a clinical interview, making it possible to analyse the data and draw out trends from subjects or participants' responses.

A disadvantage, however, is that the structured nature of this type of interview is artificial, and the respondent may not feel free to qualify their answers. This may mean the data that is gathered is limited and superficial. Being asked a list of questions in this way lacks ecological validity.

A clinical interview is where the researcher's questions follow on from what the interviewee has said. There are no set questions, but the researcher may have a list of topics or 'prompts' that he or she will ask the participant about.

Figure 8.8

An advantage of this type of interview is that a lot of detailed information, often qualitative data, can be gathered using this method.

Another advantage is that this type of interview is more like a regular conversation and is therefore higher in ecological validity than the structured interview. A disadvantage, however, is that because a broad range of topics can be discussed in detail it can be difficult to summarise the data, to analyse the data for trends or to make comparisons between participants.

Activity

1. Explain the difference between a structured interview and a clinical interview in psychological research.
2. Draw up a table to show the strengths and weaknesses of structured and clinical interviews in psychological research.

Psychometric tests

Psychometric tests are instruments (e.g. pen-and-paper tests, one-to-one tests) that have been developed to measure mental characteristics, such as intelligence tests (IQ tests), brain damage/brain function (STM capabilities), creativity, personality, job attitudes, aptitude and skills. They often provide simple, summative quantitative measurements such as IQ scores or personality scores. These summative scores are attractive to psychologists, as this makes comparison between subjects or participants and analysis of data possible.

However, there are some major problems associated with psychometric tests. They are often completed as self-reports, so data may be falsified. This affects their internal validity. Validity is a problem in general for these tests. Are they really testing what they say they are testing? It is very difficult to design a test that does not contain cultural biases and can be used for people in general.

Reliability is also important. If subjects or participants do not score significantly similar results on an equivalent test, then the tests are not reliable (and if they are not reliable, they are not valid).

Psychometric tests need to be administered and assessed by trained individuals. In the wrong hands they can be misinterpreted, for example, low IQ scores used to 'label' someone as stupid, and treating them accordingly!

An example of psychometric tests used in the core studies can be seen in Reicher and Haslam's BBC prison experiment where a battery (set) of pen and paper tests measuring clinical, social and organisational variables were administered to the participants over the period of the study.

Correlations

The fourth of the topics you need to study for the psychological investigations examination is correlations.

For the Psychological Investigations examination you need to be able to:

- explain what we mean by a correlational study in psychology

- explain what is meant by a positive correlation and negative correlation

- suggest ways of measuring variables for a correlational study

- sketch scattergrams, to show the pattern for strong and weak positive and negative correlations, and to illustrate data in source material

- interpret scattergrams (draw conclusions from them)

- frame hypotheses (null and alternate, one and two-tailed) for correlations in source material

- explain the strengths and weaknesses of using correlations in psychology, both in general and in relation to source material.

Correlational studies

Correlation is a statistical technique that can tell us about the way two variables are related to each other. They may be positively or negatively correlated or not correlated at all.

Data gathering and descriptive statistics for corrections

Because correlation is a mathematical technique, correlation requires that two variables be measured quantitatively in order for any correlation between them to be established. Data for correlations is gathered by self-report, observation or by physiological measures. For an example of the latter, look at the study by Maguire *et al.* on taxi drivers' brains.

There are some descriptive statistics that are only used for correlations, including the use of scattergrams (or scattergraphs) to pictorially represent the relationship, and correlation coefficients, which describe the relationship between two variables numerically.

Graphical or pictorial representations of correlations

The graph that we draw to represent a correlation is called a scattergram. By the pattern that the scores make on the graph we can work out the following:

- the direction of the correlation – whether it is positive or negative

- the strength of the correlation – whether it is strong or weak.

The direction of the correlation is indicated by the pattern of the scores plotted on a scattergram.

If scores go 'uphill' from left to right on the scattergram this indicates a positive correlation.

Scores going 'downhill' from left to right indicate a negative correlation.

The closer the scores are to falling in a straight line, the stronger the correlation is, and the more spread out the scores are the weaker the correlation is.

A scattergram tells the researcher whether there is a correlation in the direction they predicted and how strong this correlation is. They can therefore conclude from their scattergram whether a correlation has been

A scattergram illustrating a strong positive correlation

Variable 1 / Variable 2

Figure 8.9

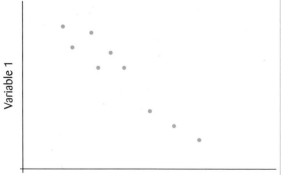

A scattergram illustrating a strong negative correlation

Variable 1 / Variable 2

Figure 8.10

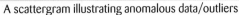

found in the predicted direction, whether this is strong or weak, and whether the data gathered supports their alternate hypothesis.

In addition, the scattergram will also show any anomalous scores, or outliers, which do not follow the general pattern, showing if the relationship is not true in all cases and if there are exceptions to the general trend observed in the data.

In this scattergram you can see a trend in general towards a strong positive correlation between the two variables. The anomalous score of 4,10 however shows that this is not true for all cases and there are exceptions to the general trend.

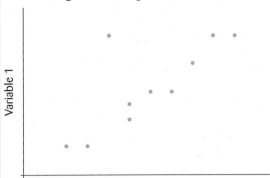

A scattergram illustrating anomalous data/outliers

Figure 8.11

Activity

1. A researcher carried out a study to see if there was a correlation between the amount of hours paid work students did a week and the amount of hours of homework they did for psychology a week.

   (a) Sketch a scattergram that shows a strong negative correlation between the amount of paid work they do and the amount of homework they did. [3]

   (Make sure you label the axes of your scattergram and give it an appropriate title – you will not get full marks if you do not!)

2. A researcher carried out a study to see if the more times a week teenagers eat junk food the less times a week they would exercise. The results were as follows.

Table 8.7

Ppt	Junk food scores	Exercise scores
1	8	3
2	10	2
3	6	3
4	4	7
5	1	6
6	8	4
7	6	6
8	4	4
9	1	8
10	3	6

(a) Sketch a scattergram to illustrate the correlation of this data. [3]

(b) Give one conclusion that could be drawn from this scattergram. [1]

3. A researcher conducted a study to see if there was a positive correlation between the average number of hours of television watched daily and teacher ratings of aggressive play in children. The scattergram below displays the results.

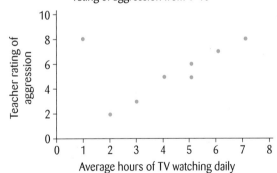

A scattergram showing the relationship between the average daily TV hours watched and the teacher's rating of aggression from 1–10

Figure 8.12

(a) Outline TWO conclusions that can be drawn from this scattergram. [2]

The correlation coefficient

A correlation coefficient is a number between -1 and +1 that describes the direction and extent of a correlation. The closer the number is to 1 or -1, the higher the correlation. The sign, +/-, tells us whether it is a negative or positive correlation. A score of, or close to, zero indicates no correlation between the variables.

Here are some examples of correlation coefficients.

Table 8.8

Positive correlations		Negative correlations	
Correlation coefficient	Meaning	Correlation coefficient	Meaning
+0.931	Indicates a very strong positive correlation	−0.865	Indicates a very strong negative correlation
+0.8	Indicates a strong positive correlation	−0.784	Indicates a strong negative correlation
+0.367	Indicates a very weak positive correlation	−0.132	Indicates a weak negative correlation

Framing hypotheses for correlations

The research hypothesis in a correlation is called an alternate hypothesis.

One-tailed (directional) alternate hypotheses for correlations say what kind of correlation is predicted, either positive or negative.

For example, 'There will be a positive correlation between the amount of independent study students complete and their A-level grades.' (The more they study, the better their grades will be and the less they study the lower their grades will be.)

Or 'There will be a negative correlation between the amount of snow on the ground and the amount of ice cream eaten.' (The more snow there is, the less ice cream will be eaten.)

Two-tailed (non-directional) alternate hypotheses for correlations just say that correlation is predicted, no direction is predicted.

For example, 'There will be a correlation between the number of hours paid work a week students do in term time and their A-level examination scores.'

The null hypothesis is the no relationship hypothesis, so for correlations the null hypothesis will always be that there is no correlation between the variables:

For example, 'There will be no correlation between the amount of independent study students complete and their A level grades.'

Or 'There will be no correlation between the amount of snow on the ground and the amount of ice cream eaten.'

Or 'There will be no correlation between the number of hours paid work a week students do in term time and their A-level examination scores.'

The uses of correlations

We will look at how correlation are used in psychology, including the strengths and weaknesses of correlational evidence.

Correlation is a useful tool in psychology as it allows us to measure the relationship between variables which it would be difficult or unethical to manipulate experimentally. For example, we might be interested in investigating the impact of student debt in university students on their general health. We could not ethically put a group of students into debt for comparison with a group of students whom we had financed through their studies. However, we could correlate the level of debt a student has in their third year of university with a measure of their general health. This correlational method would give us an ethical way to measure the relationship between student debt and health.

A common use of correlational analysis in psychological research is as a test for either reliability or validity. This can be carried out where quantitative data has been gathered and where the study can be easily replicated, as most laboratory studies can be. Correlation is therefore a useful tool for establishing inter-observer reliability (see Bandura *et al.*'s study on imitating aggression), concurrent validity (see Baron-Cohen *et al.*'s study on autism and how the concurrent validity of the eyes task was established) and the general test-retest reliability of research findings. Correlation can therefore be used to support the scientific credibility of research by establishing reliability and validity.

The major problem with correlational evidence is that correlation does not mean causation. In other words, just because two variables are correlated this does not mean that one of them has caused the other one to change. For example, if a researcher found a positive correlation between the number of ice cream sales and the number of violent crimes, could they conclude that ice cream causes violent behaviour? No, because although variables are correlated this does not mean that one variable causes the other to increase or decrease. There may be other factors which affect both variables (in this case, hot weather!).

Sampling techniques

For the OCR AS-level examinations, sampling techniques can be the focus of questions in both the Psychological Investigations examination and the Core Studies examination.

For the Psychological Investigations examination, you need to be able to:

- describe opportunity sampling, random sampling and self-selected (volunteer) sampling techniques

- identify strengths and weaknesses of opportunity, random and self-selected (volunteer) sampling techniques

- identify strengths and weaknesses of sampling techniques described in source material.

For the Core Studies examination you need to be able to:

- identify the type of sample/sampling technique for each of the 15 core studies

- describe the sample for each study in detail (Who? Where from? How many? Age? Males/females? Students? Sample type?)

- evaluate the sample used in the study – give strengths and weaknesses related to the sample type, sample size and identify any sample biases (ethnocentric biases) that threaten the generalisability of the findings to a broader population

- suggest an alternate sample for the study and speculate about the effect of such a sample on the results and generalisability of the findings.

We use a sample in psychological research when we cannot, for practical reasons (e.g. cost- and time-effectiveness) study the entire target population we are interested in.

Key concept

Target population

This is the section or group of people who we are interested in studying. For example, Baron-Cohen *et al.* had a target population of autistic and normal adults and Samuel and Bryant had a target population of children five to eight years old.

We choose our sample based on a balance between:

- getting as representative a sample as we can so that we can make generalisations from the findings to establish general rules about the target population being studied; and

- being cost- and time-effective when conducting the study.

Usually a sample size between 30 and 50 is considered enough for a psychological study, although if you are distributing a questionnaire you can have a sample size of hundreds if your target population is very big, and if you are doing an in-depth case study you may have a sample of a single subject or participant.

There are three types of sample you must know about: random samples, self-selecting (volunteer) samples and opportunity samples. You need to know definitions of each sample type and how we select each of these samples from a target population and be able to evaluate the strengths and weaknesses of these three sampling methods, often in comparison with each other and in the context of a particular psychological investigation or study.

Figure 8.13 Samples need to be as representative as possible of the target population.

Key concept

Samples

In a random sample, every member of the target population must have an equal chance of being selected to be in the sample. To obtain such a sample there has to be a clear and finite target population of whom a full list of members can be drawn up, and then a random sample can be drawn from this list. This can be done with a small target population by putting the names in a hat and drawing out the number of subjects required. For a large target population a researcher can use an RNG (random number generator) computer program to select the sample.

A volunteer sample is also known as a self-selected sample. Typical ways of getting such a sample include putting an advert in a newspaper or a notice on a notice board, and sending out postal questionnaires. Those who respond to the ad or notice and those who fill in and return the questionnaires are volunteering to take part in the study.

An opportunity sample is also known as a convenience sample. The researcher selects the most convenient people to study (e.g. Loftus and Palmer studied university students in their research on eyewitness testimony) or those who just happen to be there at the time are studied.

Evaluating the strengths and weaknesses of samples

A sample should be representative of the target population from which it is drawn. If a sample is representative, this allows us to generalise the findings: to establish general rules about the behaviour of the target population based on the behaviour of the sample.

A sample that is not representative of its target population or of people in general is called a biased sample. There are a number of biasing factors that can limit the generalisability of findings from a sample.

First, sample size has to be considered. Can 25 males and 25 females drawn from a pool of volunteers for Cambridge University truly represent 'normal males and females' in general? Is Little Hans a typical three to five-year-old boy? Samples that are not large enough to represent their target population mean we must be cautious when making generalisations from them. Similarly, we must be cautious when making generalisations where only one type of person is selected to represent a diverse population, for example, one region, one culture, one occupation, age group or gender is selected to be in the sample. These biases are known as ethnocentric biases:

* Gender bias – a sample of all males or all females is clearly not representing the omitted gender (Milgram's obedience study, Reicher and Haslam's BBC prison experiment, and Freud's case study of Little Hans all had male samples).

* Age bias – if certain age groups are omitted the sample will not be representative of people in general (any study where students are used to represent non-students or people in general, as students are generally young. Also, in Milgram's study under 20s and over 50s were not represented).

* Culture bias – only one country or area is represented (Piliavin *et al.*'s Subway Samaritan study was conducted in one place, the subway, between two stations on one line only, in New York, USA).

Certain types of sample are also fundamentally biased:

* Volunteer samples (self-selected samples) – if people volunteer to take part (Milgram, Reicher and Haslam, Griffiths) the sample will have a volunteer bias. This means that the sample is biased since only a minority of people

volunteer, therefore volunteers are atypical, so these samples are not representing people in general.

- Opportunity samples (or convenience samples) – an opportunity sample is one where the researcher uses the most convenient subjects available at the time (Samuel and Bryant used children from schools in Crediton, Devon). This means that those unavailable at the time or not in that location are not represented.

The implications of a biased sample for validity and usefulness

It is difficult, if not impossible, to select a sample that contains no biases and is representative of people in general.

If a sample is not representative, we must be cautious before we generalise the findings beyond the study to make general rules about a broader population.

If generalisability of the findings is low, we say that the study has a low population validity: the sample fails to represent its intended population.

If a study is low in population validity, this in turn limits the usefulness of the study's findings as we will be less certain that any findings from the sample truly represent behaviours demonstrated by people in the population.

The table below shows the strengths and weaknesses of random, volunteer (self-selected) samples and opportunity samples.

Table 8.9

✔ Strengths	✖ Weaknesses
Random samples	
It is assumed that by selecting participants by chance an unbiased sample will be chosen, provided that a big enough sample is selected in relation to the size of the target population. This assumption means this is considered to be the most representative of the sample types.	Can be time-consuming and therefore is more expensive to get than an opportunity sample, or a volunteer sample. Chance selection may still present biases – it is possible that minority groups in the target population, for example, may not be represented in the sample, giving it biases that limit generalisability. If the selected subjects refuse to take part, then those who do represent willing participants which may give this sample a volunteer bias and fail to fully represent those who did not, or do not, want to take part.
Volunteer samples	
A volunteer sample is cheaper and more convenient to select than a random sample generally, as you wait for responses then just contact people to arrange for them to be in your study.	Since the people who volunteer are only a minority of the target population you will always have volunteer bias in the study and it will fail to represent those people who did not or would not volunteer for such a study.
Opportunity samples	
Is cheaper and more convenient to select than a random sample or a volunteer sample as you just go where you expect the people you want to study will be and ask the first ones you meet to take part.	Since only those who were present or available at the time of the study could be selected, there are always ethnocentric biases in an opportunity sample that limit generalisability to the target population.

Activity

A researcher wants to carry out a study to see if drinking coffee helps you to concentrate better in lessons. The researcher chooses to study sixth formers in a large school in the UK where the sixth form has 500 students. A sample of 50 students in total needs to be selected to take part.

1. Explain how the researcher could obtain a random sample for the study. Give one strength and one weakness of using a random sample in this study.
   (Make sure you relate your answers to this study throughout. Contextualisation of your answers, that is, making your answers relate to the example in the source material in the examination, is very important!)
2. Explain how the researcher could obtain a self-selected sample for the study. Give one strength and one weakness of using a self-selected sample in this study.
3. Explain how the researcher could obtain an opportunity sample for their study. Give one strength and one weakness of using an opportunity sample in this study.
4. Which of these sample types would be the best one for him to use in this study? Give reasons for your answer.

Exam focus

Sampling techniques

This question is taken from the May 2009 Psychological Investigations examination.

Activity

A researcher is interested in finding out why students at a large sixth form college have decided to study psychology. He is going to use a self-report questionnaire.

(a) Suggest how the researcher could use a random sampling technique to get 40 students to complete the questionnaire. [2]

(b) Evaluate the use of random sampling in this study. [4]

This question is taken from the June 2010 Psychological Investigations examination.

Researchers conducted an independent measures design experiment in a local coffee bar, investigating whether receiving physical contact from someone increases their rating of friendliness.

The experiment took place between 11a.m. and 2p.m. on a Wednesday. As members of the public left the coffee bar after paying, some were touched lightly on the upper arm by a cashier, whereas others were not. Outside the coffee bar, members of the public were asked how friendly they thought the staff were on a scale of 1 (not very friendly) to 10 (extremely friendly).

a) Identify the sampling technique used to obtain participants for this study and suggest one weakness with it. [4]

9 Preparing for the core studies examination

Exams? Nothing to it! All you have to do is know what you need to know, learn it, then reproduce it under examination conditions. As long as you know everything, you will be all right. Easy!

Well, no, it is not easy, but performing well in examinations is something that any student can do once they learn the relevant material and the required examination techniques.

Firstly, good preparation and planning are essential. A large part of doing well in examinations depends on organisation. It is important for you to have an organised folder, in sections, perhaps one for each approach: social, cognitive, developmental, physiological and individual difference, with the perspectives included in the developmental section or given a section of their own. In addition you may have a separate 'themes' section with general information about the methods and issues: experiments, case studies, self-reports, observations, validity (including ecological validity) and reliability, longitudinal and snapshot studies, qualitative and quantitative data and the ethics of

psychological research. The themes are important for evaluation of both the core studies individually and evaluation of the approaches and perspectives in general.

Secondly, it is important to note that good revision is an ongoing process, so any tests your teacher has set, or any homework for which you have received helpful feedback will also be an essential resource for your final exam revision. Past examination papers are also useful.

Thirdly, it is essential that you revise **actively**. Engage with the material, making notes, summary sheets, tables, cue cards and mind maps. The more ways you can actively engage with the material the better you will know and understand it. *Just* reading is **not** learning!

The purpose of this chapter is to tell you what you need to learn, give you some insight into methods you can use to learn and provide you with some ways to test your learning. This should prepare you to put what you have learned to good use when you are doing your core studies examination.

Figure 9.1

What you need to know about the core studies

Remember this: The examiners are your friends in this game – they are on your side!

By now you have probably realised that there are 15 core studies to learn. The core studies examination requires you to know these inside out and backwards. The specification tells you what you need to know. Below is a list of the specific aspects of the core studies you need to learn:

- background to the studies (the context)

- theories and/or studies on which studies are based

- psychological perspectives applicable to the studies

- other research pertinent to the studies

- information in the studies

- methods used in the studies

- how the results are analysed and presented and the conclusions that can be drawn from the studies

- strengths and limitations of the studies

- general psychological issues illustrated by the studies

- evaluation of all the points set out above.

You also need to study **methods, issues, approaches** and **perspectives** and relate these to the 15 core studies. There will be more on these later in this chapter.

Revising the core studies

Some things we need to remember and some things we do not. If we are going to remember something, we will probably need to write it down and keep a record of it. Organisation is the key word here. You need a system.

You will need to organise your folder(s), to make sure you have notes on all the things you need to know. These are best sorted according to the approaches:

- cognitive

- social

- individual differences

- developmental

- physiological.

These are as in the specification, with each approach separated by file dividers. It will probably make most sense if you store them in the order in which your teacher taught them to you. You may also have a section on research methods and issues raised by the studies. The work you have done for the Psychological Investigations examination can be useful in the Core Studies examination too.

The next step is to read your folder and look for gaps. Are there any studies – or bits of studies – missing from your folder? Are there any concepts that you do not understand or do not have an explanation for? If so, you can use this book to look them up, or talk to your teacher. It is important to work out what is missing and fill in the gaps – you cannot begin your revision if you do not have the complete picture.

You are now ready to begin your revision. Remember: You are not revising if you are not writing things down. Learning/revising is an active process! You will need to equip yourself with notepaper and pens, and you might like to use coloured pens and index cards too.

Having organised your folder(s) and prepared the necessary materials, you have everything you need. Now you are ready to start learning the studies.

You need know the stories of the studies. How research papers are presented can help you here, as this provides a structure for your story:

- background and context
- aims and hypotheses
- method (design, subjects, procedure, materials, variables)
- results (are findings qualitative or quantitative? are they gathered by self-report, observation or biomedical measures?)
- discussion and conclusion.

You also need to consider the implications of the studies and evaluations that can be made of the study. You will find the commentaries at the end of every study in this book very helpful when you are considering the strengths and weaknesses of the studies.

Making summary sheets

You can make summary sheets for each of the 15 core studies. Keep these sheets at the front of your file to read through and work from later. You may have made summary sheets after you covered the study in class, when it was fresh in your mind, but it is also a useful activity for refreshing your memory of the studies towards the end of the course.

Your summary sheets should include the following:

The story of the study:

- researcher(s) and date study was published
- title of the study
- background, including any real-world events, studies or theories on which the study is based
- aims/hypotheses
- method (design, sample, location, procedure)
- results (include how any variables were measured)
- discussion points/conclusions.

Evaluation points:

You can use the questions we have used in our commentaries on the studies to help with your evaluation:

- What are the strengths and weaknesses of the research methods and data-gathering methods that have been used in the study?

- Is the study ecologically valid? Does the study raise any issues about validity or reliability?

- What are the implications of the study? Is the study useful?

- Does the study raise any ethical concerns?

Key questions about approaches and perspectives:

- Which approaches does the study illustrate?

- What are the assumptions of this approach?

- How are the assumptions of this approach made evident in the study?

- In what way is this study similar to another study from this approach?

- In what way is this study different to another study from this approach?

- What are the assumptions of the behaviourist perspective?

- What are the assumptions of the psychoanalytical perspective?

- What (if anything) does this study illustrate about the behaviourist perspective and/or the psychoanalytical perspective?

What changes could be made to the study, and what might be the effect of these changes? You need to be prepared to make suggestions about changes that could be made to the study and explain what you think the likely effect of these changes might be. Changes could be to the:

- location of the study

- type of measurement and data-gathering method used

- procedure of the study, including the research method or experimental design used

- sample used in the study

- ethical considerations of the study (what if the ethical guidelines were strictly adhered to – would this affect the study?).

Throughout this chapter you will find revision activities to help you prepare to answer questions on all these areas.

Condensing your notes

To begin with, your summary sheets may be fairly dense and you might have difficulty squeezing in all the points from the study. This is normal, so do not worry. The next stage in the revision process is to work with your notes and condense them. The reason you will be able to write less and still remember the details of the study is because you will be learning the details as you go along.

Figure 9.2 Let's make a molehill out of a mountain …

Once you can write the study on one side of A4, it is time to turn to index cards.

Index cards are very useful for revision. Once you have condensed your notes, the cards act as 'cues' for your memory and are therefore a good revision aid. Using cards gives you a portable set of revision notes, which you can put in your pocket and take with you anywhere. They are also useful for visual learning, as you can include mind maps, pictures, cartoons and diagrams to help you remember.

We have a lot of 'dead time' in our daily lives, such as when we are waiting for or travelling on a bus or train. If you have your index cards with you, you can use that time effectively, leaving you with more 'real time' for relaxing and enjoying yourself!

Testing your learning

Use specimen and past examination papers to test your learning. These will give you an idea of the kinds of questions that can be asked about the studies.

The sample in Milgram's study on obedience to authority

Figure 9.3

- A volunteer sample drawn from those answering an advert in a local newspaper to take part in a study on learning and punishment
- the sample size was 40
- all subjects were male, aged 20-50
- subjects were drawn from a range of professions.

You can use index cards to test your memory too. For example, you might make up a set of cards of samples in a study, as follows:

You can make sets of index cards on the aims of the studies, the findings of the studies, the IV and DV in the studies, controls used in the studies, and so on. They are particularly helpful if you are trying to learn definitions or key concepts for a study, as in the example below:

You don't want to spend all your time making the cards, though. Why not join up with a study buddy, share out the card-making tasks and then swap? If you can cajole your mum or dad into helping you revise, they can use the cards to test your knowledge, or study buddies can test each other.

Methods, issues, perspectives and approaches

In order to answer the examination questions, you must know about research methods, issues, approaches and perspectives, and how these relate to the 15 core studies. First, we will look at some methodological points, and then at the issues and perspectives. There will be revision activities along the way, so be prepared to join in!

Methods in the core studies

The methods are as follows:

1. Experimental method (laboratory and field)

2. Case study

Study: Piliavin et al. (subway Samaritan)
Key concept = DIFFUSION OF RESPONSIBILITY

Diffusion of responsibility means that the more people present, the less responsible each individual feels (because the responsibility is 'shared out') so the less likely someone is to receive help. This was what happened in laboratory studies of helping, but not in the Piliavin et al. study in the field.

Figure 9.4

3. Self-report

4. Observation

5. Methodological issues such as reliability and validity

The experimental method (laboratory and field)

Experiments can be carried out in the laboratory or in a natural setting. The latter is described as being 'in the field'. In a true experiment:

- the experimenter manipulates one variable – the independent variable (IV) – to see if it causes a change in another variable – the dependent variable (DV)

- all other variables (extraneous variables) are controlled or kept constant to prevent them from confounding the study; we can therefore demonstrate cause and effect – the IV causes the DV to change

- subjects/participants are randomly allocated to conditions

- a control or comparison group is used.

Experiments where these criteria are not met are known as natural experiments or quasi-experiments. We have come across examples of these where the IV occurs naturally and cannot be manipulated by the experimenter, as in Baron-Cohen *et al.*'s study of autism and Sperry's study of split-brain patients.

Revision Activity

You need to know about the strengths and weaknesses of the experimental method and apply these to the core studies. Using your knowledge of the core studies and the evaluative issues set out in the table below, copy and complete the two tables which follow.

Table 9.1

Evaluation of laboratory experiments	
✔ Strengths	✘ Weaknesses
High level of control over extraneous variables	May lack ecological validity – laboratory behaviour is artificial
IV can be manipulated and isolated as a causal factor, establishing cause and effect between the IV and the DV	Internal validity may be low because of possible biasing factors, such as subject reactivity (responding to demand characteristics) or experimenter bias
Allows the use of sensitive technical equipment (EEG, MRI scan) or complicated apparatus (e.g. Sperry's apparatus for studying split-brain patients)	Deception may be necessary as to the true purpose of the study in order to avoid subjects responding to demand characteristics – this raises ethical issues
	Restricted samples used mean it is difficult to generalise the findings to people in general
	If the study is quasi-experimental in design, this means the researcher does not have full control over the IV

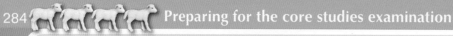

... continued

Evaluation of field experiments

✔ Strengths	✘ Weaknesses
May have high ecological validity – 'real' behaviour can be studied IV can be manipulated and isolated as a causal factor, establishing cause and effect between the IV and the DV	Not all field experiments are high in ecological validity. The introduction of stooges can reduce the realism of the study, especially if the stooge behaves unusually Low control over extraneous variables, so we cannot be entirely sure that there is a causal relationship between the IV and the DV Covert observation is often used to gather data and this raises ethical issues (deception, invasion of privacy, lack of informed consent, etc.) If the study is quasi-experimental in design, this means the researcher does not have full control over the IV

Copy and complete these tables for revision.

Laboratory experiments in the core studies

Study	IV/DV	Sample	Strengths of lab experiment	Weaknesses of lab experiment
Loftus and Palmer (eyewitness testimony)	Study 1: Study 2:			
Baron–Cohen *et al.* (autism)				
Samuel and Bryant (conservation)				
Bandura *et al.* (aggression)				

Field experiments in the core studies

Study	IV/DV	Sample	Strengths of field experiment	Weaknesses of field experiment
Piliavin *et al.* (subway Samaritan)				
Rosenhan (sane in insane places)				
Griffiths (gambling)				

The case study method

You need to know about the strengths and weaknesses of the non-experimental methods, as used in the core studies. One non-experimental method is the case study method. A case study is an in-depth study of one individual or a small group. Often a case study is carried out longitudinally, allowing development or changes to be observed over time. This method allows a great deal of qualitative data, rich in detail and high in validity, to be gathered. Techniques used in case studies include interviews and psychometric tests, and these methods bring their related strengths and weaknesses to the case. For instance, if the researchers have developed a long-standing and close relationship with the subject, their objectivity may be reduced, and therefore they may be biased in their reporting of the interview. Psychometric tests are usually self-report pen-and-paper tests and are open to falsification or manipulation by a clever subject.

Using a variety of different data-gathering methods in a study to measure the same variables is known as triangulation of methods. This can increase the validity of the findings in a case study if the different methods used all come up with similar findings, each supporting the validity of the others.

Replication of case studies is very difficult, especially as they are often of atypical or unusual cases (e.g. Little Hans, Eve White), and this means that we have to be cautious in generalising the findings to other people. This, in turn, reduces the usefulness of the findings.

Revision Activity

There are three case studies in the AS level specification. It may help you to remember these as the 'Cuddly case studies' as long as you can remember why a cuddly unicorn would represent Eve and what a cuddly (and crumpleable!) giraffe has to do with Little Hans.
Copy and complete the following table.

Strengths and weaknesses of using case studies in the (cuddly) case studies

The case studies	The cuddly clues to the case studies	Strengths of the case study method in this study	Weaknesses of the case study method in this study
Freud's case study of Little Hans	Figure 9.5		
Thigpen and Cleckley's case study of Eve White	Figure 9.6		
Savage-Rumbaugh *et al*.'s case study of Kanzi's language acquisition	Figure 9.7		

Data-gathering methods – self-report

You need to know about measurement issues such as the strengths and weaknesses of self-report methods and observational methods of data gathering.

Self-report measures include asking people questions, getting participants to fill in questionnaires, and interviewing subjects. You will learn all about these in your preparation for the Psychological Investigations examination (see Chapter 7).

Briefly, the general strengths and weaknesses of using self-report methods, such as asking questions, questionnaires, interviews, are as follows.

Table 9.2

✔ Strengths of self-report data-gathering methods	✘ Weaknesses of self-report data-gathering methods
Cost- and time-effective – can gather large amounts of data in a short time	May be falsifiable: subjects lie (e.g. responding to demand characteristics, or due to evaluation apprehension, they give socially desirable answers); if data is falsifiable, we have to question its validity
Can measure attitudes, beliefs and cognitive abilities that cannot otherwise be measured	Closed questions (forced-response questions) may frustrate the subject, who may then lose interest and not answer carefully, again reducing the validity of the study
Closed questions and rating scales on questions can provide quantitative data for analysis	Questions can be leading – suggesting the answer that ought to be given; thus the researcher is influencing the subject's responses (children may be particularly susceptible to leading questions)

Revision Activity

Using your knowledge of the core studies and the information provided above about self-report data-gathering methods, copy and complete the following table.

Study	How was self-report used?	Strengths of self-report measures	Weaknesses of self-report measures
Freud (Little Hans)			
Samuel and Bryant (conservation)			
Baron-Cohen et al. (autism)			
Loftus and Palmer (eyewitness testimony)			
Dement and Kleitman (dreaming)			
Sperry (split-brains)			
Thigpen and Cleckley (MPD)			
Griffiths (gambling)			

Data-gathering methods – observation

Observations can be carried out in a natural setting, as Piliavin *et al.* did in their Subway Samaritan study, or in the laboratory, as Bandura *et al.* did in the third stage of their study on learning aggression. Observations can be carried out covertly, without the knowledge or consent of participants, or overtly, where consent is obtained and people are aware of the observer's presence. The observer may be a part of the setting or group being observed – this is called participant observation, as in the study by Rosenhan, where the pseudopatients observed the psychiatric hospitals from the point of view of a patient. Alternatively, the observer may be outside the setting or group being studied – this is known as non-participant observation, as in the observations of the nursery school children through the one-way mirror in Bandura *et al.*'s study.

Observations often generate quantitative data by establishing codings or categories of behaviour to be observed. For example, one of the behavioural categories established by Bandura *et al.* was 'Partial imitation: sits on Bobo, mallet aggression'. This was one of nine behaviours being observed for in the 20-minute period in stage three. In the study by Griffiths, the verbal comments made by participants in the thinking aloud condition were categorised so that he ended up with 30 different categories of utterance. He was then able to measure and compare the thinking patterns of regular and non-regular gamblers, by carrying out a content analysis of all the thinking aloud recordings, observing for the 30 categories.

The general strengths and weaknesses of using observational methods to gather data are set out in the table below.

Table 9.3

✔ Strengths of observational measures	✖ Weaknesses of observational measures
Where covert observation is used, studies can be high in ecological validity, as 'real' behaviour is being observed (NB ecological validity is reduced if a laboratory is the setting for the study)	Ethical concerns are raised in covert observations
	Reductionism where quantitative methods and codings and ratings are used
In participant observations, the observer can get a real insight into the situation being observed, as they experience it first-hand	Observer bias – consciously or unconsciously affecting the results so that they fit in with the hypothesis
	Reliability – if only one observer is used, we have to question the reliability and objectivity of the results
	In overt (and participant) observations, the presence of the researcher may influence the behaviour of subjects and this will mean results are not valid
	In participant observations, the observer may lose their objectivity, as they are influenced by their experience of the situation

Revision Activity

Using your knowledge of the core studies and the information provided above about observational data-gathering methods, copy and complete the following table.

Study	What was observed and how?	Strengths of observational measures	Weaknesses of observational measures
Milgram (obedience)			
Reicher and Haslam (BBC prison experiment)			
Piliavin *et al.* (Subway Samaritan)			
Bandura *et al.* (aggression)			
Rosenhan (sane in insane places)			
Griffiths (gambling)			

Validity and reliability

A test or measure is valid if it tests what it is supposed to test. In other words, are the findings trustworthy and can we believe they are *true*?

Internal validity is determined by the extent to which a study is free of design faults which might affect the result – meaning that the test is not a true test of what it intended to measure.

Factors which reduce the internal validity of findings include the following:

- Low generalisability of findings (e.g. sample biases, ethnocentric bias, difficulty extrapolating to other groups of people or settings) – If the findings are not generalisable, they are not valid. If a sample is biased then we say it has low population validity.

- Demand characteristics – Subjects taking part in a study will try to work out what the study is about. Demand characteristics are the cues or clues present (given away by the procedure, questions and tasks, or conveyed unconsciously by those carrying out the test), which suggest to the subject what the hypothesis is. There are two responses subjects may make, having worked out what they think the study is about:

  - try to please the experimenter and get the experiment to 'work' – out of a desire to be 'right', they modify their behaviour or answers to fit in with how they think the experimenter expects them to behave

- the 'screw you' effect – here the aim is to spoil the experiment by not acting in the way they think is expected of them (this may be just for the sake of it, or because they want to make the statement, 'I am not typical').

Both these responses to demand characteristics mean subjects are falsifying their responses, and this means that the validity of the findings comes into question where subjects responding to demand characteristics is a possibility in a study.

- If it is possible that a confounding variable has operated systematically alongside the IV, this may affect the validity of the findings. For instance, in independent groups designs and matched subjects designs, it is difficult to control subject variables. In other words, there may be differences between the two groups other than the fact that one has the IV introduced. This means it is possible that subject variables have confounded the study, and therefore we have to question the validity of the findings.

In the Baron-Cohen *et al.* study on autism we came across the concept of **concurrent validity**. This means that two studies measuring the same variable have come up with similar findings. By showing that participants' scores on one advanced test of theory of mind (Happé's strange stories test) correlated with their scores on the new advanced test of theory of mind (the eyes task), the authors were able to provide evidence for the validity of their new test as a true advanced measure of theory of mind. The eyes task and Happé's strange stories test, therefore, were concurrently valid – each supporting the validity of the other.

Ecological validity is a form of external validity. We will discuss this later in this chapter as an issue in the core studies.

Reliability refers to the consistency of a measurement. A test or measure is reliable if it gives similar results when repeated in similar circumstances. In other words, if the findings prove to be replicable, which is a key feature of scientific study, then the test or measure is said to be reliable. There are two types of reliability that you need to know about: test–retest reliability and inter-observer reliability:

- **Test–retest reliability** is where the study (or test) is repeated, under similar circumstances to the original study or test. The results from the first test are correlated with the results from the second test, and if a high positive correlation is found between the two, this means that the results are consistent, and therefore reliable.

- **Inter–observer reliability** (also called inter-rater reliability) is a form of reliability designed to control for observer bias. One observer's use of a coding or rating system may be inaccurate if they have applied the system according to their own subjective interpretation or bias. To make sure that the rating or coding system (or categories of observation) is objective, another observer uses the same system to code either the same or a similar sample of behaviour. The scores from the two observers are then correlated, and if a high positive correlation is found, inter-observer reliability has been established. An example of this can be found in the study on learning aggression by Bandura *et al.* The normal aggression level ratings by the children's nursery school teacher were correlated with ratings by one of the female researchers, and the high positive correlation recorded showed that this was a reliable measure of the children's aggression.

Correlational analysis is used to test for both reliability and validity, and this is a common use of correlations in psychological investigations. Of course, this can only be carried out where quantitative data has been gathered and where the study can be replicated easily, as is the case with most laboratory studies. Researchers are least able to establish the reliability of studies that gather qualitative data, as many case studies do. This is a problem, as low reliability brings the validity of findings into question, and if a study is low in validity, this reduces its usefulness.

Revision Activity

Answer the following questions on validity and reliability in the core studies.

1. Which core studies use self-report data-gathering methods that can be falsified, leading us to question the validity of the findings?

2. Which core studies have sample biases that restrict the generalisability of the studies and mean they are not valid measures of people in general?

3. Why might brain-imaging techniques, such as the MRI scan used by Maguire *et al.*, not give valid results?

4. Why can the validity of Griffiths' thinking aloud method be questioned?

5. Identify two studies from the core studies where it would be relatively easy to test and establish the reliability of the findings, and two studies where it would be difficult to establish the reliability of the findings.

6. Explain the term 'inter-observer reliability'. Use an example from the core studies to illustrate how inter-observer reliability is established.

Issues in the core studies

The issues in the core studies are as follows:

- ethics

- ecological validity

- longitudinal and snapshot studies

- qualitative and quantitative data.

Ethics

The participants in psychological studies are people, and we should treat them with care and respect, protecting them from both psychological and physical harm. Psychologists have membership of professional organisations, such as the American Psychological Association (APA) in the USA, and the British Psychological Society (BPS) in the UK. These professional bodies oversee the work of psychologists and provide ethical guidelines to be followed when carrying out research on human subjects. These guidelines include the following:

- Participants should be informed of the nature and procedures of the study prior to taking part, so that they can make an informed choice about their involvement, and give their informed consent to participate in the investigation.

- Deception should be used only if necessary, and as little as necessary. For example, to avoid demand characteristics, it may be necessary to use a cover story to conceal the true purpose of a study. Where deception has been used, debriefing is required.

- Thorough debriefing should be provided, explaining the nature and findings of the study and providing further support, such as counselling, if required or requested.

- Participants should be protected from both physical and psychological harm, including undue stress, while taking part in the study. They should be protected from self-knowledge or experiences that have a negative impact on their self-esteem and dignity. Participants should leave the study in the same state as when they arrived.

- Confidentiality and anonymity should be assured and maintained for all those taking part in the study.

- The participants' privacy should not be invaded.

- Participants should be informed of their right to withdraw at any time, or to withdraw their data at the end of the study.

- Participants should not be coerced into taking part or continuing with a study, whether by directly refusing to allow them to stop when they want to, or by implicitly engaging their commitment to continue by payment.

The ethical guidelines represent what psychologists should aim for in their studies, but in reality it is difficult to carry out work that does not at least bend, if not blatantly flout, one or more of these 'rules'.

It has been argued that there is an ethical imperative in psychological research. In other words, there are some areas of our experience and behaviour that psychologists have a moral obligation to investigate. Some studies have shown us a great deal about how or why we behave in certain ways, or have offered effective solutions to real-life problems. Such studies can be described as ethically worthy, which means that they have made positive contributions to the development of our understanding of human behaviour, or have benefited people by suggesting ways to improve their lives. Studies that are ethically worthy can also be described as highly useful (see the section on 'The implications of the core studies' later in this chapter).

In deciding whether or not a study which breaches ethical guidelines should be (or should have been) carried out, we need to ask the following questions:

1. Does the aim of the study justify it being carried out? Is it an ethically worthy study? Will it explore areas which have not been explored before? Will the results help us to understand behaviour better?

2. If the ethical code was broken, are the findings important enough to justify this? The salient question when considering the ethics of a study involving human participants is: does the end justify the means?

An important point to note here is that some of the core studies were carried out a long time ago. The ethical guidelines that relate to current psychological practice have been amended and refined since some of these studies took place, and, in some cases, as a result of these studies. Some of the studies would probably not be allowed to be carried out in the same way if we wanted to replicate them today.

You also need to note that there are separate guidelines for animal studies, so the comparative study in the core studies (the Savage-Rumbaugh *et al.* study on Kanzi and other apes in Chapter 3) is not governed by the same ethical guidelines. For ethical concerns raised in this study, see the commentary at the end of the core study in Chapter 3.

Revision Activity

For each of the following core studies, answer the questions that follow on ethics.
- Bandura *et al.* (imitating aggression)
- Piliavin *et al.* (subway Samaritan)
- Milgram (obedience)

1. What ethical guidelines were breached by the researchers in this study?
2. Can any breaches of ethics in this study be defended on the grounds that this study is ethically worthy?
3. If this study had been carried out according to ethical guidelines, what would the effect be on the results of the study?
4. Can you suggest a way in which the researcher could have investigated their aim in an entirely ethical way?

Ecological validity

Ecological validity is a type of external validity, which means the extent to which generalisations can be made from the test environment to other situations.

A study is high in ecological validity if the behaviour which subjects are asked to perform resembles a behaviour they, or people similar to them, perform in real life. Laboratory studies tend to be low in ecological validity, since the setting is artificial and therefore unlikely to represent 'real-life' behaviour. However, it is not the case that all laboratory studies lack ecological validity, or that a study is either ecologically valid or not. For example, if you wanted to test a person's driving behaviour, you might think that there is no ecologically valid way of doing this in a laboratory. However, testing participants on a driving simulator, or using a computer program based on driving a car, may be *sufficiently* high in ecological validity for your research purposes. It would certainly be higher in ecological validity than seating a participant on a chair, with a frisbee for a steering wheel, and asking them to mime their driving behaviour!

There can be problems studying social behaviour in the laboratory, or studying the effects of environmental variables such as ambient noise, weather conditions and crowd behaviour, so there can be problems with the ecological validity of laboratory studies which investigate these areas.

There are also problems with the ecological validity of studies where children are tested individually in the laboratory, isolated from their usual social environment and tested by people they do not know.

Some researchers argue that the only method which has high ecological validity is covert observation in a natural setting, as this studies people's freely chosen and normal behaviour, without the biasing factor of their knowledge that they are being observed.

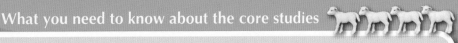

The following table gives examples of high and low ecological validity in the core studies.

Table 9.4

Study	Low ecological validity	High ecological validity
Milgram	Laboratory study, untypical task	
Reicher and Haslam	Simulated institution/prison is unlike a real prison	
Piliavin *et al.*		Covert observation of behaviour in natural setting
Loftus and Palmer	Laboratory experiment	
Savage-Rumbaugh *et al.*	The chimps were kept in captivity in a highly humanised environment, and encouraged to perform behaviours chimps do not naturally perform, including language training through instrumental conditioning in the case of the common chimpanzees, Sherman and Austin	The acquisition of symbol use through modelling is similar to how children acquire language in a natural setting
Samuel and Bryant	Laboratory experiment, children tested alone	
Bandura *et al.*	Laboratory experiment, children tested alone	
Freud		Covert observation of behaviour in natural setting (the question is: how was this behaviour interpreted?)
Dement and Kleitman	Laboratory study – we do not sleep in a laboratory or wired up to an EEG machine!	
Sperry	Laboratory experiment – subjects restricted (e.g. cannot see hands, no talking)	
Rosenhan	'Normal people' do not usually seek diagnosis of mental illness or hospitalisation	Covert observation of behaviour in a natural setting

Longitudinal studies and snapshot studies

Longitudinal studies investigate the same subjects or participants over an extended period of time: weeks, months or even years. They may be continuous, or researchers may return periodically to sample behaviour (e.g. every few months or years). This design allows us to see how behaviour changes or develops over time. Where the same researcher oversees the study, trusting relationships can be built up with the subjects so that it is possible to gather valid data on sensitive issues, since subjects are more inclined to disclose information to someone they know and trust. Studying subjects over time means a great deal of data can be gathered which is usually qualitative in nature, and this also increases the validity of the findings.

For example, in the study on the pygmy chimpanzee (bonobo) Kanzi, Savage-Rumbaugh *et al.* studied the animal intensively, recording every utterance he made using the lexigrams and/or gestures to communicate. They did this over a period of 17 months.

The studies by Freud (Little Hans) and Thigpen and Cleckley (multiple personality disorder) were also longitudinal designs. The longitudinal design is commonly used in case studies, and therefore often features in developmental studies or studies of abnormal psychology in the individual differences approach.

The strengths of longitudinal studies include the following:

- A relationship can be built up with the subject, so that they have confidence in the researcher and feel secure in providing sensitive information. The relationship of trust established over time can increase the level of detail provided by participants and therefore improve the validity of a study's findings.

- Researchers can build up a detailed picture of the subject over the course of the study. For example, Thigpen and Cleckley interviewed Eve White, Eve Black and Jane in over 100 hours of therapy, building up detailed knowledge of the three 'personalities'. The longitudinal nature of the study made it less likely for Eve White to be faking her symptoms (if she was acting, she made no errors), and this increases the credibility of multiple personality disorder as a diagnosis in this case.

The weaknesses of longitudinal studies include the following:

- Since the researcher has invested a lot of time and effort in the study, they may lose their objectivity or become too involved with the participants. This may affect the findings, reducing their validity. For example, Thigpen and Cleckley were aware of their close involvement with, and professional investment in, the case of Eve, and suggested that they might have been fooled by a very good actress.

- Longitudinal studies can be expensive in terms of both time and money, and may require a great deal of commitment from the researchers.

- Subject attrition can cause problems. Over time, a sample size may reduce as people drop out or lose contact with the researcher. This means that the researchers are left with what is, in effect, a volunteer sample, and this may not truly represent the original sample. Therefore the validity of the findings may be questioned.

- It may be difficult to establish the reliability of longitudinal studies, as societal or cultural changes that have taken place may make the study impossible to replicate. Reliability may also be difficult to establish because it is hard to find equivalent participants, especially in abnormal cases (e.g. Eve White or Little Hans).

- Once started, longitudinal studies cannot be modified or changed easily.

Snapshot studies compare different groups at the same point in time to see a 'snapshot' of behaviour. They allow us to compare groups of different ages or under different circumstances, for example, to see the effects of variables on behaviour, or to see how behaviour changes over time. They are also known as cross-sectional studies.

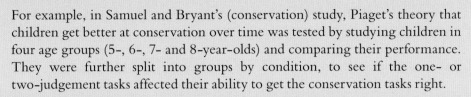

For example, in Samuel and Bryant's (conservation) study, Piaget's theory that children get better at conservation over time was tested by studying children in four age groups (5-, 6-, 7- and 8-year-olds) and comparing their performance. They were further split into groups by condition, to see if the one- or two-judgement tasks affected their ability to get the conservation tasks right.

The strengths of snapshot studies include the following:

- Snapshot studies are less time-consuming than a longitudinal study. Snapshot studies allow us to sample changes over time (e.g. in children of different ages), without having to wait for a child to grow and develop.

- Since an independent groups design is used, the likelihood of demand characteristics affecting the study is reduced, as participants are tested in only one condition of the experiment.

- Snapshot studies can be more time- and cost-effective than longitudinal studies.

- As snapshot studies are quicker and cheaper to replicate, it may be possible to establish the reliability of the findings easily.

- Snapshot studies can be easily modified or changed for further study.

The weaknesses of snapshot studies include the following:

- Since snapshot studies employ independent groups designs, snapshot studies can be affected by extraneous participant variables. Individual differences between participants may affect the DV and confound the study.

- The limited sampling of participants' behaviour may give a false impression of their typical behaviour. A longitudinal study may not be affected by this, as more detailed data are collected.

Qualitative and quantitative data

Quantitative data are numerical data such as categories and frequencies, percentages. It is attractive to gather quantitative data because of the ease with which people's performances on a test or task can be compared. The data is easy to summarise and present, and statistical analysis is possible. It is also easier to establish the reliability of numerical findings, as this can be done by retesting and correlating the results of the first and second tests to see if there is a significant positive correlation. The disadvantage is that quantitative data provides a narrow view of the person, one that is both reductionist and maybe lacking in validity.

The alternative is to gather **qualitative data**, which usually takes the form of verbal descriptions, such as reports of what has been observed or written reports of interviews. While it is more difficult to compare, analyse and draw conclusions from qualitative data, or to replicate this data to test for reliability, what you gain is an increase in the depth and detail of the findings, and therefore higher validity.

Scientific study usually implies the gathering and analysis of quantitative data, using inferential statistics to establish cause and effect or correlation between variables. Historically, therefore, psychological investigations have tended to focus on quantitative methods of analysis. However, qualitative research methods, such as discourse analysis, are now appearing more frequently in psychological literature. As you might imagine, many researchers try to incorporate the strengths of both qualitative and quantitative data in their work, and there are examples of this in the core studies.

Table 9.5

Examples of qualitative and quantitative data from the core studies

Core study	Qualitative data	Quantitative data
Milgram (obedience)	Nervous laughter and sweating was observed	65% went up to 450v, 100% went to 300v
Piliavin *et al.* (Subway Samaritan)	Comments elicited from passengers by observers (e.g. 'It's for a man to help him')	In the cane (ill) condition, victim was helped spontaneously on 62/65 trials (drunk = 19/38)
Loftus and Palmer (eyewitness testimony)		Study 1 – speed estimate was measured as an average per condition Study 2 – 16/50 subjects in 'smashed' condition reported seeing broken glass, compared with 6/50 in control condition
Savage-Rumbaugh *et al.* (ape language)	The authors report that bonobos learned symbol use by modelling and observation, whereas the common chimpanzees had to be trained (instrumentally conditioned) to use symbols	Mulika's vocabulary tests showed she understood 42 symbols
Samuel and Bryant (conservation)		DV was measured as an average number of errors out of 12 per condition
Bandura *et al.* (aggression)		Children's aggressive behaviour was recorded using categories, recording at five-second intervals for 20 minutes in stage three
Freud (Little Hans)	Study is largely qualitative (e.g. the description of Hans's fantasy of the two giraffes)	
Dement and Kleitman (dreaming)		Out of 191 REM awakenings, 152 dream recalls were recorded Out of 160 NREM awakenings, only 11 dream recalls were recorded
Sperry (split-brains)	Subjects could not name an object placed in their left hand out of their view	

Core study	Qualitative data	Quantitative data
Rosenhan (sane in insane places)	The behaviour of patients was judged to be due to their 'pathology' rather than considered normal given the environment (e.g. 'Patient engages in writing behaviour' was recorded about the diary keeping as if it were an abnormal behaviour)	In the follow-up study, 10% of the research hospital's normal intake were suspected of being pseudopatients by two members of the hospital staff
Thigpen and Cleckley (multiple personality disorder)	As this is a case report of therapeutic sessions, any episode described by the researchers is going to give qualitative data	Psychometric test scores (e.g. IQ scores and memory function scores) and EEG scores
Griffiths (gambling)	The quotes from the regular gamblers show how they were thinking irrationally (e.g. 'I'm losing heavily here … [the machine's] not giving me the numbers I want. I've just taken a quid off it so it wants its money back'	Regular gamblers made 14% irrational comments in total, compared to approximately 2.5% for the non-regular gamblers

Revision Activity

1. Write out an explanation of the difference between qualitative and quantitative data, giving an example of each type of data from one of the core studies.
2. Copy out and complete the following table to show the relative strengths and weaknesses of qualitative and quantitative data

	Strengths	Weaknesses
Quantitative data		
Qualitative data		

Implications of the core studies

A final issue that we would like you to consider here is the usefulness of psychological research. This seems very important to us, because psychology should be useful. If research does not help to explain why we think, feel and behave as we do, nor give us ideas for how we might think, feel and behave in different ways that will lead us to live happier and more fulfilled lives, then there does not seem to be much point in it!

So, are the core studies useful? The questions we need to ask are: useful for what and to whom? Findings may be useful to psychologists in that they help to explain or predict behaviour, or generally useful for helping to explain behaviours and solve problems in the real world.

On the one hand, studies can be considered useful to psychology itself by furthering our understanding of human behaviour or experience. A study or theory may also be highly generative, that is, it leads to a great deal of further research, both testing and refining the conclusions drawn in a particular area of study, and this makes it useful within psychology as a discipline.

Examples of work which has been highly generative are Freud's theory of psychosexual development, and Piaget's theory of cognitive development. It follows that studies which contribute to the debate in a particular area are also useful to psychology. For example, Samuel and Bryant's work contributes to the debate concerning children's cognitive development by providing support for the sequence of Piaget's stages, but also suggesting refinements to the timing of the stages, as their work suggests that Piaget underestimated young children's abilities.

On the other hand, usefulness can be assessed by asking: are the conclusions or findings from the study of any use in helping to solve problems in the real world? The table below considers some examples of the real–life applications of findings from the core studies.

Table 9.6

Study	Applications in real life
Samuel and Bryant/ Piaget (conservation/ cognitive development)	Understanding cognitive development in children can inform teachers about what is appropriate to teach at what stage in a child's development, and how to teach it (interactive learning environment that enables child to move from stage to stage when they are ready).
Loftus and Palmer (eyewitness testimony)	If memory is reconstructive in nature and can be altered by the use of leading questions, we must take great care about how we question people, on whose memory we rely – most importantly, witnesses to crimes, whose testimony in a court of law may be important evidence.
Griffiths (gambling)	Griffiths considers that a form of cognitive behaviour modification based on the thinking aloud method might be used in the rehabilitation of problem gamblers. Griffiths calls this 'audio playback therapy'.
Rosenhan (sane in insane places)	This work by Rosenhan was one of a number of studies that have resulted in the development of more valid and reliable diagnostic criteria for mental illnesses.

The usefulness of the core studies can also be considered in relation to the methods and issues. You should note that the usefulness of a study will be reduced if:

- the study is low in ecological validity and therefore findings cannot be generalised easily to a real-life setting

- the study is reductionist and ignores other important factors or variables which affect behaviour

- the findings of the study are not valid (e.g. if demand characteristics could have affected the findings, or if it is possible that other extraneous variables have confounded the results)

- sample biases mean the findings are not generalisable to a broad population.

Doing the core studies examination

There are **two** examinations for OCR AS level psychology:

- The **Core Studies** examination. This examination is two hours long and counts for 70 per cent of the AS marks.

- The **Psychological Investigations** examination. This examination lasts one hour and counts for 30 per cent of the AS marks.

Always keep in mind that the examiners are your friends. Their aim is to enable you to show them what you know and what you can do – they are not trying to catch you out. To help you, the examinations will follow a structure, and you need to know what this is if you are to be fully prepared. Here we will look at the structure of the Core Studies examination only, as the structure of the Psychological Investigations examination is described in Chapter 8.

Structure of the Core Studies examination

The Core Studies examination is in three sections: Section A, Section B and Section C. Below is a summary, followed by detailed descriptions of the three sections, with examples.

Table 9.7

Section A	Made up of 15 compulsory, short questions on all aspects of the core studies, and the methods, issues, approaches and perspectives. There is always one question on every core study.	Carries 60 of the 120 marks available
Section B	More in-depth questions, on a specific core study. You will choose **one** of three given studies to write about – you will be asked to write in detail about some aspects of the study, and to relate the study to the methods and issues.	Carries 36 of the 120 marks available
Section C	In-depth questions, focusing on the approaches and perspectives and how they relate to the 15 core studies, and how the core studies illustrate the strengths and weaknesses of the approaches and perspectives.	Carries 24 of the 120 marks available

You will be given a printed examination booklet with the questions on and you write your answer in the spaces given. It would be helpful for you to look at past papers so that the layout of the examination becomes familiar to you.

Section A

All questions in Section A are **compulsory**. There are 15 short answer questions in this section, worth a possible 60 of the 120 marks available on this paper. There will always be one question on each of the 15 core studies in Section A.

Questions in Section A may be in two parts (with 2 marks for each part) or one part (for a total of 4 marks). Below are examples of each type of question.

Exam focus

Core Studies Section A
Exam question examples from the June 2010 Core Studies Examination.
Marks available are shown in brackets [..]
Activity
1. The Loftus and Palmer study on eyewitness testimony used two laboratory experiments.
    (a) Identify the two experimental groups in Experiment 2. [2]
    (b) Outline one difference between the responses given by the two experimental groups in Experiment 2. [2]
2. Describe two ethical issues raised by Rosenhan's study 'On being sane in insane places'. [4]

The Core Studies examination is two hours (120 minutes) long, and there are 120 marks available. To help you use your time wisely in the exam you should plan to earn a mark a minute, which means you should spend an hour (and no more than an hour) on Section A as it is worth 60 marks.

Section B

In Section B there is **one compulsory** question, in six parts. You must therefore complete all parts of question 16. Section B is worth 36 of the 120 marks on this examination paper, so you should spend 36 minutes planning and writing your answer to section B.

In the Section B question you will be asked to write about **one** core study, from a choice of three given studies, and you will answer questions about one or more of the following: aims, research method, location, sample, controls used, data-gathering methods, types of data gathered, results and conclusions. You will be asked to write about one of the methods or issues as in relation to the study you have chosen to write about.

You will also be asked to suggest changes that might be made to some aspects of your chosen study and to consider what effects these changes might have, for example, on the outcome of the study or on the validity of the findings.

Revision Activity

To help you prepare for the questions which might ask you to suggest changes to the location, sample, method, procedure and data-gathering method, copy and complete the following three tables.

How could the location be different? What effect might a different location have on the study's findings?

Researchers	Location used	Suggested alternative location	Possible effects of this change of location on the results and validity of the study
Milgram (obedience)	Laboratory-based study at Yale University	Downtown industrial area	
Piliavin *et al.* (subway Samaritan)	Carriage in a New York subway train	In the subway station rather than on the train In a large shopping centre On the street	
Griffiths (gambling)	Amusement arcade	At a racetrack, with regular and non-regular gamblers on horse races	
Dement and Kleitman (dreaming)	Sleep laboratory on a university campus	In the subjects' own homes (natural setting)	

... Continued

How could the sample be different? What effect might a different sample have on the results of the study?

Researchers	Sample used	Suggested alternative sample	Possible effects of this change of sample on the results and validity of the study
Milgram (obedience)	40 males, aged 20–50, range of jobs, volunteers, New Haven area		
Piliavin *et al.* (subway Samaritan)	4,450 subjects, male and female, black and white, on the New York subway		
Griffiths (gambling)	60 gamblers – 30 regular gamblers and 30 non-regular gamblers		
Dement and Kleitman (dreaming)	9 adults (7 male, 2 female)		
Maguire *et al.* (taxi drivers' brains)	16 right-handed male London taxi drivers and 50 healthy, right-handed men who did not drive taxis		
Loftus and Palmer (eyewitness testimony)	University students, first 45 of them and then a further 150		

How could the aim of laboratory and field experiments using observational methods be investigated using a survey, questionnaire or self-report methods?

Researchers	Research and data-gathering method	Aim	How this study could be carried out as a survey, questionnaire or using self-report data-gathering methods	How changing to a self-report or survey method might affect the results and validity of the study
Milgram (obedience)	Laboratory-based study, observing how far a participant would go on the shock generator	To investigate how far participants would obey a malevolent authority figure instructing them to act against their conscience		
Piliavin *et al.* (subway Samaritan)	Field experiment using covert observation to record responses to staged incidents	To investigate whether an ill person who collapsed would get more help than a drunk person in the same situation		

...Continued

Researchers	Research and data-gathering method	Aim	How this study could be carried out as a survey, questionnaire or using self-report data-gathering methods	How changing to a self-report or survey method might affect the results and validity of the study
Rosenhan (being sane in insane places)	Field experiment using participant observation, carried out covertly by the pseudopatients in hospital wards	To find out how patients on a psychiatric ward were treated, and to see if a person faking symptoms could be spotted		
Bandura *et al.* (aggression)	Laboratory experiment, covertly observing aggressive behaviour displayed in stage three	Do children learn to be aggressive by imitation?		

Section C

The questions in Section C will relate the studies to the approaches and perspectives (social/individual differences/cognitive/developmental/physiological approach, and the behaviourist/psychodynamic perspective).

In Section C there will be a choice: you have to answer all parts of EITHER question 17 OR question 18 in this section. Section C is worth 24 of the 120 marks available on this paper, so you should spend 24 minutes planning and answering Section C.

This question will be in four parts (a, b, c, d) and will generally require you to know the assumptions and criticisms (strengths and limitations) of the approaches and perspectives, and how these relate to the core studies and to the topics studied in the core studies. How to revise for and answer these questions is addressed in detail in Chapter 7.

... doing examinations can be loving examinations ...

Now you have worked your way through this final chapter, you should have a good idea of what it is you need to know about core studies, and have some ideas about how you can learn them and be prepared to write about them in your examination.

Being organised and prepared can take the stress out of examinations and leave you with just enough of a buzz of arousal to really enjoy it and do your best on the day. We hope you found this book useful. Good luck!

References

Aitchison, J. (1983) *The Articulate Mammal*, London: Hutchinson, 2nd edition.

Anderson, J. (1995) *Learning and Memory: An Integrated Approach*, Chichester: Wiley.

Arendt, H. (1965) *Eichmann in Jerusalem: A report on the banality of evil*, New York: Viking.

Aronson, E. (1976) *The Social Animal*, San Francisco: W.H. Freeman & Co.

Asch, S.E. (1951) 'Effect of group pressure upon the modification and distortion of judgements' in H. Guetzkow (ed.), *Groups, Leadership and Men*, Pittsburg, PA: Carnegie Press.

Aserinsky, E. and Kleitman, N. (1955) 'Two types of ocular motility occurring in sleep', *Journal of Applied Physiology*, 8, 1, 1–10.

Atkinson, R.L., Atkinson, R.C., Smith, E.E. and Bem, D.J. (1993) *Introduction to Psychology*, New York: Harcourt Brace Jovanovich, 11th edition.

Baird, G., Simonoff, E., Pickles, A., Chandler, S., Loucas, T., Meldrum, D. and Charman, T. (2006) 'Prevalence of disorders of the autism spectrum in a population cohort of children in South Thames: The Special Needs and Autism Project (SNAP)', *The Lancet*, 368, no.9531, 210–15.

Bandura, A., Ross, D. and Ross, S.A. (1961) 'Transmission of aggression through imitation of aggressive models', *Journal of Abnormal and Social Psychology*, 63, 575–82

Banyard, P. and Grayson, A. (1996) *Introducing Psychological Research*, Basingstoke: Macmillan Press.

Banyard, P. and Grayson, A. (2000) *Introducing Psychological Research*, Basingstoke: Palgrave Macmillan.

Baron-Cohen, S. (2005) 'The neuropsychology of autism and pervasive developmental disorders – the extreme male brain theory: an expert interview with Simon Baron-Cohen, PhD, MPhil', *Medscape Psychiatry and Mental Health*, 10, no.2, available at: http://www.medscape.com/viewarticle/518449

Baron-Cohen, S. (1999) 'The extreme-male-brain theory of autism' in Tager-Flusberg, H. (ed.) *Neurodevelopmental Disorders*, Cambridge, MA: MIT Press.

Baron-Cohen, S. (1989) 'Perceptual role-taking and protodeclarative pointing in autism', *British Journal of Developmental Psychology*, 7, 113–27.

Baron-Cohen, S., Cosmides, L. and Tooby, J. (1997) *Mindblindness: An Essay on Autism and Theory of Mind*, Cambridge, MA: MIT Press.

Baron-Cohen, S., Jolliffe, T., Mortimore, C. and Robertson, M. (1997) 'Another advanced test of theory of mind: Evidence from very high functioning adults with autism or Asperger syndrome', *Journal of Child Psychology and Psychiatry*, 38, 813–22

Baron-Cohen, S., Leslie, A.M. and Frith, U. (1985) 'Does the autistic child have a theory of mind?', *Cognition*, 21, 37–46.

Bartlett, F.C. (1932) *Remembering: A study in experimental and social psychology*, Cambridge: Cambridge University Press.

Blakemore, C. (1988) *The Mind Machine*, London: BBC Books.

Bliss, E.L. (1983) 'Multiple personalities, related disorders, and hypnosis', *American Journal of Clinical Hypnosis*, 26, 114–23.

Bower, G.H., Black, J.B. and Turner, T.J. (1979) 'Scripts in memory for text', *Cognitive Psychology*, 11, 177–220.

Bowlby, J. (1951) *Maternal Care and Mental Health*, Geneva: World Health Organisation.

Bowler, D.M. (1992) 'Theory of mind in Asperger Syndrome', *Journal of Child Psychology and Psychiatry*, 33, 877–93.

British Psychological Society (1993), www.bps.org.uk

Brown, R. (1973) *A First Language*, Cambridge, MA: Harvard University Press.

Brown, R. (1986) *Social Psychology*, New York: The Free Press, 2nd edition.

Campbell, R., Baron-Cohen, S. and Walker, J. (1995) 'Do people with autism show a face advantage in recognition of familiar faces and their parts? A test of central coherence theory', unpublished ms, Goldsmiths College, University of London.

Carlson, N.R. (1986) *Physiology of Behaviour*, London: Allyn and Bacon, 3rd edition.

Corney, W.J. and Cummings, W.T. (1985) 'Gambling behaviour and information processing biases', *Journal of Gambling Studies*, 1, no.2, 111–18.

Darley, J.M. and Latané, B. (1968) 'Bystander intervention in emergencies: Diffusion of responsibility', *Journal of Personality and Social Psychology*, 8, 377–83.

Dement, W. (1960) 'The effect of dream deprivation', *Science*, 131, 1705–7.

Dement, W. and Kleitman, N. (1957) 'The relation of eye movements during sleep to dream activity: An objective method for the study of dreaming', *Journal of Experimental Psychology*, 53, 339–46

Eriksson, P.S., Perfilieva, E., Bjork-Eriksson, T., Alborn, A.M., Nordborg, C., Peterson, D.A. and Gage, F.H. (1998) 'Neurogenesis in the adult human hippocampus', *Nature Medicine*, November, 4, no.11, 1313–17.

Eysenck, H.J. (1970) *Crime and Personality*, London: Paladin.

Finkelhor, D. (1979) *Sexually Victimised Children*, New York: Free Press.

Fisher, S. (1993) 'The pull of the fruit machine: a sociological typology of young players', *Sociological Review*, 41, 446–74.

Freud, S. (1909) *Analysis of a Phobia in a Five-year-old Boy*, in *The Pelican Freud Library* (1977) Vol. 8, Case Histories 1.

Frith, U. (1989) *Autism: Explaining the Enigma*, Oxford: Basil Blackwell.

Frith, U. (1993) 'Autism', *Scientific American*, 268, no.66, 108–14.

Gardner, R.A. and Gardner, B.T. (1969) 'Teaching Sign Language to a Chimpanzee'. *Science*, 165, 664–72.

Gazzaniga, M.S., LeDoux, J.E. and Wilson, D.H. (1977) 'Language, praxis and the right hemisphere: Clues to some mechanisms of consciousness', *Neurology*, 27, 1144–7.

Griffiths, M.D. (1994) 'The role of cognitive bias and skill in fruit machine gambling', *British Journal of Psychology*, 85, 351–69

Gross, R. (2005) *Psychology: The Science of Mind and Behaviour*, London: Hodder Arnold, 3rd edition.

Haney, C., Banks, C. and Zimbardo, P. (1973) 'A study of prisoners and guards in a simulated prison', *Naval Research Reviews*, 30, no.9, 4–17.

Happé, F. (1994) 'An advanced test of theory of mind: Understanding of story characters' thoughts and feelings by able autistic, mentally handicapped, and normal children and adults', *Journal of Autism and Developmental Disorders*, 24, 129–54.

Happé, F.G.E. (1997) 'Central coherence and theory of mind in autism: Reading homographs in context', *British Journal of Developmental Psychology*, 15, no.1, 1–12.

Hayes, K.H. and Hayes, C. (1951) 'Intellectual development of a house-raised chimpanzee', *Proceedings of the American Philosophical Society*, 95, 105–9.

Hayes, N. (1994) *Foundations of Psychology: An Introductory Text*, Thomson Learning.

Heider, F. (1958) *The Psychology of Interpersonal Relations*, New York: Wiley.

Henslin, J.M. (1967) in Reith, G. (1999) *The Age of Chance: Gambling in Western Culture*, Abingdon: Routledge.

Hockett, C.F. (1959) 'Animal "languages" and human language', *Human Biology*, 31, 32–9.

Jacobs, B., Schall, M. and Scheibel, A.B. (1993) 'A quantitative dendritic analysis of Wernicke's area in human. II. Gender, hemispheric, and environmental change, *Journal of Comparative Neurology*, 327, 97–111.

Kahney, H. (1993) *Problem Solving Current Issues*, Buckingham: Open University Press, 2nd edition.

Kellogg, W.N. and Kellogg, L.A. (1933) *The Ape and the Child*, New York: McGraw-Hill.

Kline, P. and Storey, R. (1977) 'A factor analytic study of the oral character', *British Journal of Social and Clinical Psychology*, 16, no.3, 317–28.

Ladouceur, R., Gaboury, A., Bujold, A., Lachance, N. and Tremblay, S. (1991) 'Ecological validity in laboratory studies of videopoker gaming', *Journal of Gambling Studies*, 7, 109–16.

Ladouceur, R., Gaboury, A., Dumont, M. and Rochette, P. (1988) 'Gambling: Relationships between the frequency of wins and irrational thinking', *Journal of Psychology*, 122, 409–14.

Langer, E.J. (1975) 'The illusion of control', *Journal of Personality and Social Psychology*, 32, no.2, 311–28.

Latané, B. and Darley, J.M. (1968) 'Group inhibition of bystander intervention', *Journal of Personality and Social Psychology*, 10, 215–21.

Loftus, E.F. and Burns, H.J. (1982) 'Mental shock can produce retrograde amnesia', *Memory and Cognition*, 10, 318–23.

Loftus, E.F., and Palmer, J.J. (1974) 'Reconstruction of automobile destruction: An example of the interaction between language and memory', *Journal of Verbal Learning and Verbal Behaviour*, 13, 585–9

Maguire, E.A., Gadian D.G., Johnsrude, I.S., Good, C.D., Ashburner, J., Frackowiak, R.S., and Frith, C.D. (2000) 'Navigation-related structural changes in the hippocampi of taxi drivers', *Proceedings of the National Academy of Science*, 97, 4398–403

Milgram, S. (1963) 'Behavioural study of obedience', *Journal of Abnormal and Social Psychology*, 67, 371–8.

Milgram, S. (1974) *Obedience to Authority*, New York: Harper Torchbooks.

National Autistic Society, 'Autism: what is it?', available at: http://www.nas.org.uk/nas/jsp/polopoly.jsp?d=211

Ozonoff, S., Pennington, B.E. and Rogers, S.J. (1991) 'Executive function deficits in high functioning autistic children: Relationship to the theory of mind', *Journal of Child Psychology and Psychiatry*, 32, 1081–1106.

Pavlov, I.P. (1927) *Conditioned Reflexes*, London: Oxford University Press.

Perner, J., Leekam, S. and Wimmer, H. (1987) 'Three year olds' difficulty in understanding false belief: cognitive limitation, lack of knowledge or pragmatic misunderstanding?', *British Journal of Developmental Psychology*, 5, 125–37.

Pervin, L.A. (1984) *Personality*, New York: John Wiley, 4th edition.

Piaget, J. and Inhelder, B. (1956) *The Child's Conception of Space*, London: RKP.

Piliavin, I.M., Rodin, J.A. and Piliavin, J.A. (1969) Good Samaritanism, an Underground Phenomenon?, *Journal of Personality and Social Psychology*, 13, no.4, 289–99.

Reicher, S. and Haslam, S.A. (2006) 'Rethinking the psychology of tyranny: The BBC prison study', *British Journal of Social Psychology*, 45, 1–40

Rose, S.A. and Blank, M. (1974) 'The potency of context in children's cognition: an illustration through conservation', *Child Development*, 45, 499–502.

Rosenhan, D.L. (1973) 'On being sane in insane places', *Science*, 179, 250–8

Sacks, O. (1985) 'The twins' in *The Man Who Mistook his Wife for a Hat and Other Clinical Tales*, New York: Harper & Row.

Sacks, O. (1995) *An Anthropologist on Mars*, London: Picador.

Samuel, J. and Bryant, P. (1984) 'Asking only one question in the conservation experiment', *Journal of Child Psychology and Psychiatry*, 25, 315–18

Savage-Rumbaugh, E.S. (1986) *Ape Language: From conditioned responses to symbols*, New York: Columbia University Press.

Savage-Rumbaugh, E.S. and Rumbaugh, D. (1979) 'Symbolization, language and chimpanzees: A theoretical reevaluation based on initial language acquisition processes in four young Pan troglogdytes', *Brain and Language*, 6: 265–300.

Savage-Rumbaugh, S., McDonald, K., Sevcik, R.A., Hopkins, W.D. and Rubert, E. (1986) 'Spontaneous symbol acquisition and communicative use by pygmy chimpanzees (Pan paniscus)', *Journal of Experimental Psychology*, 115(3), 211–35

Savage-Rumbaugh, S. and Lewin, R. (1994) *Kanzi – The Ape at the Brink of the Human Mind*, London: Doubleday.

Schreiber, F.R. (1973) *Sybil*, Harmondsworth: Penguin.

Sears, D.O. (1986) 'College sophomores in the laboratory: Influences of a narrow data base on social psychology's view of human nature', *Journal of Personality and Social Psychology*, 51, no.3, 515–30.

Sherif, M. (1966) *Group Conflict and Co-operation: Their social psychology*, London: RKP.

Sizemore, C.C. and Pittillo, E.S. (1977) *I'm Eve*, New York: Doubleday.

Skinner, B.F. (1938) *The Behaviour of Organisms*, New York: Appleton-Century-Crofts.

Sperry, R.W. (1968) 'Hemisphere deconnection and unity in conscious awareness', *American Psychologist*, 23, 723–33

Tajfel, H. (1982) *Social Identity and Intergroup Relations*, Cambridge: Cambridge University Press.

Tajfel, H. and Turner, J. (1979) 'An integrative theory of intergroup conflict' in G.W. Austin and S. Worchel (eds), *The Social Psychology of Intergroup Relations*, Monterey, California: Brooks Cole.

Tajfel, H. and Turner, J.C. (1986) 'The social identity theory of Intergroup Behaviour' in S. Worchel and W. Austin (eds), *Psychology of Intergroup Relations*, Chicago: Nelson-Hall.

Terrace, H.S., Petitto, L.A., Sanders, R.J. and Bever, T.G. (1979) 'Can an ape create a sentence?', *Science*, 206, 891–902.

Thigpen, C.H. and Cleckley, H. (1954) 'A case of multiple personality', *Journal of Abnormal and Social Psychology*, 49, 135–51

Tulving, E. (1972) 'Episodic and semantic memory' in E. Tulving and W. Donaldson (eds), *Organisation of Memory*, London: Academic Press.

Turner, J.C. (1985) 'Social categorization and the self-concept: a social cognitive theory of group behaviour' in E.J. Lawler (ed.), *Advances in Group Processes: theory and research*, Vol. 2, Greenwich, CT: JAI Press, 77–122.

Turner, J.C. (1982) 'Towards a cognitive redefinition of the social group' in H. Tajfel (ed.), *Social Identity and Intergroup Relations*, Cambridge: Cambridge University Press.

Wagenaar, W.A. (1988) *Paradoxes of Gambling Behavior*, Hillsdale, NJ: Erlbaum.

Walker, M.B. (1992) 'Irrational thinking among slot machine players', *Journal of Gambling Studies*, 8, no.3, 245–61.

Wimmer, H. and Perner, J. (1983) 'Beliefs about beliefs: representation and constraining function of wrong beliefs in young children's understanding of deception', *Cognition*, 13, 103–28.

Zimbardo, P.G. (2006) 'On rethinking the psychology of tyranny: The BBC prison experiment', *British Journal of Social Psychology*, 45, 47–53.

Index

Page numbers in **bold** indicate key concepts.